The Juvenile Justice Century

The Juvenile Justice Century

A Sociolegal Commentary on American Juvenile Courts

John C. Watkins, Jr.
The University of Alabama

Carolina Academic Press
Durham, North Carolina

KF 9779
. W38
1998

ISBN 0-89089-992-4
LCCN 97-078345

CAROLINA ACADEMIC PRESS
700 Kent Street
Durham, North Carolina 27701
Telephone (919) 489-7486
Fax (919) 493-5668
www.cap-press.com

Printed in the United States of America

To

Sallie, Scott, Alicia, Melissa and John V.

Table of Contents

Table of Cases

Preface

In his *Introduction* to the provocative little book he recently edited,[1] Walter Truett Anderson made the following comment about the state of our postmodern existence: "We are living in a new world; a world that does not know how to define itself by what it is, but only by what it has just now ceased to be."[2] I suspect that quite a few commentators and observers of the American juvenile court would tend to agree with Anderson's observation.

The juvenile court is a peculiarly American institution, born in an age of promise and reaching its century mark in an age of profound skepticism. The juvenile court is both praised and damned by politicians, jurists, policymakers and lawyers. The general public too has its own notion of preference when juvenile justice policy issues are discussed. Juvenile courts have been a vital but rather low visibility institution on the American socio-legal scene for a century. Being a centenarian, the court has withstood a remarkable amount of criticism and change in operation, in legal philosophy, in focus and in results. In fact, I believe that one can safely predict that the American juvenile court is in the latter stages of what philosophers term a "paradigm shift." Like so many other institutions in American society, the juvenile court did not recently emerge as a radically changed institution. Instead, my guess would be that the genesis of this paradigm shift probably occurred on May 15, 1967. On that date, the Supreme Court of the United States in a 7–2 opinion decided the case formally captioned *Application of Paul L. Gault and Majorie Gault, Father and Mother of Gerald Francis Gault, a minor Appellants.*[3] Known by its more abbreviated moniker as *In re Gault*, this landmark decision not only initiated a break with both legal and historical precedent, it virtually set the stage for what I would term postmodernism in American juvenile justice.

---

1. THE TRUTH ABOUT THE TRUTH: DE-CONFUSING AND RECONSTRUCTING THE POST-MODERN WORLD (Walter Truett Anderson ed. 1995).

2. *Id.* at 6.

3. 387 U.S. 1 (1967).

What follows for the reader is a selective attempt to put in perspective some of the events in juvenile law that have brought us to this point in time. This work is by no means meant to be a complete chronicle of the juvenile court. Some readers may be disappointed, but there is a readily available literature in that area that one can turn to for more exhaustive coverage. Rather, this is an attempt to place the juvenile court, its practices, and, by extension, the juvenile justice "system" in some manageable context employing my own personal "gaze" or "slant." That gaze or slant will surely not be accepted by all readers and to expect such a consensus would be shortsighted and unrealistic.

We will begin, justifiably I think, with nineteenth-century antecedents and progress through the juvenile court's establishment, its early successes, its maturity, and its later years of controversy. Along the way, we will look at some of the mechanics of juvenile justice as it is generally practiced, and the way that both history and social science have combined to change the institution. Toward the end of the work such contemporary issues as the re-criminalization of the juvenile court, the capital punishment question and the apparent demise of the historically traditional social service juvenile court will be touched upon.

The reader should keep in mind that although this is a treatise about and on behalf of a legal institution, it is also a treatise about how certain historical, social and criminological forces have conjoined over the years to bring the court to its present state of being. The purpose of a separate tribunal for youthful lawbreakers has not, in my opinion, outlived its usefulness as some would have us believe. Law in general and juvenile law in particular does not and cannot exist in a socio-cultural vacuum. The culture of so-called postmodern, post-industrial America, however, is simply not the culture of America in the last Spring of the nineteenth century. The gaze of the Illinois "child savers"[4] and other policymakers responsible for the legislation authorizing the world's first juvenile court in Cook County, Illinois, is not the gaze of those responsible for implementing juvenile justice policy in the late 1990s. That being said, it is this centennial "just now ceased to be" juvenile court that, in a word, has spurred this endeavor.

---

4. A term employed by Anthony M. Platt in his book, THE CHILD SAVERS: THE INVENTION OF DELINQUENCY (1969).

One of the congeries of questions as yet unanswered in all of this is: Can we adapt a court whose original mission was to deal with the marginally delinquent and unsocialized children and their parents to the likes of predatory urban inner-city gang delinquents? According to some estimates, there are approximately 100,000 or so juvenile gang members in the city limits of Los Angeles alone!

Clearly, the juvenile court envisaged by the Illinois founders to deal largely with Caucasian, immigrant-driven, culture-conflict criminality is not the court that can realistically deal with the often amoral delinquents of the contemporary teenage "hood." I have a very strong suspicion that many would now look back with an intense sense of nostalgia on the offense committed by Gerald Francis Gault (an alleged lewd telephone call) as the prototypical type of juvenile criminality that the *parens patriae* juvenile court could process. In some small way, perhaps, by glancing back on what has gone before, the past will be prologue for a reconstructed institutional arrangement to deal with youth crime in its various postmodern dimensions.

What intrigues me about this field of inquiry is that its study is so ecumenical. Academic investigators can slack their thirst for answers to juvenile criminality at many waterholes—law, history, sociology, psychology, social work, criminology and anthropology, to name but seven. Like much contemporary interdisciplinary writing, what follows is not so much "new" in the sense of original, undiscovered truths. This book is not the product of "original" research except in a very limited and tentative sense. Rather, it is an admittedly dependent piece of work—dependent upon countless excellent and noteworthy scholars and researchers in both legal and social science—as well as the efforts of legislators, jurists and social commentators of every persuasion. I do owe, however, a primary debt to at least three of the seven mentioned fields, namely, law, criminology and social work. I trust this book will not do violence to their many collective contributions in juvenile justice. Without a basic fund of knowledge from these fields and satellite scholarship from related disciplines, this effort would be a poor, ill-favored, thing.

John C. Watkins, Jr.
Tuscaloosa, Alabama
March, 1998

Editorial Note

All citations conform to *A Uniform System of Citation* (16th ed. 1996). Footnotes in quoted judicial opinions are omitted. The last name of authors and co-authors of texts, treatises and periodical literature are given in text citations after their full name is first cited. The full names of all authors and co-authors cited in the text are also contained in the *References* following the *Notes* section. All United States Supreme Court decisions are cited in the *Notes*, the *Table of Cases* and alphabetically in the *Subject Index*. Lower federal court authority and state decisions appear only in the *Notes* and in the *Table of Cases*.

Acknowledgments

A number of people were instrumental in assisting in the research and preparation of this work. The final draft of this book was completed in mid-summer, 1997. From late summer, 1996, until July, 1997, the following individuals contributed immensely to its completion: Shelby Chandler, my typist and computer expert; Penny C. Gibson, and Paul M. Pruitt, Assistant Law Librarians at The University of Alabama School of Law; and my two graduate research assistants in the Department of Criminal Justice, Melanie L. Capwell and Michelle M. Kizziah. From both a professional and philosophical perspective, I would be remiss if I did not give some measure of credit to Norman Leftstein and Vaughn Stapleton, my two instructors in the seminar on Law and Juvenile Courts at Northwestern University School of Law in the fall of 1967. Their interest in and commitment to this field sparked a corresponding interest and commitment on my own behalf.

I take full responsibility for all errors that *spellcheck* did not identify and for all other acts of omission or commission that crept into the manuscript over some fourteen months of research and writing.

The Juvenile Justice Century

Chapter One

Nineteenth-Century Judicial and Social Responses to Juvenile Lawbreaking

A. The House of Refuge and Reform School Movements

Nineteenth-century America was a vibrant historical era. In countless ways, the social, political and legal life of that time was equally as mind-boggling, relatively speaking, as the post-industrial information society of the present. The challenges there faced were no less daunting than our own contemporary problems, but the tools then employed were less sophisticated than the ones we now have at our disposal. There was, however, one signal benefit that nineteenth-century America enjoyed over its twentieth-century counterpart. For lack of a better description, that benefit was a much more global value consensus in our legal, social and political economy that transcended both class and region. True, there was not and certainly could not be a total consensus regarding values in the 1800s, but, on reflection, there seems to have been an overarching edifice of widely shared socio-political values that served a very worthwhile purpose in the commonweal. As part of this commonweal, children as a class were just beginning to be recognized as both a resource and a danger to the established order of things.

From the early 1800s up until the establishment of the juvenile court, children enjoyed few benefits conferred either by law or by social convention. Childhood in the nineteenth century was a contingent and nascent groping for identity. Twentieth-century childhood, contrariwise, is almost invariably taken as a socio-legal "given"; an artifact that has its own persona and cultural identity. The concept of both childhood and adolescence in the decades preceding the juvenile court's founding, however, was both tentative and culturally relative. The law, in particular, viewed children through the prism of earlier English legal precedent. Childhood or "infancy" as it was often referred to in legal discourse was treated as a distinct legal disability of some significance. When lawbreakers in their teens or sub-teen years began to be noticed by the authorities, it was only natural for them to apply traditional criminal law remedies to a wide spectrum of juvenile misbehavior.

Early nineteenth-century America was predominately rural, communitarian in social outlook and largely Protestant in religious orientation. However, as urban centers of trade and commerce evolved, this rural-communitarian-protestant triad slowly but inevitably began to fall apart. More and more European immigrants in the East and Asian immigrants on the West coast came to populate new centers of urban development. These people brought with them a different cultural, political and religious outlook that often had counterproductive spin-offs with the authorities.

The year 1825 was a particularly significant date in the history of both juveniles and the law. On January 1, 1825, the City of New York opened its first House of Refuge for a discrete segment of juvenile malefactors. Actually, the momentum for a separate institution for juveniles in New York had begun as early as 1819 when a report by the Society for the Prevention of Pauperism highlighted the confinement of children and adults commingled in Bellevue Prison. The status of pauperism was believed to be a major causative factor in youthful law violation not only in New York, but elsewhere along the Eastern seaboard. In 1823, the Society for the Prevention of Pauperism noted:

> Every person that frequents the outstreets of this city, must be forcibly struck with the ragged and uncleanly appearance, the vile language, and the idle and miserable habits of great numbers of children, most of whom are of an age suitable for schools, or for some useful employment. The parents of these children, are, in all probability, too poor or too degenerate to provide them with clothing fit for them to be seen in at School; and knows not where to place them in order that they may find employment or be better cared for.... Can it be consistent with real justice, that delinquents of this character should be consigned to the infamy and severity of punishments, which must inevitably tend to perfect the work of degradation, to sink them still deeper in corruption... Is it possible that a Christian community can lend its sanction to such a process without any effort to rescue and save?[1]

When the New York House of Refuge opened, its initial population consisted of "six girls and three boys at an abandoned soldier's barracks."[2] Although it began operation in 1825, it was not until 1829 that public funds were secured to supplant private charity for its operation.[3] The House of Refuge movement spread to some of the more populous cities in the East with Boston and Philadelphia opening their own refuges in 1826 and 1828, respectively. In the South, New Orleans opened a refuge in 1847, followed by Baltimore in 1849. Cincinnati inaugurated a House of Refuge in 1850 followed by Pittsburgh and St. Louis in 1854. By 1860, a total of sixteen such institutions had been opened in the United States. Thomas J. Bernard[4] notes that

> Two practices in the House of Refuge were consistent with practices in poorhouses. First, these juveniles were not sentenced for a certain length of time, proportionate to the offense, as in criminal courts. Rather, boys were committed until their twenty-first birthday and girls until their eighteenth birthday. (This was later amended to be the same as the boys). Second, commitment to the institution did not require a criminal conviction. A city alderman could simply issue an order admitting the youth or a parent could apply to the board of the House of Refuge.[5]

In the fall of 1825, the operation of the New York House of Refuge was appraised. Superintendent Joseph Curtis "reported the presence of sixty-nine inmates in the House of Refuge, six of whom the Court of Sessions had committed under charges of larceny and forty-seven of whom the police had brought in under charges of stealing and va-

---

1. *Report on the Subject of Erecting a House of Refuge for Vagrant and Deprived Young People*, Society for the Prevention of Pauperism in the City of New York, reprinted in SOCIETY FOR THE REFORMATION OF JUVENILE DELINQUENTS, DOCUMENTS RELATING TO THE HOUSE OF REFUGE 13 (Hastings H. Hart ed. 1832).

2. Alexander W. Pisciotta, *Treatment on Trial: The Rhetoric and Reality of the New York House of Refuge, 1857–1935*, 29 Am. J. Legal Hy. 151, 154 (1985).

3. ROBERT S. PICKETT, HOUSE OF REFUGE: ORIGINS OF JUVENILE REFORM IN NEW YORK STATE (1969) and "The House of Refuge" in BRENDA S. GRIFFIN & CHARLES T. GRIFFIN, JUVENILE DELINQUENCY IN PERSPECTIVE 12–14 (1978).

4. THOMAS J. BERNARD, THE CYCLE OF JUVENILE JUSTICE (1992).

5. *Id.* at 63.

grancy."[6] Sixteen additional boys were committed from the almshouses for various delinquencies including vagrancy, larceny and absconding.

Pious works often masked the harsh reality of this institution. "Unfortunately for the children who were incarcerated in the NYHR, the rehabilitative rhetoric of the keepers was, in many ways, inconsistent with the actual practice of the refuge."[7] Corporal punishment, constant religious instruction primarily with a Protestant bent, a strict daily regimen and the ever-constant work ethic were some of the hallmarks of the New York House of Refuge and its sister institutions. Because the juvenile population of these refuges grew in proportion to the rising tide of immigration, the managers of houses of refuge were faced with an early nineteenth-century version of institutional overcrowding. As noted, the law generally allowed commitment of juveniles to houses of refuge until age twenty-one, but few managers retained their charges that long. Juveniles who committed a felony-type offense either within or outside houses of refuge were usually sent to the criminal courts for trial, and, if convicted, would be routinely committed to a city or county prison. Subsequent to the introduction of the penitentiary system in Pennsylvania and in New York in the late 1700s and early 1800s, many juvenile felony offenders were committed to state penitentiaries until mid-century, thence to state reformatories or training schools.

Prior to the inauguration of either the penitentiary or the reformatory, however, the massive overcrowding of houses of refuge had to be addressed. One favorite method to relieve overcrowding was the institution of the "placing out" system. Based upon the premise that urban youth would continue to be defiled by the myriad criminogenic influences of the slum and its accompanying poverty and social degradation, the managers of the houses of refuge designed a plan to transport a portion of their population to more rural sectors in their own states or to some newly opened mid-west states such as Ohio, Indiana and Illinois. In these environments, dominated as they were by agricultural pursuits, the premise was that delinquent children could work in and absorb the values, mores and industrious work habits of an agrarian way of life. It was assumed that simply by removing youth from corrupt urban venues, their rehabilitation would

---

6. Pickett, *supra* note 3, at 80.
7. Pisciotta, *supra* note 2, at 160.

be assured. After receiving some tutelage in good work habits under the watchful eyes of the house of refuge managers, the juveniles "then would be placed on trains heading west, where they would be indentured out for service until they reach 21. These apprenticeships soon accounted for 90% of releases from the House of Refuge,..."[8] Houses of Refuge "outplacement" had its roots firmly embedded in English chancery practice and the great chronicler of the common law, Sir William Blackstone, noted in his *Commentaries*[9] that

> Our laws...have in one instance made a wise provision for breeding up the rising generation since the poor and laborious part of the community, when past the age of nurture, are taken out of the hands of their parents, by the statutes for apprenticing poor children...; and are placed out by the public in such a manner, as may render their abilities, in their several stations, of the greatest advantage to the commonwealth.[10]

A broad spectrum of primarily urban adolescent misbehavior and its management in the early to mid-nineteenth century gave the refuge movement its place in history. The status of poverty, coupled with behavior that many previously considered only boisterous or rowdy in nature was now looked upon as a matter of grave social concern. This epoch marked the beginnings of some fundamental changes in the socio-legal perception of youthful miscreants. Douglas R. Rendleman[11] robustly maintains that poverty *per se* was an absolute pre-condition for state intervention into the lives of certain children. In a widely-cited law review article,[12] he stated that "[t]he American colonies, and later states, developed a system of separating children from their undeserving parents. The doctrine once established proved worthy of emulation; and the states and territories in the West copied their legislation from experiences of the earlier states."[13]

---

8. Bernard, *supra* note 4, at 65.

9. 1 WILLIAM BLACKSTONE, COMMENTARIES (William Draper Lewis ed. 1898).

10. *Id.* at 451.

11. Douglas R. Rendleman, *Parens Patriae: From Chancery to the Juvenile Court*, 23 S.C.L. Rev. 205 (1971).

12. *Id.*

13. *Id.* at 212.

Further on he observed that

> We can see in the House of Refuge, the seeds of what came to be called the juvenile court. Both were founded by "reformers" who were middle class, conservative and culturally ethnocentric. The legislation is similar to the Elizabethan poor laws because it allows the state to interpose on "behalf" of children in cases of "poverty" and "Poverty plus." The dispositional alternative of apprenticeship for the children is the thread which ties the Elizabethan poor laws to the House of Refuge and to the Illinois juvenile court.[14]

From about mid-century until the founding of the juvenile court in 1899, a newer and somewhat novel institutional arrangement arrived on the juvenile justice scene. American reformatories evolved as a place of confinement for juveniles from the earlier and privately financed houses of refuge. Five noted advocates of the reform school idea in the United States were Enoch Wines, Secretary of the New York Prison Association, Theodore Dwight, the first dean of the Columbia University School of Law, Charles Loring Brace, founder of The New York Children's Aid Society, Zebulon Brockway, the Superintendent of the Elmira Reformatory in New York, and Frank Sanborn, Secretary of the Massachusetts State Board of Charities. Each of these men, in their own way, nurtured and advanced the reformatory cause for delinquent youth. Because the numerous houses of refuge in the East had, in general, failed to slow the rate of delinquency among the urban underclass, a different approach to juvenile delinquency was now being promoted.

Reformatories, unlike their house of refuge counterparts, were state-supported institutions from the very beginning. The first reformatory in the United States was established in Massachusetts in 1848. Thereafter, the reform school notion spread rapidly among both urban and rural states with Maine establishing a reform school in 1853, Connecticut in 1854 and Ohio in 1858. Slight variations in these institutional arrangements for children appeared in New York City in 1853 with the opening of the New York Juvenile Asylum, and also in Providence, Rhode Island in 1850 and in Chicago in 1855. The character of the reformatory was shaped initially by a desire to

---

14. *Id.* at 217.

create within the institution a parent-surrogate environment for the juvenile. In order to accomplish this laudable but rather utopian goal, the reformatory pioneers adopted the ancient English chancery doctrine of *parens patriae*. The American state, as a descendent of the British Crown, would now figuratively "step into the shoes" of the juvenile's father or guardian to see to it that the minor was given both civic and moral education as well as general nurturance. Eventually, *parens patriae* would become the bellwether legal referent for state intervention in the lives of not only delinquent, but dependent and neglected youth as well.

Reformatories were not all cast from the same mold. In fact, differences in philosophy, administration and the push and pull of local and regional politics often dictated varying reformatory practices. After the 1850s, state and local governments sought new techniques to control the juvenile lawbreaker. The one technique, however, that was common to all reformatories was the idea of formal custodial training for proper citizenship.

Anthony M. Platt[15] summarized the basic reformatory principles in nine ukases:

> (1) Young offenders must be segregated from the corrupting influences of adult criminals; (2) "Delinquents" need to be removed from their environment and imprisoned for their own good...(3) "Delinquents" should be assigned to reformatories without trial...; (4) Sentences should be indeterminate...; (5) Reformation should not be confused with sentimentality...; (6) Inmates must be protected from idleness, indulgence and luxuries through military drill, physical exercise and constant supervision; (7) Reformatories should be built in the countryside...; (8) Labor, education and religion constitute the essential programs of reform...; (9) The value of sobriety, thrift, industry, prudence, "realistic" ambition, and adjustment must be taught.[16]

Reformatories were clearly coercive work-intensive custodial institutions whose object was to inculcate in recalcitrant young offenders a

---

15. Anthony M. Platt, The Child Savers: The Invention of Delinquency (2d ed. 1977).

16. *Id.* at 54–55.

due amount of respect and rectitude. The *parens patriae* "father" idiom was never really taken very seriously by most reformatory administrators. Nonetheless, much ink was spilled and much proselytizing occurred in laying out how truly "modern" the reformatory principles were and how efficient was its delinquency-eradicating potential.

When the famous Elmira Reformatory was opened for juveniles in Elmira, New York in 1876, it was hailed as a juvenile correctional milestone. Zebulon Brockway, Elmira's first superintendent, was tireless in promoting all the new innovations that had recently emerged in penology. The Elmira experiment lasted much longer than many of its counterparts. It was replicated in other states as well, but toward the end of the nineteenth century, Elmira in particular and the reformatory idea in general was losing adherents. James A. Inciardi[17] notes that "By 1910 the reformatory experiment was abandoned. Nevertheless, it left an important legacy for corrections in the years to come. The indeterminate sentence, conditional release, educational programs, vocational training, and other rehabilitative ideals fostered by the reformatory became fully a part of the correctional ideology of later decades."[18]

While some new correctional techniques did emerge from the reformatory idea, the core concept—education—failed to achieve its intended purpose. Platt[19] remarks that "[t]he most consequential deficiency of the new education was that it was primarily individualistic and used to reconcile the poor and deviant to their lot in life."[20] The rhetorical rehabilitative language of the times outpaced the grim reality of re-orienting juvenile lives enfused with different values, mores, habits and world view. Thus, the nineteenth-century reformatory began to fade from the penological and cultural landscape with the Elmira institution closing its doors in 1935. Replacements came apace, however, with the twentieth-century introduction of the industrial school, the training school and other youth service institutions for the delinquent population.

---

17. James A. Inciardi, Criminal Justice (5th ed. 1996).
18. *Id.* at 508.
19. Platt, *supra* note 15.
20. *Id.* at 57.

B. Judicial Responses to House of Refuge and Reformatory Children

1. The Age-Responsibility Factor in the Criminal Courts

The response of the judiciary to both refuge and reformatory juveniles was uneven and often contradictory. Numerous socio-cultural variables entered into a decision by a court to admit a minor to either institution. Criminal offenses committed by youngsters in the nineteenth century always had the very real potential of placing these juveniles in serious risk of severe punishment, and, at times, even death.[21] Frederick Woodbridge[22] notes that

> [i]n both the criminal law and the law relating to civil liability, an infant or child has always occupied a more favored position than an adult. In the early history of the law, when there did not seem to be a clear-cut distinction between the criminal law and the law relating to the civil liability of infants, this position was recognized and undoubtedly has had some influence upon the development of the at times rather elaborate present day statutory provisions concerning the criminal responsibility of children.[23]

Woodbridge's notation of "present day statutory provisions" probably referred to the juvenile court acts promulgated in the United States between 1899 and 1939 when his article appeared in print. In any event, the common law of crimes in this country in the nineteenth century was configured by much earlier historical and legal antecedents.

Our paucity of knowledge concerning the real source of early English criminal sanctions makes all the more difficult any reconstruction of valid hypotheses. What evidence we do possess about the early *general* liability of all but the very young points in the direction of strict accountability.[24] "When the machinery of the law finally substituted public punishment for private vengeance, the child convicted of

---

21. *See, e.g.,* M. WATT ESPY & JOHN ORTIZ SMYKLA, EXECUTIONS IN THE UNITED STATES 1608–1991: THE ESPY FILE, 3rd ICPSR ed. (1994).

22. Frederick Woodbridge, *Physical and Mental Infancy in the Criminal Law,* 87 U. Pa. L. Rev. 426 (1939).

23. *Id.* at 428.

24. A.W.G. Kean, *The History of the Criminal Liability of Children,* 53 L.Q. Rev. 364 (1937).

crime deserved and needed a pardon..."[25] Yet many children went to the gallows, reacting up to the final moment in the characteristic manner of mortally frightened youth. Even as late as the first half of the nineteenth century, Grenville, the British diarist, expressed astonishment at the incomprehensible attitude of boys about to be hanged. "Never," he is reported as saying, "did I see boys cry so!"[26]

But even the draconian laws of the Plantagenets, out of a common feeling perhaps of basic humanitarian instinct, seemed to have held to the view that the very young child ought under no circumstance suffer criminal punishment. Exhibiting medieval social restraint, Justice Spigurnel in a *Year Book* case in 1302[27] said that a child indicted for the crime of homicide should not be punished by the criminal law if he did the deed before he was seven years of age. Conversely, if either express or implied malice entered into the factual equation supported by adequate proof, even children in the immediate sub-adolescent years were subject to possible trial, conviction and death. Again, before Justice Spigurnel in 1338, a child was hung after the prosecution had proven the harboring of a "malicious will" on the part of the defendant. The *Year Book* states:[28]

> And it was said by the ancient law that no one shall be hanged within the age, nor shall suffer judgment of life or limb. But before Spigurnel it was found that an infant within the age killed his companion, and then concealed himself, and thereupon he was hanged; for he [Spigurnel] said that by concealment he [the infant] could discern between good and evil.[29]

Likewise in 1488 we are given another account of the capital punishment of a child of rather tender years.[30]

> [A] child within the age of nine years killed a child... and confessed the felony; and it was found too that when he had killed him he concealed him; and also the blood

---

25. *Id.* at 365.
26. As quoted in ANUERIN BEVAN, IN PLACE OF FEAR 177 (1952).
27. Y.B. 30–31 Edw. 1, pp. 511–13 (1302).
28. Y.B. Trin. 12 Edw. 3, p. 626 (1338).
29. *Id.*
30. Y.B. Hil. 3 Hen. 7, f. 1, p. 4 (1488).

which poured upon him he excused and said it came from his nose. And they submit that he ought to be hanged.[31]

From the thirteenth century onward, there was at least a general consensus that the criminal liability of children divided itself into the categories of absolute and conditional. Nonetheless, the exact legal boundaries between this duality of blameworthiness were not yet fixed. A divergence of authority still existed as to when the age of discretion had arrived.

Sir Anthony Fitzherbert[32] and Chief Justice Edward Coke[33] held to the view that the age of discretion began at fourteen. Sir Matthew Hale[34] likewise agreed that age fourteen was the proper dividing line for purposes of full adult responsibility. Hale actually proposed a tripartite age differential by which the criminal law could determine the responsibility question for children.[35] Subsequently, another English commentator, William Hawkins, "laid down the rule of responsibility of infants as it came to be known generally: below seven there could be no guilt, above fourteen the infant was to be judged as an adult, and between seven and fourteen there was a presumption against the capacity of the infant to commit crime."[36] The middle age range from seven to fourteen proved troublesome to both courts and commentators alike. Malice was the judicial totem which might "supply age,"[37] although in principle, the child was *doli incapax*.

---

31. *Id.*

32. ANTHONY FITZHERBERT, NEW NATURA BREVIUM 248 (8th ed. 1755). Fitzherbert said that if a child of age eight, for example, committed murder, the record of the proceeding should be removed to the Court of Chancery by *writ of certiorari* in order for the child to be pardoned. In Norman usage, the prefix "Fitz" before one's name indicated "son of," although it originally was a prefix applied to illegitimate children. *See also* Y.B. Mich. 6 Edw. II (1312).

33. COKE ON LITTLETON § 405, lib. 3, f. 247B (Francis Hargrave & Charles Butler eds. 1809).

34. 1 MATTHEW HALE, PLEAS OF THE CROWN 25 (1716).

35. Kean, *supra* note 24.

36. Kean, *supra* note 24, at 365.

37. 4 WILLIAM BLACKSTONE, COMMENTARIES 24 (William Draper Lewis ed. 1898). The arrival of puberty marked the line of mitigating punishment. From time of birth to the arrival of puberty, criminal responsibility of minors generally turned on a combination of several factors, among them: (1) the chronological age of the child; (2) the nature of the crime committed; and (3) the mental capacity of the child. Those children coming within the amorphous "infant" category (*proximi infantiae*) were generally exonerated,

"Another example," says Sir Leon Radzinowicz,[38] "is provided by the death sentence passed in 1800 on a ten-year-old boy for secreting notes at the Chelmsford Post Office."[39] Baron Hotham wrote to Lord Auckland concerning this case as follows:

> All the circumstances attending the transaction manifested art and contrivance beyond his years, and I therefore refused the application of his counsel to respite the judgment on the ground of his tender years being satisfied that he knew perfectly well what he was doing. But still, he is an absolute child, now only between ten and eleven...The scene was dreadful on passing sentence, and to pacify the feelings of a most crowded court, who all expressed their horror of such a child being hanged, by their looks and manners, after stating the necessity of the prosecution and the infinite danger of its going abroad into the world that a Child might commit such a crime with impunity, when it was clear that he knew what he was doing, I hinted something slightly of its still being in the Power of the Crown to interpose in every case that was opened to Clemency.[40]

Before birth registration in England became mandatory by statute,[41] the judges oftentimes had to rely on mere intuition and guess to determine the age of a child brought before them charged with a criminal violation. This was, at best, a rather haphazard procedure, and explains in part the early vagueness of cases discussing age limits. Parish registration of baptisms began in the reign of Henry VIII (1509–1547) and were regulated by an ecclesiastical canon of 1603. An abortive attempt at civil registration of births was made by the Long Parliament in 1653, but it was not until the early nineteenth century that the present system of birth registration was introduced in England.[42]

---

whereas those children closer to puberty (*proximi pubertate*) were often held criminally responsible even though they were chronologically under the age of fourteen.

38. 1 LEON RADZINOWICZ, A HISTORY OF ENGLISH CRIMINAL LAW (1948).

39. *Id.* at 12.

40. Quoted from the British Home Office Papers of John L. Hammond and Barbara Hammond, *The Town Labourer* 75 (1941).

41. 6 & 7 Will. 4, c. 86 (1836).

42. *Id.*

Legal history then clearly substantiates the proposition that the phrase "too young for punishment" was relative in the common law. As a matter of both administrative convenience and simple justice, age lines had to be drawn at some point, but this demarcation did not always mean that a juvenile charged with crime would be the recipient of mercy at the hands of the criminal law.

A typical early American judicial explication of the common law age sequences appeared in an opinion written by Chief Justice Kirkpatrick of the Supreme Court of New Jersey in 1818. In a murder prosecution of a black slave child captioned *State v. Aaron*,[43] the Court observed that

> It is perfectly settled, that an infant within the age of seven years cannot be punished for any capital offence, whatever circumstances of mischievous intention may be proved against him, for the presumption of the law, he cannot have discretion between good and evil, and against this presumption no averment can be admitted. It is perfectly settled also that between the age of seven and the age of fourteen years, the infant shall be presumed to be incapable of committing crime upon the same principle, the presumption being very strong at seven, and decreasing with the progress of his years; but then this presumption... may be encountered by proof; and if it shall appear by *strong* and *irresistible* evidence that [the child] had sufficient discernment to distinguish good from evil, to comprehend the nature and consequences of his acts; he may be convicted and have a judgment of death. (Emphasis in original).[44]

Judicial language such as the above invested courts with the option to place juvenile lawbreakers who fell into the seven to fourteen age category in both houses of refuge and in reformatories. But, this intermediate age cohort also created an opening for adult criminal courts to retain jurisdiction over a large number of children who were not "proper subjects" for either refuge or reformatory solicitude. In fact, children who were what we would term today chronic, predatory delinquents, would seldom, if ever, be committed to either a house of

---

43. 4 N.J.L. 231 (1818).
44. *Id.* at 271.

refuge or a reformatory. However, an in-depth history of the legal dispositions for this class of children in the nineteenth century has yet to be written.

When the history of capital punishment for juveniles arose, however, a more complete historical record appears. For example, Platt in the second edition of his important work on the American juvenile court,[45] presents a table in an appendix labeled "Leading Cases in the Criminal Responsibility of Children in American Law, 1800–82,"[46] showing fourteen cases implicating the death penalty. In Platt's listing, only two of the fourteen children were actually executed with a third child's sanction listed as "Not specified."[47] Ten juveniles were acquitted while one received a prison sentence of three years. Considering the total juvenile population in rural and urban America during those eighty-two years who might conceivably be death-eligible, Platt's findings are incomplete. In fairness to Platt, however, his juvenile execution table was probably for illustrative purposes only. Apparently, due to a number of variables, adult criminal court juries were often quite reticent to find a child guilty of a capital crime. Sentencing judges also were often able to avoid handing down a judgment of death by manipulating the variables in the "lesser included offense" category, by evidentiary rulings favorable to the defense and by consciously or subconsciously considering youth as a mitigating factor. Thus, jury nullification coupled with judicial avoidance mechanisms and the simple fact of age itself insulated a number of juveniles from the criminal law's ultimate sanction. That being said, however, does not detract from the fact that there were a number of children who did suffer death at the hands of the criminal law between 1800 and 1899.

In a major piece of research conducted at The University of Alabama by death penalty researcher M. Watt Espy,[48] he concluded that

---

45. Platt, *supra* note 15.

46. *Id.* at 208–09.

47. *Id.*

48. The ESPY FILE documents a total of 114 juveniles below the age of eighteen executed in the United States between the years 1801–1899. Of those children who faced capital punishment, 58 were African-American; 39 Caucasian; 9 Native American; 4 Hispanic; 1 Asian-Pacific Islander and 3 unknown. Ten states led in juvenile executions during the 1800s. These were Alabama (12); Georgia (8); Ohio (8); Arkansas (7); Texas (7); South Carolina (6); Tennessee (6); Kentucky (5); Maryland (5) and California, New York and Virginia tied for tenth place with 4 executions apiece.

a total of 114 children under age eighteen were put to death in the United States during the nineteenth century. Of those 114, 108 were male and 6 were female. The two offenses that placed the most children in the death-eligible category were murder and robbery-murder, the latter category being known as felony-murder in traditional criminal law offense classification schemes.

Capital punishment aside, the cultural and legal hegemony of refuge and reformatory operations between 1800 and 1899 was rarely questioned. Although houses of refuge began to give way to the reformatory model about mid-century, both institutional arrangements dominated the juvenile peno-correctional scene in the nineteenth century. Because of the social, political and community reputation of some of the refuge-reformatory mavens, courts were generally not anxious to intervene in the operations of these organizations. In fact, like their subsequent twentieth-century counterparts, nineteenth-century courts simply assumed that refuges and reformatories were altruistic establishments that were, for the most part, beyond the reach of traditional legal oversight.

2. Judicial Affirmation of Refuge-Reformatory Principles

Nineteenth-century judicial reticence to actively involve the courts in decision-making routines was natural for the time. While the *parens patriae* power of the twentieth-century juvenile court was being nurtured in select cases in the nineteenth century, a more or less hands-off attitude prevailed when it came to involving the judiciary in refuge and reformatory matters.

The *parens patriae* doctrine was beginning to assume an important legal niche in certain decisions involving early house of refuge children. On January 5, 1839, the Supreme Court of Pennsylvania in a *per curiam* opinion on a *habeas corpus* petition,[49] for the first time invoked the *parens patriae* doctrine on behalf of the reformation of a delinquent child. The father of Many Ann Crouse filed a petition for a writ of *habeas corpus* to have his daughter released from the Philadelphia House of Refuge. Mary Ann had been previously committed on a justice of the peace warrant signed by her mother. The allegation in that Warrant read "That the said infant by reason of vicious conduct, has rendered her control beyond the power of the said

---

49. *Ex parte Crouse*, 4 Whart. (Pa.) 9 (1839).

complainant [mother], and made it manifestly requisite that from regard to the moral and future welfare of the said infant she should be placed under the guardianship of the managers of the House of Refuge;..."[50] The lawyer for the petitioner-father contended that the provisions in the Pennsylvania law authorizing committal of juveniles to the House of Refuge was unconstitutional because it allowed detention without a trial by jury. The Court, nonetheless, sustained the state's power to commit Mary Ann Crouse in these words:[51]

> The House of Refuge is not a prison, but a school where reformation, and not punishment is the end.... The object of the charity is reformation by training its inmates to industry; by imbuing their minds with principles of morality and religion; by furnishing them with means to earn a living; and, above all, by separating them from the corrupting influences of improper associates. To this end, may not the natural parents, when unequal to the task of education, or unworthy of it, be superceded by the *parens patriae*, or common guardian of the community?[52]

In commenting on the historical significance of the *Crouse* decision, Sanford J. Fox[53] notes that

> So long as the declared purposes of the Philadelphia House were morally and socially acceptable, the court made no effort to inquire into what was actually happening to Mary Ann or to determine whether...the design and operation of the House were heavily laden with punitive and suppressive elements barely distinguishable from those of an adult prison.[54]

Note also that the Pennsylvania opinion spoke eloquently of "industry," "morality," "religion," and "separating" as major elements in an effort by the state, via *parens patriae*, to segregate and single out children for the benevolent purpose of reformation. The court noted that the confinement of Mary Ann Crouse "is no more than what is borne, to a greater or less extent, in every school; and we know of no

---

50. *Id.*
51. *Id.* at 11.
52. *Id.*
53. SANFORD J. FOX, MODERN JUVENILE JUSTICE: CASES AND MATERIALS (1972).
54. *Id.* at 27–28.

natural right to exemption from restraints which conduce to an infant's welfare."[55] But even more fundamentally as Peter D. Garlock notes[56]

> The *Crouse* court itself recognized that the refuge managers' primary motive was crime prevention,...Had philathropists merely wanted to create separate almshouses for poor but 'innocent' children to avoid housing them with adult paupers, there would have been no need for statutes authorizing incarceration of children on grounds of proto-criminal behavior.[57]

No doubt confinement for both education and one's welfare took legal primacy over most countervailing arguments. The *Crouse* decision thus formally invoked the *parens patriae* rubric in a manner and form that would ultimately become the legal lode star of the American juvenile court sixty years later. As the *Crouse* opinion revealed, however, nineteenth-century legal challenges attacking the incarceration of juveniles for what today would be termed incorrigibility were relatively uncommon.

Thirty years after the *Crouse* ruling, in an appeal from the Supreme Bench of Baltimore City, the Supreme Court of Maryland had before it a cause filed by a gentleman named Martin Roth.[58] Mr. Roth was the father of Frank Roth, a twelve-year-old confined in the Baltimore House of Refuge. The gist of the complaint was that Frank Roth was committed to the House of Refuge without his father's consent and that the father was both financially and morally capable of caring for his son. "The petitioner prayed for a writ of *habeas corpus* to have his child brought before the Court and relieved from such unlawful imprisonment."[59] After a lengthy discussion surrounding certain procedural issues involving the writ of *habeas corpus*, Justice Alvey concluded rather tersely that

> ...we deem it proper, in view of the great public importance of the subject, to say, without stating at large the rea-

55. *Ex parte Crouse*, 4 Whart. (Pa.) 9, 11 (1839).

56. Peter D. Garlock, *Wayward Children and the Law*, 1820–1900: *The Genesis of the Status Offense Jurisdiction of the Juvenile Court*, 13 Ga. L. Rev. 341 (1979).

57. *Id.* at 367.

58. *Roth v. House of Refuge*, 31 Md. 329 (1869).

59. *Id.* at 330.

sons of the conclusion, that we are clear in the opinion that the power conferred upon the Managers of the House of Refuge...is in no wise in conflict with the...Constitution of this State....[60]

Thus, custody of his son eluded Martin Roth. He would be among the first parents in a long line of appellate precedent to be denied parental rights when the state haltingly began invoking the *parens patriae* precept in early child welfare proceedings.

In the same year that the Maryland court was invoking *parens patriae* in *Roth*, the Supreme Court of Ohio had before it a case coming up on a Writ of Error from the common pleas court of Van Wert County.[61] It seems that Benjamin Prescott, age fourteen, was charged with arson of a barn, and that, in addition, "he was vicious and incorrigible, and a suitable person to be committed to the guardianship of the directors of the house of refuge or to the reform farm in Ohio ..."[62] The lower court ordered the juvenile committed to the reform farm "until he became of age, or was reformed, and duly discharged according to law;..."[63] Benjamin's lawyer argued on appeal that the state's decision committing the minor to the Ohio reform farm deprived his client of liberty without due process of law and also deprived him of a trial by jury. In addressing these contentions, Justice White made short shrift of the due process contention noting, among other things, that legislation already in place in Ohio at the time "authorizes the commitment to be made to the guardianship of the board of commissioners for reform schools,..."[64] Speaking to the issue raised by counsel for the juvenile regarding a right to trial by jury, the judge noted that in cases such as this

> [t]he proceeding is purely statutory; and the commitment ...is not designed as a punishment for crime, but to place minors of the description, and for the causes specified in the statute, under the guardianship of the public authorities named for proper care and discipline, until they are reformed or arrive at the age of majority. The institution to

60. *Id.* at 334.
61. *Prescott v. State*, 19 Ohio St. 184 (1869).
62. *Id. at 185.*
63. *Id..*
64. *Id.* at 187.

which they are committed is a school, not a prison; nor is the character of their detention affected by the fact that it is also a place where juvenile convicts may be sent...[65]

Unlike some earlier cases, however, the Ohio court here was faced with allegations of actual crime commission by the juvenile and that fact may have been determinative in ruling that Benjamin Prescott be detained in state custody. But we see in an opinion like *Prescott* an almost cavalier willingness by the court to disregard charges of constitutional violation in the face of what also appears to be an out-of-control juvenile; *parens patriae* superceded due process!

By the late 1860s, then, there was a slow but steady judicial recognition that houses of refuge, reformatories and other predominately rural institutions for juveniles were not actually liberty-depriving devices. In the somewhat convoluted idiom of the day, these socio-legal arrangements were transmuted into "schools." In an 1885 decision[66] in New Hampshire, the state supreme court had before it a *habeas corpus* petition demanding the release of a sixteen-year-old from the custody of the state industrial school. A local justice of the peace had committed young John Cunningham to the custody of the industrial school upon a burglary complaint. It was the petitioner's contention that this minor judicial functionary had no jurisdiction to impose such a sentence for a felony. The court granted the writ releasing Cunningham from custody for lack of subject-matter jurisdiction, and, in discussing the relationship between juvenile crime and the state industrial school, Justice Smith remarked magisterially that

> ...the commitment and detention of the relator's son is justified by the respondent [superintendent] upon the ground that the industrial school is not a prison, that the order of commitment was not a sentence, and that their detention is not a punishment. The contention is that the industrial school is a part of the school system of the state, and the state as *parens patriae* may detain in the school such scholars as may need its discipline. It is a privilege to be admitted a member of the school, it is a privilege limited to "offenders against the laws."[67]

---

65. *Id.* at 187.
66. *State ex rel. Cunningham v. Ray*, 63 N.H. 406 (1885).
67. *Id.* at 408.

While the above language was merely that of the court paraphrasing the arguments of the industrial school superintendent, it was language nonetheless that subsequent courts seized upon to justify coercive intervention in children's lives under the expansive *parens patriae* power. In other words, these early jurisdictional arguments propounded by state correctional bureaucrats in due course became the selfsame arguments to legally reaffirm former correctional ukases. What we were witnessing was the transmutation of early correctional orthodoxy into a legal doctrine that would profoundly affect twentieth-century juvenile law.

Note also the reference in several of these early opinions to the concept of guardianship as a predicate for intervention in the lives of children. The *Crouse* court spoke approvingly of the "common guardian of the community"[68] being synonymous with *parens patriae* and the guardian-ward relationship that fit quite neatly into the overall state-as-parent surrogate scheme. One of the articles of faith in juvenile justice in both the nineteenth and twentieth centuries has been "[t]he fundamental idea... that the state must step in and exercise guardianship over a child found under such adverse social conditions as develop crime.... It proposes a plan whereby he may be treated... as a ward of the state."[69]

Guardianship and wardship in various forms were the early touchstones of juvenile justice philosophy and still play a significant role in contemporary practice. The assumption here was that the state adapt the guardian-ward relationship to situations where the natural (parental) guardian or guardians were either absent or guardians in name only. If the natural guardians of the juvenile were somehow less eligible in the eyes of the law to meet the daunting challenges of parenthood, the state could intervene and take the parents' place under the authority of *parens patriae*. But these parental powers of the state were of a different order and legitimacy from those that one would normally associate with natural affection bestowed upon a child by its biological parents. As Hasseltine B. Taylor aptly observed, "[t]he metaphysical entity of the state cannot serve as an actual guardian."[70] In the latter half of the nineteenth century we begin to detect the judi-

---

68. *Ex parte Crouse*, 4 Whart. (Pa.) at 11.
69. As quoted in *Report of the Committee of the Chicago Bar*, 1899.
70. HASSELTINE B. TAYLOR, LAW OF GUARDIAN AND WARD 5 (1935).

ciary using the legal rhetoric of benevolence to distance itself from the hard choices it faced in dealing with juvenile criminality. Thomas Ross[71] notes that "[r]eal human suffering vanishes as we conjure up the spectre of righteousness. Rhetoric becomes the smooth veneer on the cracked surface of the real and hard choices in law."[72] The state as super parent and its attendant verbal gymnastics in justification for such a role was well entrenched by the 1870s. However, this era produced a rather unique appellate decision from Illinois that, momentarily at least, lifted the rhetorical veil shrouding *parens patriae.*

In the 1860s, the Illinois legislature had enacted several pieces of legislation dealing with the Chicago Reform School. In sum, that legislation authorized the commitment of juveniles between the ages of six and sixteen to the reform school who were either destitute or were growing up in idleness and vice, among other things. These early forms of what later would become so-called status offenses gave the authorities an extremely broad jurisdictional net. The sole authority to discharge juveniles from the Chicago Reform School was vested in the Board of Guardians during the juvenile's minority which terminated at age twenty-one.

Daniel O'Connell was an inmate in the Chicago Reform School and his father, Michael O'Connell, filed a writ of *habeas corpus* seeking Daniel's release.[73] The gravamen of the writ was that this minor was held in the reform school without having been either charged or convicted of any crime, and, because of this, Daniel's custody was alleged to be in contravention of the state Bill of Rights. The loss of liberty without due process of law specifically pointed up the legal dilemma confronting the Illinois tribunal.

In the mittimus committing O'Connell, the writ stated, among other things, that Daniel "has been found, by competent evidence, to be a proper subject for commitment in the said reform school, and whose moral welfare and the good of society require that he should be sent to said school for instruction, employment and reformation, ..."[74] Notice here the three-fold justification for Daniel O'Connell's

---

71. Thomas Ross, *The Rhetorical Tapestry of Race: White Innocence and Black Abstraction,* 32 Wm. & Mary L. Rev. 1 (1990)

72. *Id.*

73. *People ex rel. O'Connell v. Turner,* 55 Ill. 280 (1870).

74. *Id.* at 281.

confinement—educational, economic and correctional. The Supreme Court of Illinois framed the issue by announcing that "[t]he only question for determination is the power of the legislature to pass laws, under which this boy was arrested and confined."[75] In order to make that determination, the court had to juxtapose the state legislation alongside the higher organic law contained in the state Constitution and its Bill of Rights. The question then came down to whether or not the Illinois laws giving broad powers to police magistrates, justices of the peace, and other criminal justice functionaries to commit children to the Chicago Reform School squared with constitutional mandates.

In his wide-ranging opinion in the case, Justice Thornton began by discussing the legislation authorizing certain criminal justice personnel to involuntarily confine certain children in this reformatory. The jurist then makes this telling observation: "[t]he warrant of commitment does not indicate that the arrest [of Daniel] was made for a criminal offense. Hence, we conclude that it was issued under the general grant of power *to arrest and confine for misfortune.*"[76] (Emphasis added). In a nutshell, the Illinois court stripped away any pretense that confinement of Daniel O'Connell was justified on anything other than a sociolegal artifact unconnected with any substantive criminal wrongdoing. The juvenile was being imprisoned for "misfortune." Further on, in an even more scathing indictment of reform school practice, the court noted that "[I]n our solicitude to form youth for the duties of civil life, we should not forget the rights which inhere both in parents and children. The principle of absorption of the child in, and its complete subjection to the despotism of, the State, is wholly inadmissible in the modern civilized world."[77] That comment could have easily been written by the majority in the *Gault* decision ninety-seven years later.

The *O'Connell* court was clearly disturbed by the rather routinized practice of criminal justice officials populating the Chicago Reform School with youngsters from the underclass whose only "crime" was either pauperism or some variety of perceived social maladjustment. For some forty-five years from the establishment of the New York

---

75. *Id.* at 282.
76. *Id.* at 283.
77. *Id.* at 284.

House of Refuge in 1825 until the *O'Connell* case in 1870, the courts began breathing the pure oxygen of *parens patriae* and resisted all efforts to recognize any legal rights that might perchance devolve upon the juvenile. *O'Connell*, for a brief moment, jolted the judges from their disengagement from reality and laid bare the true nature of reformatory policy and practice.

In the latter portion of his eight-page opinion, Justice Thornton cast a jaundiced eye at the imprisonment of youth for misfortune. He caustically remarked that

> This boy is deprived of a father's care, bereft of home influences; has no freedom of action; is committed for an uncertain time; is branded as a prisoner; made subject to the will of others; and thus feels that he is a slave. Nothing could more contribute to paralyze the youthful energies, crush all noble aspirations, and unfit him for the duties of manhood. Other means of milder character;...would better accomplish the reformation of the depraved, and infringe less upon inalienable rights.[78]

The Illinois court ordered Daniel O'Connell released from custody. It almost goes without saying that the *O'Connell* decision did not meet with a groundswell of favorable opinion, especially among the juvenile correctional bureaucracy. The case vividly documented for all to see the mask thrown up around the pre-juvenile court correctional system to effectively marginalize any legal rights that children might claim. Naturally, the *O'Connell* ruling left many latter nineteenth-century juvenile reformers aghast at the prospect of having to release juveniles from reform schools on *habeas corpus*, simply because an appellate court happened to view the incarceration violative of constitutional guarantees. As the child savers and their acolytes became more politically sophisticated, however, the *O'Connell* case was viewed by them simply as a judicial oddity. The closer the end of the century approached, the less frequently *O'Connell's raison d'etre* was considered of any real precedential value by courts or policymakers alike. The decision was ultimately looked upon as an aberrant pronouncement that could not and would not stand in the way of Progressive social engineering. Platt[79] noted that the "[c]hild saving orga-

---

78. *Id.* at 287.
79. Platt, *supra* note 15, at 104.

nizations regarded the O'Connell case as an irresponsible decision designed to discredit and retard their efforts."[80] In short, *O'Connell* did raise a red flag to those who sought, by whatever method, "to intervene in the lives of 'pre-delinquent' children and maintain control over them until they were immunized against 'delinquency'..."[81] Nonetheless, *O'Connell* did have some limited impact in both Chicago and in Illinois generally. In its aftermath, the Chicago Reform School ceased operation and the Illinois legislature repealed court jurisdiction over "misfortune" cases.[82]

The same year *O'Connell* was decided, the National Prison Association, the precursor of the American Correctional Association, met for the first time in Cincinnati, Ohio. The membership of that organization was made up of numerous child saving advocates who had both a social and political agenda to promote. *O'Connell's ratio decidendi* was disturbing to the Cincinnati convocation, for that organization saw itself as the pied piper of the nascent correctional profession. In that light, its theories and newly emerging practices could not be hamstrung by a single state appellate court decision. Indeed, *People v. O'Connell* was ultimately relegated to a judicial footnote in nineteenth-century jurisprudence dealing with children's rights. The social, cultural, political and criminological indices all pointed toward a children's rights agenda totally at loggerheads with the laudable premises enunciated by the Supreme Court of Illinois. Guardianship, *parens patriae* and the ubiquitous concept of pauper control, along with and coincident to the newly emerging "scientific" theories of criminality all contributed to the dissonance of the *O'Connell* holding.

In 1876, six years after *O'Connell*, the Supreme Court of Wisconsin decided *Milwaukee Industrial School v. Supervisors of Milwaukee County*.[83] This matter came to the highest court in Wisconsin on an appeal from the circuit court of Milwaukee County. The industrial school sought to recover monies expended for board and tuition of certain children under its care from the county. The county supervisors denied the claim and an appeal was taken to the circuit court. After a hearing in the circuit court, that tribunal rendered a judgment for the industrial school and the county appealed. In upholding the

80. *Id.*
81. *Id.* at 107.
82. Act of May 3, 1873, § 17, 1873 Ill. Laws 145.
83. 40 Wis. 328 (1876).

circuit court judgment, Chief Justice Ryan began his opinion by noting that "...the political necessity and duty of the sovereignty to make provision for the care of subjects or citizens, unable...to take care of themselves...has been too long recognized in all civilized countries...to be regarded as an open question."[84] As if to preempt any criticism of any statutes allowing industrial schools to confine both the pauper and the delinquent with only nodding obedience to due process, Ryan intoned that "[t]here might be constitutional difficulties or defects...in statutes of this character."[85] Nonetheless, he was quick to add that "...not only their humanity, but their propriety"[86] are "within a proper legislative function, and not a meddlesome interference with private discretion or discipline."[87]

The *Milwaukee Industrial School* case was also notable for its demarcation of behaviors that would become boiler plate legislative language in subsequent juvenile codes. In an attempt to arrest juvenile crime in its early stages, the Wisconsin legislation provided that male children under twelve and females under sixteen who came within the following conditions were candidates for commitment to the Milwaukee Industrial School:

> ...begging or receiving alms,...or being in any public street or offering for sale anything...or that is found wandering and not having any home or settled place of abode, proper guardianship or means of substinence; or is found destitute either by being an orphan or having a parent or parents who is undergoing imprisonment or otherwise; or that frequents the company of reputed thieves, or of lewd, wanton or lascivious persons in speech or behavior; or notorious resorts of bad character; or that is found wandering in streets, alleys or public places, and belonging to that class of children called "ragpickers"; or that is an inmate of any house of ill fame or poor house...or who has been abandoned...or who is without means of substinence or support.[88]

---

84. *Id.* at 331.
85. *Id.* at 333.
86. *Id.*
87. *Id.*
88. *Id.* at 334–35.

Notice the catalog of behaviors thought to reveal pre-delinquency in all its manifestations: begging; receiving alms; wandering; without proper guardianship; destitute; orphan; frequents company of deviants of all persuasions; "ragpickers"; child prostitution; abandoned children; and finally those who have no financial means for food or support. This reflected the reality of much underclass lifestyle in the latter third of the nineteenth century. The *leitmotif* of the child savers here was the erection of a legislative and judicial structure responsive to the ideology of altruism and beneficence on the one hand, and to coercive state intervention on the other.

In June of 1882, the Supreme Court of Illinois again had a case before it that raised troubling questions of civil liberties and state intrusiveness.[89] In an appeal from Cook County Court, a nine-year-old female by the name of Winifred Breen was petitioned before that court because she "had repeatedly been picked up by the police and others while wandering about the streets [of Chicago] at night; was a truant from school, and had not proper parental care, and was in imminent danger of ruin and harm..."[90] The lower court adduced three witnesses who testified to the rather shallow character of the child. Collectively, their testimony indicated that Winifred had a "weak-minded" mother and a stepfather who was frequently absent from the family and often was unable to control the child. The hearing ended with a jury returning a verdict that the juvenile was a dependent child. Thereupon, the judge of the county court committed Winifred to the Industrial School for Girls in Evanston.

On appeal to the Supreme Court of Illinois, Justice Sheldon, in remarking upon the procedural protections afforded juveniles committed to the industrial school in question, was at pains to point out that "anxious provision" was incorporated in the statute to protect "all just rights." He then, like his predecessors in Illinois and elsewhere, reiterated that classical escape clause so frequently finding its way into appellate decisions. Said Sheldon:

> This institution [the industrial school] is not a prison, but it is a school and the sending of a young female child there to be taken care of who is uncared for, and with no one to care for her, we do not regard imprisonment. We perceive

89. *In re Ferrier*, 103 Ill. 367 (1882).
90. *Id.* at 368.

hardly any more restraint of liberty than is found in any well regulated school. Such a degree of restraint is essential in the proper education of a child, and it is in no just sense an infringement of the inherent and inalienable right to personal liberty so much dwelt upon in the argument.[91]

There is no doubt, of course, that the Girls Industrial School was, in fact, a school. Educational uplift was a key component of the entire juvenile correctional apparatus. But this industrial school and others like it were, in reality, an educational system *plus*. The *plus* included a host of other routine regimens and teacher-student roles not found in the typical free-world public schools. Drawing on chancery's kingly prerogative under *parens patriae*, Justice Sheldon gave it due recognition. In the latter portion of his opinion, he placed the role of teacher and pupil alongside that of parent and child and guardian and ward. Apparently, the premise here was that an industrial "school" had an incontestable right to exercise custody over the children of the undeserving poor as schoolmaster *par excellent*. The teacher-student, guardian-ward and parent-child roles "...are legal and just restraints upon personal liberty which the welfare of society demands..."[92] Thus, the judgment of the Cook County Court committing Winifred Breen to the industrial school was affirmed. With this decision, the Supreme Court of Illinois essentially repudiated its *O'Connell* precedent. In speaking to the issue of a child's right to liberty, the *Ferrier* court noted that

> The right to liberty which is guaranteed is not that of entire unrestrainedness of action.... There are restrictions imposed upon personal liberty which spring from the helpless or dependent condition of individuals in the various relations of life, among them being those of parent and child, guardian and ward, teacher and scholar.[93]

What happened in Illinois between 1870, the date of the *O'Connell* ruling and 1882, the date of the *Ferrier* decision happened in appellate tribunals across the land. The courts were unceremoniously turning a blind eye to the many faults of the refuge-training school-industrial school trilogy. From their very inception, it was earnestly

---

91. *Id.* at 371.
92. *Id.* at 373.
93. *Id.* at 372.

contended that these institutions were not penal in character. Sadly, most of their non-punitive policies were temporary; punitive practices drove institutional routine on a regular basis. In the last third of the nineteenth century, the houses of refuge still in existence, the juvenile training schools and the reformatories became custodial in both architecture and in character. High walls surrounded many of them and their dormitories often resembled cellblocks. Although apprenticing children out and transporting them to distant states for rehabilitation purposes had become less frequent, their labor within institutional walls was highly prized. The earning capacity of institutionalized juveniles was regularly exploited by the managers, wardens and overseers. The courts, apparently, ignored such exploitation while trumpeting, instead, the educational opportunities these institutions afforded. Despite this judicial rhetoric, however, educational opportunities for committed juveniles were meager at best.[94] In speaking of the accommodations of a typical house of refuge in the latter half of the 1800s, David S. Snedden[95] notes that

> ... prison and penitentiary methods were used and are still in use. The youth was confined at contract labor. Only the most meager educational advantages were afforded him. His superior officers' first thought was the amount of money to be gained from his labor. When boys entered the institution, no matter what they had been committed for, they received the same treatment, and, according as they were big or little, the same classification... When bed time came he was taken to a large cell-hall, for decency's sake called a dormitory; in each hall were from 150 to 200 narrow cells, 5 x 8 x 6, tier on tier, with a single barred slit in one wall called a window and in the other a grated iron door fitted with a padlock or brake.... When work was slack or wanting, long hours of idleness were his in which to morally degrade himself and his fellows and to plan all kinds of villainy.[96]

---

94. *See generally* F.H. Nibecker, *Education of Juvenile Delinquents*, 23 Annals 483 (May, 1904).

95. David S. Snedden, Administration and Educational Work of American Juvenile Reform Schools (1907).

96. *Id.* at 14; 16.

Descriptions such as this were commonplace but were terribly at odds with the received wisdom of the conservative reformers of the era as well as with the judges who occasionally had to address civil liberty issues in these places. It was a common practice of house of refuge managers to play up all favorable endorsements by notable visitors. For example, Barry Krisberg and James F. Austin[97] note that "[p]rominent visitors to the institutions, like Alexis de Tocqueville and Doreathea Dix echoed the praise of the founders."[98] Further on these same commentators observed that "[p]ublic relations efforts proclaiming the success of the houses of refuge helped lead to a rapid proliferation of similar institutions."[99]

C. Late Nineteenth-Century Developments

In the forty-year period stretching roughly from about 1880 to 1920, American society witnessed a major socio-structural rearrangement. This was an era marked by an enormous influx of European and Asian immigrants, an expanding urban population, a radical shift from an agrarian to a manufacturing economy and an abiding belief in the idea that government at all levels should be a major partner in addressing social ills. Historians generally refer to this time span as the Progressive Era.

In juvenile justice, the Progressive reformers were not at all timid in taking credit for the introduction of some of the more humane aspects of existing reformatories and training schools. However, these reforms were aimed always at achieving goals deemed worthy by the predominantly Caucasian middle class. It was during the first half of the Progressive Era, from 1880 to 1900, that certain events occurred which cast a long shadow over juvenile justice for most of the twentieth century. In the final two decades of the nineteenth century, the legal determination of guilt or innocence for crimes committed by children over age fourteen was essentially preordained. American criminal law, then as now, was wedded to the centuries-old common law doctrine of *mens rea* and blameworthiness as legal markers for criminal responsibility. That philosophy continued during the late

---

97. BARRY KRISBERG & JAMES F. AUSTIN, THE CHILDREN OF ISHMAEL: CRITICAL PERSPECTIVES ON JUVENILE JUSTICE (1978).

98. *Id.* at 18.

99. *Id.*

nineteenth century to place juvenile offenders over age fourteen on a par with adult violators. Progressive Era thought viewed this treatment of teenage youth over age fourteen as both unnecessary and unwise. In almost every aspect of American life, Progressives ardently desired to remold existing institutions to suit their own world view. The devotees of Progressivism in juvenile corrections desired to refashion their charges into something different, something more "American." Because many juvenile institutions housed a large immigrant cohort, Progressive administrators wanted to literally "make over" these children into persons fitting their idealized conception of the American adolescent of the time. William A. Williams[100] notes that Progressives believed that "[p]eople were capable of improvement, but improvement was defined as becoming more like Americans,"[101] thus the Progressive reformatory and training school of the late nineteenth century became the incubus for much of their later twentieth-century replicas.

Progressive era reformers became enamored with many of the new developments in the emerging social sciences. Sociology, psychology, anthropology, social work and criminology, among others, were developing theories and ideas and hypotheses about crime and delinquency that animated Progressive thought. In their book on benevolence and the altruistic enterprise, Willard Gaylin and others[102] remarked about the Progressives that "[t]heir ranks were composed of the graduates of the new universities, those who had typically spent most of their classroom hours learning the canons of social science. They had been taught to investigate social reality with a clear eye to its improvement."[103] Armed with the newly acquired knowledge of social science and with a resolve to make over the children of the underclass, they sallied forth to achieve higher goals. Rhetoric and reality, nonetheless, failed to coalesce in many of their endeavors, but such failure simply spurred them on to a greater effort. "[T]hey could not begin to understand that the programs [they sought] might be administered in the best interests of officials, not clients."[104]

---

100. William A. Williams, The Contours of American History (1961).

101. *Id.* at 400.

102. Willard Gaylin, Ira Glasser, Steven Marcus & David J. Rothman, Doing Good: The Limits of Benevolence (1978).

103. *Id.* at 75.

104. *Id.* at 79.

Developing alongside these reforms but yet at some distance philo-sophically from the inflexible responsibility criteria of the criminal law, was an institutional concept destined to have a profound impact on the men and women of the Chicago "experiment" of 1899. Though it is a relatively recent form of correctional treatment, proba-tion has a substantial history.

The probation concept—one that allows a convicted offender to remain free from the physical confines of jail or prison—has roots probably going back to the concept of benefit of clergy.[105] Sol Rubin[106] states that benefit of clergy was a device "by which the rep-resentatives of the Church, and later orders, could avoid the penal-ties of the criminal law....A successful defense through benefit of clergy transferred the criminal trial to the ecclesiastical court, which had the power to imprison for life but actually exacted little punish-ment beyond degradation."[107] This was benefit of clergy in its pure theistic form whereby a cleric could be tried in a bishop's court by a jury of clerks upon the oath of twelve compugators.[108] In 1350 the statute of *pro clero*[109] extended this ecclesiastical privilege to secular clerks and eventually to any male defendant who could read. By pleading benefit of clergy, an accused charged with a capital crime could escape the death penalty. Like so many other concepts in the law, however, abuse of the benefit of clergy became widespread.

---

105. LEONARD B. ORFIELD, CRIMINAL PROCEDURE FROM ARREST TO APPEAL 494–95 (1947). *See also* GEORGE W. DALZELL, BENEFIT OF CLERGY AND RELATED MATTERS (1955); S.F.C. MILSOM, HISTORICAL FOUNDATIONS OF THE COMMON LAW at 368 (1969). David Mellinkoff writes that "the customary test for the right to claim *bene-fit of clergy* (and so escape the harshness of the King's criminal justice) was the ability to read, later formalized as the ability to read the 'neck verse' in Latin: 'Miserere mei Deus' (Have mercy upon me, God)." DAVID MELLINKOFF, THE LANGUAGE OF THE LAW 86 (1963). (Emphasis in original).

106. SOL RUBIN, THE LAW OF CRIMINAL CORRECTIONS (1963).

107. *Id.* at 17.

108. Theodore F.T. Plucknett notes in describing the ancient English practice of "wager of law," an early form of trial, that "[t]he party who was called upon to make his law had to find a number of people, twelve or some other number fixed by the court according to circumstance, and then to take a solemn oath that he was innocent. His companions, or 'compurgators' as they were called, then swore that the oath which he had taken was clean....the court calls upon the accused to produce a specified number of people...who are prepared to swear that in their opinion his oath is trustworthy." THEODORE F. T. PLUCKNETT, A CONCISE HISTORY OF THE COMMON LAW 115 (1956).

109. 25 Edw. III St. 3, c. 4.

Thus, in the late 1400s Parliament enacted curative legislation removing what would now be considered murder with malice from the
benefit. By 1692, benefit of clergy was finally extended to women.[110]
Seeing it overextended and misused, however, England abolished the
concept entirely in 1827.[111]

Although benefit of clergy never became an accepted legal practice
in American criminal law, its core ideas of mercy, grace and redemp-
tion took hold in American correctional ideology. Paul W. Tappan[112]
takes the position that, in addition to benefit of clergy, the judicial re-
prieve and the recognizance were two additional forerunners of probation. In speaking of the idea of recognizance, Tappan states that

> This device of "binding over for good behavior" appears
> to have developed in England in the fourteenth century
> both as a means of preventive justice and as a means of
> avoiding punishment. Its use was specifically authorized by
> the English Criminal Law Consolidation Act of 1861 and
> the Summary Jurisdiction Act of 1879 for persons con-
> victed of misdemeanors and felonies. It was introduced
> early in the colonies and was very commonly employed, es-
> pecially in Massachusetts, as a means of avoiding the harsh
> and rigid penalties of the penal law.[113]

In the United States, historians of penology usually trace the active
beginnings of probation to the Boston bootmaker by the name of
John Augustus.[114] It is believed that Augustus was the first reformer
to actually use the word "probation" in the special sense of giving
bail under supervision. In August, 1841, Augustus first received on
bail from the Boston police court an inebriate who otherwise would
have been locked up in the contemporary equivalent of the "drunk
tank." Representing the Washingtonian Total Abstinence Society, the

---

110. 4 Wm. and Mary c. 9.

111. 7 & 8 Geo. IV, c. 28. This statute abolished benefit of clergy for all except the
peerage. As to them, the matter was finally put to rest by 4 & 5 Vict., c. 22 enacted in
1841.

112. PAUL W. TAPPAN, CRIME, JUSTICE AND CORRECTION (1960).

113. *Id.* at 540.

114. A Report of the Labors of John Augustus for the Last Ten Years in Aid of the
Unfortunate 5 (1852) and CHARLES CHUTE, JOHN AUGUSTUS: FIRST PROBATION OFFI-
CER: JOHN AUGUSTUS' ORIGINAL REPORT OF HIS LABORS, 1852 (1939).

Boston cobbler applied his curative techniques and reported a favorable result. In Augustus' own words:

> He [the offender] was ordered to appear for sentence in three weeks from that time. He signed the pledge and became a sober man; at the expiration of this *period of probation*, I accompanied him into the court room; his whole appearance was changed and no one, not even the scrutinizing officers, could have believed that he was the same person who less than a month before had stood trembling on the prisoner's stand.[115] (Emphasis added).

Probation's immediate evolution on the judicial scene evidently came about through the efforts of the nineteenth-century temperance movement; a movement, incidentally, not lost on the architects of later juvenile court legislation. Augustus spent the greater portion of the next eighteen years devoting his energies to the supervision and rehabilitation of offenders in the local courts of Boston.[116] Through the year 1858, it was reported that he had bailed some 1,946 persons.[117] Augustus' "...efforts had expanded during this period *to cover children* [in 1843], women, and offenders of many types. He claimed a very high proportion of success."[118] (Emphasis added).

The branching out of the idea of probation to include children in 1843 was the beginning of the juvenile probation concept. It gained credence in the adult courts where children were tried for a variety of offenses and the judges saw probation as a judicial and penological escape valve for youngsters who could be supervised in a non-custodial setting. Probation also had another attractive quality, especially to the Progressive mind set of the late 1800s. This was the belief that juveniles, especially, should be given a "second chance"; a chance to be an eligible candidate for the ministrations of developing social science treatment techniques. The ideology of probation for juveniles

---

115. *Id.*

116. For a more detailed analysis of both the history and the administration of probation, see 1 NICHOLAS S. TIMASHEFF, ONE HUNDRED YEARS OF PROBATION (1941); TODD CLEAR & VINCENT O'LEARY, CONTROLLING THE OFFENDER IN THE COMMUNITY (1984); JOHN ORTIZ SMYKLA, PROBATION AND PAROLE: CRIME CONTROL IN THE COMMUNITY (1984); and Edward Sieh, *From Augustus to the Progressives: A Study of Probation's Formative Years*, 57 Fed. Probation 67 (1993).

117. CHARLES CHUTE & MARJORIE BELL, CRIME COURTS AND PROBATION 44 (1956).

118. Tappan, *supra* note 112, at 544.

was closely tied to the concept of the probation officer as a surrogate parent figure. While not employing the *parens patriae* rubric with as much verve and intensity as was done post-1899, pre-1899 juvenile probation practice nevertheless was not averse to drawing parallels between the state and the *pater familias*.

Allied with the idea of probation in general child welfare was an equally strong animus among Progressive thinkers toward criminal punishment of children *per se*. The punishment of children in the eighteenth and nineteenth centuries, both here and abroad, would certainly not claim the accolades of enlightened penology. In the two centuries immediately preceeding the founding of the juvenile court, the philosophy of retribution and deterrence held full sway in criminal law administration. Public opinion in this era was noticeably disinterested in the plight of children accused, tried and sentenced for criminal violations. In her testimony before the British Select Committee on Criminal and Destitute Juveniles in 1852, reformer Mary Carpenter provided a vivid word-picture of the inconsistencies of the common law in treating child offenders as adults. In her polished but forceful style, she noted:

> In the English law, as far as I can understand it, children are considered incapable of guiding themselves, they are therefore entirely submitted to the guidance of their parents; they are not permitted to perform so good an act as apprenticing themselves to a trade; that cannot be done without permission of their parents.... A child likewise, has not the power of disposing of his own earnings. The parent has a right to demand from him his earnings if he is not apprenticed till 21.... The father is considered responsible for his maintenance; and if he neglects to provide him with proper food, the child can appeal to the parish, who will punish the father for so neglecting him. *But the moment the child shows he is really incapable of guiding himself by committing a crime, from that moment he is treated as a man....* He is tried in public, and all the pomp and circumstance of law is exercised towards him as to a man.[119] (Emphasis added).

---

119. *Report from the Select Committee on Criminal and Destitute Juveniles; Together With the Proceedings of the Committee*, para. 935, p. 118 (1852), as quoted in Grace Abbott, The Child and the State 323 (1938).

This report, like numerous other written during the period, clearly indicts the common law for its severity in the handling of juvenile lawbreakers. Felonies perpetrated by juveniles in this period of time were usually punished by death or transportation, and misdemeanors by whipping[120] branding, mutilating and by exposure to public ridicule.[121] The laws enacted in the early American colonies, particularly in Puritan New England, were excessively draconian by our standards. For example, in the *General Laws* of the New Plymouth Colony enacted in 1671, we read:

> If any Childe or Children above sixteen years old, and of competent Understanding, shall Curse or Smite their Natural Father or Mother; he or they shall be put to death, unless it can be sufficiently testified that the Parents have been very Unchristianly negligent in the Education of such Children, or so provoked them by extreme and cruel correction that they have been forced thereto, to preserve themselves from Death or Maiming.[122]

Note here that there was, in effect, a legal escape clause for specific parental wrongdoing. But, absent evidence of parental aggravation of some sort, a child's physical assault on or a vituperative ephitet hurled at a parent would seriously imperil the child's life. Out of this puritanical heritage of punishment for youthful wrongdoers came an attempt to ameliorate criminal punishments for children. Clearly, the early House of Refuge movement and its later counterparts trace their origins, in part, to this desire to diminish the criminal sanction and its more odious forms of punishment for the child.

Operating on the periphery of nineteenth-century judicial reforms were several socio-legal theories derived from the budding science of

---

120. For an American example of this form of punishment, *see* ROBERT CALDWELL, THE RED HANNAH, DELAWARE'S WHIPPING POST (1947).

121. A general discussion of some of the more bizarre and humiliating forms of punishment inflicted on both juvenile and adult in eighteenth and nineteenth century Anglo-American law can be found in GEORGE IVES, A HISTORY OF PENAL METHODS (1914); HEINRICH OPPENHEIMER, THE RATIONALE OF PUNISHMENT (1913); Arnold D. Margolin, *The Element of Vengeance in Punishment*, 24 J. Crim. L. & Criminology 755 (1933); and Thorsten Sellin, *Corrections in Historical Perspective*, 23 Law & Contemp. Probs. 585 (Autumn, 1958).

122. As quoted in CLIFFORD E. SIMONSEN, JUVENILE JUSTICE IN AMERICA 16 (3d ed. 1991).

criminology. In its purest sense, "criminology" refers to the scientific study of the causes of crime.[123] From its very inception, however, criminology has been a discipline hobbled by theoretical inconsistencies and some outright nonsense. That being said, only the major so-called "schools"[124] of criminological thought will be mentioned. The various schools of criminology, as philosophical and policy constructs, have generally been above the fray that exists in other components of the discipline. In fact, both criminal law and juvenile law have operated over the years within an overarching scaffold of criminological principles.

Man has always been a defining and classifying creature because definitions give us at least a surface feeling of security when we are forced to deal with abstruse concepts. The word "crime," unfortunately, is a notoriously abstruse term if we incorporate both the legal and the social science definitions into one interpretation. In a narrow legal sense, the term means a violation of a criminal law passed by a legislative body or a rule established by judge-made case law. Contrariwise, in a social science sense, the word crime takes on a broader definition because social scientists see crime not only emerging from recognized official categories, but also from unofficial non-reported data and from a series of perceived wrongs legally unrecognized. Hence, the search for a global, all-encompassing definition continues to elude us.

In its efforts to explain the multiple causes of criminal behavior, criminology developed trends of thought, each having at least some bearing on the principles and methods of the juvenile justice system. Writing as early as 1764, Cesare Beccaria[125] expressed a philosophic sympathy for the criminal and stoutly protested against the standard-

---

123. Edwin H. Sutherland and Donald R. Cressey, however, give a broader meaning to the term. They say: "Criminology consists of three principal divisions, as follows: (a) the sociology of law, which is an attempt at systematic analysis of the conditions under which criminal laws develop...(b) criminal etiology, which is an attempt at scientific analysis of the causes of crime; and (c) penology, which is concerned with control of crime." EDWIN H. SUTHERLAND & DONALD R. CRESSEY, CRIMINOLOGY 3 (9th ed. 1974).

124. "A 'school of criminolgy' is a system of thought, together with the supporters of that system of thought, The system of thought consists of a theory of crime causation integrated with policies of control implied in the theory." *Id.* at 49.

125. CESARE BONESANA BECCARIA, AN ESSAY ON CRIMES AND PUNISHMENT (1764).

less and unprincipled forms of punishment, especially the death penalty. Jerome Hall[126] noted that Beccaria's "...essay led not only to the greatest penal reforms in modern history, it also stimulated acceptance of the Humean philosophy of 'a moral [*i.e.*, social] science' modeled after physics and based on the precise application of the pleasure-pain principle...."[127]

It was Beccaria who made one of the first significant contributions to what is now termed the Classical School of Criminology. He, along with such other philosophic notables as Rousseau, Montesquieu and Voltaire[128] advocated the doctrine of psychological hedonism. American criminologists Edwin H. Sutherland and Donald R. Cressey[129] remarked that "[t]he general proposition of the classical school was that it is necessary to make undesirable acts painful by attaching punishment to them."[130] This was thought necessary in order that the criminal, through a form of mental calculus, could discern between the pleasure of the act versus the pain of impending punishment. By contemporary standards, of course, this form of thinking may seem somewhat archaic, but it nonetheless represented quite an advance in thought for its time. Despite their avowed interest in improving criminal law administration and penology, the classical writers eschewed any noticeable concern with the issue of criminal responsibility. Classical criminology was largely an administrative and legally-specific criminology, giving primacy to the reordering of the criminal law itself and emphasizing in particular the criminal act and its consequences. The classical writers spurred a shift in thought from the older notions of disparate penalties for a long list of wrongs, to a thesis which embodied the notion of proportionality; let the punishment fit the crime. Once the criminal act could be identified and fit into a particular legal category, the punishment for that act would follow as a matter of course from the doctrine's proportionate sanctions. Tappan[131] summed up quite well the Classical School's ideology when he wrote that "[t]he Classical School adopted the position that

126. Jerome Hall, General Principles of Criminal Law (2d. ed. 1960).
127. *Id.* at 603.
128. Marcello T. Maestro, Voltaire and Beccaria as Reformers of the Criminal Law (1942).
129. Sutherland & Cressey, *supra* note 123, at 301.
130. *Id.*
131. Tappan, *supra* note 112.

punishment should be administered for practical reasons to prevent crime and to protect public interests through deterrence, rather than gratuitously or for moral reasons...."[132]

However, classical criminology was not long in giving way to some of the more enlightened compromises of the so-called Neo-classical School.[133] The neo-classicists' basic charter of reform was by no means pedestrian. It held that the criminal law administrative and sentencing reforms promoted by the classical writers were too tentative and conservative in nature. To the neo-classical commentators certain groups of individuals such as children and the mentally disabled could not be expected to rationally calculate pain and pleasure, hence, they should not be regarded as blameworthy by the criminal law. Since blameworthiness was one of the core concepts in classical ideology, those persons suffering from certain legal disabilities could not, in good conscience, be *blamed* or be held *responsible* for their criminal behavior. Thus, under neo-classical criminology, reaction to crime should no longer be considered purely punitive; mitigating circumstances should and must be taken into account in order to perfect true justice. The nineteenth century witnessed the full development of neo-classicism in the legal systems of both Great Britain and the United States. By the late 1800s, neo-classic criminology, while not generally alluded to by name, nevertheless informed many appellate court decisions in cases dealing with youthful offenders and the mentally ill. As long as juveniles were being tried under the blameworthy icon of the adult criminal law, the very concept of "child" or "youth" could be interposed to lessen the sanctions imposed. A great many jurists intuitively adopted a neo-classical approach to both guilt-determining and punishment phases of criminal law practice. Although there were a number of juveniles who suffered the supreme legal sanction during the nineteenth century, towards the end of that century far more children became the recipients of neo-classical ideas already in place. The absorption by the judiciary of neo-classical teachings was not, of course totally instantaneous. However, in the last

---

132. Tappan, *supra* note 112, at 266.

133. A more detailed discussion of the Neo-classical and other "schools" of criminological thought can be found in the earlier work by GEORGE B. VOLD, THEORETICAL CRIMINOLOGY (1958) and in chapters two and three of the more recent revision of the Vold work by GEORGE B. VOLD & THOMAS J. BERNARD, THEORETICAL CRIMINOLOGY (3d ed. 1986).

third of the century the *idea* of special mitigation for a special population was an idea whose time had arrived. Juveniles were beginning to be seen as individuals less eligible for the application of the rigid responsibility-free-will classification of adult criminal law.

A third and final school of criminology that began in the latter 1800s provided the definitive rationale for the establishment of a separate justice system for children. Cesare Lombroso, Enrico Ferri and Raffaele Garofalo collectively formed the grand trinity of what was to be labeled the Positive School of Criminology. Radzinowicz[134] notes that "[v]irtually every element of value in contemporary criminological knowledge owes its formulation to that very remarkable school of Italian criminologists who took pride in describing themselves as 'positivists.'"[135] The first among equals in that Italian triumvirate was Lombroso "a physician and professor of psychiatry before acquiring a reputation as a criminal anthropologist."[136] Although little interested in theory, Lombroso was certain that there existed a distinct clinical entity which he called "the born criminal." He and his professional colleagues were adamant in their initial belief that the typical criminal was an atavistic "throw-back" to a lower form of primate life. "Their principal evidence that criminality was atavistic," writes Sutherland and Cressey,[137] "was the resemblance of the criminal subjects to the savage, but the characteristics of the savage were assumed, not determined by reliable methods."[138] In fairness to Lombroso's total outlook, however, it must be mentioned that he later modified his original thesis about the atavistic criminal and came to recognize the importance of the social causes of crime as well.[139]

One salient fact stands out when we look back on the rather unscientific approach of the Lombrosian formulation. No matter how crude his methodology and regardless of the fact that the Englishman

---

134. Leon Radzinowicz, In Search of Criminology (1961).

135. *Id.* at 3.

136. Marvin L. Wolfgang, *Criminology and the Criminologists*, 54 J. Crim. L.C. & P.S. 155, 156 (1963).

137. Edwin H. Sutherland & Donald R. Cressey, Principles of Criminology 123 (7th ed. 1966).

138. *Id.*

139. *See* Cesare Lombroso, Crime, Its Causes and Remedies (1913).

Charles Goring later demolished his entire "born criminal" theory,[140] Lombroso, nevertheless, brought to the study of criminals the advantages of what Hall described as a "crude empiricism."[141] In other words, criminological interest now focused on the offender and not on the criminal act. The act-oriented law of crimes held no interest *per se* for the disciples of criminal anthropology. Philosophically, the underpinnings of the positivist approach to the study of crime denied individual responsibility and reflected, instead, an avowed non-punitive response to criminal wrongdoing. The positivists would replace punitiveness with a more humane social defense rationale, emphasizing treatment and rehabilitation as the only true solution to widespread criminality. Positivism and social science emerged in the last part of nineteenth-century America as the twin answers to much that was troubling in the criminal law's treatment of children.

The Progressive Era reformers of the 1890s had finally found, what seemed to them at least, both a legal and a scientific basis for erecting a new jurisprudence for children. Drawing on the premises of the legal disabilities of youth, the doctrine of *parens patriae*, probation practice and the innovative teachings of positive criminology, the Illinois child savers discovered a ready-made justification for a separate juvenile court. Somewhat like a set of discordant strands being pulled through a common eyelet, the concepts of youth as mitigation, *parens patriae*, probation and positivism in criminology became welded into a single philosophy that emerged full-blown in the form of the Cook County Juvenile Court in 1899. There are, of course, revisionists in several fields who make it a point to suggest that other avenues of juvenile court formation were of more or equal importance to those just mentioned. Nonetheless, when one looks at the more immediate factors which coaleased in the Spring of 1899 to move the Illinois juvenile court legislation through the political process, one must, it is believed, give due weight to the four legal and criminological concepts that heavily influenced the minds of the reformers, politicians and jurists alike.

---

140. Charles Goring published his work, THE ENGLISH CONVICT in 1913, which statistically refuted Lombroso's concept of the "born criminal." In speaking to this point, Leon Radzinowicz said: "It is significant that the first major contribution by an Englishman to criminology...concentrated mainly on destroying the anthropological assumptions of the Lombrosian myth." *supra* note 134, at 173.

141. Hall, *supra* note 126, at 605.

Chapter Two

Establishment of the Juvenile Court

A. The Illinois Juvenile Court Act of 1899

The judicial system of the United States in the latter half of the nineteenth century was severely criticized in several quarters for its apparent inability to adapt to new social realities.[1] "Specialization of the courts was hopefully a panacea for the ills of the former system," said H. Ted Rubin and Richard Schaffer.[2] The *Illinois Juvenile Court Act* of April 21, 1899, was the prototype for subsequent legislation establishing a special court for a special purpose. This law put an end to the exclusive jurisdiction of criminal courts over minors under age sixteen charged with a violation of the state penal code. As a consequence of this Act, the Juvenile Court of Cook County, Illinois, opened on July 1, 1899. "To some," said Gustav Schramm,[3] "the Chicago doctrine was a strange one. The juvenile court was to act for the state ... as a parent, ... to recognize the individuality of the child and adapt its orders accordingly."[4] An entire new cluster of legal categories was established and the delinquency, dependency and neglect criteria of the original statute still survives today in slightly altered form in many juvenile codes. The initial Illinois law defined "delinquent child" as any minor under age sixteen "who violates any law of this State or any city or village ordinance."[5] This language incorporated all violations of the state penal code with the exception of capital felonies which remained within the jurisdiction of the adult criminal courts. The dependent and neglected child was then defined in a series of six separate categories as follows:

---

1. *See generally* JAMES W. HURST, THE GROWTH OF AMERICAN LAW, ch. 8 (1950) and Roscoe Pound, *The Causes of the Popular Dissatisfaction With the Administration of Justice*, 19 A.B.A. Rep. 395 (1906).

2. H. Ted Rubin & Richard S. Schaffer, *Constitutional Protections for the Juvenile*, 44 Denver L.J. 66 (Winter, 1967).

3. Gustav L. Schramm, *Philosophy of the Juvenile Court*, 261 Annals 101 (Jan. 1949).

4. *Id.*

5. *An Act to Regulate the Treatment and Control of Dependent, Neglected and Delinquent Children*, Ill. Laws 1899, 131.

(1) any child who for any reason is destitute or homeless or abandoned; (2) has not proper parental care or guardianship; (3) who habitually begs or receives alms; (4) who is found living in any house of ill fame or with any vicious or disreputable person; (5) whose home, by reason of neglect, cruelty, or depravity on the part of its parents, guardian or other person in whose care it may be, is an unfit place for such a child; (6) any child under the age of 8 years who is found peddling or selling any article or singing or playing any musical instrument upon the street or giving any public entertainment.[6]

Individually and collectively, these behaviors were thought to ultimately lead to a life of delinquency and crime, hence they had to be judicially identified and extirpated wherever possible. Going now by the more contemporary designation of "status" offenses, these statutory categories were the forerunners of a lengthening list of pre-delinquent behaviors that policymakers and the courts deemed critical for the control of juvenile misbehavior.

The second section of the Illinois statute precluded children under age twelve being committed to either "a jail or police station." The statute made separate provisions for the disposition of the delinquent, dependent and neglected children as well as provisions for probation services and certain types of guardianship arrangements. A juvenile court judge operating under this legislation had a much broader range of dispositional alternatives than his or her criminal court counterpart. Probation was the cornerstone of all dispositional options. This was followed by commitment to either an orphanage or foster home, or a guardianship placement to "any association or individual." Associations or individuals would then have the authority "to place such child in a family home, with or without indenture, and may be made party to any proceeding for the legal adoption of the child..." The final alternative was to commit the juvenile to either a training school (for males) or to an industrial school (for females) up to age twenty-one. The idea of a separate specialized court with a new treatment ideology was intense. "Delinquent children were to surrender to the state the powerful cloak of autonomy they had worn as citizens, possessing the rights guaranteed by state and federal constitutions, and in exchange they would be relieved of moral responsi-

---

6. *Id.* at § 8.

bility for, and cured of, incipient criminality."[7] Within five years of 1899, eleven states[8] had enacted statutes giving juvenile jurisdiction to either new or already existing tribunals. By 1909, the District of Columbia and twenty additional states had established juvenile courts. By 1927, all but Maine and Wyoming had some form of juvenile court in operation and these latter two holdouts had enacted juvenile court acts shortly after the end of World War II. In organizational structure, juvenile courts were far from unidimensional. For example, they could be organized along one or more of the following guidelines: (1) they could be a special branch or session of another court such as a district court, a superior court or a circuit court whose main function is to try civil and criminal cases at the adult level; or (2) the juvenile court may be a free standing, independent court which may or may not also hear and determine domestic relation cases dealing with matters of family law; or (3) the juvenile court may be defined with reference to a particular geographical space, such as a county court, a city court or a court having jurisdiction in an area specifically set forth by legislation. Despite variations in structure, however, all followed more or less the premises laid out in the original Illinois statute making allowances for legislative tinkering in specific jurisdictions.

The Illinois legislation represented a culmination of years of behind-the-scenes activity on behalf of children to separate and distance them from adult criminal law hegemony. As far back as 1870, the City of Boston had initiated separate hearings for children under age sixteen for certain types of offenses and New York City followed this same practice in 1877. The State of Massachusetts enacted a law in 1869 that mandated a member of the State Board of Charities to be present at juvenile trials to oversee their best interests. In Illinois, in particular, the Illinois Conference of Charities in 1898 proposed a radical departure from the past by lobbying for a separate court for child lawbreakers. Likewise, the legal profession in Chicago through the Chicago Bar Association added significant professional and political support to the Illinois Conference of Charities' position. Other influ-

---

7. *Comment*, Sherry B. Holstein, *Slamming the Door on Prodigals: Changing Conceptions of Childhood and the Demise of Juvenile Justice*, 9 No. Ky. L. Rev. 517, 527 (1982). *See also*, Albert J. Harno, *Some Significant Developments in Criminal Law and Procedure in the Last Century*, 42 J. Crim. L.C. & P.S. 427 (1951).

8. California, Colorado, Indiana, Iowa, Maryland, Missouri, New Jersey, New York, Ohio, Pennsylvania, and Wisconsin.

ential groups such as the Chicago Woman's Club and prominent individuals in the social welfare and legal communities lent their collective voices to the juvenile court idea.[9] The modern concept of childhood—so different from that of an earlier time—became the sociolegal grist for the new juvenile court mill. The 1899 statute was the first of many successive legislative blueprints establishing legal and social welfare jurisdiction over a wide array of American youth. The break with the criminal law past was more or less complete, or so it was believed. New terminology, new procedures and an entirely new gaze by a new statutory court immediately commanded the interest of professional and layperson alike.

B. Founding Theories and Philosophies of Juvenile Justice

In their desire to disassociate the juvenile from centuries of common law doctrine in criminal justice and to realign the court with a decided social welfare outlook, the child saving reformers proposed a new terminology more in keeping with their own world view. First, the juvenile court would have original and exclusive jurisdictional autonomy over three classes of children previously mentioned, the delinquent, the dependent and the neglected. The delinquent child would be considered the most serious malefactor because he or she would now be committing acts which otherwise would violate the penal law. Conversely, the dependent and neglected child categories were jurisdictional artifacts oriented toward the social agency role of the court. Unfortunately, as time went on and more states enacted juvenile codes, the clear legal distinction between delinquency, dependency and neglect began to blur. In fact, depending upon the phrasing of a particular juvenile code, dependency and neglect could and often did become commingled with the generic term "delinquency." This commingling of jurisdictional categories eventually led to some very serious civil liberty issues which will be addressed in a later chapter.

---

9. For an in-depth discussion of child saving in Illinois prior to the passage of the first juvenile court legislation, *see* ANTHONY M. PLATT, THE CHILD SAVERS: THE INVENTION OF DELINQUENCY ch. 5 (2d ed. 1977). *See also* WILLARD GAYLIN, IRA GLASSER, STEVEN MARCUS & DAVID J. ROTHMAN, DOING GOOD: THE LIMITS OF BENEVOLENCE 69–96 (1978); Henriette G. Frank, Jerome Amalie & Hofer Amalie, *Annals of the Chicago Woman's Club for the First Forty Years of Its Organization, 1871–1916* (1916) and THOMAS D. HURLEY, ORIGINS OF THE ILLINOIS JUVENILE COURT LAW (1907).

Besides this jurisdictional trinity, the founders of the juvenile court initiated a wholesale change in procedure and accompanying terminology. Juvenile court facilities were separate from adult criminal courtrooms and all terminology that harkened back to criminal law practice was abandoned. For example, instead of having phases in a juvenile proceeding called pre-trial, trial and sentencing, the new juvenile courts' vocabulary termed these pre-adjudicatory, adjudicatory and dispositional. The aim here was to rid juvenile justice terminology of any language reminiscent of the word "trial" since a juvenile was not before a juvenile court to be "tried" for a "crime," but simply to be "adjudicated" or not in one of the three jurisdictional categories. Another major departure in terminology was incorporated in the charging process. Instead of being charged by a complaint, indictment or information, a juvenile came before the court by virtue of a "petition." This charging document could be initiated by numerous state agents and private parties, not simply by a prosecuting attorney, grand jury or by a victim. Once in court, the child's procedural due process rights evaporated under the paternal glare of *parens patriae*. Under the *parens patriae* ideology, both the probation officer and the juvenile judge would assume the mantle of a surrogate parent-counselor-confessor to the child, hence there was no need for formal legal representation on the child's behalf. An even more radical break with the past was the view adopted early on that juvenile court proceedings were *civil* in nature, not criminal. Thus, long-standing constitutional due process protections that heretofore may have been employed to protect the juvenile tried in a criminal court were automatically dismissed as an impediment to the court's parental mission. The so-called "civil label of convenience" was a major source of legal empowerment not only for juvenile court personnel *per se*, but also for those responsible for community and institutional correction for the child. Such play on words had significant consequences for many children and permeated juvenile law well into the 1960s and beyond. In essence, calling a juvenile court hearing "civil" created a due process vacuum allowing unfettered state intervention in children's lives on a massive scale. Constitutional protections heretofore employed on behalf of juveniles in criminal court were routinely dismissed as an impediment to rehabilitation. The *parens patriae* liturgy was elevated to a sacrosanct position and anyone who had the temerity to question this benevolent doctrine was viewed as anti-child and anti-progressive. Years later, the United States Supreme Court would note in its *Gault* opinion that "[t]hese results [the reformation of the whole child] were to be achieved without coming to conceptual and constitutional grief, by insisting that the proceedings were not adversary, but that the state was proceeding as *parens patriae*."[10]

Once a petition was lodged against a child, the juvenile was not "arrested" but rather "taken into custody." The rationale for this terminological twist was that an arrest was a criminal law process, not one suited for identifying a process initiating state power over children. Subsequently, an elaborate screening or "intake" procedure was developed to determine whether a particular juvenile actually needed court protection. Screening or intake took the place of traditional criminal law procedures such as the first appearance before a magistrate, preliminary hearing, arraignment and plea negotiations.

If it was determined that a juvenile should be retained in the court system and held for eventual adjudication on the merits, the question of legal representation arose. But, in the cultural dynamics of the time, little thought was seriously given as to whether a lawyer should be representing a juvenile before this court. There were several contemporary arguments that kept legal assistance for juveniles a low visibility issue. In the vast majority of cases coming before the early (and later) juvenile courts were children suffering a dual handicap— poverty and educational deficiency. It probably did not even occur to them or even to their parents (who were often similarly situated) that legal representation might be of some value. In those few cases where an attorney was sought, the general reply from the juvenile courts and their probation offices was that lawyers were an impediment to the court's work and were not welcome. It was common knowledge among the Progressive juvenile court vanguard that legal counsel for children in this new tribunal would only serve to repudiate all they had worked for. Lawyers, it was said, would move the court retrogressively to a pre-1899 *status quo ante* of legal formalism that would stifle the court's creative mission. When the mission of a new branch of jurisprudence is uplift, benevolence and curative therapeutics, the re-introduction of a guilt-determining, adversarial procedure that lawyers would surely bring to the proceedings would be antediluvian. The ready reply to why lawyers were not welcome was that both the judge and the probation personnel would see to it that the

---

10. *In re Gault*, 387 U.S. 1, 16 (1967).

juvenile's legal rights were recognized and protected. Legal counsel for the child in such a scenario would be superfluous.

Another terminological variance from adult criminal law practice was employed by the juvenile judge in finding that a child had committed a statutory violation of the juvenile code. The juvenile was "adjudged" either to be delinquent, dependent or neglected; not found to be "guilty." Two reasons were advanced for this change: first, since juvenile court hearings were now considered *civil* in nature, the term "guilty" had no place in juvenile court jargon and secondly, an adjudication of "guilty" implied responsibility and personal blameworthiness. Clearly, condemnation and community and personal stigma were to be avoided at all costs. Juvenile law doctrine presupposes a non-criminal law adjudication that is basically non-judgmental and a resolution having no adult criminal law counterpart. The term "adjudged" was considered to be less pejorative and stigma-neutral. When all of this was tied to the non-public nature of juvenile court proceedings, the assumption of the Progressive word-Smiths was that such terminology, in tandem with confidentiality, would foster a body of law that would promote a more responsive solution to a juvenile's predicament.

All of these innovations and others in terminology, in structure and in practice augured well for the novel approach taken to secure a new court for troubled children. It is often said that philosophic constructs sometimes impede and at other times promote both legal and social change. For the emerging juvenile court in the early years of the twentieth century, its philosophic constructs fit admirably with the felt needs of the era regarding child welfare. Behind both the Illinois law and the establishment of the Cook County Juvenile Court stood a cluster of ideas that served to promote a national movement for a separate juvenile justice system. In sum, there were at least five essential ideas or aims of the juvenile court founders that, even to this day, still animate some segments of juvenile justice. These were: (1) the establishment of a tribunal that was organized to specifically avoid the stigma of criminalizing the young; (2) a tribunal whose processes would largely avoid public scrutiny through closed-door proceedings and the judicial sealing of juvenile records; (3) a tribunal whose treatment ethos would attempt to reduce youth crime by eradicating delinquent behavior in its "budding" stages; (4) a tribunal whose probation division would, in effect, open to the juvenile a "supermarket of social services"[11] under the aegis of a new social science; and (5) a tribunal whose personnel, for the most part, held an almost pathological prejudice against adult criminal law and practice.

Philosophies, however, are often both evanescent and sterile unless they are transformed into real-world policy choices. The Progressive reformers in the juvenile justice arena were quite adept at seeing their policy choices gain full implementation in the legislative and judicial councils of state government. The five philosophical aims for a jurisprudence for children were implemented by gaining legislative recognition of five parallel criteria for legal hegemony over youth. The first and probably the foremost control device was the recognition that the state, as such, enjoyed a superior right of parenthood over all the children within its geo-political boundaries. The state as a "higher" parent of the child was premised upon the doctrine of *parens patriae*. That doctrine gave the state a legal monopoly to intervene under appropriate circumstances. Along with the state as super-parent came a corollary civic obligation to individualize justice for each errant youth brought before the juvenile court. The reformers took quite seriously the dicta of the positive school of criminology that the *offender* and not the offense was the proper starting point for dealing with youth crime. By constructing a novel legal concept— delinquency—the child savers, in effect, deconstructed an entire body of law. In its place they re-constructed for the juvenile a statutory, non-criminal, stigma-neutral, treatment-oriented jurisprudence. In order to further their criminological and social service aims, the reformers established non-adversary proceedings to insure that the identification of the "root causes" of a child's lawbreaking could be dissected in an atmosphere unsullied by rigid formality and adversarial hyperbole. The last policy choice selected by the child savers was the adoption of non-punitive and remedial goals for the juvenile offender. Thus, these intentional policy choices in conjunction with the five main aims noted previously all served to transform philosophic rhetoric into judicial reality. Many of the pioneering juvenile court judges and lay persons having a stake in juvenile court expansion all trumpeted these new realities. One of the early juvenile jurists who was totally confident that a separate court for young lawbreakers

---

11. This phrase is attributed to the late Monrad G. Paulsen, formerly law dean at the University of Virginia and Yeshiva University's Benjamin N. Cardozo School of Law and nationally recognized scholar of the juvenile court.

was the only way to proceed was Julian W. Mack of Chicago. Writing in the *Harvard Law Review*[12] soon after the turn of the century, Judge Mack noted:

> Why is it not just and proper to treat these juvenile offenders as we deal with neglected children as a wise and merciful father handles his own child whose errors are not discovered by the authorities? Why is it not the duty of the state, instead of asking merely whether a boy or a girl has committed a specific offense, to find out what he is physically, mentally, morally, and then if it learns that he is treading the path that leads to criminality, to take him in charge, *not so much to punish as to reform, not to degrade but to uplift, not to crush but to develop, not to make him a criminal but a worthy citizen.*[13] (Emphasis added).

But Judge Mack and his successors in Illinois and elsewhere were increasingly becoming prisoners of their own rhetoric. Jane Addams, founder of Chicago's Hull House and a key spokesperson for social work and child welfare exuberantly noted that

> There was almost a change in mores when the juvenile court was established. The child was brought before the judge with no one to prosecute him and none to defend him—the judge and all concerned were merely trying to find out what could be done on his behalf. The element of conflict was absolutely eliminated and with it all notions of punishment as such with its curious connotation.[14]

Ben Lindsey, a noted early juvenile judge in Denver, was of the opinion that under the newly enacted Colorado juvenile code, a child who, for example, merely enters or visits certain undesirable places, is *automatically delinquent*! It mattered not whether such a child's entrance or visit was innocent in purpose. Lindsey characterized delinquency as a "condition" and he brushed aside any criticism that the powers wielded by this new court might somehow be abused. "Such fears," he wrote,[15] "have proved entirely groundless, since out of hundreds of cases brought to the juvenile court, no such charge

---

12. Julian W. Mack, *The Juvenile Court*, 23 Harv. L. Rev. 104 (1909).
13. *Id.* at 107.
14. As quoted in JUSTICE FOR THE CHILD 14 (Margaret K. Rosenheim ed. 1962).
15. Ben Lindsey, *The Juvenile Laws of Colorado*, 18 Green Bag 126 (1906).

has ever been taken to, or appealed from, a single judgment."[16] Judge Lindsey saw only a wise and beneficent judicial suzerainty flowing from juvenile court intervention; not outcomes whose results would, in any way, foster abuse of state power. There was no reason to question the juvenile courts' handling of young offenders, for any type of juvenile court intervention was far less harmful than what a child would experience at the hands of the criminal court. Herbert Lou,[17] expressed a then typical approach to this new court structure when he wrote that "[i]n this new court we tear down punitive prejudice, hatred and hostility toward the law breaker in that most high bound of all human institutions, the court of law, and we attempt as far as possible, to administer justice in the name of truth, love, and understanding."[18]

By 1932, there were over six hundred independent juvenile courts throughout the United States. Like other sociolegal trends that came to prominence in the first third of the twentieth century, juvenile justice was stoutly defended.[19] Few commentators raised their voice in opposition to this new legal structure. For those who did, the reply was quite simple: there was really nothing "new" or "different" about the juvenile court. Its genius emerged, by analogy, from the supervisory and benevolent powers of the courts of chancery over wards of the state via the doctrine of *parens patriae*.

The chancery background of juvenile court development, however, did not go totally unquestioned. Roscoe Pound believed that "the jurisdiction of equity over infants was not a factor in creating...[juvenile courts]."[20] He had a different theory. To Pound, juvenile court jurisdiction over the child "arose on the criminal side of the courts, because of the revolt of those judges' consciences from legal rules that

---

16. *Id.* at 129.

17. HERBERT H. LOU, JUVENILE COURTS IN THE UNITED STATES (1927).

18. *Id.* at 2.

19. Between the founding of the court in 1899 and the year 1904, eleven states had enacted juvenile codes. By 1909, twenty additional jurisdictions and the District of Columbia had passed juvenile court legislation and by the late twenties the movement had blanketed the nation.

20. ROSCOE POUND, INTERPRETATIONS OF LEGAL HISTORY 135 (1923). *See also* John Hagan & Jeffrey Leon, *Rediscovering Delinquency*, 42 Am. Soc. Rev. 587 (1987) for the argument that the juvenile court's establishment was premised upon existing legal policies rather than on any new or novel approach to juvenile crime.

required trial of children over seven as criminals... "[21] In perhaps an example of historic exaggeration, Pound alleged in 1913 that the powers of the infamous English Court of Star Chamber[22] were a trifle in comparison to those of the American juvenile court.

One fertile source for wider netcasting that would bring a number of children to the courts' attention was the jurisdictional ambivalence between a "true" delinquent and the wayward or unruly behavioral categories. Seeing that many just-emerging juvenile courts were rarely making any distinction between the juvenile who had violated a penal law and one who was either dependent or neglected, a few jurists began expressing their concern with this jurisdictional smorgasbord. In 1921, for example, Judge Edward Waite warned that "[h]as not the time arrived when no tribunal should claim the title of juvenile court...without distinction in aim and essential method between delinquent, dependent and neglected wards of the state...?"[23] Paul Tappan, a legally trained sociologist, noted that "[t]he procedures employed by these [juvenile] courts are based not upon chancery but upon the effort to act so far as possible like general agencies of child welfare rather than courts of law that administer what are fundamentally correctional measures.[24] Herbert Bloch and Frank Flynn[25] saw a combination of factors giving birth to the juvenile court system. "Actually, the evidence," they say, "indicates that the legal roots of the juvenile court lie both in the special treatment of children under the

---

21. Pound, *supra* note 20.

22. The Court of Star Chamber has come to symbolize the arrogance and inquisitorial overreaching of judicial power. With the fall of the House of Lancaster and the ascension of Edward IV (1461–1483) to the British Throne, the administration of certain matters of state, and, in particular, the criminal law of the medieval King's Council increasingly became the business of that body meeting in a room called the Star Chamber. Charles Rembar notes that "[t]he Tudors fostered what are sometimes called the Courts of the Royal Prerogative. Star Chamber is the best known, symbol of tyrannical injustice.... Star Chamber at first served more than a selfish royal purpose, but later it was turned to evil ends. The prerogative courts had a short life; they disappeared in the seventeenth century when the monarchs were subdued." Charles Rembar, The Law of the Land: The Evolution of Our Legal System 70–71 (1980).

23. Edward F. Waite, *How Far Can Court Procedure Be Socialized Without Impairing Individual Rights?*, 12 J. Crim. L. & Criminology 339, 340 (1921).

24. Paul W. Tappan, Crime, Justice and Correction 392 (1960)

25. Herbert Bloch & Frank Flynn, Delinquency: The Juvenile Offender in America Today (1956).

criminal law and in the chancery courts."[26] These differences aside, by the weight of both textual and appellate authority, it was the *parens patriae* rubric that seemed to be the dominant referent for deploying juvenile court power.

Parens patriae's theoretical nexus is the clearest in the civilly oriented dependency and neglect situations. It is the jurisprudential leap from that area to the delinquency jurisdiction as some form of quasi-criminal substitute for "true" crime that was disturbing to some. The Progressive reformers were well aware that they could not mount a frontal assault on the criminal law *per se* in the hope of humanizing its principles when they were applied to children. They devised, instead, a sociolegal end run around the criminal law to achieve their purposes. Since blaming and condemnation were not in their statist vocabulary, the reformers were forced to invent an alternative strategy. Jurists and lawmakers in the states were well aware that there was abundant precedent in chancery doctrine to make appropriate disposition of both the property and the person of children who were not well cared for. Judge Julian Mack wrote that "[w]e know that whatever may have been the historical origin of the practice, for over two centuries as evidenced by the judgments of the House of Lords and of the Chancellors, the courts of chancery in England have exercised for the protection of the unfortunate child."[27] Note here, however, Mack's use of the word "unfortunate." The *social condition* of being either in poverty or in some other "unfortunate" circumstance in life was never, *by itself*, sufficient to invoke the machinery of the criminal law. It was social condition *plus* that invoked criminal jurisdiction during the pre-juvenile court era. The "wayward" child with all the connotations such a term implied had been dealt with quite frequently in nineteenth-century America, albeit in criminal courts.[28] The "plus," of course, was the seminal idea that unless society moves to first identify and then ameliorate the vice of waywardness, criminal behavior would follow as a matter of course. The new vanguard of child savers in the early twentieth century were quite willing and

---

26. *Id.* at 308.

27. Mack, *supra* note 12.

28. For a seminal article addressing the legal treatment of wayward children by the American courts in the nineteenth century, *see* Peter D. Garlock, *Wayward Children and the Law, 1820–1900: The Genesis of the Status Offense Jurisdiction of the Juvenile Court,* 13 Ga. L. Rev. 341 (1979).

indeed eager to establish a linkage with misfortune and criminality. At least for children, one rarely existed without the other. Armed with this linkage, the child savers were then able to de-couple crime from a rigid age-specific formulae in penal law and re-couple it to a civil law idea that embodied the essence of sovereign protection.

> The truly revolutionary feature of...juvenile court legislation [was] the extension of state authority through civil and equity courts involving children charged with committing acts of a criminal nature. The jurisdiction of the juvenile court in this instance [was] probably a product of civic conscience revolting against the inhuman aspects of post-conviction treatment accorded youthful offenders.[29]

The chancery principles of guardian-ward, *parens patriae*, flexible procedure, dispositional flexibility and the court's ability to operate *in personam* (on the person) instead of simply *in rem* (on property), all contributed to chancery's attraction. The Progressive child savers were comfortable with this body of jurisprudence and juvenile court ideology was drawn firmly into the orbit of equity. Nonetheless, much of the foregoing was a doctrinal illusion. Courts of chancery never exercised any *criminal law* power over children at all prior to 1899. But, illusions and legal fictions of amazing variety have been a staple of Anglo-American law for centuries and the introduction of this particular illusion was both intensively seductive and pragmatic. "If an illusion helps men live..." wrote Jerome Frank,[30] "then to insist upon exposing the falsity of the illusion...is at best pedantry... and at worst malicious mischief."[31] The Progressive architects of the juvenile court had no intention of exposing any false illusions. Their ideology was boxed in and protected by *parens patriae* and the falsity of their illusions went unexamined for sixty-eight years.

During the juvenile courts' adolescent and early adult years, few legal scholars took issue with the equitable accommodation to criminal justice. Roscoe Pound, however, continued to be one of a small number who discerned a problem few of his colleagues even acknowledged. In 1930, Pound wrote that "[n]o legal machinery of

---

29. Note, *Misapplication of the Parens Patriae Power in Delinquency Proceedings*, 29 Ind. L.J. 475, 476 (1953–54).

30. JEROME FRANK, LAW AND THE MODERN MIND (1935).

31. *Id.* at 118.

which we have any knowledge is equal to doing everything which we might like to achieve through social control by law."[32] He made direct reference to the juvenile court as an example of the law's impotence in ordering certain aspects of community life. Such impotence, however, did not become fully acknowledged until much later.

In addition to constructing a novel legal base for state intervention in the lives of children, the juvenile court gained widespread legitimacy by supplementing that legal base with a parallel social science base. There was an implicit, if not explicit, *quid pro quo* argument operational in the system's two-track jurisdiction net. If the judiciary chooses to intervene in children's lives, that intervention should be connected to a social science able to deliver treatment and rehabilitation to some of society's most vulnerable members. To address the problem of criminally deviant youth, both the early and then the later mid-century juvenile court became a laboratory for testing new theories in criminology and related disciplines. Yet the predominant conception of juvenile delinquency, certainly after mid-century, was jaded by the contemporary social *zeitgeist*. In the formative years of the juvenile court, however, the public's perception of juvenile wrongdoing was closely tied to the twin hobgoblins of poverty and social disorganization. These two areas were the chief foci of the nascent field of social work. As an embryonic discipline striving for professional status, social work began to concern itself with moral and social uplift. Social work processes, especially casework, began to exert a noticeable influence on the operational practices of the juvenile court.

In the decades preceding the establishment of the juvenile court, several developments in the general field of social welfare assumed prominence. From about 1885 on there emerged in urban American certain group-serving social agencies such as the Boy's Clubs, the YMCA and the YWCA. The policy of these organizations was to provide, among other things, appropriate role models for young persons in an environment stressing both a religious orientation and youth activities. The idea of Christian benevolence and outreach melded with a community organization model exerted a profound influence on child savers and Progressive reformers of all persuasions. H. Wayne Johnson[33] notes also that

---

32. Roscoe Pound, Criminal Justice in America 62 (1930).
33. The Social Services: An Introduction, 2d ed. (H. Wayne Johnson ed. 1986).

One of the most fascinating social innovations in urban
centers...was the settlement house....One of the best
known was Hull House in Chicago, established in 1899 by
Jane Addams, one of the striking early personalities in
American social work. Settlement houses were typically located in the inner city in areas populated by working people and immigrants....Settlements also impacted upon
other social movements such as the juvenile court...[34]

Jane Addams herself noted[35] that the settlement house workers
"must be open to conviction and must have a deep and abiding sense
of tolerance" while at the same time the "residents must be emptied
of all conceit of opinion and all self-assertion..."[36] The ideas of conviction to a purpose, tolerance for cultural and behavioral differences
and the notion of what is best for settlement tenants dovetailed quite
neatly with the ukases of the child saving ethos. In 1910, for example, Harvey Baker wrote that the proper approach to juvenile court
practice would be to conceptualize the juvenile judge as a sort of *social physician* and the probation officer as his *medical assistant*. Said
Baker,[37] "The [juvenile] judge and the probation officer consider together, like a physician and his junior, whether the outbreak [of delin-
quency] was largely accidental, or whether it is due chiefly to some
inherent physical or moral deficit of the child, or whether some feature of his environment is an important factor..."[38]

While the settlement house concept of social work community organization practice emphasized, in part, the environmental correlates
of juvenile delinquency and social disorganization in general, criminology and medicine were collaborating to put an empirical "face"
on the aetiology of delinquency. Harvey Baker and his followers were
among the first in juvenile justice to introduce what was later to be
known as the "medical model" of rehabilitation. H. Ted Rubin[39] ar-

---

34. *Id.* at 35–36
35. JANE ADDAMS, TWENTY YEARS AT HULL HOUSE, as quoted in DONALD
BRIELAND, LELA B. COSTIN & CHARLES R. ATHERTON, CONTEMPORARY SOCIAL WORK:
AN INTRODUCTION TO SOCIAL WORK AND SOCIAL WELFARE 101 (2d ed. 1980).
36. *Id.*
37. Harvey H. Baker, *Procedure for the Boston Juvenile Court* as quoted in PREVEN-
TIVE TREATMENT OF NEGLECTED CHILDREN (Hastings H. Hart ed. 1910).
38. *Id.* at 322.
39. H. TED RUBIN, THE COURTS: FULCRUM OF THE JUSTICE SYSTEM (1976).

gued that the juvenile court in its formative years was "[c]reated in an aura of benevolent paternalism, it would be law and social work, control and help, the good parent and the stern parent; it would be all things to all people."[40]

A new social work phrase that would also have important consequences for the juvenile court came into being in early twentieth-century America. The term "social services" identified a congeries of interwoven techniques designed to improve and remediate the lot of the urban underclass. Ira Glasser[41] trenchantly observed that this terminology was employed

> especially by political liberals as entirely humanitarian and benevolent, an undifferentiated and untroublesome *social* extension of humanity's best individual *instincts....* This undifferentiated view of social services and the political context in which the struggle to provide social services took place, tended to blind liberals to certain unintended consequences of their good works.[42] (Emphasis in original).

Child welfare advocates in social work in the early twentieth century noted that there was little, if any, national effort to promote their particular agenda. In 1909, however, President Theodore Roosevelt, at the behest of such prominent social workers as Edward Devine, Florence Kelly and Paul Kellogg, among others, invited professionals in child welfare to the first White House Conference on the Care of Dependent Children. A broad agenda was adopted at this gathering that rejected the notion that children should be removed from their parents because of simple misfortune or poverty. Among the recommendations of special interest was the one that promoted the idea

---

40. *Id.* at 66. Sociologist Edwin M. Lemert noted, however, that "[t]he establishment of the first juvenile courts reveal them to have been less a carefully planned innovation than the climax of a nineteenth century reform movement to rescue children from the depravity and immorality of lower class urban environments. The envisioned ideal that delinquent children would thereafter be defined and treated as 'neglected' proved false; in practice, the reverse often was true, that is, dependent and neglected children fell under the pall of delinquency and in many cases were subjected to the same kinds of sanctions." EDWIN N. LEMERT, INSTEAD OF COURT: DIVERSION IN JUVENILE JUSTICE 5–6 (1971).

41. WILLARD GAYLIN, IRA GLASSER & STEVEN MARCUS, DOING GOOD: THE LIMITS OF BENEVOLENCE (1978).

42. *Id.* at 101–07.

that the federal government should establish an official agency for children. Following up on this recommendation, the United States Congress created the Children's Bureau in 1912. President William Howard Taft appointed Julia Lathrop, a close personal friend of Jane Addams, as the first director of the Children's Bureau. This agency had a varied mission. Besides dealing with issues of infant mortality, child labor, and social legislation affecting children, the Children's Bureau also had an interest in the juvenile court and its operations.

The nexus between the Children's Bureau and juvenile courts became immediately apparent. Because of the plight of the urban poor, those in the Bureau that worked closely with juvenile court personnel were of the opinion that steps should be taken by juvenile courts to aggressively identify and separate out those children who have need of social service intervention. Probably most of the social work personnel in the Children's Bureau, as elsewhere in this new profession, were not doctrinaire partisans for any one particular solution or intervention technique for use in juvenile justice. Instead, in Robert Bremmer's words on the role of social workers in the reform movements of the early twentieth century,[43] "they made their appeal to altruism rather than to ideology. Generally speaking, they were content with piecemeal progress.... Abolish the misery of the most miserable, they counseled, and repeat the process as long as want and suffering persist."[44]

The Children's Bureau, the Child Welfare League of America founded in 1920, and the subsequent White House Conferences on child welfare and children's health and protection all set the stage for a collaborative effort between private and governmental social work agencies. The social work ethos of non-judgmental intervention to help the helpless found receptive soil in the early juvenile court. Like social work, juvenile justice was in its infancy in the early 1900s and these two emerging fields—social services and juvenile justice—were both idealistically and pragmatically merged to form a lasting partnership. In the early years of accommodation there was little aware-

---

43. Robert Bremmer, *A Note on the Role of Social Workers in the Reform Movement* as quoted in PERSPECTIVES ON SOCIAL WELFARE: AN INTRODUCTORY ANTHOLOGY (Paul Weinberger ed. 1969).

44. Id. at 89. For a detailed history of the United States Children's Bureau through the 1950s, see DOROTHY E. BRADBURY, FIVE DECADES OF ACTION FOR CHILDREN: A HISTORY OF THE CHILDREN'S BUREAU (1962).

ness of the awesome power both law and social work wielded over certain segments of America's young population. By themselves neither juvenile courts not the social work profession had the ability to address the rising criminality of urban youth. But, demography, social circumstance, economic and public choice decisions forged a bond between these two areas of American life that has lasted throughout the twentieth century. Juvenile courts became one of the official "suppliers" to social work of a group of children viewed as prime candidates for innovative social service ministrations. There was, in sociologist Robert Merton's phraseology, a "path dependence" between juvenile courts and the social work establishment. Without a separate court for troubled youth that would funnel their charges into a social service continuum, the juvenile judge would not, in most cases, be fulfilling his or her *parens patriae* role. Each was dependent upon the other not only for "clients," but also for political and economic support. This was a symbiotic relationship involving the juvenile judge, the probation staff of the court and various social service agencies. Denver juvenile court judge Ben Lindsey captured this law-social work relationship quite well when he wrote in 1904[45] that

> [the juvenile court's] purpose is...to prevent crime before crime is actually committed....the inception of crime is in the waywardness of misdirected children. It would take care of these children in adolescence, when character is plastic and can be molded as clay in the potter's hands. It would help to form character and not postpone the evil day in a burglary attempt to reform it.[46]

Note here the emphasis in judge Lindsey's characterization of the role of the juvenile court: prevention, a "plastic" adolescent character and the court's mission to mold delinquents into law abiding citizens. What better way to do this than by calling upon the expertise of the child welfare branch of the social work profession. Thus there was in a real sense both a marriage of ideology and of convenience between the juvenile court and social justice exemplified in the methods and practices of social work.

---

45. Ben Lindsey, *The Juvenile Court of Denver* in INTERNATIONAL PRISON COMMISSION, CHILDREN'S COURTS IN THE UNITED STATES: THEIR ORIGIN, DEVELOPMENT AND RESULTS (1904).

46. *Id.* at 30–31.

C. Early Case Law and Legislative Developments

"Well before the invention of the juvenile court," says Peter Garlock,[47] "statutes authorizing the state to intervene coercively in the lives of wayward children, whether on grounds of general misbehavior such as 'incorrigibility' or specific offenses for youth such as truancy, were prevalent in the United States."[48] When the reformers established the additional jurisdictional grounds for juvenile court intervention based upon delinquency and neglect in 1899, there was nearly a century of legal precedent and statutory authority justifying the inclusion of the status offender as well. During the early years of its existence, roughly from 1899 to about 1935, the juvenile court enjoyed the benefits of a significant "hands-off" policy practiced by the nation's appellate bench. Delinquency, dependency (or waywardness) and neglect decisions by juvenile courts all across the country were met with almost complete approbation by state courts of appeal. What follows is a selected sampling of the appellate mind-set that established the tone of juvenile law for nearly seventy years.

While still the subject of jurisprudential debate, one can at least argue that what "the law" is in a particular field is what appellate courts say it is. Despite the fact that the overwhelming majority of juvenile cases never go beyond the trial court level, the "law" of juvenile justice is developed, if at all, at the appellate stage. The appellate opinion is a form of discourse that both enlightens and instructs. It enlightens lawyers and juvenile court practitioners on the application of legal doctrine while instructing them in the manner in which future fact patterns may be resolved. James Boyd White[49] observes that

> While the law works as a system of discourse, this does not happen in isolation but in interaction with the other systems of discourse that make up our world. Law is a language that must establish relations with virtually all other languages spoken in our world: scientific and technical

---

47. Garlock, *supra* note 28.
48. *Id.* at 434.
49. James Boyd White, *Imagining the Law*, as quoted in THE RHETORIC OF LAW 38 (Austin Sarat & Thomas R. Kearns eds. 1994).

talk, psychological and sociological language, the speech habits of the parties and the witnesses, and so forth.[50]

In the formative period of the body of case law that established the juvenile court, appellate courts clearly interacted "with the other systems of discourse" to uphold lower court decisions involving juvenile justice questions. Implicitly realizing that a new jurisprudence needed a corresponding new corpus of case law to legitimate its existence, appellate courts early on began to expound upon and develop that corpus.

In 1900, the Supreme Court of Nebraska had before it a case involving a fourteen-year-old child by the name of Sarah Jane Flowers.[51] Among other things, this minor was alleged to be "incorrigible and from lack of proper parental care and control, and is growing up in idleness and vice."[52] The juvenile was committed to the state Industrial School for Girls, but was later released after an *ex parte* hearing. By her next friend, Lucretia Flowers, the child commenced a civil action for damages against F. W. Scott for both false imprisonment and malicious prosecution. A verdict by a jury in the amount of $2,500 for false imprisonment was rendered and Scott appealed. Although sustaining the damage award on appeal, the Nebraska Supreme Court noted that

> the complaint charged this girl with incorrigibility. Who is more likely to eventually become a criminal than a youth who is so far advanced in following [her] own will as to have become incorrigible...Clearly, an incorrigible youth is "growing up in crime," within the meaning of this term, taking it in its broadest sense,...[53]

In speaking to the penal character of the Industrial School, the court ruled that "[t]hese institutions are not of a penal character, but are reformatory. Many who are sent there are not criminals..."[54] and their inmates are there "for the purpose of reforming them."[55] Here we begin to see early appellate language intentionally employed to validate the ideology of child saving!

---

50. *Id.*
51. *Scott v. Flowers*, 84 N.W. 81 (Neb. 1900).
52. *Id.*
53. 84 N.W. at 82.
54. *Id.*
55. *Id.*

Six years later in 1906, the Supreme Court of Georgia had a case[56] before it involving a writ of *habeas corpus* filed by the plaintiff to regain the custody of her child from the managers of an institution called the "Home for the Friendless." The juvenile had been committed to that institution by the Recorder's Court of the city of Atlanta. The plaintiff attacked numerous provisions of a Georgia statute enacted in 1894 that regulated benevolent institutions in that state. The trial court heard all of the plaintiff's arguments and then issued an order denying the writ and remanding the child to the custody of the Home for the Friendless. In reviewing the denial of *habeas corpus*, the Supreme Court of Georgia took special pains to expound on one argument made by the appellant. Appellant asserted, among other things, that the Georgia legislature in enacting certain statutes affecting benevolent institutions for children had violated the Thirteenth Amendment to the United States Constitution. That amendment prohibits slavery and involuntary servitude except for punishment of crime. The gist of appellant's argument here was that this juvenile was being forced by the State of Georgia into a posture of involuntary servitude because she had not been charged with nor convicted of a "crime" in the traditional sense of that term. Although the state high court reversed the lower court ruling on other grounds, it is noteworthy to focus on the language employed by the Georgia Supreme Court in addressing the involuntary servitude argument:

> When the state as parens patriae,...takes under its custody and control those unfortunates who are unable to take care of themselves on account of physical or mental infirmity, or on account of the fact that those charged with the duty of caring and providing for such persons fail to discharge this duty...it cannot be said that,...such persons are placed within slavery within the meaning of the constitutional provisions denying the power of the state to establish that condition of servitude.... [I]t necessarily follows that, when the state has to assume the control and custody of the child, its conduct towards it would be the same as that of a dutiful parent would exercise...and the action of the state...would neither amount to a placing of a child in slavery, nor depriving it of its liberty in an unlawful way.[57]

---

56. *Kennedy v. Meara et al.*, 56 S.E. 243 (Ga. 1906).
57. *Id.* at 247.

From the language of these two early appeals, one can begin to adduce the statist assumptions that courts of appeal were employing to uphold whenever possible the hegemony of state superintendence over youth. In 1907, the Supreme Court of Utah[58] decided a matter involving a thirteen-year-old male charged with the petty larceny of a box of cigars. In a ringing endorsement of the juvenile court laws of Utah, the court remarked that

> Such laws are most salutary and are in no sense criminal and not intended as a punishment, but are calculated to save the child from becoming a criminal. The whole and only object of such laws is to provide the child with an environment such as will save him to the state and society as a useful and law-abiding citizen... [T]he proceedings of the juvenile court do not fall, nor are they intended to come within what is termed criminal procedure, nor are the acts therein mentioned, as applied to children, crimes.[59]

Despite such language, however, the *Mill* case was an early aberrant exception that overturned the commitment of a juvenile by a juvenile court. The Utah appellate judges were adamant that before any juvenile court could split up families and infringe upon their natural rights, two additional findings were necessary: (1) that the child was, in fact, "delinquent," and (2) that the parent or guardian be proven antecedently incompetent or neglectful of parental duties in the care, training and education of the child. The child's commitment to the state Industrial School was set aside to allow the boy's father to substantiate his fitness as a parent in another proceeding.

Since juvenile law derived its animating characteristics from chancery, jury trials in a juvenile court were a non-issue. Traditionally, courts of chancery did not employ juries as fact-finders except in rare cases; the chancellor was both judge and jury. In the juvenile justice context in those rare situations where the jury trial issue was raised, appellate courts spoke with essentially one voice. In 1911, the Court of Appeals of Kentucky decided a case[60] wherein it was contended that the enactment of the Kentucky juvenile court statute denied a delinquent child the right to trial by jury and was hence unconstitutional. Justice Lassing,

---

58. *Mill v. Brown*, 88 Pac. 609 (Utah 1907).
59. *Id.* at 613.
60. *Marlow v. Commonwealth*, 133 S.W. 1137 (Ky. 1911).

noting that this was a case of first impression in Kentucky, utilized a common notion and precedent from thirteen other jurisdictions to deny a jury trial to the juvenile in question. Said Lassing:

> The last objection urged to the [juvenile court] act is that it is unconstitutional because it deprives the delinquent or dependent child of its liberty without due process of law, in that no jury trial is provided for.... [S]imilar acts have been in force in other states, and this same objection has been made to their validity, and the courts have, with a degree of uniformity, upheld them.[61]

Citing thirteen separate state supreme court opinions ruling on the jury trial issue for juveniles, Lassing noted that "[a]ll these opinions are rested upon the theory that the [juvenile] proceedings are not criminal, but merely the *services of the government* calling into play ...protecting, training, and correcting a class of children who, through *misfortune*...are unable or unwilling to care for themselves."[62] (Emphasis added). The words "services," "protecting," "training," and "correcting" those who are suffering "misfortune" were now firmly embedded in the juvenile justice lexicon by the end of the court's first decade of operation. Social work, criminology, psychology, sociology and corrections now had a firm ideological foundation in juvenile court philosophy and practice.

Nineteenth-century reformatories and training schools often attempted to inculcate religious orthodoxy among their young charges. Various Protestant viewpoints dominated custodial institutions. Appellate courts in the early years of juvenile court development would often assume, *sub silentio*, that the Christian faith was the dominant religion of choice to be propagated among incarcerated youth. In 1913, however, the Supreme Court of Illinois, in the case of *Lindsay v. Lindsay*,[63] announced an opinion that deviated from this norm. In *Lindsay*, the appellant Charles R. Lindsay, filed a petition in the juvenile branch of the Circuit Court of Cook County charging that William Lindsay, a male child under age seventeen, "was a dependent child, and did not have proper parental care; that his father was dead, and that he was in the care of his mother and one Otoman Zar-

---

61. *Id.* at 1141.
62. *Id.* at 1142.
63. 100 N.E. 892 (Ill. 1913).

Adusht Hanish..."[64] Apparently, the child's mother was a follower and probable religious convert to the Mazdaznan religion "said religion purports to be the teaching of oriental philosophy and religion."[65] At the time of the filing of the petition, the juvenile and his mother were visiting Illinois, but were residents of another state. Before the day appointed for the hearing, the mother and the juvenile disappeared and the Circuit Court of Cook County, sitting as a juvenile court, entered a default decree against both mother and son. The court made a finding that the juvenile was "a neglected and dependent child..."[66] Subsequently on appeal, the Supreme Court of Illinois noted that "[i]t is the connection of Mrs. Lindsay with this religious society [Mazdaznan] and the association of the boy with Hanish, that afford the basis for the allegation in the petition that she is an improper guardian of her boy."[67] Nonetheless, in an opinion by Justice Farmer, the court found no evidence of parental neglect and reversed the decree of the Circuit Court of Cook County. The Illinois high court noted that the mother "has great faith in Hanish as the head of the Mazdaznan religion and...there is no evidence that she is in any way an unfit or improper person to have the care and custody of her boy."[68] Furthermore, "[t]here is no proof in the record that the Mazdaznan religion is an immoral religion, or that Hanish himself is an immoral man or engaged in immoral practices..... There should be evidence that the child is being exposed to immorality and vice."[69] Finding none, the court overturned the juvenile court ruling. Perhaps this was an early twentieth-century opinion favoring religious pluralism, but aberrant nonetheless in the overall scheme of orthodox Christian teachings. Few appellate courts would so easily overturn a lower court decision that essentially equated religious heterodoxy with "neglect."

Appellate rulings during the Progressive era of juvenile court history also served as legislative teacher. The Supreme Court of Missouri in 1914 had before it an appeal wherein a probate court judge refused to hear a case involving a charge of petty larceny against a

---

64. *Id.* at 893.
65. *Id.*
66. *Id.*
67. *Id.* at 896.
68. *Id.*
69. *Id.* at 897.

twelve-year-old boy.[70] It was the probate judge's contention that the Missouri act conferring jurisdiction on probate courts to hear juvenile cases violated certain sections of the state constitution. In an action for a writ of mandamus to compel the probate judge to hear and determine the case, a state circuit court ultimately sided with the probate judge and refused to grant a preemptory writ. The prosecuting attorney than appealed that refusal to the Supreme Court of Missouri. In a lengthy opinion, the latter court ruled, in effect, that the state probate courts were without jurisdiction to hear cases against a juvenile charged with either a felony or a misdemeanor *per se*. Per Justice Walker, the court noted that

> While this act extends the prima facie rule of an infant's non-liability for crime to 17 years, it could not, without revolutionizing the entire system of the criminal law... change the class of character of offenses designated in the Constitution and the statutes as felonies and misdemeanors. These classes or character of offenses not being changed, the same procedure must be observed in their prosecution whether the offender be an adult or an infant ...While such [juvenile court] legislation should be sustained and encouraged, it cannot be when it is, as in this case, in conflict with the organic law and as a consequence out of accord with our entire system of criminal jurisprudence.[71]

As appellate teacher, *Tincher* admonished the legislature to take another look at the juvenile statutes of Missouri. The *Tincher* opinion sought to bring legislative creativity to bear on the question of requiring state probate courts, as chancery tribunals, to exercise jurisdiction over "delinquency" used in its generic sense by the child savers. Under Missouri law, probate courts were without jurisdiction over offenses whose initiation must commence by either indictment of by information. A "true" crime must be charged by a formal accusatory pleading, and since that was not possible in probate, the decision was both doctrinally and procedurally correct.

By the end of the first twenty years of juvenile court operation, the institutionalization of that court was a *fait accompli* in American law.

---

70. *State ex rel. Cave v. Tincher*, 166 S.W. 1028 (Mo. 1914).
71. *Id.* at 1032-33.

In *Ex parte King*,[72] the Supreme Court of Arkansas fell under the spell of Progressive era rhetoric in 1919. There a juvenile named Pearlie King was adjudged delinquent by the juvenile court of Independence County in May, 1919. A petition for a writ of *habeas corpus* was sought against the superintendent of the Girl's Industrial School of Arkansas where the juvenile was held. The petition was denied in the lower court, and on appeal to the state supreme court, that tribunal affirmed the lower court decision awarding custody of the juvenile to the state institution. In the opinion of the Arkansas Supreme Court, the creation in 1911 of juvenile courts by the state legislature was constitutional because

> the sole purpose of this act seems to be to supply those who are "destitute, homeless, abandoned," wayward or incorrigible, who have not yet arrived at the age where they are entitled by the law of nature or of the state to absolute freedom, with such environments as will conduce to their physical, moral, and intellectual well-being. This law undertakes to *reclaim* and *reform* rather than to condemn and punish. For these *unfortunate minors* who come within the terms of the act it opens the doors of an *asylum, but not a jail.*[73] (Emphasis added).

Further on, the court noted its parent surrogate role when it observed that "[c]ertainly no higher duty could devolve upon the government than to throw proper safeguards around that helpless class..."[74] In concluding his opinion, Justice Wood was moved to observe that "[t]he progressive and enlightened policy of such [juvenile court] legislation is everywhere recognized and commended. Happily for the unfortunate class benefited and for the public weal we find no barrier in our organic law to the act in its present form."[75] The magical litany of words like "reclaim," "reform," "unfortunate class," and "asylum" were skillfully combined to convince any reader, professional or lay alike, that social welfare doctrine had become legal doctrine as well.

Not surprisingly, the 1920s era produced more of the same. The gist of appellate decisions in that decade both repeated and elabo-

---

72. 217 S.W. 465 (Ark. 1919).
73. *Id.* at 467.
74. *Id.* at 469.
75. *Id.* at 470.

rated upon that cluster of ideas animating the first juvenile court. In terms of less serious crime and for cases of dependency and neglect, appellate judges were having little difficulty in promoting the idea of juvenile court hegemony over children. But, in cases involving some of the more serious felonies, especially homicide, there was still the issue of whether to proceed against the youth in juvenile or in adult criminal court. In 1920, the Supreme Court of North Carolina had before it just such a case. In *State v. Burnett*,[76] two males under the age of ten years were indicted for murder. On a motion to quash the indictment, the trial court assented and remanded both juveniles to the juvenile court instead. The state appealed. Justice Hoke ruled, among other things, that "the prosecution of these infant children, both under 10 years of age at the time of the alleged offense, cannot be maintained."[77] He went on to note that "children under 14 years of age are no longer indictable as criminals, but are, in the cases specified, committed for reformation and primarily to the juvenile department of the superior court."[78] The juvenile law of North Carolina, said Hoke, "purports to deal with delinquent children *not as criminals*, but *as wards*..."[79] (Emphasis added). After citing numerous examples of courts in other states upholding the constitutionality of juvenile court acts, Justice Hoke remarked that "there could not well be conceived, in this day and time, a case where the enlightened public sentiment of the state would approve the capital execution of a child under 14...."[80] The advocates of reformation, he noted, "have the better of the argument."[81] That being stated, the North Carolina high court upheld the lower court's order to remand the youths to the juvenile court for disposition.

In its reticence to incarcerate juveniles with adult felons and to favor certain children with the benefits of juvenile court procedures, the Criminal Court of Appeals of Oklahoma noted in a 1921 decision[82] that "[t]he courts, in construing these [juvenile court] statutes, have universally treated them as beneficial and entitled to liberal con-

---

76. 102 S.E. 711 (N.C. 1920).
77. *Id.* at 713.
78. *Id.* at 714.
79. *Id.*
80. *Id.* at 715.
81. *Id.*
82. *Ex parte Parnell*, 200 Pac. 456 (Okla. 1921).

struction."[83] In that decision, a juvenile below the age of sixteen, was charged with larceny of an automobile. The child plead guilty to the larceny charge in criminal court and was immediately transferred to the state penitentiary at Granite, Oklahoma, to be "held and confined in said penitentiary, at hard labor, for a period of two years... "[84] The mother of the juvenile petitioned for a writ of *habeas corpus* and the appellate court, without hesitation, granted the process. The Oklahoma judges on the Criminal Court of Appeals were of the opinion that the lower court did not have jurisdiction to try the juvenile because such jurisdiction was superseded by the state juvenile court act. Mindful of their duty to strike a balance between adult criminality and juvenile delinquency, the judges observed that "statutes of this [juvenile] character are not criminal in their nature, and are designed to protect and save the child from *evil* or *criminal influence* for his own sake... "[85] (Emphasis added). Employing a favorite appellate device by alluding to the law of cognate jurisdictions, the court went on to note that "[a]n investigation discloses that in recent years *in every state of the Union* there have been enacted juvenile laws and courts, in the main similar to our own."[86] (Emphasis added).

In 1923, the Supreme Court of Missouri ruled in an *en banc* opinion,[87] that a male juvenile under age seventeen charged with rape is to be proceeded against in juvenile court because "[i]t is not sought to punish him as a rapists, but to reform him from his state of delinquency."[88] Likewise, the Supreme Court of California in 1924 followed the general tenor of both the Missouri *Buckner*[89] decision and the North Carolina decision of *State v. Burnett*[90] regarding juvenile court jurisdiction over youths committing serious felonies. In *Ex parte Daedler*,[91] the California Supreme Court reviewed the legality

---

83. *Id.* at 458.

84. From the judgment of the District Court of Comanche County, Oklahoma, Feb. 18, 1921, as quoted in 200 Pac. at 457.

85. *Id.* at 458.

86. *Id.* Actually, the Oklahoma court was in error regarding the italicized words. By 1921, most, but not "every state" in the country had enacted juvenile court statutes. Maine and Wyoming were the last to do so in the immediate post-World II era.

87. *State ex rel. Matacia v. Buckner*, 254 S.W. 179 (Mo. 1923).

88. *Id.* at 182.

89. *State ex rel. Matacia v. Bucker*, 254 S.W. 179 (Mo. 1923).

90. *State v. Burnett*, 102 S.E. 711 (N.C. 1920).

91. 228 Pac. 467 (Cal. 1924).

of a juvenile court commitment of a fourteen-year-old male in *habeas corpus*. The minor, Paul Daedler, was charged with the murder of one Arthur Martinez "willfully and with malice aforethought."[92] The juvenile court, after conducting a hearing, found that Paul Daedler had committed a felony and declared the juvenile a ward of the court, sentencing him to the Preston School of Industry. Daedler was in the temporary custody of the superintendent of the Los Angeles Juvenile Hall when the writ of *habeas corpus* was sought by his parents.

The parents' main contention was that since their son was charged with the crime of murder, he was entitled to be tried by a jury on that charge. Because he was summarily found to be a ward of the juvenile court without a jury trial, the parents sought *habeas corpus* for his release, contending that his detention violated due process of law. The court, per Justice Richards, then proceeded in a lengthy opinion to justify Paul Daedler's incarceration without a jury determination. The judge delved into the long history of equity and its relation to children both in England and in the United States. Citing earlier precedent in California in *Moore v. Williams*,[93] the judge quoted approvingly these statements from the *Williams* decision: "These juvenile courts... are the creation of *modern philanthropic endeavor*, and are designed to and in fact do provide a most excellent means of restraining and reforming wayward persons who, unchecked, may become a menace to society."[94] (Emphasis added). Further warming to his subject, Justice Richards noted that early on in California and elsewhere there was some "disposition" by courts to strictly apply certain constitutional guarantees in juvenile proceedings. However, he then made this cogent remark: "the main trends of modern authority has been *away from this* [constitutional] *viewpoint...*"[95] (Emphasis added). The writ was denied and the juvenile ultimately recommitted to the Preston School.

In 1928, the Supreme Court of Mississippi decided an appeal from an order of the Forrest County Chancery Court involving a commitment of a juvenile to the state industrial school.[96] At the time in question, Mississippi had a dual court structure involving common law

---

92. *Id.* at 468.
93. 127 Pac. 509 (Cal. 1912).
94. *Moore v. Williams*, 127 Pac. 509 (1912).
95. *Id.*
96. *Bryant v. Brown*, 118 So. 184 (Miss. 1928).

and chancery tribunals. The juvenile, Howard Bryant, was a thirteen-year-old male residing with his parents and he had a lengthy offense record. In upholding the commitment order to the juvenile institution, Justice Ethridge noted that if a juvenile's case is transferred from a court of general jurisdiction to a chancery court, "the proceeding is changed from a criminal to a civil proceeding, and is governed by the rules of procedure in other civil cases."[97] The parents of the juvenile in their appellate pleadings had argued in their assignments of error that their son had been denied a trial by jury under the juvenile laws of Mississippi and therefore the juvenile statutes would not pass constitutional muster. Note, however, how the Mississippi court dealt with such an allegation. Simply by identifying juvenile violations with traditional equitable principles, the case had suddenly become "civil" in nature. Since juries were not a historic component of equity jurisprudence and since "civil" litigants did not enjoy the same panoply of constitutional rights accorded "criminal" litigants, the parents' arguments fell on deaf ears. One must realize, however, that the Mississippi court was not extolling a minority viewpoint by 1928. By then, there was a fully developed body of appellate authority in the United States that readily conceded that juvenile court proceedings were civil in nature. Because of this ideological and legal slant, few traditional pre-trial or trial rights of constitutional dimension were being accorded any deference in juvenile hearings.

By the 1930s there was in place a broad and, in many cases, an intrusive judicial policy regarding delinquent youth. In a footnote in his work *Love and the American Delinquent*,[98] Steven Schlossman observed that

> Not surprisingly, then, social reformers in the Progressive era found the juvenile court an excellent base on which to build their more general plea for increased governmental powers of intervention and surveillance over families of the poor. This derived from the unusual position of the juvenile justice system vis-a-vis other child welfare proposals. The juvenile justice system was, in a sense, the "granddaddy" of governmental programs in child welfare (together, of

---

97. *Id.* at 188.

98. Fn. 31, chap. 1, as quoted in STEVEN SCHLOSSMAN, LOVE AND THE AMERICAN DELINQUENT: THE THEORY AND PRACTICE OF "PROGRESSIVE" JUVENILE JUSTICE, 1825–1920 212 (1977).

course, with the public schools). It was an institutional network in which the right of the State to disrupt natural family relations of the poor was well established.[99]

In the thirteen appellate decisions discussed, a distinct pattern emerges. Since there was no extant precedent in juvenile law *per se* prior to 1899, it fell to the lot of American appellate courts to literally manufacture precedent out of whole cloth. There came to be a grand set of interlocking ideologies, part legal, part philanthropic, part sociological, part political and part criminological that nourished juvenile court development. While courts were not always and everywhere in complete accord on all issues, there was an astounding unanimity on the central tenets of juvenile law. To contemporary eyes, this unanimity may seem somewhat illogical, given the civil libertarian ethos that engulfed juvenile law in the immediate post-*Gault* juvenile court. However, the one thing to remember here is that in the roughly thirty-year period between 1899 and 1930, all the legal techniques that characterized and embraced state power over children were in place. The child savers and Progressive era doctrine had developed a new legal order that would be both praised and repudiated in the years to come.

99. *Id.*

Chapter Three

The Matter of Jurisdiction

A. Jurisdiction and Its Meaning

In law, the matter of jurisdiction is generally considered to be a division of labor device assuring the successful operation of multiple tasks. In the juvenile court, jurisdiction both promotes and at the same time limits the ability of the court to do its work. The original Illinois law broke juvenile court jurisdiction down into two major components—age and conduct. Since 1899, that dual concept of jurisdiction was adopted by all subsequent juvenile court acts. What has changed over the decades has been the upper age limits for court intervention and the types of conduct giving rise to that intervention. More recently, a phenomena known as exclusion statutes have effectively precluded certain classes of juvenile law violators from juvenile courts altogether. As the juvenile court reaches its century mark, the jurisdictional markers for late twentieth-century youth are on a somewhat different order than those of their late nineteenth-century counterparts. This chapter will explore some of the developments and some of the differences in the juvenile court jurisdictional context during the twentieth century.

What appears to have taken place this century has been a movement to legislatively expand the type of conduct that would trigger intervention as well as increase the chronological age at which that conduct would be relevant. Age twenty-one seems to be the universally agreed maximum age for continuing jurisdiction, although for practical purposes, age eighteen is generally the norm for intervention.[1] Once a teenager has passed his or her eighteenth birthday, juvenile court jurisdiction ceases in the original sense of that term. Thereafter, the individual is proceeded against as an adult in the criminal courts

---

1. Samuel M. Davis notes that "[b]y far, the most common jurisdictional age is eighteen, which is accepted as the jurisdictional age in more than two thirds of the states and in the District of Columbia." SAMUEL M. DAVIS, RIGHTS OF JUVENILES: THE JUVENILE JUSTICE SYSTEM 2–2 (2d ed. 1996).

unless a special "youthful offender" statute carves out special treatment for those youth in the eighteen to twenty-one-year-old category.[2]

In the early decades of the twentieth century, there was debate in many jurisdictions that had established a juvenile court as to exactly where the chronological age cut-off should be for intervention. In a 1919 address before the New York City Conference of Charities and Correction, Arthur W. Towne noted these concerns and voiced then exactly some of the problems still bedeviling the juvenile court today. Said Towne,[3] "[w]hatever age cleavage is legally adopted must necessarily be more or less arbitrary; it cannot conform to the varying degrees of development among those individual children either above or below the boundary line who deviate from the normal."[4] Clearly, the jurisdictional age question was not well-settled even twenty years after the establishment of the juvenile court. By 1929, there was some type of legislation regarding age limits in forty-six of the then forty-eight states. Fourteen states[5] established age sixteen as the upper jurisdictional age. Thirteen states[6] and the District of Columbia increased that age limit to seventeen years, while an additional seventeen states[7] established age eighteen as the upper age limit. Maryland and California, however, did not fit precisely into any of these three traditional groupings. In Maryland, there was an age differential based on the gender of the juvenile with age eighteen being the upper age limit for females while age twenty was the upper age limit for males. California, on the other hand, established age twenty-one for both males and females. The original Illinois statute set age sixteen as the upper age for juvenile court intervention, but that

---

2. Youthful Offender Acts are examples of an interim approach to youth wrongdoing that essentially allow a "juvenile court approach" to certain offenses committed by young persons in the 18–21 age group with appropriate court approval.

3. Arthur W. Towne, *Shall the Age Jurisdiction of Juvenile Courts Be Increased?*, 10 J. Crim. L. 493 (1920).

4. *Id.* at 499.

5. Alabama, Colorado, Georgia, Indiana, Iowa, Kansas, New Jersey, New Mexico, New York, Oklahoma, Pennsylvania, Rhode Island, Tennessee and Vermont.

6. Arkansas, Delaware, Florida, Illinois, Kentucky, Louisiana, Massachusetts, Michigan, Missouri, Montana, New Hampshire, Texas, Wisconsin and the District of Columbia.

7. Arizona, Connecticut, Idaho, Minnesota, Mississippi, Nebraska, Nevada, North Carolina, North Dakota, Ohio, Oregon, South Carolina, South Dakota, Utah, Virginia, Washington and West Virginia.

statute was further amended in 1905 and then again in 1907 to add additional interventive acts. States which followed the Illinois model did not begin enacting this form of legislation until after 1901, but it can be assumed that those fourteen jurisdictions setting age sixteen as their maximum jurisdictional age probably patterned their legislation after the Illinois statute in its broadened 1907 form.

Between 1899 and 1929, then, we begin to witness what subsequently would become a jurisdictional crazy quilt of statutes that varied both in age and in conduct regarding the child offender. One would have realistically surmised that the Illinois prototype would have been replicated nationwide, but that was not the case. Among other things, Progressivism was still a dominant socio-political force in these formative years of juvenile court development and that concept meant different things to different constituencies. In state legislatures there were competing Progressive agendas vying for a voice in social legislation, not the least of which was juvenile court legislation. Statutory enactments in the several states were not at all in one accord on the question of how far a specialized court for children should extend its grasp over a multitude of behaviors ranging from felonies and misdemeanors to status offenses. "Progressives," notes Barry C. Feld,[8] "envisioned an informal court whose disposition reflected the 'best interests' of the child."[9] However, it was the constructing of a "best interest" model that was the chief topic of debate. Different state legislatures had different views on this matter, and, as a result, there was not one national, overarching *Grundnorm* applicable to the jurisdictional issue. Feld further remarked that "[p]rogressives felt no reservations when they attempted to 'Americanize' the immigrants and poor through a variety of agencies of assimilation and acculturation...."[10] Since state legislatures of the time were largely representative of white middle-class values, it was no accident that those value preferences should, on a regional basis, exhibit differences in how the law should react to juvenile delinquency. Correspondingly, the legislative flexibility regarding juvenile court jurisdiction was simply a mirror of the times.

---

8. Barry C. Feld, *Criminalizing the American Juvenile Court* 17 Crime and Justice: A Rev. of Research 197 (Michael Tonry ed. 1993).

9. *Id.*

10. *Id.* at 202.

At the risk of oversimplification, it may be ventured that these early foundational statutes concerning conduct fell into two broad categories: (1) the "specific enumeration" statute and (2) the "generalized" statute. The Illinois statute of 1907 is the earliest legislation we know of that follows the legislative technique of specifically enumerating various behaviors that would trigger juvenile court intervention. That statute specifically listed fourteen separate "acts" of delinquency beyond simply violating a state law or ordinance that would allow state intervention. In many ways, these fourteen legislative characterizations were evidence of the profound influence the Positive School of criminology exerted on the minds of the Illinois lawmakers. In criminology, positivism in the main is a way of thought that concentrates on the study of the offender, not the offense. Closely allied with that thesis is the corollary doctrine that assumes that delinquency and crime emerge from a multi-causal constellation of factors. In Feld's words,[11] positivism asserts "a scientific determinism of deviance," seeks "to identify the causal variables producing crime and delinquency, and informed many Progressive criminal justice reforms."[12] Legislatures who adopted the Illinois "specific enumeration" juvenile statute format were probably at least somewhat conversant with the positivist thinking of their time. The fourteen enumerated acts of delinquency in this organic legislation came in large measure from the purported "causal variables" deemed crucial to the identification of factors that might lead a child to a lifetime of criminality. The juvenile's associates, the places he or she frequents, the language spoken with its intonations and argot and the general disobedience to authority, both parental and state, were seen as crucial indices of pre-delinquency in the abstract and of actual delinquency in the concrete! This 1907 statute opened the door to legislative replication of a jurisdictional conduct base that has been both advantageous and troubling in juvenile justice.

The other category of conduct jurisdiction legislation is the so-called "generalized" statute. Here, the legislature eschews the temptation to set forth a lengthy list of factors it may deem criminogenic. Instead, it chooses to employ broad language to cover what would otherwise be separate and discrete acts of delinquency. In statutes such as these, one may find provisions that declare a child delinquent

---

11. *Id.*
12. *Id.*

if he or she "is growing up in idleness or crime," or "so deports themselves as to injure or endanger the morals, health or welfare of themselves or others." A generalized delinquency statute conferring jurisdiction over children coming within such omnibus conduct terminology did not, at first, seem to matter. The aim, of course, was to encompass the widest possible conduct of delinquent and pre-delinquent youth and to then employ the ministrations of social science to correct their deviance through juvenile court intervention. Both enumerated and generalized conduct statutes proliferated in the first thirty years of juvenile court existence with little thought being given to any civil liberty problems that might exist. Later, of course, the procedural laxness that became endemic in the juvenile court created by these vague and all-encompassing statutory proscriptions would return to seriously constrict delinquency adjudications.

On the thirtieth anniversary of the founding of the juvenile court in 1929, Charles L. Chute,[13] the general secretary of the National Probation Association, noted with some sense of urgency that

> The surveys made by the National Probation Association and the United States Children's Bureau prove that many of these laws [regarding delinquency] are seriously inadequate and should be amended. In certain states the laws are limited to a few large cities or counties. In some the courts are not given full jurisdiction to deal with delinquent children, while in others no jurisdiction is granted to deal with adults responsible for the delinquency or neglect of children.[14]

Chute lobbied for and was instrumental in convincing some state legislatures to raise the jurisdictional age level to eighteen. The National Probation Association at the time was on public record as advocating that juvenile courts be given exclusive jurisdiction of juveniles up to age eighteen and to also broaden the court's jurisdiction to deal directly with adults who contribute to a minor's delinquency.

By its thirtieth birthday, the juvenile court, as a court, was a significant institutional component in the overall child welfare scheme of things in the United States. By 1929, forty-six states had enacted some form of juvenile court legislation. By that date juvenile delin-

---

13. *Current Events, Juvenile Court Celebrates Thirtieth Birthday,* 15 A.B.A. J. 329 (June, 1929).
14. *Id.*

quency was predominately defined, conduct-wise, to include acts vi-olative of state, county and municipal laws as well as conduct which applied only to children. Neglect jurisdiction was also typically pro-vided for within the general delinquency statutes. Age-wise, these statutes varied from a low of age sixteen to a high of age eighteen with a few jurisdictions opting for a seventeen year middle range for intervention. It was within this general time frame that juvenile court jurisdiction, both conduct and age-wise, became relatively fixed in American law. But this statutory variability involving jurisdiction was both a blessing and a curse. It was a positive development in the sense that it facilitated some true legal and social experimentation in the intervention and treatment of delinquency. Negatively, it sowed the seeds for some contemporary views in juvenile justice that argue that this court has served its usefulness and that its glaring twentieth-century procedural shortcomings cannot be adequately addressed in its present institutional posture. "Abolishing the juvenile court," writes Feld,[15] "would force a long overdue and critical reassessment of the entire social construct of 'childhood.'"[16] Retreating for the mo-ment from the question of abolition, however, does allow us to piece together a tapestry of an institutional arrangement that promoted its ukases through the dual concepts of age and conduct. It was the Pro-gressives' idea of "childhood" and the sovereign ideal of *parens pa-triae* that conjoined to produce the widely varying jurisdictional bases for juvenile court intervention. By 1930, there were several ju-risdictional models in place throughout the United States that bore witness to this partnership. From that point until the late 1960s, the jurisdictional markers of age and conduct set the stage for the coming constitutional reordering of the juvenile court.

B. Status Offense Jurisdiction

As an arm of state government, the juvenile court is officially set up to intervene in a child's life under a given set of circumstances. As a socio-legal agency of child welfare, it can forcibly change, for both the short and for the long run, a child's life chances. In their attempt to promote both criminological and Progressive dogma, legislators in-vested the juvenile court with a jurisdiction over children peculiar in

---

15. Feld, *supra* note 8, at 261–67.
16. *Id.*

Anglo-American law. The status offense category in juvenile jurisprudence is a shining example of the elevation of form over substance.

In the criminal law, persons are arrested, tried and convicted because they are involved in either acts of commission or omission that are detailed either by statutory or case law edict. These acts may vary, but the one constant is that what is done by the accused is verifiable by objective investigation, or certainly inferred therefrom. On the other hand, the status offense jurisdiction of the juvenile court can be triggered on the basis of criteria far less objective or inferential in nature. When the term "status" is employed in the juvenile justice idiom, what is generally meant by that designation is that a youth so charged has not violated a penal law *per se*. Rather, the involved juvenile has been found to be in some "condition" or in some "vicinity" or in some "relationship" with parents, peers or others that those in authority perceive to be conducive to *future* delinquency. In other words, children charged with a status offense are those who are in the unenviable position of being accused of committing an *offense only for children*. There is no adult criminal law counterpart to the juvenile status offense, with the possible exception of statutes punishing "vagrancy" or "loitering" still found today in some penal codes. Because it has been traditional wisdom that legislatively enacted "statuses" may be precursors to true delinquency (that is, delinquency that also happens to mimic adult crime), the "nip it in the bud" syndrome became operational in juvenile practice. Since the juvenile court establishment early on was enamored with the combined traditions of *parens patriae*, the "best interest" of the child paradigm, the "rehabilitative ideal,"[17] and equitable remedial flexibility, the stage was set for a robust employment of "status" jurisdiction to stem delinquent behavior.

The practical and theoretical basis for status offense jurisdiction was the unwavering assumption that juvenile status offenders could somehow be "helped" in the process of being exposed to juvenile court intervention. But, according to John Henry Wigmore,[18] the promoters of this type of juvenile court legislation "in their enthusiasm for its benefits and their determination to eliminate the conditions of

---

17. A phrase coined by law professor Francis A. Allen in his book entitled THE BORDERLAND OF CRIMINAL JUSTICE: ESSAYS IN LAW AND CRIMINOLOGY (1964).

18. WIGMORE, EVIDENCE 5 (3d ed. 1940).

the usual criminal court, have gone to the borderline of prudence in their iconoclasm."[19] In hindsight, this "borderline of prudence" was probably reached in the language of juvenile court acts by the year 1930. But, one must also remember that it was during that era that the marriage of social science and juvenile law became a *fait accompli*. Thirty years later in 1960, Aldous Huxley scathingly criticized social science for pretending to be the depository of all true wisdom in such organizations as the juvenile court. Said Huxley,[20] "Like Sir Galahad's their strength is the strength of ten because their heart is pure—and their heart is pure because they are scientists and have taken six thousand hours of social studies."[21]

Taking a long view of twentieth-century history, what is particularly troublesome to many modern observers was the cavalier attitude of lawmakers, jurists and lawyers alike in the wholesale affirmance of differential definitions of juvenile delinquency. Perhaps to a contemporary civil libertarian, constitutional law scholar or perceptive jurist, the commingling of "true" criminal violations by juveniles with protocriminal "status" offenses is confounding. On the other hand, perhaps, its confounding nature may be unraveled.

By 1930, the United States already had a rather well-established sociological criminology in place. Sociological positivism which began at the turn of the century in the research and writings of such men as Robert E. Park, Ernest W. Burgess and Louis Wirth, exerted a profound influence on the juvenile court. Park, Burgess, Wirth and other collaborators in the sociology department at the University of Chicago developed a social ecology theory of urban crime and delinquency which became a mainstay in criminology. While this was certainly not the first attempt at sociological explanations of criminality, it did command widespread legal and social science attention due to the status of the researchers and the university at which they taught. In a nutshell, the combined research of Park, Burgess, Wirth, Clifford R. Shaw, Henry D. McKay and others found that there were discrete "delinquency areas" in Chicago and that these were more or less concentrated in what were called "interstitial" or transitional areas of the city. These demographic areas had a correspondingly high rate of residential turnover, a lack of community ethos and were populated

19. *Id.* at 145.
20. Aldous Huxley, Brave New World Revisited (1960).
21. *Id.* at 26.

by a large number of the urban immigrant underclass. Many of the children hailed into the Cook County Juvenile Court came from these interstitial locales. Out of all of this developed a distinct "Chicago School" of delinquency explanation whose methodology and ideological bent was picked up and replicated in other cities across America. The social disorganization of the inner cities and the criminogenic children of their inhabitants energized lawmakers to continue to add to the definitions of delinquency new status offenses in the hope of controlling this serious social problem. Probably one of the most famous community action programs in delinquency prevention in this century emerged from the writings of these University of Chicago sociologists. The noted Chicago Area Project (CAP) was initiated in the 1930s to deal with juvenile delinquency in selected blighted areas of Chicago. Steven Schlossman and Michael Sedlak praised the Chicago Area Project as "a legendary experiment in community-based delinquency prevention."[22] Arnold Binder, Gilbert Geis and Dickson Bruce noted, however, that "[i]n the end, Shaw and McKay themselves remained uncertain whether their bold attempt to translate some loose theoretical concepts into a practical action program had been successful. They did become convinced that, given the chance, local residents in high-crime areas could organize themselves effectively to address common problems...."[23]

Also in the early 1930s a group of newly-emerging scholars in the field of social psychology added a new dimension to the conundrum of juvenile delinquency. These researchers began to investigate the relationship between reciprocal groups such as the family, one's peers and the educational experience to determine if these interactions affected behavior. The assumption here was that if a child experiences social and psychological trauma in, say, family interactions, in school, or among peers, such trauma may indeed lead to a law-violating lifestyle. More importantly, so the argument went, was the fact that if the juvenile had close associations with deviant peers and was thus exposed to procrime influences, the juvenile would "absorb" such influences through the normal learning process and ultimately become a lawbreaker. Other researchers focused on the tensions be-

---

22. Steven Schlossman & Michael Sedlak, *The Chicago Area Project Revisited*, 29 Crime & Delinq. 398 (1983).

23. Arnold Binder, Gilbert Geis & Dickson Bruce, Juvenile Delinquency: Historical, Cultural, Legal Perspectives 152 (1988).

tween internal and external controls on the child while still others investigated the many behavioral restraints which the socialization process exacted.

While psychological explanations of delinquency were proliferating in academe during the first three decades of the century, psychological theories *per se* were rarely invoked in the legal debates surrounding status offense delinquency. Psychology found its niche in juvenile justice in the treatment orientation employed by the juvenile court. Juvenile corrections adopted many psychological techniques in an attempt to rehabilitate their inmates, but rarely would one find any distinct nexus between the legal descriptions of status offense behavior and psychological or psychiatric nosology. The juvenile court *as a clinic* rather than the juvenile court *as a court* did manage to employ psychology in numerous treatment regimens. Such a law-social science partnership continues to exist to this day in those juvenile courts who enjoy the financial resources to employ psychology professionals in delinquency control.

The real sleeper in the status offender jurisdiction category is the relationship between law and sociology. When the legislators of forty-six states had enacted some form of juvenile code by 1927, the received wisdom of the time was that a congeries of social conditions predisposed children to law violating behavior. By the late twenties and early thirties, the work of the Chicago School of sociology was well-known in juvenile justice circles throughout the nation. Likewise, there was a parallel belief that social disorganization, broadly defined, was a major determinant of youth crime. The logical step it seemed would be for the state to enact statutes that gave the police, probation personnel and the juvenile court itself an interventive weapon in the struggle against delinquency. As a result, status offense jurisdiction was viewed by many at the time to literally be the "point of the spear" in the state's armamentarium against delinquency. But even here there was disagreement on exactly what "status" would necessarily lead youth down the slippery slope to adult criminality. As a result of this normative dissonance embedded in such legislation, the country had no definitive idea of exactly what status offense legislation would accomplish. Although perhaps deficient in concept, what status offense jurisdiction did accomplish was to funnel into the juvenile court countless numbers of children who under a more legally confined jurisdiction would have never been adjudicated. The sense of purpose animating the Progressive reformers and the child savers was fueled in large measure by their sincere belief that social science *could* make a difference in the lives of children. Yet, now we must admit that the verdict on the success of status offense jurisdiction in the juvenile court is still not in.

More likely than not, one of the main reasons for such pessimism is the fact that the social and legal forces of the 1920s were such that no counterweights were available to caution lawmakers in their headlong rush to legislatively demonize protocriminal behavior in the young. Positivism in social science meant the employment of the "scientific method" to heretofore untouched arenas. There was much talk by 1927 of the "hard facts" discovered by the sociologists and the psychologists regarding delinquency. The behavioral markers of children of underclass incumbents led many researchers to the confirmed belief that they had at last found some scientific solution to an intractable human condition. Sociological criminology was unearthing "facts" that pointed toward discrete social antecedents of more incipient criminality. But, in Jerome Frank's critical notation,[24] "[f]acts . . . are not immortal. They are made by mortals and may be changed by other mortals. Because a fact represents a selection, . . . it follows that in the contriving of every fact some aspects of experience have been suppressed or disregarded."[25] Despite the "mortal" nature of facts generated by this new scientific criminology, the urge to adopt a positivist explanation of delinquency far overshadowed any doubts that either the legal or social science community held about their validity. But such global excitement tended to exacerbate an already counter-productive aspect of juvenile law that has been in existence since the second revision of the original Illinois statute in 1907. That aspect was the Janus-faced concept of "liberty" that very early on came into universal practice in juvenile law. During the twentieth century the juvenile court has assuredly been a force for good in American society; few would deny that fact. But, regretfully, it has also been something else. While on the whole it has mitigated the rigidity of adult penal practice, it has also created a serious collateral civil liberties problem. The juvenile court "idea" was premised upon

---

24. Jerome Frank, *The Place of an Expert in a Democratic Society*, as quoted in THE SELECTED WRITINGS OF JUDGE JEROME FRANK: A MAN'S REACH (Barbara Frank Kristein ed. 1965).
25. *Id.* at 15.

a scientific criminology that cared a great deal about the aetiology of delinquency but little at all about the procedures through which that ideology would be applied to youth. As Isaiah Berlin warned in his presidential inaugural address at Oxford University in 1958,[26] "[W]hen ideas are neglected by those that ought to attend to them... they sometimes acquire an unchecked momentum and an irresistible power over multitudes of men that may grow too violent to be affected by rational criticism."[27] Beginning in 1907 and continuing to the present time, the idea of "justice" for the child may have become, in a figurative sense, "an irresistible power" incapable of lending itself to rational and constructive criticism. The juvenile court and its implicit idea of "justice" for the child confronts a paradox: since juvenile delinquency, dependency and neglect are not crimes, freedom from coercive state intervention in these jurisdictional segments is not assured. The "liberty" to be free from state intervention could only be safeguarded in juvenile justice by the wise discretion of the judiciary. But, the juvenile court judiciary had no "habit," no historical precedent molded in the give and take of advocacy and no received wisdom from the ages to fall back upon. There simply was not in-place a body of case law or statutory formulations to assure even rudimentary adherence to the concept of due process and ordered liberty in the juvenile court setting. The "freedom" that adults enjoyed and took for granted under both constitutional, statutory and case law protection in the criminal law sector of jurisprudence was simply not there in the juvenile law sector. At best, a juvenile enjoys a truncated "freedom"; a freedom so-called to be hauled into a children's court of conscience there to be ministered to by a surrogate parent-judge under the aegis of an all-encompassing positive criminology. One prong of this newly-developed freedom promised a benevolent correction; the other promised state oversight of this corrective apparatus through a legal pedigree going back over seven centuries. What went either unnoticed or unmentioned was that a rehabilitative idea was intentionally fused with a *parens patriae* doctrine that, in combination, gave birth to a "freedom" for children heretofore unrecognized. This was the symbolic "other face" of Janus that was submerged in the rhetoric and enthusiasm of the time. The child savers

---

26. Isaiah Berlin, *Two Concepts of Liberty*, an Inaugural Lecture delivered before the faculty at Oxford University, England, on October 31, 1958.

27. *Id.* at 4.

and their Progressive minions had literally manufactured a new legal order out of admittedly old cloth. It was one with a radical mission driven with the zeal of a religious convert. The concepts of a positive criminology, the state as parent-surrogate, probation as second chance and treatment as counterweight to the "disease" of delinquency, all became welded together into an institutional embodiment of public policy. This public policy, however, has been severely tested and strained in the last quarter of the twentieth century due to a multiplicity of factors. In fact, there are those who now view the juvenile court as an almost *criminogenic* institution—an institution that has for far too long marginalized the seriousness of juvenile criminality and often unintentionally fostered continuing delinquency!

American politicians of late have used the "crime problem" as a so-called "wedge issue" in local, state and national campaigns. Beginning in earnest in the late 1960s with the election of Richard Milhous Nixon, politicians of every stripe began raising the spectre of crime to garner votes. It worked with ball-bearing efficiency! At the national level, from presidents Nixon through William Jefferson Clinton, America's "crime problem" has been excellent political cannon fodder. Beginning in the early 1970s and continuing unabated to the present day is a generalized notion that serious, repetitive and predatory juvenile delinquency is a major component of late twentieth-century social disorganization. One can pick and choose from a variety of alleged "causes" for this outbreak of pervasive social concern about juvenile crime. The disintegration of the nuclear family; the media saturation accounts of high-profile juvenile crime; the debasement of morals and social values that previously acted as a buffer to delinquent behavior; the marginalization of religion in many sectors of American life; the exponential growth of an underclass culture created at least in part by the enormous maldistribution of economic resources; the literal "reinvention of childhood" by the literati; the overwhelming ease of access to firearms; the pervasive drug culture and its rosy promise of a "crime tariff"[28] being bestowed upon youth willing to undertake the risks—and the list goes on and on. All, or a discrete combination of the above, mixed no doubt with many more

---

28. The term coined by law professor Herbert L. Packer in his book entitled THE LIMITS OF THE CRIMINAL SANCTION (1968). Packer's characterization involved a concept from economics that suggested that large amounts of money, a "monopoly profit," so to speak, could be accured by those willing to deal in drugs and other contraband which have a steady or "flat" demand curve in American society.

"causes" not even mentioned, have conveyed to the public mind the notion that the juvenile court has become an ineffective instrument of social control. Beginning around the middle of the 1970s a move sprouted to tighten the rather open-ended definitions of delinquency and to begin a narrowing process that continues to this day. Writing in the early 1970s, Samuel M. Davis of the University of Mississippi School of Law noted that "...there are subtle indications that many states have never fully accepted the notion of specialized treatment of juveniles who have violated the criminal code."[29] In speaking to the numerous forms of statutory innovations that in one form or another keep certain youth out of the juvenile court, Davis further noted that "...all of these provisions manifest a basic mistrust of the juvenile court and represent the absence of a firm commitment to the juvenile court's rehabilitative philosophy."[30] Into such a social reality of the 1970s stepped a "new solution" aimed at both disenfranchisement and empowerment simultaneously. Legislatures began the enactment of a variety of *exclusion* statutes aimed primarily at what the public at large saw as a new youth crime wave; the increasing reporting of violent, predatory delinquency by a group of youth whose moral compass had long been directionless.

C. Exclusion Statutes and Juvenile Delinquency

Since juvenile law and the courts that administer it are entirely creatures of the legislative will, the lawmakers can and do frequently change that law to address problems of the moment. After the decision in *In re Gault*[31] in 1967, there was debate in juvenile justice about how to address the constitutional rights newly conferred by that decision on juveniles charged with an act of delinquency. Whatever else *Gault* did in juvenile law, it left substantially intact the juvenile court's traditional processing methods involving children charged with a status offense. On the other hand, the *Gault* plurality let it be known quite clearly that the former rules of juvenile court engagement for youth charged with a delinquent act would be altered. *Gault* established a new legal order, on paper at least, for minors

---

29. Samuel M. Davis, *The Jurisdictional Dilemma of the Juvenile Court*, 51 N.C.L. Rev. 195, 196 (1972).

30. *Id.* at 199.

31. 387 U.S. 1 (1967).

charged with delinquency violations. It selectively imported the rules and processes of constitutional law into a narrow slice of juvenile misbehavior—the adjudicatory phase of a delinquency hearing where a loss of liberty was possible. Correspondingly, it also sensitized lawmakers to the idea that if selected constitutional rights were now available to certain delinquents, perhaps it was time to re-think juvenile codes as well. Part and parcel of this re-thinking was the introduction and expansion of the exclusion statute as a near-term legislative device to deal with chronic and violent acts of delinquency.

Placing a certain segment of youth beyond juvenile court protection is not a new phenomenon. The original Illinois act of 1899 excluded children over age sixteen from juvenile court jurisdiction as well as those minors charged with a serious felony. But, in the intervening years, a gradual inclusionary focus came into play. Homicide was generally excluded in the early laws, but as the juvenile court's power and political prestige became more dominant in its first thirty five to forty years of operation, even homicide was often tried and punished within the juvenile justice system. By the time the United States Supreme Court became involved in juvenile court processes in the 1960s, juvenile codes for the most part limited the classification of "delinquency" to acts violative of state or federal law or some local ordinance. Homicide and other serious forms of delinquency were often incorporated by reference into such legislation. The urge for inclusion was further complicated by the fact that numerous "delinquency" classifications also incorporated status offenses into a generic definition of delinquency. However, after the *Gault* ruling, there developed a move to legislatively rearrange not only the legal definition of delinquency, but also to sharply curtail its reach. There was precedent for this change. From the mid-1950s through the 1960s, some jurisdictions had exclusion statutes in force that served as models for the post-*Gault* approach.[32] Feld[33] maintains that at

---

32. Examples from seven states and the District of Columbia include the following: *1952* — MISS. CODE ANN. § 7185-15 (excluding crimes punishable by death or life imprisonment committed by child age 13 or older); *1953* — DEL. CODE ANN. tit. 10, § 1159 (excluding capital offenses); *1962* — S.C. CODE ANN. § 15-1103(9)(a) (excluding crimes punishable by death or life imprisonment); *1966*—W. VA. CODE ANN. § 49-1-4(2) (excluding capital offenses); *1968* — LA. REV. STAT. ANN. § 13:1570(A)(5) (West 1968) (excluding capital offenses and attempted aggravated rape, if committed by child age 15 or older); *1969* — COLO. REV. STAT. ANN. § 22-1-3(b) (West, Supp. 1969) (excluding crimes of violence punishable by death or life imprisonment when committed

least three major outside forces converged to change legislative thinking about juvenile crime and indirectly had an impact on exclusion legislation. He notes that "left-wing critiques of rehabilitation that characterized all governmental programs as coercive instruments of social control...liberal disenchantment with the unequal and disparate treatment of similarly situated offenders..., and conservative advocates of a 'war on crime' during the turbulent 1960s who favored repression over rehabilitation"[34] were major social realities that changed legislative approaches to juvenile crime.

Exclusion from juvenile court jurisdiction can be accomplished through several approaches. Among them would be: (1) lowering the chronological age for adult court jurisdiction via the waiver device; (2) listing specific offenses that would place the affected juvenile beyond juvenile court jurisdiction; (3) providing for either, or both, prosecutorial and judicial waiver of jurisdiction to the adult criminal court under a variety of circumstances; and (4) the employment of a "concurrent" jurisdiction device that allows both the juvenile court and the criminal court jurisdiction over a child under certain circumstances. Davis[35] laments this state of affairs when he notes that

> This limited faith on the part of legislatures (and in some instances the courts) is exasperating. Their interpretation of what occurs in the juvenile process is distorted; they seem to be saying that the redemptive philosophy of the juvenile court is laudable when dealing with "wayward" youth or childish pranks, but that when serious criminal offenses are committed, the rehabilitative ideal must be abandoned in favor of the retributive processes of the criminal law.[36]

One can argue at length about this distortion of purpose in juvenile justice exemplified by exclusion statutes. The reality is that in the last

---

by child age 14 or older); *1971* — D.C. CODE ANN. § 11-2301(3)(A) (Supp. IV, 1971) (excluding certain enumerated felonies when committed by child age 16 or older); *1971* — MD. CODE ANN. art. 26 § 70-2(d)(1) (Supp. 1971) (excluding crimes punishable by death or life imprisonment committed by child age 14 or older, unless case be transferred to juvenile court from criminal court).

33. Feld, *supra* note 8.

34. *Id.* at 205.

35. Davis, *supra* note 29.

36. *Id.* at 199.

twenty-five years of the twentieth century, legislators have exercised an approach to serious juvenile crime that may portend the eventual split between the traditional *parens patriae* juvenile court in place for most of the century with a more act-oriented retributive approach to juvenile crime.

An act-oriented approach to the more socially threatening forms of juvenile lawbreaking may also be, in part, at attempt to de-couple felonious predatory delinquency once and for all from the non-felonious delicts of youth. Lee A. Teitelbaum[37] writes that

> [t]he controversy over responses to youth crime is precisely an argument about the kind of legal rules that should be employed. . . . American criminal law is usually considered to be the context in which a *regime of rules* is most consistently and appropriately applied. The juvenile court's treatment of youth crime, for its part, is the domain most strongly identified with *governance by standards and individualized justice*; indeed, there may be no close second.[38] (Emphasis added).

By drawing a distinction between an act and rule-oriented body of law and one that operates largely by general standards employing wide discretion, Teitelbaum lays bare the public policy choices that contemporary juvenile lawmakers must face. Apparently, in increasing numbers, our newer juvenile codes adopt a legislative compromise between the tensions pulling lawmakers away from the *parens patriae* model and toward a more succinct rule-oriented jurisprudence for serious acts of delinquency. This rule-oriented standard, with new attention being paid to a juvenile's *conduct*, has brought the juvenile court almost full-circle. It was precisely the desire to *remove* the rule and act-oriented penal law of the nineteenth century from juvenile adjudications that came to be the central concern of the Progressive reformers. Since the nation is apparently well on its way back to a rule and offense-based juvenile justice for seriously delinquent minors, we confront a dilemma. Is it appropriate, both philosophically and policy-wise, to continue giving lip-service to the *parens patriae* version of the American juvenile court, while, at the

---

37. Lee A. Teitelbaum, *Youth Crime and the Choice Between Rules and Standards,* 1991 B.Y.U. L. Rev. 351.

38. *Id.* at 356.

same time, denigrating and marginalizing its benefits for a substantial segment of delinquent youth? What we have witnessed in the juvenile justice century is both the development of a *parens patriae* traditionalist approach to juvenile crime alongside a more recent penal law neo-traditionalist stance. The epiphany of this neo-traditionalist approach began as early as the 1960s. It came into its own, however, in the early to mid-1980s and has been a guiding force in the reconstruction of a number of juvenile court acts since that time. In roughly a thirty-five year time span between 1960 and the mid-1990s, the *sanctum sanctorum* of juvenile law (*parens patriae*) has given way to a divided ideology for wrongdoing that amounts to a form of *delinquency mala in se* beyond the pale of the state as super parent. For traditionalists, a term such as the above is oxymoronic. The *mala in se* concept has never been applied in juvenile law; it is a criminal law designation only. Nonetheless, current political, ideological and legal perceptions of certain types of delinquency have blurred almost to the point of extinction the differences that once existed between juvenile delinquency *as delinquency* and juvenile delinquency as *blameworthy criminality*.[39]

Beginning in the last decade of the twentieth century, legislative tinkering with the jurisdictional bases of juvenile delinquency continues apace. The increased employment of the waiver device by both judicial and prosecutorial agents has also dramatically changed the landscape of juvenile law. More will be said about waiver and its implications in a following chapter.

For exclusion legislation, however, one thing can be said with certainty. As we approach the centennial anniversary of the juvenile court, the scope of juvenile justice litigation has been considerably narrowed. The jurisdictional "reach" of the juvenile court, while theoretically still quite expansive, has, in reality, been significantly downsized. For the violent, older predatory delinquent in post-indus-

---

39. Compare the 1973 argument of Samuel M. Davis contained in his article *The Jurisdictional Dilemma of the Juvenile Court, supra* note 29 for both original and exclusive jurisdiction being vested solely in the juvenile court *in all cases* up to the maximum allowable age limit for juvenile court intervention with the 1993 article by Barry C. Feld, *supra* note 8, where it is argued that because there is no real national concensus on the role of the juvenile court in the late twentieth century, especially for the upper-age seriously delinquent youth, "[a]bolishing the juvenile court would force a long overdue reassessment of the entire social construct of childhood." *supra* note 8, at 267.

trial America, the reality is that the criminal law and juvenile law are now one and the same. In Feld's cogent assessment, "[t]he substantive and procedural convergence between juvenile and criminal courts eliminates virtually all of the conceptual and operational differences in strategies of social control of youths and adults."[40] This "convergence" is no where better illustrated than in three statutory examples of recent juvenile court legislation. Statutes in California, Florida and Kansas clearly exemplify this trend.

Provisions contained in the 1996 California *Welfare and Institutions Code*[41] typically follow provisions in other states concerning the maximum age limit for juvenile court intervention and for retention jurisdiction. Ages eighteen and twenty-one, respectfully, are California's statutory age limits. The California legislation then sets forth criteria for the criminal prosecution of a minor if that individual is not a "proper subject" for juvenile court jurisdiction. In order to determine that issue, the statute provides for a fitness hearing to determine the future disposition of the case.[42] Presumably, a "fit" subject would be petitioned into the juvenile justice system and there dealt with under the *parens patriae* model. The legislation then goes on, however, to list *twenty-nine* separate categories of wrongdoing wherein a juvenile over age sixteen may be tried as an adult in criminal court.[43] A separate section then lists *twenty-four* additional offense categories[44] wherein a juvenile between the ages of fourteen and sixteen may be declared "unfit" for juvenile disposition and charged with a criminal law violation. Thus, California has at least *fifty-three* statutory categories that may, in appropriate situations, defer juvenile court jurisdiction pending an award of that jurisdiction to an adult criminal court for trial. Clearly, the California statutes presently in force do not promote what one would term a late twentieth-century Progressive version of the Illinois statute of 1899.

On the opposite side of the nation, the state of Florida has recently enacted a highly detailed juvenile statute that mimics its *parens patriae* roots, but is, in reality, light years distant from its 1899 ancestor. The Florida Juvenile Code sets a maximum jurisdictional age

---

40. Feld, *supra* note 8, at 199.
41. CAL. WELF. & INST. CODE § 602 (West 1996).
42. CAL. WELF. & INST. CODE § 606 (West 1996).
43. CAL. WELF. & INST. CODE § 707(b) (West 1996).
44. CAL. WELF. & INST. CODE § 707(d)(2) (West 1996).

limit at seventeen[45] and a retention jurisdiction provision up to age nineteen for delinquent acts.[46] Effective January 1, 1995, however, Florida law provides that *regardless of a child's age at the time of an offense*, a state attorney must file an *information* against such child who has been previously adjudicated for any offense that would have been an adult felony.[47] Additionally, these aforementioned felonies must have triggered three or more *delinquency* adjudication hearings in juvenile court and each of those hearings must have terminated in a residential commitment of the youth.[48] An additional provision enacts that subsequent to January 1, 1995, a child either fourteen or fifteen who is charged with the commission of one or more of *fourteen* enumerated felonies will be subject to criminal prosecution provided the state attorney feels that adult sanctions should be imposed.[49] This type of legislation, somewhat akin to that in California, seems to statutorily commingle exclusion provisions with waiver language. Nonetheless, the end result is that both pieces of legislation allot prosecuting authorities almost *carte blanche* discretion in whether or not to jurisdictionally invoke the criminal law instead of the juvenile code.

In Middle America, the state of Kansas in its *Juvenile Offender Code* of 1993, embarks on its own form of "convergence." The Kansas Statute defines a "juvenile" as one under age eighteen for purposes of delinquency jurisdiction[50] and sets age twenty-one as the maximum age for retention jurisdiction.[51] At this point, Kansas deviates somewhat from the other two jurisdictions cited. The *Kansas Juvenile Code* provides for adult prosecution of minors under an unusual set of circumstances. In essence, a juvenile may be proceeded against in criminal court if that individual is sixteen or older and charged with a felony. The statute then goes on to add that if the juvenile has been adjudicated in two separate prior juvenile proceedings of an act which would be a felony if committed by an adult and that adjudication occurred *prior* to the date of the new act charged,

45. FLA. STAT. ANN. § 39.01(10)(Supp. 1995).
46. FLA. STAT. ANN. § 39.02(4)(a) (Supp. 1996).
47. FLA. STAT. ANN. § 39.052(5)(c) (Supp. 1995).
48. *Id.*
49. FLA. STAT. ANN. § 39.052(5)(a) (Supp. 1995).
50. KAN. STAT. ANN. § 38-1602(a) (1993).
51. KAN. STAT. ANN. § 38-1604(c) (1993).

the juvenile can be prosecuted as an adult.[52] Another section provides for adult prosecution if the juvenile is sixteen or older and charged with a felony while confined in any state training school or rehabilitation facility.[53] The final example of "convergence" occurs in the provision regarding fourteen and fifteen year olds who are charged with a class "A" or "B" felony after July 1, 1993, a so-called "off-grid" felony or a non-drug felony ranked at a certain "severity level." Under any or all of these scenarios, the county or district attorney may file a motion requesting prosecution as an adult.[54]

These three examples of Feld's "convergence" concept essentially vests prosecuting authorities in these states with a broad array of behaviors that could at once make juvenile delinquents criminal law eligible. Collectively, these examples of recent legislation reveal the statutory emasculation of the original and exclusive jurisdiction of the juvenile court over youthful criminality. While other similar legislative provisions could be documented, these typify the national mood toward serious delinquency in the 1990s. They essentially "legislate out" of juvenile court jurisdiction those offenses deemed particularly threatening to community solidarity and public order. In effect, the prosecutor has now become the alter ego of the juvenile court judge by virtue of language contained in modern waiver and exclusion legislation. While overall community protection, rehabilitation and social reintegration remain a goal, both the agents and the means employed to attain that goal have dramatically changed. The American juvenile court in the 1990s is in an era of jurisdictional transition. By century's end, assuming current trends continue, that transition may have completely revamped the jurisdictional power of what is left of the *parens patriae* juvenile court in matters touching on delinquency.

---

52. KAN. STAT. ANN. § 38-1602(b)(3) (1993).
53. KAN. STAT. ANN. § 38-1602(b)(7) (1993).
54. KAN. STAT. ANN. § 38-1636(a)(1) & (a)(2) (1993).

Chapter Four

The Juvenile in the Arms of the Law — the Police

A. Police Interaction with Juveniles Generally

On the whole, one can hazard the guess that during most of the twentieth century, law enforcement handling of juveniles has been both ambivalent and inconsistent. However, before we excoriate the police for this state of affairs, it is also important to remember a corollary truth. Since law enforcement is an institution that in many ways reflect the mores, values and attitudes of the times, police interaction with law-violating children have simply mirrored those concepts. Throughout the twentieth century, American social policy toward the delinquent child has been one of vacillation and uncertainty. We have been consistently inconsistent in our definition of "childhood," and on how our law and social policies should be directed in the service of that concept. One reason there are calls for both the abolition and the resurrection of the original juvenile court idea is that we are still wrestling with the magnificent ambivalence of that 1899 development. As the twentieth century draws to a close, we are no further along the path toward solving this dilemma than we were in the juvenile court's formative era.

In many respects, how the police handle youthful law violators has always been tied as much to the demographics, the gender, the race and ethnic background and the socio-economic status of the offending youth as to his or her perceived misbehavior. Differential law enforcement processing of delinquents has become a staple in American police practice despite periodic calls for more uniformity, more standardization and more adherence to the rule of law. Because the juvenile court was established to decriminalize a significant range of youthful lawbreaking and to direct its charges toward a more law-abiding lifestyle in a civil law context, police were immediately confronted with a dilemma. Early on this dilemma became apparent in deciding how to deal with a wide spectrum of misbehaviors that were neither purely "criminal" nor purely "civil." In consequence, police were asked to perform their law and order, protective and public service functions in the context of a quasi-criminal milieu. Although the juvenile court was not a criminal court and although it proceeded under the civil *parens patriae* rubric, there was always prevalent an implicit or undercurrent police ideology that juvenile court clients were "sort of" criminal. Since police are trained by and large to act on behavioral markers exhibited by adult suspects allegedly violating a penal law, the amorphous delinquency, dependency and neglect jurisdiction of the juvenile court immediately created ambivalence. As the century progressed and the juvenile court began to come under widespread pressure after the 1970s to relinquish its protective jurisdiction in a wide array of circumstances, police behavior towards juveniles became more consonant with their behavior toward adults. Particularly during the last quarter of the twentieth century, American law enforcement seems to have adopted a less ambivalent role in dealing with serious delinquency. On the other hand, it still exhibits a significant amount of role ambiguity in its dealing with the status offender and neglected child.

This chapter will not deal with the whole of juvenile-police encounters. What will be discussed are five areas that reflect both the early ambiguity of police-juvenile interactions and the now more stringent and rule-oriented policies that have emerged since the mid-1970s. Arrest, search and seizure, interrogation, pre-trial identification and record confidentiality will be examined. How law enforcement deals with these areas will, in part at least, reflect a national policy-shift away from the *parens patriae* model and toward a more formalistic due process, just deserts model of juvenile law.

B. Triggering the Apparatus:
Arrest, Search and Seizure

By the middle of the 1970s, one could begin to discern in American case law a gradual deterioration of the juvenile-adult distinction in the police handling of older, more experienced predatory delinquent youth. In actuality, however, such a blurring of the juvenile-adult distinction probably began as early as 1966 with the United States Supreme Court's decision in *Kent v. United States.*[1] In an opin-

---

1. 383 U.S. 541 (1966).

ion dealing with the transfer of a District of Columbia juvenile to the criminal court for trial, Justice Abe Fortas warned that "There is evidence...that there may be grounds for concern that the child receives the worst of both worlds: that he gets neither the protection accorded to adults nor the solicitous care and regenerative treatment postulated for children."[2] That phrase became a rallying cry for both sides of the juvenile court debate in the 1960s and beyond. In particular, however, it begat the now long and continuous thirty-plus year slide towards further eroding the juvenile-adult distinction for crimes committed by teenagers under revamped waiver and exclusion legislation.

As a precursor to a more legalistic and formal style of police intervention in the lives of suspected delinquents, mention must first be made of the so-called "criminal law revolution"[3] in adult penal practice. The twentieth century had passed its halfway point well before the Supreme Court of the United States began venturing into the so-called constitutional criminal procedure field. Law enforcement in the United States has always been primarily local[4] with the exception being the various state police organizations and federal law enforcement agencies operating under specific statutory directives. Because of the nature of police work, the bulk of the day-to-day law enforcement in the United States was, and still is, carried on by local police agencies. These agencies operate under municipal, county, and statewide penal laws that establish both jurisdictional and substantive boundaries for intervention. Adult criminal law enforcement through the 1950s was left to run primarily on its own, with only occasional

---

2. *Id.* at 556.

3. *See generally* THE CRIMINAL LAW REVOLUTION AND ITS AFTERMATH: 1960–1975 (Anthony E. Scudellari, John G. Miles, Jr., Richard E. Crouch & George F. Knight eds. 1975).

4. Writing in 1929, Bruce Smith noted that "[a]n outstanding feature of police administration in the United States is its local character." Bruce Smith, *Municipal Police Administration* 26 Annals 1 (Nov. 1929). He then cites fourteen "special activities" of a typical municipal police organization as follows: "(1) Licensing, (2) Traffic Regulation, (3) Public Ambulance Service, (4) Supervision of Paroled Convicts, (5) Inspection, (6) Registration of Voters and Verification of Poll Lists, (7) Police Census, (8) Ice Breaking in Navigable Waters, (9) Examination of Prostitutes for Venereal Disease, (10) Temporary Lodging for the Homeless, (11) Emergency Relief for the Destitute, (12) Free Employment Agencies, (13) Neighborhood Entertainment, and (14) Dog Pound." *Id.* at 2. Note the absence in the above list of any activities that refer specfically to children or delinquency prevention or control.

federal oversight. What cases did eventually come to the federal courts of appeal from the turn of the century through the late 1950s were those which involved egregious behavior against adult suspects by local constabularies.[5] If juveniles were the object of police indiscretion or brutality, evidence of that fact was essentially non-existent insofar as appellate case law was concerned.

In their legal anthology of United States Supreme Court opinions in the fourteen-year period between 1960 and 1974, the editors of the Bureau of National Affairs work on the "revolution" in criminal law noted in their *Introduction*[6] that "[m]eterologists need but glance at a wind-measuring device to discern the point at which a gale becomes a hurricane. No such simple calculation is available to measure the point at which the 'winds of change' in the criminal law passed from evolution to revolution."[7] But, in 1914, only fifteen years into the juvenile court experiment, the nation's highest court decided in *Weeks v. United States*[8] that at least in a *federal* prosecution, evidence seized in violation of the commands of the Fourth Amendment could not be introduced against a defendant. Between 1914 and 1961, a forty-seven year time span, state law enforcement agents were free to introduce evidence seized in violation of the Fourth Amendment in state criminal prosecutions. While some states adopted the federal exclusionary rule, the United States Supreme Court did not foreclose the issue until 1961. In that year, the Warren Court in *Mapp v. Ohio*[9] "incorporated" the Fourth Amendment commands into state criminal jurisprudence thus ending a state's

---

5. *See, e.g., Brown v. Mississippi*, 297 U.S. 278 (1936); extracting a confession by hanging, severe beating and threats; *Ashcraft v. Tennessee*, 322 U.S. 143 (1944); relay police interrogation continuously for some thirty-six hours before confession was obtained; *Haley v. Ohio*, 332 U.S. 596 (1948); reversed the convictin of fifteen year old juvenile who had signed an alleged confession after an all-night, intensive police interrogation; *Williams v. United States*, 341 U.S. 97 (1951); physical brutality and torture of suspect rendered confession unreliable and hence inadmissible; *Fikes v. Alabama*, 352 U.S. 191 (1957); illiterate suspect signed an alleged confession after police questioning; and *Spano v. New York*, 360 U.S. 315 (1959); the "false friend" confession decision that criticized police use of a friend of the suspect to play on suspect's emotions that eventually led to an alleged confession.

6. Scudellari *et al., supra* note 3, at v.

7. *Id.*

8. 232 U.S. 383 (1914).

9. 367 U.S. 643 (1961).

right to ignore the dictates of the Fourth Amendment in the pretrial stages of police investigation. *Mapp* was one of the first in a long line of subsequent high court cases that initiated a complete overhaul of investigative practices by police before trial. With the Fourth Amendment's nascent "privacy" analysis coming to the forefront in pre-trial adult procedure, the stage was ultimately being prepared for a corresponding application when an appropriate juvenile justice issue was similarly raised. Prior to high court judicial activism during the 1960s, police behavior in the pre-adjudicatory stages of a juvenile court proceeding ranged from a detached but polite professionalism to a complete abdication of constitutional fundamentals. For nearly six decades, juvenile court processes and especially the investigative activities of law enforcement were essentially invisible.

For example, in 1921, commentators such as Edward F. Waite could say with confidence that "[w]hen a court is acting not as an arbiter of private strife but as the medium of the state's performance in its sovereign duties as *parens patriae* and promotes the general welfare, it is *natural* that some safeguards of judicial contests should be laid aside."[10] (Emphasis added). Note the author's use of the word "natural" in that observation. Judge Waite, of course, was referring to the juvenile court. Such a comment clearly reflected the general tenor of the times. Appellate case law buttressed such assertions in their widespread approval of non-adversarial, non-criminal, reformation-minded ideals. In a series of selected state appellate court opinions between 1900 and 1930,[11] we find such terms as "reformatory,"

---

10. Edward F. Waite, *How Far Can Court Procedure Be Socialized Without Impairing Individual Rights?*, 12 J. Crim L. & Criminology 339 (1921).

11. *See, e.g., Scott v. Flowers*, 84 N.W. 81 (Neb. 1900); "These institutions [in this case the state Industrial School for Girls] are not of a penal character, but are reformatory." *Id.* at 82; *Kennedy v. Meara*, 56 S.E. 243 (Ga. 1906); "When the state as *parens patriae*,...takes under its custody and control those unfortunates...it cannot be said that...such persons are placed within slavery within the meaning of the constitutional provisions..." *Id.* at 247; *Ex parte Small*, 116 Pac. 118 (Idaho 1910); "It [state juvenile delinquency law] is rather intended to be an educational and charitable statute..." *Id.*; *Mill v. Brown,* 88 Pac. 609 (Utah 1907); "the proceedings of the juvenile court do not fall, nor are they intended to come, within what is termed criminal procedure, nor are the acts therein mentioned, as applied to children, crimes." *Id.* at 613; *Marlow v. Commonwealth*, 133 S.W. 1137 (Ky. 1911); "All these opinions are rested upon the theory that the proceedings are not criminal, but merely the services of the government called into play for the purpose of protecting, training, and correcting a class of children, who, through misfortune...are unable or unwilling to care for themselves." *Id.* at 1142; *State*

"unfortunates," "educational," "charitable," "guardianship," "reclaim," and "welfare" voiced over and over again in opinions that spoke to either the juvenile court itself or to juvenile court legislation. The public, more likely than not, assumed that since the juvenile court was, in Waite's words, "not an arbiter of private strife," what it did to and for children as a class was relatively benign. Since most

---

ex rel. Cave v. Tincher, 166 S.W. 1028 (Mo. 1914); "The legislation [juvenile delinquent act] exemplified by the act in question may not only be characterized as progressive, but humanitarian as well." *Id.* at 1029; *Childress v. State*, 179 S.W. 643 (Tenn. 1915); "Such proceedings before a juvenile court do not amount to a trial of the child for any criminal offense.... The court...does not undertake to punish the child for the crime committed, but...to remove him from bad influences...to eradicate evil propensities by education, wholesome training, and moral instruction." *Id.* at 644; *In re Brodie*, 166 Pac 605 (Cal. 1917); "These acts have always been sustained, and the summary procedure therein provided for approved as not being a procedure which would effect a criminal conviction, but rather one providing guardianship." *Id.* at 606; *Ex parte King*, 217 S.W. 465 (Ark. 1919); "This law undertakes to reclaim and reform rather than to condemn and punish. For these unfortunate minors who come within the terms of the act it opens the doors of an asylum, but not a jail." *Id.* at 467; *State v. Burnett*, 102 S.E. 711 (N.C. 1920); "these and other authorities well make answer that such legislation deals, and purports to deal, with delinquent children not as criminals, but as wards, and undertakes rather to give them the control and environment that may lead to their reformation..." *Id.* at 714; *Ex parte Parnell*, 200 Pac. 456 (Okla. 1921); "in every state of the Union there have been enacted juvenile laws and courts,...The courts, in construing these statutes, have universally treated them as beneficial and entitled to liberal construction." *Id.* at 458: *Ex parte Peterson*, 187 N.W. 226 (Minn. 1922); "The whole tenor of the act indicates that the sole purpose is the welfare of the delinquent as well as the dependent or neglected child....That the delinquency charge is not intended as a proceeding to punish for a crime is evident..." *Id.* at 227; *State ex rel. Roberts v. Johnson*, 194 N.W. 202 (Iowa 1923); "The dominant purpose and aim of the juvenile law is not to punish but to change the line of direction of the conduct of the boy or girl, and to impress upon the plastic mind the necessity of good habits and correct conduct." *Id.* at 203; *State ex rel. Matacia v. Buckner*, 254 S.W. 179 (Mo. 1923); "A proceeding under the [juvenile court] act...is the exertion of the state's power, parens patriae, for the reformation of a child and not for his punishment under the criminal law...and the constitutional guarantees respecting defendants in criminal cases do not apply." *Id.* at 181; *Bryant v. Brown*, 118 So. 184 (Miss. 1928); "The proceeding in the chancery court is not for the purpose of inflicting punishment or entertaining criminal jurisdiction. It is the remedial proceeding designed to reform and educate the child into habits of industry, good morals, and conduct." *Id.* at 188; *Harris v. State*, 129 So. 795 (Ala. 1930); "In construing the foregoing statute, we have in mind the great advance in the public policy of the state in dealing with youthful violators of the law looking to reformation rather than extreme punishment." *Id.* at 796.

police work with juveniles was aimed then, and, to a lesser extent now, with general welfare promotion, one can fairly see why police-juvenile encounters were not crucial pubic policy concerns. The matter becomes muddled, however, when the welfare orientation of the juvenile court comes head to head with its law enforcement function. As the innocence of American childhood began to evaporate and be rubbed away by raw reality in mid-century, the welfare-law enforcement dichotomy of juvenile justice was likewise being rubbed away. While there was certainly some pre-1960 adult precedent for constitutionalizing a slice of criminal investigation, there was no significant precedent in juvenile law that pointed toward the same processes in the pre-adjudicatory or adjudicatory stages prior to the 1960s.

Law enforcement administration in juvenile search and seizure situations was unremarkable largely because in the first half of the century it was simply assumed that police had *carte blanche* authority to do as they pleased with youth. It cannot be gainsaid that there were abuses and decisional laxity in both the seizure of youngsters and the collection of inculpatory evidence from them by the police. But, for certainly at least half a century or more, the words of legal historian Lawrence M. Friedman are particularly apt regarding the justification for such a state of affairs. Said Friedman,[12]

> The juvenile court was an example of the new professionalism: no jury, but (ultimately) a flock of social workers and other experts. The whole baggage of rights and rules were gotten rid of; and the emphasis was on the offender, not the offense;...Juvenile court was a reform hatched by ...[i]ts paternalism, middle-class bias, and absence of due process...[13]

The condemnation of the criminal law for juveniles was abolished in 1899. When an event of that magnitude took place, law enforcement thus became unsure of its primary mission in dealing with delinquent youth. Since the *social mission* of the juvenile court was *de rigueur* for over half a century, the law enforcement mission became truncated. Hence, it was not at all uncommon for police to regularly violate procedural due process in the greater service of the court's social mission.

---

12. LAWRENCE M. FRIEDMAN, A HISTORY OF AMERICAN LAW (2d ed. 1985).
13. *Id.* at 599.

In 1980, the Joint Commission on Juvenile Justice Standards of the Institute of Judicial Administration and the American Bar Association, published a twenty-three volume work[14] of standards to serve as guidelines for both legal and non-legal agencies in juvenile law. In the volume titled *Standards Relating to Police Handling of Juvenile Problems*, The Joint Commission noted that

> Of all the institutions of government dealing with juveniles, none are charged with, or have assumed, as wide and diffuse a range of responsibilities as the police.... [B]ecause of their early involvement in the exercise of public care and control, the police are in the position to give complex problems a presumptive definition and thereby impel subsequent treatment in certain directions.[15]

Further on, the Joint Commission suggested in *Standard 3.2*[16] a radically different approach to pre-adjudicatory practices in the juvenile court. The Commission recommended that

> Police investigation into criminal matters should be similar *whether the suspect is an adult or a juvenile.* Juveniles, therefore, should receive at least the same safeguards available to adults in the criminal justice system. This should apply to:
>
> A. preliminary investigation (e.g., stop and frisk);
>
> B. the arrest process;
>
> C. search and seizure;... [17] (Emphasis added).

Bearing in mind that these *Standards* are advisory only and hortatory in nature does not detract in the least from their significance. Eighty-one years after the birth of the juvenile court, two premier national organizations of the legal profession recommended a return to adult investigatory practices in juvenile law administration. Perhaps the drafters of *Standard 3.2* were at least dimly aware of the warning uttered by law dean John Henry Wigmore of Northwestern in 1926 that[18]

---

14. *IJA/ABA Juvenile Justice Standards* (1980).

15. *Standards Relating to Police Handling of Juvenile Problems* 13 (1980).

16. *Id.* at 54.

17. *Id.*

18. John Henry Wigmore, *Juvenile Courts vs. Criminal Courts*, 21 Ill. L. Rev. 375 (1926).

the social workers and the psychologists and the psychiatrists know nothing of crime and wrong....These people need to have the moral law dimned into their consciences every day of the year. The juvenile court does not do that. And to segregate a large share of daily crime into the juvenile court is to take a long step toward undermining the whole criminal law....[19]

While *In re Gault*[20] in 1967 focused exclusively on the *adjudicatory* stage of a *delinquency* hearing, there were many who believed that *Gault* was the opening wedge in the complete "constitutional domestication"[21] of the juvenile court. However, this has not come about. One should keep in mind that the *Juvenile Justice Standards* project was an attempt to possibly forestall further United States Supreme Court tinkering with the pre-adjudicatory aspects of juvenile law. After *Mapp v. Ohio* in 1961, *Kent* in 1966, and *Gault* in 1967, the thinking of the juvenile justice *cognoscenti* slanted toward a complete revamping of juvenile court procedures from initial custody to reform school. Nonetheless, despite the seeming move to incrementally "constitutionalize" the juvenile court, the United States Supreme Court braked that move in the 1970s. After *Kent* and *Gault*, the Court moved a bit more cautiously.

In respect to a decision to take a juvenile into custody, such decision is fraught with a number of imponderables. Law professor Samuel M. Davis[22] notes that "[a] youth usually has preexisting attitudes toward the police that, depending on the officer's handling of the situation, will be confirmed or changed by his initial encounter with a police officer....Juveniles possess unique characteristics that demand a specialized form of handling."[23] Are there some unique socio-legal factors that determine whether to take a juvenile into custody, and, if so, what are they? First of all, we must remember that in the United States (unlike England) no private party can initiate an *ex*

---

19. *Id.*

20. 387 U.S. 1 (1967).

21. A phrase employed by Monrad G. Paulsen after the United States Supreme Court decision in *In re Gault* in 1967. *See* Monrad G. Paulsen, *The Constitutional Domestication of the Juvenile Court*, 1967 Sup. Ct. Rev. 233.

22. SAMUEL M. DAVIS, RIGHTS OF JUVENILES: THE JUVENILE JUSTICE SYSTEM (2d ed. 1996).

23. *Id.* at 3–15 (Release #16, 4/96).

parte proceeding in either a criminal or juvenile court. Charges of law violation must be processed through official channels and in most cases of juvenile violations this means through formal police contact. A juvenile's attitude, gender, race, victim preference, if any, and a host of other non-quantifiable indices all may play into a police officer's decision to intervene. In a 1970 study by sociologists Donald Black and Albert J. Reiss, Jr.,[24] they found that in their sample at least, a significant number of *juvenile complainants* did not express a clear command for police action in the case. Steven M. Cox and John J. Conrad in 1978[25] and Carl E. Pope[26] in 1984 concluded, respectively, that both sex and race were factors in police-juvenile contacts, but their influence in the custody-no custody decision was not as direct as had been assumed. As Albert R. Roberts notes,[27] "[i]ndeed, for patrol officers, attitude is probably the most relevant factor next to offense. But this may be by default,... because of the paucity of other available information at the time the officer has to make the judgment."[28] Elyce Z. Ferster and Thomas F. Courtless[29] citing a sociological study by Irving Piliavin and Scott Briar,[30] note seven ways in which, once taken into custody, police can "process" arrested juveniles. They write that

> in order of increasing severity are: (1) release; (2) release accompanied by an official report describing the encounter with the juvenile; (3) an official "reprimand" with release to parent or guardian; (4) referral to other agencies when it is believed that some rehabilitative program should be set up after more investigation; (5) voluntary police supervision used when it is felt that an officer and parent can assist a child cooperatively; (6) referral to the juvenile court

---

24. Donald Black & Albert J. Reiss, Jr., *Police Control of Juveniles*, 35 Am. Soc. Rev. 63 (1970).

25. STEVEN M. COX & JOHN J. CONRAD, JUVENILE JUSTICE (1978).

26. Carl E. Pope, *Blacks and Juvenile Crime: A Review*, as quoted in CRIMINAL JUSTICE SYSTEM AND BLACKS 75 (Daniel Georges-Abeyie ed. 1984).

27. ALBERT R. ROBERTS, JUVENILE JUSTICE: POLICIES, PROGRAMS, AND SERVICES (1989).

28. *Id.* at 97–98.

29. Elyce Z. Ferster & Thomas F. Courtless, *The Beginning of Juvenile Justice: Police Practices and the Juvenile Offender*, 22 Vand. L. Rev. 567 (1964).

30. Irving Piliavin & Scott Briar, *Police Encounters With Juveniles*, 70 Am. J. Soc. 206 (1964).

without detention; and (7) referral to the juvenile court with detention.[31]

In 1968, political scientist James Q. Wilson published a seminal work on law enforcement[32] in which he identified three types or "styles" of police organization in the United States and their general behavioral mode of operation. Wilson's styles were (1) the *watchmanlike* department; (2) the *legalistic* department; and (3) the *service* department. As Wilson would be quick to point out, no police organization captures a "pure" style of one to the exclusion of the other two. What these three styles or models of police organization allow us to do is to understand with greater clarity the *response behavior* police exhibit to juvenile offending. When the factors of sex, race, location, victim preference and attitude of a juvenile is factored into the equation, Wilson's trilogy of police organization and management style may give one a fairly accurate clue on custodial or non-custodial outcome. All other factors being equal, watchmanlike and service style department personnel may be more accommodating to compromise in certain cases by allowing for either outright release, reprimand, or referral to a social service agency if indicated. Contrariwise, a department with a strong legal orientation that essentially "goes by the book," may well invoke provisions of the juvenile code to refer a youth to juvenile court with or without detention. Absolutes here should be avoided. Clearly, if a juvenile is accosted and taken into custody for a serious felony-type act of delinquency, the range of non-court dispositions today are far less assured than they would have been thirty years ago. All of this seemingly indicates that probably up until the 1960s, the vast majority of police-juvenile initial contacts would result in non-court disposition. The 1960s changed things in this nation, not only legally, but culturally and morally as well. The sociological significance of "intermediate institutions" of social control came under relentless strain in that watershed decade. The traditional nuclear family, our public educational infrastructure and our Judeo-Christian ethic were seriously degraded and compromised. Writing in the late 1940s, Martin H. Neumeyer[33] noted that "[a] community can have almost any degree of law observance...

31. Ferster & Courtless, *supra* note 29, at 573.
32. JAMES Q. WILSON, VARIETIES OF POLICE BEHAVIOR (1968).
33. MARTIN E. NEUMEYER, JUVENILE DELINQUENCY IN MODERN SOCIETY (1949).

The attitude of youth toward law observance and enforcement reflects the community attitude. If there is respect for law, children naturally develop the attitude."[34] Regretfully, it seems that beginning in the 1960s and continuing on into post-industrial America, the "respect for law" Neumeyer spoke of in 1949 is far more contingent on both the adult and the juvenile level. Because of this, police custodial decisions involving juvenile law violators have become, in the main, more "legalistic" in the Wilsonian sense of that term. Because of this, police are now more vigilant of limited constitutional due process rights for children. At the same time, however, they are now more frequently invoking either the juvenile or the criminal justice apparatus on a formal basis. What then has this shift in emphasis portended for the law of search and seizure for juveniles?

Like it does in so many of its adult decisions, the United States Supreme Court in the *Gault* ruling eschewed any wide-ranging pronouncements about juvenile procedures in general. Although *Gault* did take the juvenile court establishment to task in a lengthy portion of its opinion, the 7–2 majority focused on the due process and fair treatment issues in a delinquency adjudication only. The Court did not address either the pre-adjudicatory or the dispositional phases of the juvenile process, although the question remained how far the *Gault ratio decidendi* could be extended to other segments of juvenile law.

Since 1967, the search and seizure issue as applied to juveniles has tracked the *Mapp* exclusionary rule rationale. However, nothing in the language of either *Gault* or *Mapp* necessarily pre-ordained that the Fourth Amendment's commands would automatically be applicable to juvenile lawbreakers. In his second edition of *Rights of Juveniles: The Juvenile Justice System*,[35] Davis remarks that "[a]ll courts that have specifically considered the question of the applicability of the fourth amendment to the juvenile process have held in favor of its applicability,..."[36] In incorporating the exclusionary rule's commands into the juvenile process, appellate courts are also incorporating by reference all or most of the ancillary formulations developed since the 1961 *Mapp* decision. For example, the so-called "plain-

---

34. *Id.* at 215.
35. Davis, *Supra* note 22.
36. *Id.* at 3–17 (Release #16, 4/96).

view" doctrine,[37] the "stop and frisk" rationale,[38] and the warrantless search of a juvenile incident to a lawful "taking into custody"[39] have all been judicially approved in appropriate case law. Moreover, there has been a move since the mid-1980s to legislate Fourth Amendment principles into various juvenile codes. California, Georgia, Illinois, Mississippi, North Dakota, Pennsylvania, Tennessee, Texas and Vermont represent nine jurisdictions that have, in one form or fashion, recently extended Fourth Amendment jurisprudence to juveniles via legislative mandate.

One of the more intriguing contemporary issues confronting appellate tribunals in the juvenile Fourth Amendment context is the public school search and seizure question. Prior to the mid-1980s when the landmark decision of *New Jersey v. T.L.O.*[40] was handed down, public school search and seizure situations were viewed primarily as a matter touching educational mission, control and student discipline. These issues were generally considered beyond the ambit of constitutional inquiry. Those courts that did venture into this particular realm generally sided with the educational establishment in its desire to maintain an orderly and decorous teaching-learning environment. Several time-honored legal doctrines were frequently invoked by public school authorities to buttress their arguments that public school children had little, if any, constitutional protections regarding search and seizure. As far back as 1969, however, the United States Supreme Court in the *Tinker*[41] ruling noted that "students or teachers [do not] shed their constitutional rights...at the schoolhouse gate."[42] That

---

37. "Plain view" applied in the Louisiana case of *State ex rel. Jynes*, 626 So. 2d 452 (La. Ct. App. 1993).

38. California, Pennsylvania and New York appellate courts have upheld the stop and frisk practice as applied to juvenile suspects in such decisions as *In re Tony C.*, 21 Cal. 3d 888, 582 P. 2d 957, 148 Cal. Rptr. 366 (1978); *In re James D.*, 43 Cal. 3d 903, 741 P. 2d 161, 239 Cal. Rptr. 663 (1987), *cert. denied*, 108 S. Ct. 1222 (1988); *In re Lang*, 44 Misc 2d 900, 255 N.Y.S. 2d 987 (Fam. Ct. N.Y. Co. 1965); and *In re Jermaine*, 399 Pa. Super. 503, 582 A. 2d 1058 (1990).

39. *In re Marsh*, 40 Ill. 2d 53, 237 N.E. 2d 529 (1968) and *In re J.F.F.*, 164 Wis. 2d 10, 473 N.W. 2d 546 (Wis. Ct. App. 1991).

40. 469 U.S. 325 (1985).

41. *Tinker v. Des Moines Independent Community School District*, 393 U.S. 503 (1969) was a free speech and expression decision, not a public school search and seizure case.

42. *Id.* at 506.

language did not clear up the matter. As usual, statements such as this by the Court often raise as many questions as answers. In the intervening years between *Tinker* and *T.L.O.*, the prevailing view seemed to be that public school students enjoyed a remarkably truncated right to privacy in their lockers, desks and other educationally related fixtures. Beyond these specific areas, the law provided little guidance.

In general, one can say that at least three overlapping legal doctrines provided public school administrators with almost unbridled authority to search and seize materials from certain student-occupied areas within a school complex. These three were the (1) *parens patriae* doctrine broadly conceived; (2) the *in loco parentis* doctrine; and (3) proprietary interest theory. The *parens patriae* and *in loco parentis* arguments gave primacy to the authority of teachers and administrators to search and seize certain items from school children on the premise that they were the parental alter ego while the child was in school and hence since parents could generally search at random for illegal items, school authorities could likewise do so. The proprietary interest theory was bottomed on the property law concept that the school had a superior property interest in desks, lockers and other school fixtures and that superior property interest allowed searches at random with the child being only a tenant at will at best. Courts which sided with school authorities in allowing search and seizures often were not completely forthcoming on which doctrine or theory, or combinations thereof, supported their decision. Some opinions would speak of one concept as controlling, while others, in grand obfuscation, would merge, distill and combine one or more tenets from each to reach a desired conclusion.

The *parens patriae* rationale in particular was frequently invoked *sub silentio* as a supporting leg of either or both the *in loco parentis* or the proprietary interest argument. While the child was in attendance at a public school and since public education is an arm of state bureaucracy, the state as the supreme parent of the child in that context is free to allot authority to public school officialdom to represent it in these situations. In the normal course of things, a child's natural parents or guardian do not need the child's "permission" to look for inculpatory evidence in the home or elsewhere, hence, the school as super-parent agent correspondingly needs no such permission. More often than not, however, the lawfulness of pre-*T.L.O.* search and seizure decisions was premised upon a combination of *in loco parentis* and the theory of proprietary interest.

The *in loco parentis*[43] doctrine invokes the parent-surrogate theme and the parental proxy argument. Standing behind this particular public school proxy to search and seize is the view that there is no need for school personnel to honor the legal formalities of probable cause, neutral magistrate and the issuance of a formal search warrant. No public school in the nation, of course, has the resources nor indeed the will to afford its students complete constitutional due process in this context. The *in loco parentis* argument demurred to the civil libertarian thesis that all children are fully protected by the commands of the Fourth Amendment while attending a state-supported institution. Since, by hypothesis, a parent or guardian does not have to comply with the commands of the Fourth Amendment in the ordinary situation of privacy violation involving their own child or children, so too the public school official is likewise exempt.[44] *In re Donaldson*,[45] a 1969 California decision, discusses all the legal bases for upholding the authority of public school officials to search students and student enclaves.

Overarching all three bases justifying privacy rights intrusions in the public schools is a relatively obscure 1921 decision[46] by the United States Supreme Court. In *Burdeau v. McDowell*,[47] the Court ruled that the commands of the Fourth Amendment do not reach to protect an individual against search and seizures that are privately initiated. In other words, the proscriptions of the Fourth Amendment apply only to so-called "state action." This means simply that school authorities who undertook search and seizures on their own without calling in formal law enforcement assistance, were acting as a private citizen, not as state agents. Hence, the argument proceeded, any incriminating items found implicating a juvenile pupil was evidence seized by a "private" citizen under the *McDowell* rationale and thus

---

43. This Latin term means "in place of the parent." An example of this concept being employed in juvenile law can be found in the decision of *Mercer v. State*, 450 S.W. 2d 715 (Tex. Civ. App. 1970).

44. Illustrative cases include the California decision of *In re Donaldson*, 269 Cal. App. 2d 509, 75 Cal. Rptr. 220 (1969); the Florida decision of *Nelson v. State*, 319 So. 2d 154 (Fla. Dist. Ct. App. 1975); the New York case of *People v. Overton*, 20 N.Y. 2d 360, 283 N.Y.S. 2d 22, 229 N.E. 2d 596 (1967) and the Washington state case of *State v. McKinnon*, 88 Wash. 2d 75, 558 P. 2d 781 (1977).

45. 269 Cal. App. 2d 509, 75 Cal. Rptr. 220 (1965).

46. *Burdeau v. McDowell*, 256 U.S. 465 (1921).

47. *Id.*

not subject to Fourth Amendment constraints. Collectively, these doctrines, theories and concepts allowed an exploratory blank check for public school authorities to search students and their property.

Public school search and seizure issues did not become a matter of significance until the 1960s. In large measure, then and now, the driving forces behind these types of intrusiveness are drug-related. The fruits, instrumentalities and contraband of the American drug culture have changed the legal landscape of public school search and seizure law over the past thirty years. It certainly cannot be said that all of our public primary and secondary schools are drug-infested, for that is simply not the case. There are, nonetheless, numerous examples of certain school systems that have been particularly hard hit by the ready availability of controlled substances. It was out of one of these schools that a situation arose to both change and to clarify public school search and seizure law in the 1980s.

New Jersey v. T.L.O.[48] was remarkable in the sense that it was so unremarkable. A New Jersey high school instructor discovered a fourteen-year-old female student smoking a cigarette in the girl's rest room and took the student to the principal's office. There the juvenile was questioned by an assistant vice-principal and during that encounter she denied smoking in the restroom. The vice-principal demanded to see the contents of T.L.O.'s purse, opened it, and found therein cigarettes, cigarette rolling papers, a small amount of marijuana, plastic bags, index cards with names of students who owed T.L.O. money, a substantial quantity of money in one-dollar bills and two incriminating letters implicating the juvenile in drug dealing. At that point, the school notified T.L.O.'s mother and the local police and turned the evidence of drug dealing over to the police. A subsequent confession by the juvenile implicating her in drug dealing formed the basis for delinquency charges against her.

At her delinquency hearing before the Juvenile and Domestic Relations Court of Middlesex County, New Jersey, T.L.O., through her attorney, moved to suppress all evidence found in her purse by the vice-principal on the thesis that it was tainted by an unlawful search. The juvenile court denied the motion to suppress and concluded that although the Fourth Amendment did apply to school official searches,[49]

---

48. 469 U.S. 325 (1985).
49. *State ex rel. T.L.O.*, 178 N.J. Super. 329, 428 A. 2d 1327 (1980).

a school official may properly conduct a search of a student's person if the official has a reasonable suspicion that a crime has been or is in the process of being committed, or reasonable cause to believe that the search is necessary to maintain school discipline or enforce school policies.[50]

The New Jersey court then concluded that the search of T.L.O.'s purse was "reasonable" and was based upon a well-founded suspicion that T.L.O. had violated a no-smoking rule of the school. A divided Appellate Division affirmed the juvenile court's findings that there had been no Fourth Amendment violation.[51] The Supreme Court of New Jersey reversed the judgment of the Appellate Division and ordered the evidence found in T.L.O.'s purse suppressed.[52] In late 1983, the United States Supreme Court granted the State of New Jersey's petition for *certiorari*[53] to review the entire issue of public school search and seizures.

In a lengthy opinion by Mr. Justice White, the Supreme Court dismantled the state action-private citizen dichotomy when it concluded, among other things, that public school personnel *are* "state agents" for Fourth Amendment purposes. Said White, "[i]t is now beyond dispute that 'the Federal Constitution, by virtue of the Fourteenth Amendment, prohibits unreasonable searches and seizures by state officers.'"[54] But he then went on to note that "[e]qually indisputable is the proposition that the Fourteenth Amendment protects the rights of students against encroachment by public school officials:"[55] In a partial answer to the *Tinker* dictum about students and teachers not losing constitutional rights "at the schoolhouse gate," the Court focused its attention on the *reasonableness* of the school authorities' search and seizure in the instant case. What is "reasonable" intoned the majority, varies from circumstance to circumstance. The Court then invoked a balancing test; that is, a need for public school officialdom to conduct searches over against a student's privacy interest invaded by the search. In the end, the majority concluded that the Fourth Amendment's formal warrant requirement was inapplicable

---

50. *Id.* at 341, 428 A. 2d at 1333.
51. *State ex rel. T.L.O.*, 185 N.J. Super. 279, 448 A. 2d 493 (1982).
52. *State ex rel. T.L.O.*, 94 N.J. 331, 463 A. 2d 934 (1983).
53. 464 U.S. 991 (1983).
54. 469 U.S. 325, 334 (1985).
55. *Id.*

to public school officials and, by hypothesis, inapplicable to public school searches.[56] Since the word "reasonableness" is subject to varying degrees of interpretation, the Court stipulated a two-point inquiry: (1) was "the...action...justified at its inception" and (2) was the search conducted by these officials "reasonably related in scope to the circumstances which justified the interference in the first place?"[57] Applying this two-part criteria, the Court concluded that the Supreme Court of New Jersey's ruling was erroneous, representing what Justice White characterized as "a somewhat crabbed notion of reasonableness."[58]

On balance, the state of New Jersey's public school officials and those nationwide were given fairly broad leeway to interpret what a "reasonable" search and seizure entailed. The adult criminal procedure model of probable cause, examination of affidavit for warrant by a neutral magistrate, issuance of a warrant and service thereof were realistically abandoned in this context. The Court, however, left unanswered several issues that may spur future litigation. For example, Davis[59] notes the following unresolved issues left by the T.L.O. decision:

> whether evidence illegally obtained as a result of a search by school personnel is admissible in court, whether the same rules applicable to searches of the person apply to searches of lockers and desks, whether the rules outlined by the Court are affected if school personnel act as agents of the police, and whether school personnel must have individualized suspicion before searching a particular student.[60]

A decade after the T.L.O. ruling, the Supreme Court had occasion to amplify what it meant by "reasonableness." In 1995 in a case from Oregon[61] involving authorized but random drug testing of student athletes, the Court approved a school district policy to that effect. Mr. Justice Scalia apparently revived the *in loco parentis* doctrine in *Vernonia School District 47J v. Acton*. Most commentators had as-

---

56. *Id.* at 340.
57. *Id.* at 341.
58. *Id.* at 343.
59. Davis, *supra* note 22, at 3–23 (Release #16, 4/96).
60. *Id.* at 3–23; 3–24 (Release #16, 4/96).
61. *Vernonia Sch. Dist. 47J v. Acton*, 115 S. Ct. 2386 (1995).

sumed that *T.L.O.* had judiciously interred *in loco parentis* in the public school search and seizure context. Not so, according to Justice Scalia. In the previous bench trial, the United States District Court in Oregon had denied the claims of the juvenile's parents that the school district policy on random drug testing violated both the Fourth and Fourteenth Amendments to the Federal Constitution and Article I, sec. 9, of the Oregon Constitution.[62] However, the judgment of the District Court was reversed by the Ninth Circuit Court of Appeals[63] predisposing the United States Supreme Court to grant *certiorari* to review the issue. Reaffirming the "reasonableness" doctrine of *T.L.O.,* Justice Scalia then noted that[64]

> a warrant is not required to establish the reasonableness of all government searches; and when a warrant is not re-quired...probable cause is not invariably required either. A search unsupported by probable cause can be constitu-tional, we have said, "when special needs, beyond the nor-mal need for law enforcement, make the warrant and probable cause requirement impracticable...[65]

Scalia then applied the "special needs" test to situations involving "(1) children, who (2) have been committed to the temporary cus-tody of the State as schoolmaster."[66] With the sovereign as "school-master" and with the additional fact that "[l]egitimate privacy expec-tations are even less with regard to student athletes,"[67] the Court, by a vote of 6–3, ruled that James Acton's Fourth and Fourteenth Amendment rights were not infringed and vacated the judgment of the Ninth Circuit remanding the case to determine what protections, if any, the Oregon Constitution afforded the juvenile. *Acton* thus reinvigorated *in loco parentis* in the "State as schoolmaster" idiom. Perhaps equally as plausible as a justificatory rationale for the deci-sion is the judiciary's intense concern for upholding, whenever possi-ble, drug enforcement policies in public education that appear both facially fair and narrowly drawn.

---

62. *Acton v. Vernonia Sch. Dist.* 796 F. Supp. 1354 (D. Or. 1992).
63. 66 F.3d 217 (9th Cir. 1995).
64. *Vernonia,* 115 S. Ct. at 2391.
65. *Id.*
66. *Id.* at 2392.
67. *Id.*

For over thirty years now, the law of search and seizure has been applied in varying degrees to juveniles in both educational and non-educational settings. Clearly, the *Acton* decision does not diminish the Fourth Amendment's commands in other case-specific scenarios. Although there is a split of authority in drug enforcement policies involving trained dogs to detect controlled substances in an educational setting,[68] the Fourth Amendment does entitle the juvenile to an enforceable privacy interest in areas outside the home and school. Except in emergency or "exigent" circumstances and in those situations where valid legal authority exists, a juvenile should have and enjoy the same Fourth Amendment protections accorded adult suspects.

C. Interrogating the Juvenile

Police questioning of juveniles poses special problems not generally encountered with adult suspects. First of all, unlike adults, juveniles are subject to the peculiar but nearly century old trichotomy of being a suspect in delinquency, dependency or neglect situations. Because two of these three categories involve behavior that is inapplicable in a comparable adult context, police interrogation in certain cases may take on a perspective not ordinarily routine.

Like so many other areas in juvenile law, police interrogation practices in the pre-adjudicatory phase was not a major concern in pre-

---

68. *See, e.g., Doe v. Renfrow*, 475 F. Supp. 1012 (N.D. Ind. 1979); *Doe v. Renfrow*, 631 F. 2d 91 (7th Cir. 1980), *cert. denied*, 451 U.S. 1022 (1981), wherein the court upheld the *in loco parentis* rationale for a lock-down and school search for narcotics where police were present, but those conducting the search were school personnel and a prior agreement between the school and law enforcement was that no arrests would be made if any drugs were discovered. However, a strip search of one female thirteen-year-old student was performed and, although the district court granted only declaratory relief, the Seventh Circuit United States Court of Appeals remanded that portion of the case dealing with the nude search of the juvenile for a determination of the measure of damages, if any, incurred by that act. In *Jones v. Latexo Independent School Dist.*, 499 F. Supp. 223 (E.D. Tex 1980), a federal district court in Texas ruled that employing trained canines to make a drug "sweep" through a public school in an indiscriminate search for drugs was unconstitutional and that the *in loco parentis* doctrine does not automatically insulate school officials from Fourth Amendment strictures. For juvenile street search and seizure practices, as opposed to those at a school, *see generally* Lourdes M. Rosado, *Minors and the Fourth Amendment: How Juvenile Status Should Invoke Different Standards for Search and Seizures on the Streets*, 71 N.Y.U.L. Rev. 762 (1996).

1960 practice. The vast majority of juveniles who were routinely interrogated by law enforcement personnel cooperated with the authorities, often at the behest of either their parents or guardian. The "civil" nature of juvenile justice coupled with the intense *parens patriae* mind-set of the judiciary exhaulted the cooperative nature of police-juvenile interrogation. As law enforcement agencies became more professional and juvenile justice case law became more rights-specific after the 1960s, interrogation practices tended to track adult procedures. Prior to the advent of the Warren Court, juvenile interrogation, and indeed, adult interrogation as well was a relatively low-visibility issue in criminal procedure. In adult practice, however, there were some notable exceptions that ultimately had an impact on juvenile law as well.

In the 1930s, the United States probably reached a low point in police interrogation practices. While only a small fraction of police questioning procedures ever reached the appellate level for review, those that did shed a disturbing light on what was too often routine police abuse of adult suspects. Perhaps the archetypal abuse by police of the interrogation process reached the United States Supreme Court in 1936 in the *Brown*[69] decision. There, a confession was extracted from a black male suspect by egregious police brutality.[70] Citing a portion of the dissenting opinion by the Mississippi Supreme Court,[71] the United States Supreme Court per Chief Justice Hughes, reversed the defendant's conviction holding that the confession given by Brown to the police was unconstitutionally coerced. *Brown v. Mississippi* effectively enshrined the so-called "voluntariness" test of confession admissibility and appellate courts were to look at all the surrounding circumstances to determine if a confession was made of a person's own free will. If not, the confession was presumed coerced, involuntary, and hence inadmissible as evidence.

---

69. *Brown v. Mississippi*, 297 U.S. 278 (1936).

70. *Brown* involved the Court in what two commentators termed "a case marked by the worst excesses of racially motivated brutality." MARVIN ZALMAN & LARRY J. SIEGEL, CRIMINAL PROCEDURE: CONSTITUTION AND SOCIETY 472 (2d ed. 1997). The case involved three black males charged with murder. The defendant Brown was hung twice and cut down and when he continued to protest his involvement in the crime, sheriff deputies tied him to a tree and whipped him. Subsequently Brown was whipped again and was told the whipping would continue until he confessed. He finally agreed to confess and was then taken to jail.

71. *Brown v. State*, 173 Miss. 542, 574–75; 161 So. 465, 471 (1935).

Between *Brown* in 1936 and *Miranda v. Arizona*[72] in 1966, juvenile interrogation practices were apparently of little concern in constitutional law. There were, however, two decisions rendered in that thirty-year interim that involved juvenile interrogations, although in each case the juvenile in question was tried as an adult in criminal court. In 1948 in *Haley v. Ohio*,[73] the Supreme Court initially began to differentiate juveniles from adults in the interrogation process. The fifteen-year-old juvenile in that case confessed to murder after a five-hour interrogation by police absent family, friends or legal assistance. The Court noted that a youth of Haley's age "cannot be judged by the more exacting standards of maturity. That which would leave a man cold and unimpressed can overawe and overwhelm a lad in his early teens..."[74] Haley's conviction was overturned as being involuntary and consequently a violation of due process of law. Fourteen years later in 1962, the United States Supreme Court again had before it a case involving a youth who was tried and convicted in adult criminal court. In *Gallegos v. Colorado*,[75] the Court reasoned that

> [A] fourteen year old boy, no matter how sophisticated, is unlikely to have any conception of what will confront him when he is made accessible only to the police.... [W]e deal with a person who is not equal to the police in knowledge and understanding of the consequences of the questions and answers being recorded and who is unable to know how to protect his own interests or how to get the benefits of his constitutional rights....[76]

The Court went on to note that a fourteen-year-old should be provided with some form of competent protection against the overwhelming power of the state represented by the police. It remarked that Gallegos "would have no way of knowing what the consequences of his confession were without advice as to his rights—from someone concerned with securing him those rights—..."[77] Haley and Gallegos were juveniles in age but were prosecuted in adult court; hence there

---

72. 386 U.S. 436 (1966).
73. 332 U.S. 597 (1948).
74. *Id.* at 599.
75. 370 U.S. 49 (1962).
76. *Id.* at 54.
77. *Id.*

was no *juvenile law* precedent prior to *In re Gault*[78] that specifically addressed the general issue of a juvenile's due process interrogation protections in a juvenile justice context.

All this changed between 1966 and 1967. Arguably, three United States Supreme Court rulings, two involving juveniles and one involving an adult, reconfigured both juvenile and adult pre-trial procedures, including the confession question. *Kent v. United States*[79] and *Miranda v. Arizona*[80] in 1966 and *In re Gault*[81] in 1967 began a paradigm shift in certain pre-trial practices in juvenile and in criminal justice. Justice William O. Douglas in his majority opinion in the *Haley* decision noted that "when, as here, a mere child—an easy victim of the law—is before us, special care in scrutinizing the record must be used."[82] It was this "special care" issue that sensitized not only the Supreme Court, but lower courts as well, to be more mindful of the due process rights of minors during police custodial interrogation. The courts which did address juvenile confession issues prior to the *Miranda* case employed a "totality of the circumstances" test to assist in the determination of whether or not the questioned confession was truly voluntary. The judicially crafted *Miranda* litany in the interrogation context did not arrive until 1966 and at least initially seemed to apply only to adult suspects. However, landmark constitutional decisions often have a way of spilling over into other related branches of the law and this was certainly the case in the interrogation and confession field. Lifting language directly from the 1948 *Haley* decision, the United States Supreme Court in *Gault*[83] ruled that the privilege against compulsory self-incrimination was applicable to juveniles charged with a delinquency violation via the Fourteenth Amendment.[84] *Gault*, however, did not directly rule on the applicability of *Miranda* warnings to juveniles. The Court in that decision took pains to avoid the entire juvenile-police investigation scenario.[85] Nonetheless, after the *Miranda* ruling, some state legislative bodies

---

78. 387 U.S. 1 (1967).
79. 383 U.S. 541 (1966).
80. 386 U.S. 436 (1966).
81. 387 U.S. 1 (1967).
82. *Haley v. Ohio*, 332 U.S. 596, 599 (1948).
83. 387 U.S. 1 (1967).
84. *Id.* at 45–46.
85. In 1979 in *Fare v. Michael C.*, 442 U.S. 707, 717 n. 4, the Court specifically noted that it had not ruled on *Miranda's* applicability to juvenile interrogation practices.

undertook to provide *Miranda*-type safeguards to juveniles either by statute or in rules of juvenile procedure.[86]

Today, a legitimate guess can be hazarded that since the late 1960s, with *Kent, Miranda* and *Gault* on the books, no court would deliberately withhold the *Miranda* safeguards from juveniles undergoing custodial police interrogation. The contemporary debate is not so much whether *Miranda* warnings should be given, but rather whether or not juveniles may, *ex parte*, waive their *Miranda* rights and subject themselves to police questioning. The issue is further complicated by the fact that there has been some concern over whether or not a juvenile's parent, guardian, custodian or attorney must also be present with the juvenile and correspondingly waive the *Miranda* warnings along with the juvenile.[87] The law here is unsettled, but the far safer rule would be to err on the side of caution and have the police always "Mirandize" the juvenile suspect unless they are under a strict departmental or legal policy mandate to deliver the minor to a juvenile detention facility without custodial interrogation. In that event, the police would merely act as a processing agent for the juvenile court and the child's constitutional right to silence ought, in theory at least, be honored in the committing process. Ever since the *Gault* decision, there has been some concern in juvenile justice circles that juvenile confessions, except perhaps in the most streetwise and sophisticated of youth, are suspect *per se*. In the relatively short history of constitutional due process in the juvenile interrogation sector, as elsewhere,

---

86. *See, e.g.,* CAL. WELF. & INST. CODE §§ 625, 627.5 (West 1984); COLO. REV. STAT. ANN. § 46b-137(a) (West 1986); OKLA. STAT. ANN. tit. 10, § 1109(A) (West 1987). Alabama provides in its juvenile rules of procedure that *Miranda* warnings be given and, in addition, requires that the juvenile be specifically warned that he or she has the right to consult with an attorney or parent or guardian. If the child is not so counseled, no statement subsequently made while in police custody is admissible. ALA. R. JUV. PROC. 11(A). In this connection, *see Ex parte Whisenant*, 466 So. 2d 1006 (Ala. 1985) and *Payne v. State*, 487 So. 2d 256 (Ala. Cr. App. 1986). In the *Payne* decision, the Alabama Court of Criminal Appeals held that the juvenile's grandmother was not his "guardian" within the meaning of Rule 11(A), ALA. R. JUV. PROC. unless evidence could be adduced that she was his primary caretaker.

87. Vermont, for example, by case law has adopted the "interested adult" requirement for consultation before waiver in *In re E.T.C.*, 449 A. 2d 937 (Vt. 1982). Statutory provisions in New York mandate that *Miranda* warnings be given not only to the juvenile, but to parents or other custodian if they are present at the questioning. *See* N.Y. FAM. CT. ACT § 305.2(7) (McKinney 1983).

we still have a gap between "official" or "book law" and what might be described as "law in action." Nonetheless, as we move inexorably toward the juvenile court's century mark, the preadjudicatory interrogation processes for delinquency suspects seem to be moving, in Lawrence M. Friedman's words, "toward a single legal culture—a trend that is persistent, genuine, and significant."[88]

The United States Supreme Court focused its 1967 *Gault* rulings on a *delinquency* adjudication only. Clearly, up until the late 1960s, juvenile law exhibited a looseness in both its substantive and procedural contexts not tolerated on the adult level. *Gault* changed all of that in juvenile fact-finding hearings held to determine whether an act of *delinquency* had taken place. Writing for the seven justice majority in *Gault*, Abe Fortas noted that "We do not mean...to indicate that the [delinquency] hearing must conform with all the requirements of a criminal trial..."[89] What did the Court have in mind here? Of course, one of the "requirements" of a criminal trial is the development of pre-trial evidence, part of which may include the results of a police interrogation. Since *Gault* dealt with only a charge of delinquency, not dependency or neglect, how should police handle interrogations of children taken into custody for alleged dependency or neglect? The Court was silent on that matter and probably for good reason. Since there were numerous jurisdictions in the 1960s that had, in effect, "commingled" dependency and neglect within their definition of delinquency, it would have created a terribly confusing issue to decipher "true" delinquency from a congeries of status and parental fault categories.

Certainly juveniles who are categorized in any of the three jurisdictional pigeonholes are not free to refuse to answer questions of an informational nature such as name, age, residence and parental or guardian names, addresses and phone numbers. Such ministerial inquiries are not designed to elicit inculpatory responses from the juvenile. Even assuming, however, that police questioning focuses on the dependency or neglect issue does not, one would presume, preclude that form of questioning for these activities are not the adult equivalent of *crimes* in the ordinary sense of such terminology. There is little commentary on the silence issue in either the status or neglect situations.

---

88. Friedman, *supra* note 12.
89. *In re Gault*, 387 U.S. at 30.

This is probably salutary. Invoking a criminal procedure model here would be time-consuming and simply wrong-headed social policy.

D. Juvenile Records and Confidentiality

Courtroom and documentary confidentiality has always been a hallmark of the *parens patriae* juvenile court. The confidentiality concept was advanced to foster a complete and unfettered information flow among and between the juvenile, and the court and probation staff. If certain sensitive information about the youngster were made public, the fear was that extra-judicial pressures in some form might be brought to bear on the decision-making process. Since 1899, however, we have undergone several "revolutions" in information technology and there are those today that seriously question the hidden decision-making processes of most juvenile courts. Since the juvenile court has operated more or less under a social welfare philosophy for most of the twentieth century, the collection of a maximum amount of personal data on a child is considered a necessary predicate for equitable judgments. Under *parens patriae*, the generating of information on a juvenile is considered part and parcel of the special obligation incurred by the state to assure proper dispositional alternatives. In 1980 in the *IJA/ABA Juvenile Justice Standards* project, the Joint Commission on Juvenile Justice Standards noted that "[j]uveniles often have less choice than adults about giving or consenting to the disclosure of information when requested to do so.... they are the captive subject of a particular institution, perhaps a school or welfare department... it is difficult for the child to resist."[90] The *Standards* volume entitled *Juvenile Records and Information Systems* sets forth a series of recommendations on confidentiality too detailed to cover in this context. What will be discussed, however, is the apparent late twentieth-century move in some quarters to rent the confidentiality veil that has shrouded juvenile proceedings since their inception.

In 1995, the National Council of Juvenile and Family Court Judges in a policy statement remarked that[91]

---

90. *IJA/ABA Juvenile Justice Standards, Standards Relating to Juvenile Records and Information Systems* 2 (1980).
91. National Council of Juvenile and Family Court Judges, *Children and Families First: A Mandate for America's Courts* 3 (1995).

Traditional notions of secrecy and confidentiality should be reexamined and relaxed to promote public confidence in the court's work. The public has a right to know how courts deal with children and families. The court should be opened to the media, interested professionals and students and, when appropriate, the public in order to hold itself accountable, educate others and encourage greater community participation.[92]

Consequently, ninety-six years after the establishment of the Cook County Juvenile Court, the national organization of juvenile and family court jurists have issued a call for a more open juvenile court process. Doubtless, many judges in America's juvenile court system willingly subscribe to this policy statement, due perhaps in part to the perceived increase in violent juvenile crime in the United States. There are others, however, who still hold to the traditional view that court and record confidentiality is a key element in the overall rehabilitative process and should not be abandoned. Regardless of which view one takes, it is clear that the United States Supreme Court has yet to rule on the merits of a "right to confidentiality" in juvenile court proceedings. This reticence by the Court to involve itself in this issue may be due in part to the fact that a number of states have either by legislation or otherwise allowed a diverse number of individuals access to juvenile hearings if they have an "interest" in the outcome of those proceedings.[93]

---

92. *Id.*

93. A representative sample of 1990s legislation involving persons "with a proper interest" in the outcome of a juvenile hearing include the following: *Alabama* — ALA. CODE § 12.15.65 (Supp. 1994); *Arkansas* — ARK. CODE. ANN. § 9.27325 (Michie 1993); *California* — CAL. WELF. & INST. CODE § 676 (West Supp. 1995); *District of Columbia* — D.C. CODE ANN. § 16.2316 (Supp. 1994); *Georgia* — GA. CODE ANN. § 15.11.28 (1994); *Iowa* — IOWA CODE ANN. § 232.39 (West 1994); *Kentucky* — KY. REV. STAT. ANN. § 610-070 (Baldwin Supp. 1994); *Massachusetts* — MASS. GEN. LAWS ch. 119, § 65 (West 1992); *Minnesota* — MINN. STAT. ANN. § 260-155 (West Supp. 1995); *Mississippi* — MISS. CODE ANN. § 43.21.203 (1993); *New Mexico* — N.M. STAT. ANN. § 32A.2.16 (Michie 1993); *North Dakota* — N.D. CENT. CODE § 27.20.24 (1991); *Ohio* — OHIO REV. CODE ANN. § 2152.35 (Anderson 1994); *Oklahoma* — OKLA. STAT. ANN. tit. 10, § 1111 (West Supp. 1995); *Texas* — TEXAS FAM. CODE ANN. § 5408 (West Supp. 1995); *Utah* — UTAH CODE ANN. § 78.3a.33 (Supp. 1994); *West Virginia* — W. VA. CODE § 49.5.1 (1995); *Wisconsin* — WIS. STAT. ANN. § 48.299 (West Supp. 1994) and *Wyoming* — WYO. STAT. § 14.6.224 (1994).

In the late 1970s, the Supreme Court began to lay the conceptual groundwork for a wider public "right to know" policy in juvenile litigation. In two cases, *Oklahoma Publishing Co. v. District Court*[94] in 1977 and in *Smith v. Daily Mail Publishing Co.*[95] in 1979, the Court seemed to strongly favor the widespread dissemination of juvenile court data in proceedings either open to the public or where a newspaper divulged the name of a juvenile homicide suspect during a press interview involving the case. In 1982, the Court in *Globe Newspaper Co. v. Superior Court*[96] upheld the First Amendment free press principle when it came into conflict with the confidentiality precepts of juvenile court hearings. In *Globe*, for example, the press was allowed access to an adjudication in juvenile court involving the testimony of a child sex abuse victim under the age of eighteen. In balancing the interests of the juvenile victim against the public's "right to know," the Court came down on the side of the Fourth Estate. However, the public's right to access in juvenile proceedings generally are still *relative*, not absolute. What the United States Supreme Court has wisely done here is to allow lower courts a wide degree of discretion in determining whether or not certain aspects of juvenile proceedings should remain beyond public scrutiny. In *Globe*, for instance, the Court noted that "[a] trial court can determine on a case-by-case basis whether closure is necessary to protect the welfare of the minor victim."[97] A juvenile court judge may feel far more comfortable applying discretionary decision-making in delinquency adjudications, especially serious delinquency, than in, say, situations involving either status or neglect scenarios. The openness of court proceedings in the status and neglect categories have not attracted as much legal or scholarly comment as has the delinquency cases. A well-reasoned argument can be made for the proposition that in most status or neglect hearings, the right to the full reporting of such proceedings would not be in the interest of either the public or the private parties involved. Where status and neglect jurisdiction is still a component of broad juvenile court hegemony, it is questionable whether the "right to know" over-shadows the right to personal autonomy and privacy in these particular situations.

---

94. 430 U.S. 308 (1977) (*per curiam*).
95. 443 U.S. 97 (1979).
96. 457 U.S. 596 (1982).
97. *Id.* at 608.

The question of juvenile confidentiality in the fingerprint context has also given rise to professional dissonance. On the one hand, there are those who maintain that a juvenile taken into custody by the police for delinquency is not being charged with a "true" crime, hence, there is no official need for a fingerprint record. Arrayed against that argument and one that has gained increased credence in the last quarter of the twentieth century is the proposition that juvenile offenders charged with at least a felony-type act of delinquency should be fingerprinted as a matter of course. It was in 1969 that the United States Supreme Court decided the first crucial case dealing with juvenile fingerprint evidence. In that year, in a rape case from Mississippi,[98] the Court overruled the state supreme court decision which had allowed the wholesale fingerprinting of not only the juvenile suspect, but also twenty-three other black male youths who were taken to police headquarters in a dragnet arrest. All were questioned and fingerprinted without even a perfunctory compliance with constitutional directives. However, in the years since this late 1960s opinion, there has been a corresponding shift in thinking regarding juvenile fingerprint evidence even in situations that attract little public attention. Today, wider authority has been granted to law enforcement personnel to fingerprint juvenile suspects, especially felony suspects regardless of age. In this connection, H. Ted Rubin[99] notes that "[f]ingerprint cases ...turn on compliance with statutory provisions, procedural fairness, and individual determination as to when judicial approval is necessary."[100] No iron-clad formula can be established here. What can be said is that in postmodern America, the confidentiality principle that cloaked juvenile offenders from public scrutiny, ridicule and social stigma has been seriously eroded. There are a number of reasons for this and one would be hard-pressed to single out the one *single* driving force behind the evaporation of juvenile law confidentiality. But there is a feeling abroad that began ever so tentatively with *In re Gault* in 1967 and has continued unabated, that serious juvenile wrongdoers should not enjoy the cloak of anonymity the child savers reserved for them in 1899.[101] While confidentiality against public disclosure is still the norm even in the 1990s, the long-term *trend* in ju-

---

98. *Davis v. Mississippi*, 394 U.S. 721 (1969).

99. H. TED RUBIN, JUVENILE JUSTICE: POLICY, PRACTICE AND LAW (2d ed. 1985).

100. *Id.* at 112.

101. For an argument that counters this trend, *see* Paul R. Kfoury, *Confidentiality and the Juvenile Offender*, 17 New. Eng. J. on Crim. & Civ. Confinement 55 (1991).

venile justice is toward an overall reduction in the low-visibility, anonymous juvenile decision-making process. When the juvenile court becomes a centennarian in 1999, the *parens patriae* model of tribunal and record confidentiality will have succumbed to social, political and legal forces unimagined one hundred years earlier.

Chapter Five

The Juvenile in the Arms of the Court — Pretrial Processes

A. Preliminary Judicial Procedures: Intake and Diversion

Intake and diversion practice in the juvenile court sets the stage for either outright dismissal, a modified form of less-formal intervention, or the initiation of more formal court procedures. During this century, the intake and diversion roles of the juvenile court are two areas of practice that have been least affected by changing legal doctrine. It is still a truism in juvenile law that what a court decides at this pre-adjudicatory phase dramatically determines the ultimate outcome of the matter. Robert M. Mennel[1] notes that "[t]he popularity of the juvenile court derived in some measure from the fact that it served as a laboratory for the professional study of delinquency."[2] The door to this laboratory is the intake and diversion process. As social work sought professional recognition in the early years of the twentieth century, its practitioners in the juvenile court immediately began to see the advantage inherent in information gathering techniques for their client population. The more information that could be compiled about a juvenile, the better. Intake and diversion practices were seen as a form of social diagnosis that would ultimately lead to a particular type of intervention in the life of the juvenile under the *parens patriae* mantle. While a significant portion of delinquent youth will ultimately become law-abiding if left to their own devices, both public safety and public trust is and must remain a major concern for the juvenile court. Social scientists generally view the delinquent as an individual who has strayed to varying degrees from the normal path of development due to some psychological, social or demographic

---

1. Robert M. Mennel, *Attitudes and Policies toward Juvenile Delinquency in the United States: A Historiographical Review,* 4 Crime and Justice: An Annual Rev. of Research 191 (Michael Tonry & Norval Morris eds. 1983).

2. *Id.* at 208.

deficit. The intake and diversion process allow juvenile court professionals to intervene with lawbreaking youth and utilize that opportunity to work toward correcting behavior that may and often does lead to more serious criminality.

Douglas J. Besharov[3] notes that "[i]ntake...is a court related process which diverts from the juvenile court those cases which are considered inappropriate or better handled elsewhere. Its predominant purpose is to stand between the complainant and the court to prevent the initiation of unnecessary proceedings."[4] Intake diversions come from one of three sources: the police, after a juvenile is taken into custody and transferred to a detention facility, through the complaint or citation process when the child is considered non-dangerous and not a flight risk, and through direct referral through some nonlaw enforcement agency or individual such as a school, a welfare agency, physicians, attorneys, parents or guardian or victim.

Age, race, demography and socio-economic background have continually been some of the key variables identifying delinquent or predelinquent children during the twentieth century. In the 1990s, *official* statistics seem to indicate that the prototypical juvenile delinquent is male, between the ages of ten and seventeen, of African-American descent, and comes from a low or marginal socioeconomic strata.[5] One should recognize, however, that this profile is a prototype only and that any given delinquent will fit the profile only to varying degrees.

Intake practice operates essentially as an initial gate-keeping or screening mechanism.[6] Since the vast majority of juvenile courts operate under both time and caseload constraints, the intake officer (usually a probation professional) will make a determination of whether or not to file a formal petition against the youth or to "adjust" the matter by other less formal methods. The term "adjustment" is often used in conjunction with intake and refers simply to a decision to make a referral of the juvenile to some other agency. Besharov re-

---

3. Douglas J. Besharov, Juvenile Justice Advocacy 157 (1974).

4. *Id.*

5. Gary F. Jensen & Dean G. Rojek, Delinquency and Youth Crime 115 (2d ed. 1992).

6. *See, e.g.*, John A. Wallace & Marion M. Brennan, *Intake and the Family Court*, 12 Buff. L. Rev. 442 (1963) and Robert M. Terry, *The Screening of Juvenile Offenders*, 58 J. Crim L.C. & P.S. 179 (1967).

marks that "[t]he alternatives to court action range from a warning to referral to various community agencies, including churches, YMCA's and family service or other social service agencies, to restitution, apology or assignment to a special work detail."[7] At this stage in the process, the intake officer will meet with police, the child, his or her parents, the complainant if available, and, on occasion, with the juvenile's attorney. According to the *IJA/ABA Juvenile Justice Standards*[8]

> the intake function... is one of the most critical points in the juvenile justice system, for it is there that a decision is made as to what action to take regarding a juvenile who is allegedly delinquent and who has been brought to the attention of the juvenile court.... The importance of intake screening can be seen from the fact that nationwide approximately half of the total number of juveniles brought to the attention of juvenile and family courts are handled at intake without the filing of a petition.[9]

The *Standards* further note in a separate volume[10] that "[t]he intake official's primary function is to make interim status decisions."[11] In making such a decision,

> The intake official should: 1. inform the accused juvenile of his or her rights...; 2. inform the accused juvenile that his or her parent will be contacted immediately to aid in effecting release; and 3. explain the basis for detention, the interim status alternatives that are available, and the right to a prompt release hearing.[12]

Standard 6.6, Guidelines for Status Decision, "represents the heart of the Interim Status volume and one of the most controversial of its formulations."[13] The controversy centers around the so-called "preventive detention" concept that has come to the fore within the last

---

7. Besharov, *supra* note 3, at 158.

8. *IJA/ABA Juvenile Justice Standards, Standards Relating to the Juvenile Probation Function* (1980).

9. *Id.* at 2.

10. *IJA/ABA Juvenile Justice Standards, Standards Relating to Interim Status* (1980).

11. *Id.* at 75.

12. *Id.* at 76.

13. *Id.* at 79.

quarter of the twentieth century. Under Standard 6.6, the intake officer is required to release the juvenile from custody unless the juvenile
is charged with a violent felony which, if proven, will result in a secure institutional commitment and

One or more of the following additional factors is present:

a. ...crime charged is a class one juvenile offense;

b. ...juvenile is an escapee from an institution or
other placement facility...

c. ...juvenile has a demonstrable record of willful
failure to appear at juvenile proceedings, on the basis of
which the official finds that no measure short of detention
can be imposed to reasonably ensure appearance; or

2. has been verified to be a fugitive from another
jurisdiction, an official of which has formally requested
that the juvenile be placed in detention.[14]

The pros and cons of pre-trial or pre-adjudicatory preventive detention will be addressed in the following section. Note that the
IJA/ABA Juvenile Justice Standards do not attempt to establish any
non-legal rationale for either release or detention of the juvenile. The
Standards concern simply whether or not the juvenile before the intake officer has committed a certain type of offense, is an escapee
from a placement facility after adjudication, or represents a flight risk
if released before an adjudication hearing is set. The other factor not
specifically enumerated is the rare, but nonetheless potential danger
to witnesses or a victim if the juvenile is released. Juvenile courts have
plenary power to deny release with or without some form of bail if
the court deems that third party safety may be compromised. Thus,
this particular *Standard* addresses only the most serious juvenile
malefactor. By far, however, the majority of youth coming before the
intake officer in most courts are there for the less serious felony or
misdemeanor-type offense or are in the ubiquitous status offender or
neglected child category. It is with this cohort that the intake process
can call upon its historic social science roots to provide the juvenile
with treatment options and delinquency prevention processes to interrupt deviant behaviors. Alfred J. Kahn[15] notes that "[w]hat is espe-

---

14. *Id.* at 78.

15. Alfred J. Kahn, *Social Work and the Control of Delinquency* as quoted in DELIN-
QUENCY AND SOCIAL POLICY (Paul Lerman ed. 1970).

cially interesting about delinquency as a unifying concept is that twentieth-century society has been willing to develop a treatment rationale for its broad control measures...positive action following case-finding in instances of alleged or emerging delinquency is a complex process involving...careful integration and coordination..."[16] Unfortunately, due to a range of factors beyond the control of most intake processes, "positive action" to treat and to prevent future delinquency is often more rhetoric than reality.

The intake process varies from court to court in certain particulars and such variance, within limits, is to be expected. Overall, however, intake presumes a series of sanction decisions that will materially affect both the juvenile the juvenile's family. Intake personnel enjoy a limited but significant set of options that can be brought to bear on the juvenile to include, besides what Besharov previously mentioned, the following: (1) outright dismissal, with or without conditions attached; (2) outright dismissal accompanied by a warning or some other verbal cue; (3) placing the juvenile on what frequently is known as "informal probation" with conditions and often limited in duration by statutory criteria; (4) referral of juvenile to a local family counseling or community mental health center. Such arrangements are usually established through inter-agency agreement contracts where the juvenile alone or in company with family members attend specified treatment programs for a certain duration. Upon successful completion, provision is usually made for the juvenile's record to be expunged; and (5) "filing" against the juvenile. In the latter situation, a child has usually been referred to the court or has been brought in by virtue of a formal complaint. The intake officer will determine the nature of the referral or complaint and then "file" a formal petition alleging delinquency, dependency or neglect.

Studies in the past twenty-five years have reflected upon the difficulty of attributing intake dispositions *solely* to race, ethnicity, or socioeconomic status. A 1975 study of three juvenile courts by Lawrence E. Cohen[17] for the United States Department of Justice noted that "[o]ur study has yielded no empirical evidence to sustain

---

16. *Id.* at 423.

17. Lawrence E. Cohen, *Delinquency Dispositions: An Empirical Analysis of Processing Decisions in Three Juvenile Courts*, U.S. Department of Justice, National Criminal Justice Information & Statistics Service (NCJISS), Washington, DC: U.S. Government Printing Office (1975).

the charge that [youth of] lower socioeconomic status are systematically accorded the most severe treatment by agents of the juvenile court. Similarly, there is no direct evidence to suggest minority youths are the objects of discriminatory treatment."[18] Conclusions such as the above must be taken advisedly and with a healthy dose of skepticism. A host of non-quantifiable indices often intrude into an intake decision in juvenile courts and, despite ever more sophisticated statistical and methodological instruments, the universal reality remains that underclass children continue to provide the major grist for the intake mill. A constellation of factors, some subtle, some overt, will continue to have a profound influence on who does and who does not become a candidate for full juvenile court processing. This is not to say that juvenile justice has failed to reign in some of the more pernicious influences that affect intake decision making. It is only to say that since the court is dealing with a teen and often sub-teen population whose socialization has been marginal at best, factors that exist outside a researcher's tool kit often provide the *raison d'etre* for certain intake decisions. Also, situational and social factors interact with personal variables to determine behavioral outcomes. To do a credible job of sorting out those youth who do and those who do not need juvenile court intervention requires far more solid information than normally possessed even by the most skilled intake division. The juvenile's environment serves to provide feedback about behavior and that environment either strengthens or weakens the likelihood that their delinquent behavior will be repeated. Yet, neither intake personnel nor the broader juvenile justice system can impact a criminogenic environment *per se*. All the court can do is either send the youth back into that same environment with or without program support in the forlorn hope that he or she will muddle through without further lawbreaking or push the juvenile further into a system that may be equally as criminogenic as the youngster's free-world environment. The intake function in juvenile law was originally conceived to be a sort of quasi-prevention program. The thesis here was that a certain number of youth could be returned to their parents and home environments with a warning and an admonition. From 1899 through the 1950s, this form of "warn and release" tactic worked reasonably well for a significant number of youth because, even though their home life was not altogether the most desirable, most lived in an in-

---

18. *Id.* at 53–54.

tact family structure where there was at least some modicum of socialization and social control being exerted. All of this began to perceptibly disintegrate during the 1960s and beyond, and, one sees at century's end the social and cultural detritus left behind by this state of affairs. Robert H. Bork,[19] in his recent account of the decline of American culture and values notes that "[t]here is no longer any doubt that communities with many single parents, whether because of divorce or out-of-wedlock births, display much higher rates of [delinquency], drug use, school drop-outs, voluntary unemployment, etc...."[20] He then quotes political scientist James Q. Wilson's observation[21] about the family structure deficit that exists in the United States in the late twentieth century:

> [T]he presence of a decent father helps a male child learn to control aggression; his absence impedes it.... When the mother in a mother-only family is also a teenager, or at least a teenager living in urban America, the consequences for the child are even grimmer. The most authoritative survey of what we know about the offspring of adolescent mothers concluded that the children suffer increasingly serious cognitive deficits and display a greater degree of hyperactivity, hostility, and poorly controlled aggression than is true of children born to older mothers of the same race, and this is especially true of the boys.[22]

What connection, if any, does all of this have to do with juvenile court intake? The answer should be both obvious and profoundly troubling. Since most of the more serious forms of delinquency are committed by prepubescent and teenage males, and since a large number of these children fit Wilson's profile and exist almost in a feral state, American society has cause for alarm. Substantively, the juvenile justice system, *as a system*, simply cannot positively impact the vast majority of these children. Exchanging the unfitness of a home environment for the equally unfit environment of institutional life is not a positive tradeoff. Many of these children, perhaps most, come to the juvenile court unsocialized, non-habilitated and with little, if any, life skills that

---

19. ROBERT H. BORK, SLOUCHING TOWARDS GOMORRAH: MODERN LIBERALISM AND AMERICAN DECLINE (1996).

20. *Id.* at 157.

21. JAMES Q. WILSON, THE MORAL SENSE (1993).

22. Bork, *supra* note 19, at 157.

could possibly insulate them from a criminogenic lifestyle. Juvenile court intake effectiveness began its long and steady decline after mid-century and has not yet and probably cannot resurrect itself from its present state. Its choices are now limited more than ever with the re-criminalization of juvenile deviance that has come to the fore since the mid-1980s. Moreover, there appears to be little slack in the on-going practice of some prosecuting authorities at the intake level to essentially preempt intake decisions involving certain youth who are both age and felony-eligible. By this is meant that certain youth who have reached a chronological age cut-off and who have been charged with a certain type of felony are being intercepted at this gateway before they enter the juvenile system. If prosecutorial intake intervention continues and expands, as some contend it should, the juvenile court intake function may well be restricted to the handling of status offenders and neglected children only. If the initial point of entry is foreclosed to felony-type delinquency, the juvenile court in the twenty-first century may well become only a former shadow of itself; time and circumstances will tell.

B. Pretrial Detention

Jonathan Simon[23] notes that "[t]he transformation of the juvenile court into a punitive instrument to address an increasingly marked and isolated population, has been ongoing for some decades."[24] One prong of this "punitive instrument" is the increasing use of the pretrial detention device for juveniles since the 1970s. Pretrial, preadjudicatory or "preventive" detention is exactly what the names implies. It is a conscious policy aimed at keeping certain juveniles in custody pending a hearing on the merits of their delinquency petition. In its most benign form, preventive detention has been utilized on occasion to retain custody of status or neglected juveniles until either their parents or other caretakers could be located or a proper social service placement arranged. In this strictly *parens patriae* context, little controversy arose. What has caused concern among civil libertarians and other child welfare advocates is the more recent employment of pre-

---

23. Jonathan Simon, *Power Without Parents: Juvenile Justice in a Postmodern Society*, 16 Cardozo L. Rev. 1363 (1995).
24. *Id.* at 1365.

ventive detention as both a punitive and protective device; punitive as to the juvenile and protective as to public safety.

Although both legal and public policy still generally favor release of most juveniles who are caught in the juvenile court net, there is a discernible trend in the United States favoring preventive detention for an increasing number of delinquent acts. In the late 1960s, both legal and public policy sided with release as a matter of course.[25] Model codes and state statutes of that era were hesitant to impose blanket restraints on a juvenile's freedom, even when that particular juvenile had been charged with a rather serious felony unless there was a legitimate risk of flight or the juvenile, if released, would be a danger to himself or herself, or others. The *IJA/ABA Standards* took the view in their *Interim Status* volume[26] that "[r]estraints on the freedom of accused juveniles pending trial and disposition are generally contrary to public policy. The preferred course in each case should be unconditional release."[27] But, unanimity on this volatile issue is ephemeral. As early as 1961, the National Council on Crime and Delinquency urged policymakers to reject *carte blanche* release criteria and detain juveniles in appropriate cases for treatment purposes. The NCCD noted that[28] "[i]nstead of being merely a 'waiting period,' detention should begin the process of rehabilitation and lay the groundwork for later treatment.... Although the detention home is not a training school, staff attitudes can and should begin the training process."[29] A relatively obscure but nonetheless important decision on this issue was decided in 1979 by the Supreme Court of Appeals of West Virginia. In *State ex rel. R.C.F. v. Wilt*,[30] a *habeas corpus* petition was filed for the release of a seventeen-year-old indigent resident of the Jefferson County, West Virginia jail. During the year 1978, the youth had been incarcerated in the county jail for more than twenty-seven days on three separate occasions on delinquency petitions charging him with various theft offenses. In granting

---

25. *See generally* Elyce C. Ferster, Edith N. Snethen & Thomas F. Courtless, *Juvenile Detention: Protection, Prevention and Punishment*, 38 Fordham L. Rev. 161 (1969).

26. IJA/ABA Juvenile Justice Standards, *supra* note 10, at § 3.1.

27. *Id.* at 50.

28. National Council on Crime and Delinquency, *Standards and Guides for the Detention of Children and Youth* (1961).

29. *Id.* at 36.

30. 252 S.E. 2d 168 (W. Va. 1979).

the writ and releasing R.C.F. from custody, the court, per Justice Mc-Graw observed that[31] "[t]he legislature has recognized in its wisdom that the incarceration of juveniles in a jail with adult offenders violates the fundamental rehabilitative purpose of a juvenile court."[32] Warming to his subject, Justice McGraw noted that "[t]he confinement of juveniles in jails is a precursor to suicide, to sexual and physical abuse and to psychological harm; the confinement of juveniles with adults in poorly constructed, ill-equipped and sometimes mismanaged jails may well contribute to crime rather than reduce it."[33] The *Wilt* decision was followed three years later in 1982 by *D.B. v. Tewksbury*,[34] a United States District Court opinion from Oregon. *Tewksbury* involved a civil rights class action lawsuit questioning the constitutional validity of confining juveniles in the Columbia County Correctional Facility, an adult jail. All juveniles in the jail were pretrial detainees, ranging in age from twelve to eighteen, many of whom were alleged status offenders. After listing a number of shortcomings in the facility insofar as it applied to juveniles, Judge Frye stated that[35]

> current literature in the field of juvenile justice indicates that behavior modification of socially deviant children is best achieved when children are diverted from the criminal justice system and its jail and punishments whenever possible....restraints are best carried out through diversion programs, home detention, shelter care, crises or emergency centers, or through intensive counseling or monitoring.[36]

Citing the United States Supreme Court decisions of *Robinson v. California*,[37] *In re Gault*,[38] and provisions from the *Oregon Revised Statutes*,[39] among others, Judge Frye ruled that "[n]o child who is a *status offender* may be lodged constitutionally in an adult jail."[40]

---

31. *Id.*
32. *Id.* at 171.
33. *Id.*
34. 545 F. Supp. 896 (D.C. Or. 1982).
35. *Id.*
36. *Id.* at 903.
37. 370 U.S. 660 (1962).
38. 387 U.S. 1 (1967).
39. Or. Rev. Stat. § 419.507, 419.509 (1982).
40. *Tewksbury*, 545 F. Supp. at 906.

(Emphasis added). Employing the *parens patriae* doctrine as one of its major legal referents, the court noted that[41]

> Juvenile proceedings...are in the nature of a guardian-ship imposed by the state as *parens patriae* to provide the care and guidance that under normal circumstances would be furnished by the natural parents....A jail is not a place where a truly concerned natural parent would lodge his or her child for care and guidance. A jail is not a place where the state can constitutionally lodge its children under the guise of *parens patriae.*[42]

Thus, pretrial or preventive detention of purely status offenders in an adult lock-up was held to be a violation of Fourteenth Amendment due process. *Tewksbury* employed the *parens patriae* rubric here in a legitimate case of juvenile justice error. The *Uniform Juvenile Court Act* of 1968[43] does provide for situations where a juvenile may be held in detention if

> (1) his detention or case is required to protect the person or property of others or of the child or (2) because the child may abscond or be removed from the jurisdiction of the court or (3) has no parent, guardian, or custodian or other person able to provide supervision and care for him and return him to court when required, or (4) an order for his detention or shelter care has been made by the court pursuant to this Act.[44]

Despite this language and similar language in other legislation, there remains a strong presumption in favor of releasing a juvenile before an adjudicatory hearing even for a criminal offense. However, family circumstance, a juvenile's record, possible out of state detainers and a host of other impediments may preclude outright release in a number of situations. Nonetheless, in the *Tewksbury* situation, a group of children who apparently had not been charged with a true crime were being incarcerated in an adult jail and that practice was deemed constitutionally infirm. The *Uniform Juvenile Court Act* makes al-lowance for detention under varying circumstances, but nowhere

---

41. 545 F. Supp. 896 (D.C. Or. 1982).
42. *Id.* at 901–07.
43. *Uniform Juvenile Court Act* (1968).
44. *Id.* at § 14.

does it sanction the blanket detention of children charged with a status offense.

The bellwether case in juvenile pretrial detention law came in 1984 when the United States Supreme Court decided *Schall v. Martin.*[45] The *Schall* case involved an interpretation of a New York state statute that authorized pretrial detention of certain juveniles who might commit another act of serious delinquency if they were released before the return date of their present charge.

In December, 1977, Gregory Martin, age fourteen, was arrested and charged with first-degree robbery, second degree assault and the criminal possession of a firearm. Martin and two other youths had allegedly assaulted a youth, hit the victim on the head with a loaded gun and then proceeded to steal the victim's jacket and shoes. This was simply another in a long and tiresome line of urban juvenile upon juvenile assaults involving the acquisition by force of clothing that was highly prized by certain teenagers unable to afford similar apparel. Because the juvenile was fourteen at the time of the act, by New York law he came within the exclusive jurisdiction of the New York Family Court.[46] When Martin initially appeared in court, he was ordered into pretrial detention pursuant to a provision in the New York statute.[47] After a week in detention had transpired, Martin was found guilty of robbery and the criminal possession of a weapon, adjudicated a juvenile delinquent and then placed on probation for two years. During his pretrial detention, Martin filed a class action *habeas corpus* writ for himself and all other juveniles held in preventive detention awaiting their adjudication on or after December 21, 1977.[48] The juvenile sought a declaratory judgment that would uphold his contention that section 320.5(3)(b) of the *New York Family Court Act*[49] violated both the due process and the equal protection clauses of the Fourteenth Amendment to the United States Constitution.

---

45. 467 U.S. 253 (1984).

46. The N.Y. FAM. CT. ACT provided that a person between age seven and less than age sixteen cannot be held criminally responsible for his or her conduct because of infancy. N.Y. FAM. CT. ACT § 301.2 (1) (McKinney 1983).

47. N.Y. FAM. CT. ACT § 320.5(3)(b) (McKinney 1983).

48. The original lawsuit was captioned *United States ex rel. Martin v. Strasburg,* 513 F. Supp. 691 (S.D.N.Y. 1981).

49. *Supra* note 47.

The United States District Court for the Southern District of New York ruled that the New York legislation violated due process, but it denied Martin's equal protection claim.[50] This holding was affirmed by the United States Court of Appeals for the Second Circuit in 1982.[51] On appeal from that affirmance, the Supreme Court of the United States noted probable jurisdiction[52] and reversed the Second Circuit.[53] Justice Rehnquist joined by Chief Justice Burger and Justices White, Blackmun, Powell and O'Connor noted that pretrial preventive detention does not violate due process, but instead serves a legitimate state interest in protecting both the juvenile and the community from the potential effects of further pretrial delinquency.[54] The Court also noted that the New York statute in question provided adequate procedural protections for pretrial detainees.[55] In a two-part analysis, the Court first took under consideration whether pretrial preventive detention serves any legitimate state interest under the *New York Family Court Act*, and secondly, whether this legislation's procedural provisions safeguarded a juvenile's pretrial detention rights for "at least some" accused delinquents. Discussing the first issue, Justice Rehnquist stated that[56]

> The substantiality and legitimacy of the state interests underlying this statute are confirmed by the widespread use and judicial acceptance of preventive detention for juveniles. Every state, as well as the United States in the District of Columbia, permits preventive detention of juveniles accused of crime. A number of model juvenile justice acts also contain provisions permitting preventive detention....we conclude that the practice serves a legitimate regulatory purpose compatible with "fundamental fairness" demanded by the Due Process Clause in juvenile proceedings.[57]

Turning to the procedural fairness issue, the Court noted that "[t]he required statement of facts and reasons justifying the detention and

---

50. *United States ex rel. Martin v. Strasburg*, 513 F. Supp. at 717.
51. *Martin v. Strasburg* 689 F. 2d 365 (2d Cir. 1982).
52. 460 U.S. 1079 (1983).
53. 467 U.S. 253 (1984).
54. *Id.* at 274.
55. *Id.* at 277.
56. *Schall v. Martin*, 467 U.S. 253 (1984).
57. *Id.* at 261–67; 268.

the stenographic record of the initial appearance will provide a basis for the review of individual cases. Pretrial detention orders in New York may be reviewed by writ of habeas corpus..."[58] Although the *Schall* decision has given rise to some rather heated academic debate,[59] the general concensus in late twentieth-century detention practice is that juveniles who are petitioned into juvenile court for serious delinquent behavior and are flight and public safety risks are proper candidates for preventive detention. This trend is in line with the continual criminalizing philosophy of the juvenile court in the post-1975 time frame. Historical accounts of the juvenile court's early years give little, if any, recognition to the issues raised in the *Schall* decision. In fact, for at least three quarters of the twentieth century, the juvenile court system as a whole was not conviction oriented at all and this particular slant or mind-set caused little concern for juvenile pretrial detainees. The detention of most juveniles was to be accomplished, if at all, simply as a preliminary procedure to diversion. Diversion and probation were the crux of the *parens patriae* juvenile court and a child's detention to determine a proper diversionary placement for probation was of little concern to most juvenile court judges. Only after the juvenile court's treatment and rehabilitative ethos was seriously called into question in the 1970s did pretrial detention take on the trappings of constitutional importance.

To reflect just how different late twentieth-century symbols of delinquency are from their earlier counterparts, one has to go no further than to the writings of Herbert H. Lou in 1927.[60] In his history of the juvenile court in that year, Lou noted twelve "commonly defined" statutory provisions regarding delinquency. A delinquent child in Lou's list was one who

---

58. *Id.* at 280.

59. *See e.g.,* Irene M. Rosenberg, *Schall v. Martin: A Child is a Child is a Child,* 12 Am. J. Crim. L. 253 (1984); Cynthia M. York, *Casenote, Constitutional Law —Pretrial Preventive Detention—Pretrial detention of an accused juvenile delinquent who poses a serious threat of recidivism does not violate due process,* 62 U. Det. L. Rev. 145 (1984); Mary Jane Boswell, Notes, *Where Have All The Children Gone? The Supreme Court Finds Pretrial Detention Of Minors Constitutional: Schall v Martin,* 34 DePaul L. Rev 733 (1985); and Deborah A. Lee, Comment, *The Constitutionality Of Juvenile Preventive Detention: Schall v. Martin —Who Is Preventive Detention Protecting?,* 20 New Eng. L. Rev. 341 (1984–85).

60. HERBERT L. LOU, JUVENILE COURTS IN THE UNITED STATES (1927).

(1) violates a state law or local ordinance...(2) is wayward, incorrigible, or habitually disobedient; (3) associates with thieves, criminals, prostitutes, vagrants, or vicious persons; (4) is growing up in idleness or crime; (5) knowingly visits a saloon, pool room, billiard room, or gambling place; (6) knowingly visits a house of ill-fame; (7) wanders about streets at night; (8) wanders about railroad yards, jumps on moving trains, or enters any car or engine without authority; (9) habitually uses or writes vile, indecent, or obscene language; (10) absents himself from home without just cause or without the consent of parent or guardian; (11) is immoral or indecent; or (12) is a habitual truant.[61]

Serious, violent and repetitive criminality, while normally excepted from both early and later juvenile court legislation, was never really considered a problem for the *parens patriae* juvenile court. In most cases, the child savers and their progeny focused on relatively minor criminal conduct and ascriptive teenage behaviors that had no criminal law counterpart. Of the twelve "acts" of delinquency that Lou noted in 1927, only the violation of a state law or local ordinance had a direct tie-in to the adult criminal justice system. All of the remaining eleven were acts that affected children. As to these, the condemnation sanction of the criminal law was removed, for the *parens patriae* rationale, in conjunction with the civil nature of most delinquent acts forbid the impressment of stigma upon a child adjudicated "delinquent." Post-1975 juvenile justice takes an entirely divergent view of serious predatory delinquency committed by a largely non-habilitated cohort of lower class minority youth. After a spate of United States Supreme Court decisions in the late 1960s and the early 1970s affecting procedural justice for the child, the emphasis shifted back again to state court adjudication and legislation that, on the whole, was both more conservative and more punitive in orientation. The *Kent*[62] decision in 1966 was accorded constitutional respectability in the *Gault*[63] opinion the following year. However, the *Kent* holding on waiver and its implications for the juvenile did not gain any significant momentum until after the mid-1970s when the so-called

61. *Id.* at 53.
62. 383 U.S. 541 (1966).
63. 387 U.S. 1 (1967).

"rehabilitative ideal"[64] lost almost all of its legitimacy in adult penology. This loss of respect for an ideology that had been the cornerstone of American adult and juvenile correction for most of the twentieth century had a profound impact on the employment of the waiver device in juvenile law.

Others may take different views on this issue,[65] but there is general concensus that the 1970s ushered in an era that viewed retribution superior to restoration when it involved official state responses to serious delinquency. Nowhere has the retribution-restoration dichotomy been played out more completely than in the waiver procedures constitutionally annointed in *Kent v. United States*.[66]

C. Waiver, Transfer or Certification of Juveniles to Adult Criminal Court

Actual adjudication or trial of juveniles was a rare event for about the first sixty odd years of the American juvenile court. Adversary "truth-finding" was a device to be avoided by juvenile court jurists in all but the most serious situations. The *parens patriae* grip on the court was so complete and suffocating that there was little serious thought given to a determination of the true factual issues. Such practices belonged, if at all, to adult courts—not a children's court. Correspondingly, most delinquencies in the juvenile courts' first six decades of existence were handled through the cooperation of the judge, the probation officer, the parents and the child. There was a commingling of adjudication and disposition, most of which took place at a single

---

64. A phrase employed by law professor Francis A. Allen in his work titled THE BORDERLAND OF CRIMINAL JUSTICE: ESSAYS IN LAW AND CRIMINOLOGY (1964). Allen later chronicled the demise of the "rehabilitative ideal" in his book THE DECLINE OF THE REHABILITATIVE IDEAL: PENAL POLICY AND SOCIAL PURPOSE (1981).

65. *See, e.g.*, Roger J.R. Levesque & Alan J. Tompkins, *Revisioning Juvenile Justice: Implications of the New Child Protection Movements*, 48 Wash. U.J. Urb. & Contemp. L. 87 (1995); Ralph A. Rossum, *Holding Juveniles Accountable: Reforming America's Juvenile Justice System*, 22 Pepp. L. Rev. 907 (1995); Gordon Bazemore & Mark Umbreit, *Rethinking the Sanctioning Function in Juvenile Court: Retributive or Restorative Responses to Youth Crime*, 41 Crime & Delinq. 296 (1995); and Katherine H. Federle, *The Abolition of the Juvenile Court: A Proposal for the Preservation of Children's Legal Rights*, 16 J. Contemp. L. 23 (1990).

66. 383 U.S. 541 (1966).

hearing. Lawyers were most unwelcome in the juvenile court during this era because the presence of an attorney would usually signify that an adversary posture would be taken by the juvenile involved or the state and adversariness was the *bete noire* of the *parens patriae* juvenile court. As M. Marvin Finkelstein[67] noted, "[t]he participation of a state prosecutor would have implied the existence of some particular state interest which required advocacy.... But such a conception was considered contrary to the traditionally prevailing notion that only one interest—the child's—was at stake in juvenile court proceedings."[68] *In re Gault*[69] began the move toward greater lawyer participation in the juvenile court process and with the national mood in the 1970s shifting toward crime control and retribution, it was only a matter of time before courts and legislatures began redefining the prosecutor-as-lawyer role in serious delinquency situations.

We start in 1966 with the *Kent*[70] decision. Some fourteen months prior to the watershed ruling in *In re Gault*,[71] the United States Supreme Court had before it a case from the District of Columbia involving a juvenile by the name of Morris A. Kent, Jr. Unlike Gerald Gault in the next precedent-shattering decision by the Court, Morris Kent was a juvenile who exhibited traits of criminality that foretold possible serious adult malfeasance. At the time Kent was taken into juvenile custody, he was sixteen. However, he had been placed on probation for a series of earlier offenses involving multiple housebreaking and attempted purse snatching. In September, 1961, an intruder entered an apartment in the District of Columbia, stole a wallet and raped the female occupant. Kent was subsequently identified and taken into custody, and, at age sixteen, was still within the exclusive jurisdiction of the District of Columbia Juvenile Court. During his previous probationary period, a "social service" file had been developed. Although Kent's attorney sought a court order for psychiatric evaluation and access to the social service file in the juvenile court's possession, neither request was granted. Without a hearing,

67. M. Marvin Finkelstein *et al., Prosecution in Juvenile Courts: Guidelines for the Future*, National Institute of Law Enforcement and Criminal Justice, Law Enforcement Assistance Administration, Washington, DC: U.S. Government Printing Office (1973).

68. *Id.* at 9.

69. 387 U.S. 1 (1967).

70. 383 U.S. 541 (1966).

71. 387 U.S. 1 (1967).

the juvenile judge *sua sponte* transferred Kent to the criminal court for trial as an adult. Subsequently tried as an adult before a jury, Kent was found guilty of housebreaking and robbery, although the jury for some inexplicable reason found Kent not guilty by reason of insanity on the rape charge. The youth was thereupon sentenced to serve a ninety-year prison term on the housebreaking and robbery counts. Through his attorney, Kent challenged the validity of the decision by the juvenile judge to waive juvenile court jurisdiction and transfer him to adult court for trial without a prefatory hearing in juvenile court. The United States Supreme Court was now faced with deciding whether or not Morris Kent had appropriately been waived to adult court for trail after an allegedly "full investigation" of the issue in juvenile court. Upon a reexamination of the facts, it became clear that the juvenile judge had not informed himself of the background of this juvenile before he had perfunctorily transferred Kent to the United States District Court for trial as an adult. In nullifying the juvenile judge's decision to waive under these circumstances, Justice Abe Fortas remarked that[72]

> These considerations raise problems of substantial concern as to the construction of and compliance with the Juvenile Court Act. They also suggest basic issues as to the justifiability of affording a juvenile less protection than is accorded to adults suspected of criminal offenses, particularly where, as here, there is an absence of any indication that the denial of rights available to adults was offset, mitigated or explained by action of the Government, as *parens patriae*, evidencing the special solicitude for juveniles commanded by the Juvenile Court Act. However, because we remand the case on account of the procedural error with respect to waiver of jurisdiction, we do not pass upon these questions.[73]

This language was a harbinger of things to come in *Gault*, but *Kent* was a decision that affected only a statutory procedure in the District of Columbia, not one *at that moment* that affected a wider audience. The Court found that Morris Kent's waiver to adult criminal court was deficient and it then enumerated a set of minimum due

---

72. 383 U.S. 541 (1966).
73. *Id.* at 551.

process criteria that has served as a prototype for subsequent legislation and as precedent for case law nationwide.[74]

Justice Fortas' opinion in *Kent* began laying the groundwork for the selective incorporation of certain constitutional amendments into the heretofore closed system of juvenile justice. Taking on *parens patriae,* Fortas rejected that doctrine's rationale for informal procedures in the juvenile court. The Court proceeded to announce several due process minima that must be observed before a juvenile in the District of Columbia could be waived to adult court for trial.

In order for a waiver order to be valid and meet constitutional muster, the juvenile court must hold a hearing on the waiver question, the juvenile must be afforded a right to counsel at that hearing, the juvenile's lawyer must have a right of access to the social service records the court may hold on that particular youngster, and, lastly, if the juvenile judge determines to waive, then a written statement of reasons must accompany the waiver order. Thus, procedural due process was enshrined in the waiver context insofar as the District of Columbia was concerned. The Court noted trenchantly that "there is no place in our system of law for reaching a result of such tremendous consequences without ceremony—without hearing, without effective assistance of counsel, without a statement of reasons."[75] This one opinion in the mid-1960s was destined to significantly diminish the juvenile courts' unfettered discretion on which child should and which should not be transferred to criminal court for trial. The waiver decision was elevated to a "critical stage" in juvenile proceedings and ultimately the *Kent* ruling laid the groundwork for a nationwide reform movement in the juvenile-criminal court interactive process. The Court appended to its decision a "Policy Memorandum" drafted by the District of Columbia juvenile court outlining the policies and rules to govern waiver decisions.[76] A voluminous litera-

---

74. It should be noted, however, that as early as 1962, the Supreme Court of Alabama had ruled that a juvenile could not be waived to an adult court for trial until the juvenile court had made a thorough investigation of the juvenile's background and had correspondingly supported its findings in writing. *See Stapler v. State,* 273 Ala. 358, 141, So. 2d 181 (1962).

75. *Kent,* 383 U.S. at 554.

76. *Policy Memorandum* No. 7, November 30, 1959, provided, in part, the following "determinative factors" a juvenile judge should consider before a waiver order is issued: "1. The seriousness of the alleged offense to the community and whether the protection of the community requires waiver. 2. Whether the alleged offense was committed in an

ture in its own right has emerged since 1966 on the waiver question and its importance in juvenile justice administration.[77] Immediately after the *Kent* ruling, some doubt developed regarding its constitutional pedigree.[78] However, when the Supreme Court in *In re Gault*[79] made several pointed references to *Kent*,[80] the developing concensus

---

aggressive, violent, premeditated or willful manner. 3. Whether the alleged offense was against persons or against property...4. The prosecutive merit of the complaint, i.e., whether there is evidence upon which a Grand Jury may be expected to return an indictment...5. The desirability of trial and dispositon of the entire offense in one court when the juvenile's associates in the alleged offense are adults...6. The sophistication and maturity of the juvenile...7. The record and previous history of the juvenile...and 8. The prospects for adequate protection of the public and the likelihood of reasonable rehabilitation of the juvenile..." 383 U.S. 541, at 565–68 (1966).

77. A representative sample include the following: Miriam S. Alers, *Transfer of Juvenile From Juvenile to Criminal Court,* 19 Crime & Delinq. 519 (1973); Robert B. Keiter, *Criminal or Delinquent? A Study of Juvenile Cases Transferred to Criminal Court,* 19 Crime & Delinq. 528 (1973); Paul R. Kfoury, *Prosecutorial Waiver of Juveniles Into Adult Criminal Court: The Ends of Justice...or the End of Justice?,* 5 Nova L.J. 487 (1981); Paul R. Kfoury, *Relinquishment of Jurisdiction For Purposes of Criminal Prosecution of Juveniles,* 8 No. Ky. L. Rev. 377 (1981); M.A. Bortner, *The Young Offender: Transfer to Adult Court and Subsequent Sentencing,* 6 Crim. Just. J. 281 (1983); Charles W. Thomas & Shay Bilchik, *Prosecuting Juveniles in Criminal Courts: A Legal and Empirical Analysis,* 76 J. Crim. L. & Criminology 439 (1985); M.A. Bortner, *Traditional Rhetoric, Organizational Realities: Remand of Juveniles to Adult Court,* 32 Crime & Delinq. 53 (1986); Dean Champion, *Teenage Felons and Waiver Hearings: Some Recent Trends, 1980–1988,* 35 Crime & Delinq. 577 (1989); Jeffrey Fagan & Elizabeth P. Deschenes, *Determinants of Juvenile Waiver Decisions for Violent Juvenile Offenders,* 81 J. Crim. L. & Criminology 314 (1990); Donna M. Bishop & Charles E. Frazier, *Transfer of Juveniles to Criminal Court: A Case Study and Analysis of Prosecutorial Waiver,* 5 Notre Dame J.L. Ethics & Pub. Pol'y 281 (1991); Franklin E. Zimring, *The Treatment of Hard Cases in American Juvenile Justice: In Defense Of Discretionary Waiver,* 5 Notre Dame J.L. Ethics & Pub. Pol'y 267 (1991); Susan Wagner, Casenote, *Constitutional Law—State Classification of Certain Juvenile Offenders—Does It Offend Equal Protection Or Due Process Rights Of Juvenile Defendant,* 29 J. Fam. L. 201 (1991); and Donna M. Bishop, Charles E. Frazier, Lonn Lanza-Kaduce & Lawrence Winner, *The Transfer of Juveniles to Criminal Court: Does It Make a Difference?,* 42 Crime & Delinq. 171 (1996).

78. *See, e.g., State v. Acuna,* 78 N.M. 119, 428 P. 2d 658 (1967); *Stanley v. Peyton,* 292 F. Supp. 209 (W.D. Va 1968); *Hazell v. State,* 12 Md. App. 144, 277 A. 2d 639 (1971); *In re Bullard,* 22 N.C. App. 245, 206 S.E. 2d 305, *appeal dismissed.* 285 N.C. 758, 209 S.E. 2d 279 (1974); and Tom A Croxton, *The Kent Case and Its Consequencies,* 7 J. Fam. L. 1 (1967).

79. 387 U.S. 1 (1967).

80. *Gault,* 387 U.S. at 12; 30–31.

in legal circles was that the *Kent* waiver criteria had taken on the mantle of constitutional law. Since the late 1960s, juvenile waiver criteria have made their way into juvenile court transfer legislation in every jurisdiction, although other means of referring children to criminal courts have emerged as well.

Legislative and prosecutorial waiver have become either adjuncts to the more common form of judicial waiver, or, in some situations are employed more frequently than the *Kent* prototype. The variety of statutory schemes allowing for transfer of jurisdiction are enormous and their differences will not be catalogued here. What can be said, however, is that waiver accomplished by legislative edict is generally more circumscribed and rigid. These so-called "exclusion" statutes place certain age-specific and offense-specific children beyond the jurisdiction of the juvenile court *ab initio*.[81] They treat "child-

---

81. Some of the more recent examples of statutory exclusion legislation include the following: *Alabama* — ALA. CODE § 12.15.34.1 (Supp. 1996); Any juvenile age 16 or over who has committed the following offenses: (1) Capital offense; (2) Class "A" Felony; (3) Felony committed with a deadly weapon; (4) Felony having element of causing death or serious physical injury; (5) Felony having element of use of dangerous instrument against the following persons: (a) law enforcement officer; (b) corrections officer; (c) parole or probation officer; (d) juvenile court parole or probation officer; (e) district attorney or other prosecuting official; (f) judge or judicial official; (g) grand juror, juror, witness in any legal proceeding whatever…(h) teacher, principal or employee of public education system; (i) trafficking in drugs; and (j) Any lesser included offenses charged or any lesser offense charged arising from the same facts or circumstances and committed at the same time; *California* — CAL. WELF. & INST. CODE § 707(b) (West 1996) provides for an appropriate "fitness" hearing for juvenile to determine whether child is a proper subject for juvenile court jurisdiction and then lists twenty-nine separate offenses where a juvenile, age sixteen or older, may be waived to criminal court for trial. § 707(d)(2) (West 1996) lists twenty-four separate offenses where a juvenile, ages fourteen to sixteen, may be "unfit" for juvenile court jurisdiction and presumably transferred to adult court for trial; *District of Columbia* — D.C. CODE ANN. § 11-2301(3) (Supp. 1996) provides that the term "child" means an individual who is under age 18…except that the term "child" does *not* include an individual who is age sixteen or older and is (A) charged by the United States Attorney with (i) murder, first-degree sexual abuse, burglary in the first degree, robbery while armed, or assault with intent to commit any said offense, or (ii) an offense listed in clause (i) and any other offense properly joinable with such an offense; *Florida* — FLA. STAT. ANN. § 39052(5)(c) (West Supp. 1995) enacts that *regardless of child's age* at time of offense, state attorney *must* file an information against child previously adjudicated for offenses which, if he or she were an adult, would be felonies and such offenses occurred at three or more delinquency adjudicatory hearings and those hearings resulted in a residential commitment; *Illinois* — ILL. ANN. STAT. § 405/5-4(6)(a) (Smith-Hurd Supp. 1996) provides that the definiton of a "delinquent

hood" or "juveniles" as legally irrelevant because no minor falling within the age and act category of these enactments ever sets foot in juvenile court. This spate of post-1975 legislation is a direct repudiation of the *parens patriae* juvenile court in the sense that in most cases prior to that time, even seriously delinquent children would often be adjudicated and sentenced within the system.

What has attended this floodgate of legislation that some contend has marginalized the juvenile court experience? We can begin perhaps with the eroding influence of American culture during and following the 1960s. Law, to a greater or less degree, has followed institutional, cultural, economic and social change in the United States since the republic was formed. Although there often is a "legal gap" between socio-cultural and other forms of change, sooner or later the law will adjust to these variations, albeit often only by bits and pieces. It has taken the American juvenile court the greater part of the last thirty years of the twentieth century to adjust itself to a changed and truncated conception of childhood. This changed (and changing) conception of childhood has nowhere been more accurately reflected than in juvenile court waiver practice. One of the great imponderables in the 1990s is whether or not this changed waiver policy is part and parcel

---

minor" shall *not* apply to any minor who at time of offense was 15 years of age and who is charged with first-degree murder; aggravated criminal sexual assault; armed robbery with a firearm; or for separate other code violations while in the buildings or grounds of any elementary or secondary school; community college; college or university. § 405/5-4(7)(a) enacts that the definition of a "delinquent minor" shall *not* apply to any minor age 15 or above charged with an offense under the *Illinois Controlled Substances Act*; § 405/5-4(8)(a) notes that the definiton of "delinquent minor" shall *not* apply to any minor charged with a violation of § 31-1(a) or § 32-10 of the *Criminal Code* of 1961 when the minor is subject to prosecution under the *Criminal Code* of 1961, § 405/5-4(9)(a), the definition of delinquent minor shall *not* apply to any minor *at least 13 years of age* who is charged with first-degree murder committed during the course of either aggravated or criminal sexual assault, criminal sexual assault or aggravated kidnapping. These five legislative variations in statutory language indicate the wide range of criteria utilized by various states in their exclusion legislation. There is no unformity that consistently appears in these provisions, allowing each jurisdiction to establish its own criteria for either outright exclusion from juvenile court jurisdiction or giving prosecuting authorities and the judiciary wide powers to dismiss children from juvenile jurisdiction and commit them to the adult criminal process. For a more complete discussion of various exclusion provisions as well as judicial and statutory waiver criteria, *see* SAMUEL M. DAVIS, RIGHTS OF JUVENILES: THE JUVENILE JUSTICE SYSTEM §§ 2.8; 2.9; 2.10 & 2.11 (2d ed. 1996).

of a draconian "new criminology" for certain youth or merely a transitory late twentieth century turning back the clock in order to get a handle on the perceived lawlessness of a small but frightening segment of American teenagers? The issue was joined in the mid-1970s. Then policymakers, politicians, academics and practitioners alike seemingly came to a rather startling conclusion—that our social science, legal and medical "tools" were simply not adequate to continue relying on them under the rubric of the rehabilitative ideal. Especially urban delinquency and its streetwise practitioners became a genuine threat to public safety. This attitudinal awakening, while separate and apart from the procedural re-tooling of the juvenile court, nonetheless dovetailed quite nicely with the United States Supreme Court's withering critique of the *parens patriae* juvenile court in the essay portion of its *Gault* opinion.

In the Beccarian "proportionality" sense of the term,[82] the juvenile court establishment in the 1960s and early 1970s was perceived to be badly out of touch with the "reality" of a nascent strain of violent, repetitive, predatory delinquency. For most of its history, the juvenile court has conceived its mission to be offender oriented, not offense oriented. Offender oriented policies and practices have allowed the court broad leeway in the manner and form through which it exercised its *parens patriae* prerogative. This all changed after *In re Gault*. This offender-offense dichotomy has always caused some genuine confusion of purpose in juvenile court operation and the *Gault* decision and other major juvenile rights cases since 1967 have tended to exacerbate this issue.

In the last three decades of the twentieth century, systemic reaction to serious delinquency has divided along two principal fault lines: (1) increased employment of both the judicial and prosecutorial waiver device for an increasingly larger cohort of violent youth, and (2) the enactment of exclusion statutes to disallow these youths the benefit of juvenile court jurisdiction. While both of these devices have their own proponents and detractors, they have become a common staple in juvenile court procedure in the 1980s and 1990s. In his discussion of what he terms delinquency "cycles," Thomas J. Bernard[83] asserts

---

82. CESARE BONESANA BECCARIA, AN ESSAY ON CRIMES AND PUNISHMENT (Henry Padlucci trans. 1963).
83. THOMAS J. BERNARD, THE CYCLE OF JUVENILE JUSTICE (1992).

that judicial policymakers should draw a clear distinction between those juveniles who are, in his words, "rational calculators,"[84] as opposed to those who are "naive risk-takers."[85] To Bernard, the rational calculator should be subject to universal waiver under any one of several criteria, whereas the naive risk-taker should remain within the traditional juvenile court structure and be subject to whatever techniques are contemporarily applied in juvenile correction. This rational calculator/naive risk-taker dichotomy may hold promise as one possible stepping stone in the re-design of a juvenile code that breaks away in certain important particulars from the total culpability criteria of adult criminal statutes.

Only after the 1970s did juvenile court legislation turn away from its language of "standards" and move more towards a language of "rules" in specific waiver formats, be they judicial, prosecutorial or statutory. Dean Lee Teitelbaum was not suggesting that even in criminal law, "standards" and "discretion" do not play a part, for they invariably do. What he is suggesting, one would suppose, is that the entire juvenile court apparatus, its ethos, its culture and its dynamics have all centered upon *standards* of adjudication and sanction that would not, and indeed could not, be circumscribed by the inflexibility of *rules*. The *parens patriae* juvenile court was the archetype standard-oriented legal institution. When dealing with the adolescent and pre-pubescent child, flexible processes are essential. The pre-*Gault* juvenile court, however, ran afoul of these processes because it apparently was often too eager to adjudicate by standards that would allow procedural rule-oriented justice to fail the child at precisely the moment it was needed. The *parens patriae* civil proceeding assumptions were so strong, so institutionalized and so easy to administer that the juvenile bench in the United States became the victim of its own rhetoric. In any system of dispute resolution, but more especially in a quasi-formal system like the juvenile court, there has to be a balance between rules and standards. Between 1899 and the mid-1960s, the American juvenile court employed its *parens patriae* civil *standards* jurisprudence to a wide variety of situations with remarkable success. There were few who dared criticize its decision-making processes before the 1960s. When criticism did come, however, it

---

84. *Id.* at 169.
85. *Id.* at 168.

came from an institution that commanded a far wider audience than the juvenile court had previously faced. Juvenile justice existed largely in a cocoon culture until the first two constitutional volleys were fired at its *parens patriae* edifice by *Kent* and *In re Gault*. In a phrase that captured the United States Supreme Court's discomfort with juvenile court operations, Justice Fortas remarked[86] "that *the child receives the worst of both worlds:*"[87] (Emphasis added). Thus emerged the rubric that was to have a significant impact on the "standards" oriented *parens patriae* juvenile court for the remainder of the twentieth century. Up until Justice Fortas' astute observation in the *Kent* decision in 1966, the juvenile court had operated for some sixty-seven years behind the scenes of social concern in its own rather cloistered atmosphere secure in the belief that its principles and methods were immune from mordant criticism. When this belief system was assaulted by the Warren Court, the foundation was laid for the juvenile court's decline as a *parens patriae* tribunal and its bifurcation into a quasi-criminal court with an institutional mind-set at odds with its historical antecedents. This mind-set subordinates in-house accommodation of serious delinquency and superordinates waiver as the "rule" rather than as a "standard."

Waiver, transfer, certification, regardless of title, is the postmodern juvenile courts' answer to the late twentieth-century juvenile crime problem. The ready access of juveniles to adult criminal courts via waiver will permanently affect the youth's life chances in more ways than one. If the juvenile transferee is a serious repeat offender who has little, if any, chance of reformation at the hands of the juvenile justice system, then trial as an adult is perhaps society's final judgment. Once waived, the minor has additional procedural protections he or she would not normally enjoy in juvenile court, but they come with a heavy pricetag. If tried and convicted as an adult "felon," the now "juvenile" criminal automatically loses certain civil rights, and a host of occupational and professional possibilities. These so-called "collateral consequences" of a criminal conviction[88] will invariably

---

86. *Kent v. United States*, 383 U.S. 541 (1966).

87. *Id.* at 556.

88. *See Special Project: The Collateral Consequences of a Criminal Conviction*, 23 Vand. L. Rev. 941 (1970).

operate as a second unofficial punishment and can and often does provide the grist for further criminality.[89]

One of the due process principles considered necessary for possible review was the requirement in *Kent* that a statement of reasons accompany a juvenile court judge's order transferring a child to criminal court for trial. Generally, most commentators and observers of juvenile justice over the past thirty years have almost invariably assumed that a waiver order must be accompanied by written findings. However, depending upon who decides waiver, there is not total unanimity on this issue. For example, the Seventh Circuit United States Court of Appeals in Chicago as far back as 1974[90] ruled that "[t]here is not an inflexible requirement" that a juvenile judge always meet *Kent's* statement of reasons provision. What the Seventh Circuit addressed was the difference between a *judicial waiver* and a *prosecutorial waiver* and held that only a judicial waiver required a formal statement of reasons. The United States Supreme Court subsequently denied certiorari in an appeal from the Seventh Circuit holding.[91] Consequently, there remains a split of judicial opinion as to whether, *in all cases of waiver,* a written statement of reasons is constitutionally required.

One would have supposed that, regardless of the mechanics of waiver initiation, due process of law would, at a minimum, require a written statement of reasons for possible appellate review. However, the very issue of appellate review of waiver orders has itself become a contentious subject in its own right. For example, should a decision by a juvenile court judge to waive the minor to criminal court be subject to immediate appeal? Contrariwise, should that very same order await the outcome of the criminal trial and be appealable only after conviction? Case law here is in disarray often turning on the issue of whether a transfer order is interpreted as *interlocutory only,* and hence not subject to appeal, or whether that very same order is a *final judgment* subject to appellate review? Statutory law, on the other hand, may offer more consistent guidance on this issue especially if it makes specific provision for those orders which are and which are not "final" in the

---

89. *Id.* and Barry C. Feld, *The Juvenile Court Meets the Principle of the Offense: Legislative Changes in Juvenile Waiver Statutes,* 78 J. Crim L. & Criminology 471 (1987).

90. United States ex rel. *Bombacino v. Bensinger,* 498 F. 2d 875 (7th Cir. 1974).

91. 419 U.S. 1019 (1974).

appellate sense of that term. There is no apparent national concensus on this question which further complicates the entire waiver practice in juvenile courts. The far better rule, it is ventured, would be to require written reasons for waiver in both judicial and prosecutorial transfer decisions. Waiver is crucial, regardless of which legal functionary makes the decision. A waiver order unaccompanied by reasons is tantamount to something akin to khadi justice and should be foreclosed throughout the juvenile court establishment. Both juvenile judge and prosecutor have a legal and moral obligation to spread on the record the factors which weigh in their decision to try the juvenile in a criminal court. *Kent* clearly mandated this requirement for the bench, but prosecutorial waiver is on a par with judicial waiver in all respects and allowing some prosecutorial waivers to be made without reasons is simply shortsighted policy.

One problem that has continually plagued juvenile justice since 1899 and is still a problem at century's end is the statutory vagueness endemic not only in waiver criteria, but more importantly in the legal criteria separating delinquency, dependency and neglect. For waiver, especially, the legislative language leaves a great deal to be desired. In many waiver statutes one finds language that supports waiver if the juvenile "is not amenable to treatment or rehabilitation" in the juvenile justice system. What precisely does this mean? Especially after the 1970s with the advent of the "nothing works" syndrome, the words "treatment" and "rehabilitation" have become phantom phrases in juvenile law. Criminology and the social sciences are not complete failures in this arena, but their overall track record has not been salutary. Nonetheless, do juvenile courts simply employ nonamenability as an easy rationale for ridding themselves of juveniles who may profit from some other form of correctional intervention simply to satiate community sentiment? One would have to hazard an affirmative reply to that *quare*. Utah's Dean Teitelbaum may have suggested a way out of the correctional-punitive dilemma that has bedeviled the juvenile court form the beginning. Teitelbaum notes that[92]

> codes are generally content simply to incorporate by reference the generally prevailing rules for adjudicating adult criminality. Those rules even applied to adults, have been

---

92. Lee E. Teitelbaum, *Youth Crime and The Choice Between Rules and Standards,* 1991 Brigham Young L. Rev. 351.

criticized for their failure to consider the culpability of individuals before the court. Whatever may be true in that domain, punishment justified by deserts and dependent on categories of offense supposes a normative clarity about conduct and mental state that cannot routinely be supposed for children. Accordingly, it seems sensible to consider adopting, for this special population, formulations that depart from the usual Anglo-American approach to adult wrongdoing.[93]

In a word, Teitelbaum is apparently suggesting no less than a *criminal code for children* that takes into account some recognized differences in their behavior patterns when compared with adults. This has not been done, of course, but the time may be upon us when serious consideration needs to be given to a complete re-vamping of the concept of "childhood" in statutory law. The waiver process points up the discordant pulls and pushes that juvenile courts have experienced since the 1960s and the often questionable legal and public policy choices juvenile court judges and prosecutors must make in waiver determinations. Thirty-plus years after *Kent v. United States*,[94] we are still experiencing the "worst of both worlds" scenario for far too many youngsters and the waiver decision process ranks high on that worst worlds list. Feld cogently observed[95] "[a]s sentencing criteria, 'amenability to treatment' and 'dangerousness' implicate some of the most fundamental and difficult issues of penal policy and juvenile jurisprudence....Because judges interpret and apply the same law inconsistently, discretionary statutes [like waiver] are not administered on an evenhanded basis."[96] So long as we have the mind-boggling variety of waiver statutes and accede to the judge, the prosecutor and the legislature full or partial hegemony over the transfer decision, waiver practice in juvenile courts will continue to be a jurisprudential conundrum.

---

93. *Id.* at 400.

94. 383 U.S. 541 (1966).

95. Barry C. Feld, *Criminalizing the American Juvenile Court*, 17 Crime & Justice: A Rev. of Research 197 (Michael Tonry ed. 1993).

96. *Id.* at 234–35.

Chapter Six

The Juvenile in the Arms of the Court — Adjudication

A. Adjudication Generally

The adjudication stage of the juvenile justice process is the fact-finding or "trial" stage of the proceedings. After a petition has been filed against a juvenile and the matter cannot be disposed of at intake, the juvenile is moved further along the judicial continuum. The adjudicatory segment determines whether or not the allegations contained in the petition are true. In the early years of juvenile court development, the adjudicatory stage was treated as a more or less informal but structured decision point along the road to treatment and rehabilitation. The formal and set-piece accouterments of a criminal trial were dropped, and, in their place came a procedure that raised informal fact-finding to an art form. Petitions were filed without the necessity of determining "probable cause" and once an adjudicatory hearing was commenced, the procedural protections surrounding juvenile suspects in pre-1899 hearings evaporated. The concept of due process of law whose idea can be traced to Magna Charta gave way, overnight as it were, to a non-adversary but intensely inquisitorial posture advocated so successfully by the child savers of Chicago. Here the juvenile—not the act committed—was the key determinant. The juvenile court was in the child-saving business, not the guilt-allocation business. The criminal court was anathema. As Anthony M. Platt[1] noted, the "invention" of delinquency was the major legal construct allowing the decoupling of youthful lawbreaking from the grip of the criminal law. Monrad G. Paulsen[2] noted shortly after *In re Gault*[3] had been decided that

---

1. ANTHONY M. PLATT, THE CHILD SAVERS: THE INVENTION OF DELINQUENCY (2d ed. 1977).
2. Monrad G. Paulsen, *The Constitutional Domestication of the Junveile Court* 1967 Sup. Ct. Rev. 233.
3. 387 U.S. 1 (1967).

[t]he historic leaders of the juvenile court movement fully
believed that formal procedure in the court was, at best,
excess baggage and, at worst, positively harmful. Procedural nicety could not help a youngster....The court of
which the reformers dreamed, born of a passion for social
justice, dedicated to the rehabilitation of the offender,
would respond to a child's delinquency by offering treatment without imposing the stigma of criminality.[4]

Commentators on the juvenile court who preceded Paulsen and
even Paulsen himself often noted that, in theory, the juvenile court
through its adjudicatory process would open a door to a "supermarket" of social services for the delinquent. Adjudication was merely
the formalized opening step to treatment and guilt or innocence was
marginalized for the higher purpose of child saving. Herbert H. Lou[5]
noted in 1927 that the juvenile court now had "probation officers,
physicians, psychologists and psychiatrists who search for the social,
physiological, psychological, and mental backgrounds of the
child....[6] No mention was made of a search for culpability, fault or
blameworthiness. When a tribunal's key reason to exist is premised
upon Lou's catalog of actors, there is simply no room left for an adversarial, guilt-determining process. In a real sense the *parens patriae*
juvenile court represented to the Progressive child saving devotees a
utopian visage similar in kind to what John Winthrop's 1630 "City

---

4. Paulsen, *supra* note 2, at 239.

5. HERBERT H. LOU, JUVENILE COURTS IN THE UNITED STATES (1927). But in that
same year (1927), the New York Court of Appeals in *People v. Fitzgerald*, 244 N.Y. 307,
155 N.E. 584 (1927) unanimously overturned a conviction of a juvenile whose guilt was
established in the Children's Court largely by testimony of a juvenile accomplice and by
virtue of an illegal confession. Said Justice Crane: "Our activities in behalf of the child
may have been awakened but the fundamental ideas of criminal procedure have not
changed. They require a definite charge, competent proof and a judgment. Anything less
is arbitrary power." 244 N.Y. at 316, 155 N.E. at 588 Five years later, Justice Crane in
dissent in *People v. Lewis*, 260 N.Y. 171, 183 N.E. 353 (1932), *cert. denied* 289 U.S.
709 (1933), raised this issue:

> Do the Constitution of the United States and the Constitution of the State of
> New York apply to children or only to adults? May a child be incarcerated and
> deprived of his liberty in a public institution by calling that which is a crime by
> some other name; and, if so, at what age may the Legislature take from him that
> constitutional right? 260 N.Y. at 181, 183 N.E. at 356.

6. Lou, *supra* note 5, at 219.

Upon a Hill" sermon[7] represented to the Puritan faithful upon reaching what was to become the Massachusetts Bay Colony.

With lawyers shunned and unwelcome in this new court for children, the accompanying legal processes traditionally employed in criminal courts were de-emphasized and abolished. Since the adjudicatory hearing was considered to be a civil process, the issue was no longer a child's criminal responsibility, but rather what caused the "problem" leading this particular minor to violate the juvenile code? The immediate need was not to reconstruct in court the factual scenario of the delinquent act *per se*, but rather to address the wider (and to the child savers) more troubling issue of the *etiology* of the act. This focus on etiology was not accidental, but intentional. Since punishment had been definitionally removed from juvenile justice practice, the *parens patriae* doctrine demanded a flow of information that would enable both the judge and the probation staff to adjust a disposition to the child that comported with his or her "best interests." Of course, reconstructing the past to determine a minor's "best interest" for the future is a task that has confounded the juvenile court since its inception.

For an adjudicatory hearing in juvenile court, the reformers succeeded in actually changing the physical layout of the courtroom in many instances. Although today juvenile courtrooms in many cases reflect a traditional courtroom setting, the child savers opted for a setting less ceremonial and intimidating than the traditional criminal courtroom. In order to optimize a closer relationship between the judge, the child, the parents and the probation staff, early juvenile courtrooms were often designed without an elevated bench and more often than not, the judge discarded the traditional black robe in favor of professional office attire. Gone too were the usual coterie of criminal court officials who were regularly in attendance at a criminal trial. Since the juvenile court was not traditionally a court "of record," the automatic transcription of the proceedings by a court reporter were usually not taken, although this practice varied from jurisdiction to jurisdiction. The entire tone and atmosphere was more akin to a child-guidance clinic than to a judicial proceeding and this

---

7. Winthrop said in his famous sermon that "wee must Consider that wee shall be as a City upon a Hill, the eies of all people are uppon us…" Robert N. Bellah, *American Civil Religion in the 1970s*, as quoted in AMERICAN CIVIL RELIGION 267 (Donald G. Jones & Russell E. Richey eds. 1990).

informal, free-information flow called an adjudicatory hearing became commonplace in juvenile courts across the land. When any institution places an emphasis on informality, intense information
input, ingratiating interchange between the parties and a seeming
benevolent search for a "solution," traditional legal processes become the first victim. The reasons are self-evident. Criminal law is a
powerful engine of formal social control and because it has the potential for affecting both liberty and life, it must be hedged about
with procedures whose aim, among others, is to see to it that an accused receives a legal process that is "due"—in other words, one
whose regularized procedures are carried out in the name of fairness.
Due process has always been a crown jewel in the American system
of criminal justice with only occasional historical lapses. However, in
the hands of the pre-*Gault* juvenile court, the concept of due process
was strangely tilted on its head. To the judges and probation officers
who were the descendants of the 1899 juvenile court, the process that
was "due" a juvenile in an adjudicatory hearing was a process un-
adorned with centuries-old legal protections. In the arms of the court
in an adjudicatory hearing, the alleged delinquent was totally at the
mercy of the judge-probation officer duo. While in many cases this
decision-making format was instrumental in redirecting young
lives—especially status and neglect offenders—it left a great deal to
be desired for those children charged with more seriously culpable
wrongdoing. Stripped of their pre-trial and trial constitutional rights
due to the civil rubric of the proceeding, the truly delinquent minor
faced the "worst of both worlds" in the *parens patriae* juvenile court.
On May 15, 1967, however, all of that changed. *In re Gault*[8]
emerged on the scene involving a case notably pedestrian in its factual context. Nonetheless, *Gault* changed the entire juvenile justice
adjudicatory landscape and laid the foundation for significant legal
changes throughout juvenile law in the last three decades of the twentieth century.

B. *In re Gault* and the Adjudicatory Process

To characterize the *Gault* decision as pedestrian is itself perhaps an
understatement. What happened to this Arizona juvenile did not
seem, at first blush, to be the "stuff" of constitutional litigation, let

---

8. 387 U.S. 1 (1967).

alone the ingredients for a landmark ruling by the Warren Court. Yet, as in so many other Warren era cases involving the tensions between the state and the individual, the case of Gerald Francis Gault did come to the attention of the Court at a propitious time in juvenile court history.

Gault[9] was, on its face, a wide-ranging and omnibus opinion "not closely tied to the facts of the case, thus suggesting that nothing less than a thorough reform of juvenile court procedure would satisfy its requirements."[10] The benefit of some thirty-plus years of hindsight now allows us to conclude that while some reforms have taken place in juvenile law since 1967, the "thorough reform" expected soon after the case was decided has not come to pass. Institutional inertia, legal and otherwise, has been a powerful deterrent to meaningful juvenile court reform in the post-*Gault* era. What *Gault* did accomplish, however, was a reform of sorts in the *adjudicatory stage* of a delinquency hearing where a juvenile's liberty interests were at stake. The immediate impact of the decision saw the selective incorporation[11] of several criminal procedure safeguards placed within the adjudicatory scheme.

On the adult level, the criminal law has always operated within a paradoxical frame of reference. At one end stands the substantive law of crimes which denominate those acts which society deems potentially destructive of the social fabric. At the opposite end stands criminal procedure which "is designed quite properly to avoid conviction either where substantive policy is not clear-cut or where the evidence is insubstantiated."[12] From about 1960 until the *Gault* ruling in the spring of 1967, the law of criminal procedure in the United States had undergone a major realignment.[13] The Bill of Rights had truly

---

9. *Id.*

10. *The Supreme Court, 1966 Term*, 81 Harv. L. Rev. 171 (1967). For an excellent early discussion of both *Kent* and *Gault* and the problems raised by these decisions, *see* Thomas A. Welch, *Kent v. United States and In re Gault: Two Decisions in Search of a Theory*, in *Symposium: Youth and the Law*, 19 Hastings L.J. 29 (1967).

11. For an interesting and historically relevant discussion of constitutional "incorporation" of the Bill of Rights via Fourteenth Amendment due process, *see* HENRY J. ABRAHAM, FREEDOM AND THE COURT 21–78 (1967).

12. PAUL W. TAPPAN, CRIME, JUSTICE AND CORRECTION 15 (1960).

13. For example, the incorporation of the Fourth Amendment's "exclusionary rule" into state criminal justice practice in *Mapp v. Ohio*, 367 U.S. 643 (1961); the Sixth Amendment's "right to counsel" for indigent, non-capital felony defendants in *Gideon v.*

become a national mini-code of criminal procedure for the adult offender.[14]

Prior to the 1960s, juvenile law exhibited an almost universal looseness in both substantive and procedural practice not tolerated on the adult level. *In re Gault*[15] put an end to at least some of the procedural irregularities extant in the juvenile "trial" phase. Since the procedural looseness by which Gerald Gault was adjudged "delinquent" was an excellent example of the *parens patriae* juvenile court adjudication practice, the facts of the case will be reviewed in some detail. The contemporary reader must be cautioned to understand that what follows was not at all out of the ordinary in the run-of-the-mill delinquency hearings in Arizona or in other states as well.

On June 8, 1964, nearly three years before his case reached the United States Supreme Court, Gerald Francis Gault, age fifteen, a resident of Gila County, Arizona, was taken into custody by the county sheriff on a verbal complaint. It seems that a female neighbor living in the same trailer park as the Gault family had filed a verbal complaint about an allegedly lewd telephone conversation she had received from young Gault. The United States Supreme Court in its majority opinion attempted to sanitize the actual content of the words supposedly uttered to the neighbor by the juvenile. Justice Fortas characterized the conversation to be of the "irritatingly offensive adolescent, sex variety."[16] What Gerald Gault had allegedly said to his neighbor, a Mrs. Cook, was reported to be the words "How big are your bombers?," obviously referring to a portion of Mrs. Cook's anatomy. Gault's parents were not notified of his detention and his

<hr>

Wainwright, 372 U.S. 335 (1963); the interrogation and confession case of *Escobedo v. Illinois*, 378 U.S. 478 (1964); the incorporation of the Fifth Amendment's privilege against compulsory self-incrimination made applicable to the states by *Malloy v. Hogan*, 378 U.S. 1 (1964); the introduction of a "mini-code" of criminal procedure for suspects undergoing "custodial interrogation" in *Miranda v. Arizona*, 384 U.S. 436 (1966); the broadening of the Fifth Amendment "self-incrimination" privilege in *Garrity v. New Jersey*, 385 U.S. 493 (1967) and in *Spevack v. Kein*, 385 U.S. 511 (1967); and in the Sixth Amendment field, the police line-up, right to counsel cases of *United States v. Wade*, 388 U.S. 218 (1967); *Gilbert v. California*, 388 U.S. 263 (1967) and *Stovall v. Denno*, 388 U.S. 293 (1967).

14. *See* Henry J. Friendly, *The Bill of Rights as a Code of Criminal Procedure*, 53 Cal. L. Rev. 929 (1965).

15. 387 U.S. 1 (1967).

16. 387 U.S. at 4.

mother subsequently learned of his plight later that same evening from the family of the other accused juvenile in the case, a boy by the name of Ronald Lewis.[17] Upon reaching the juvenile detention center to inquire into the cause of her son's incarceration, Mrs. Gault was informed by Mr. Flagg, a probation officer, "'why Gerald was there'"[18] and was then informed that "a hearing would be held in Juvenile Court at 3 o'clock the following day...."[19]

The first of two separate hearings inquiring into the respondent's alleged delinquency was held the following afternoon in the presence of two probation officers, the juvenile, his mother and the juvenile court judge. Gerald's father was not present at this hearing. The female complainant was not present. Testimony was taken, but not sworn, no transcript of the proceedings was kept and Gerald Gault was extensively questioned by the judge[20] without being advised either of his right to remain silent or of the right to be represented by an attorney. It must be noted parenthetically here that such a process was the common method of procedure in most juvenile courts of the period. At the conclusion of the hearing, Gault was taken back to the detention facility where he remained for several additional days.[21] In later reacting to this latter procedure, the Supreme Court stated that

---

17. The Supreme Court noted in its opinion, however, that there was testimonial conflict at the first "hearing" in juvenile court as to exactly who made the alleged phone call. Said Justice Fortas: "There was a conflict as to what he [Gault] said. His mother recalled that Gerald said he only dialed Mrs. Cook's number and handed the telephone to his friend, Ronald. Officer Flagg [the Probation Officer] recalled that Gerald had admitted making the lewd remarks." 387 U.S. at 6.

18. 387 U.S. at 5.

19. *Id.* The note Mrs. Gault received from probation officer Flagg was on a plain piece of paper, not on court letterhead. It read simply: "Mrs. Gault: Judge McGhee has set Monday June 15, 1964 at 11:00 A.M. as the date and time for further Hearings on Gerald's delinquency. /s/Flagg."

20. Under Arizona law at the time, juvenile court hearings were conducted by a judge of the Superior Court, designated by his colleagues on the Superior Court to sit as a Juvenile Court judge. ARIZ. CONST. art. VI, § 15; ARIZ. REV. STAT. ANN. §§ 8-201–202 (1956).

21. The United States Supreme Court in footnote #2 of its opinion, recalled that there was a conflict between Officer Flagg's recollection and that of Mrs. Gault as to how long Gerald remained in detention before his release. Mrs. Gault testified that her son was released on Friday, June 12, 1964, while Officer Flagg was of the opinion that the juvenile was released on Thursday, June 11, 1964, although he admitted this recollection was from memory; he kept no written record or memoranda.

"[t]here is no explanation in the record as to why he was kept in the Detention Home or why he was released."[22]

A week later, a second hearing in the nature of a "commitment" determination was held. In attendance before the judge in chambers at this hearing were Gerald Gault and Ronald Lewis, both of Gault's parents, Mr. Lewis and probation officers Henderson and Flagg.[23] Again, the complaining witness was absent. "Mrs. Gault asked that Mrs. Cook be present 'so she could see which boy done the talking, the dirty talking over the phone.' The Juvenile Judge replied that 'she didn't have to be present at that hearing.'"[24] Similar lax procedures characterized this second hearing. The judge made no attempt whatever to resolve the disputed issue of fact as to whether Gault had actually uttered offensive language in conversing with Mrs. Cook. That phone call, however, initiated a chain of events that made juvenile court history.

Gerald Gault was unceremoniously adjudged "delinquent"[25] at the conclusion of the second hearing and committed to the State Industrial School for Boys until age twenty-one. It is interesting to note in this context that had Gerald Gault been an adult found guilty of the same offense, he would, under the Arizona Criminal Code,[26] have been subject to a maximum punishment of a fifty-dollar fine and imprisonment for not more than sixty days, or both. As it was, and because Gault was adjudged to be a "delinquent" child, he was subjected to incarceration for a maximum period of six years in the state reformatory.

After taking an unsuccessful appeal to the Supreme Court of Arizona,[27] Gault's counsel petitioned the United States Supreme Court[28]

---

22. 387 U.S. at 6.

23. *Id.* at 7.

24. *Id.*

25. The legal basis for the "delinquency" finding according to the juvenile judge was Gerald Gault's violation of ARIZ. REV. STAT. ANN. § 13-337 (1956), which forbid the use of vulgar or obscene language in the presence of a woman. Because of Gault's youth, the above statute triggered the delinquency proceeding under ARIZ. REV. STAT. ANN. § 8-201(6)(a) (1956). That statute defined a "delinquent" *inter alia* as one "who has violated a law of the state...."

26. ARIZ. REV. STAT. ANN. § 13-377 (1956).

27. *Application of Gault*, 99 Ariz. 181, 407 P. 2d 760 (1965).

28. The appeal was taken under 28 U.S.C. § 1257(2) (1952); *cert. granted*, 384 U.S. 997 (1966).

alleging that the Arizona juvenile code was unconstitutional both on its face and as applied to this particular minor. Specifically, the petitioner alleged the following violations of constitutional dimension: (1) failure to give adequate notice of the charges; (2) failure to apprise the juvenile of a right to counsel; (3) right to confront and cross-examine witnesses both for and against respondent; (4) failure to accord the juvenile the privilege against self-incrimination; (5) right to a transcript of the proceedings; and (6) the right to appellate review. The efforts of Gault's appellate counsel met with substantial success.

In an exhaustive fifty-six page majority opinion per Mr. Justice Fortas, the Court, in a 7–2 decision, reversed the findings of the Arizona juvenile court. Gerald Francis Gault's name is thus "appended to the first juvenile case ever reviewed by the United States Supreme Court on constitutional grounds and is...forever linked to the decision that brought the requirements of the Fourteenth Amendment to juvenile court hearings."[29]

Justice Fortas, joined by four other colleagues and in part by Justice White[30] and a concurring opinion by Justice Black, held that "juvenile court history has again demonstrated that unbridled discretion, however benevolently motivated, is frequently a poor substitute for principle and procedure."[31] Attacking the procedural looseness of the entire handling of Gault by the Arizona juvenile authorities, the

---

29. Monrad G. Paulsen, *Children's Court —Gateway or Last Resort?*, 72 Case and Comment 3 (Nov.–Dec., 1967).

30. Justice White concurred, but was of the opinion that the Court should have eschewed decision on the issues of self-incrimination, confrontation and cross-examination in the juvenile court procedural context. Justice Black also concurred, but based his concurrence on the authority of the Fifth and Sixth Amendments rather than on the Fourteenth Amendment.

31. 387 U.S. at 18. Fifteen years before *Gault*, for example, the Indiana Court of Appeals noted in *Matter of Green*, 108 N.E. 2d 647 (Ind.Ct.App. 1952) that

[t]he petition reveals a star chamber proceeding...without a semblance of due process....The [Juvenile Court] act does not, nor could it, within constitutional limitations, sanction the action of a court in finding a juvenile guilty of a wrong against the state in disregard of his rights to a hearing in which he is apprised of the charges against him, the evidence in support thereof, and afford an opportunity to defend himself. 108 N.E. 2d at 649.

Court then held "that deficiencies in notice of charges and proceedings, in provision and explanation of the right to counsel, and in evidentiary safeguards...denied Gerald due process."[32] Even from a narrow reading of the decision, one can conclude that *In re Gault*[33] worked a procedural renaissance in the law applicable to *delinquent* children.[34] The case established that "all 'fact-finding' hearings in juvenile court [that is, hearings in which it is determined what the juvenile has done] 'must measure up to the essentials of due process and fair treatment.'"[35]

Apprehending the impact of its decision on the entire juvenile court apparatus in the United States, the Supreme Court in characteristic fashion, utilized a "this case only" approach in addressing the issue before it. Said Justice Fortas:[36]

> We consider only the problems presented to us *by this case.* These relate to the proceedings by which a determination is made as to whether a juvenile is a *"delinquent"* as a result of alleged misconduct on his part, with the consequences that he may be *committed* to a state institution. (Emphasis added).

From this, it seemed that the Court was bothered by two basic problems in juvenile law: first, the problem of *status* and secondly, the problem of *incarceration* as a result of that status. In order to assure a broader standard of fairness to the potential training school or reformatory inmate, the Court explicated the following specific criteria to be adopted in juvenile delinquency proceedings.

---

32. *The Supreme Court, 1966 Term,* 81 Harv. L. Rev. 171, 172 (1967).

33. 387 U.S. 1 (1967).

34. For examples of pre-1899 case law according minors charged with a criminal violation full constitutional rights, *see People ex rel. O'Connell v. Turner,* 55 Ill. 280 (1870); *Commonwealth v. Horregan,* 127 Mass. 450 (1879); *State v. Ray,* 63 N.H. 406 (1885); *People v. Flack,* 125 N.Y. 324, 26 N.E. 267 (1891). For more recent pre-*Gault* decisions along the same lines, *see United States v. Glover,* 372 F. 2d 43 (2d Cir. 1967); *In re Winburn,* 32 Wis. 2d 152, 145 N.W. 2d 178 (1966); *Shioutakon v. District of Columbia,* 236 F. 2d 666 (D.C. Cir. 1956); and *In re Poff,* 135 F. Supp. 224 (D.D.C. 1955).

35. Paulsen, *supra* note 29, at 3.

36. 387 U.S. at 13.

1. Notices of Charges

A minor charged with *delinquent conduct* as well as that individual's parent or guardian, as the case may be, must be given "Notice … in advance of scheduled court proceedings so that reasonable opportunity to prepare will be afforded" and this notice "must set forth the alleged misconduct with particularity."[37] Notification given at the time of the initial hearing is not timely. "[E]ven if there were a conceivable purpose served by the deferral proposed by the court below," said Fortas,[38] "it would have to yield to the requirements that the child and his parents or guardian be notified, in writing, of the specific charge or factual allegations to be considered at the hearing." Due process in this context requires notice which, from either a civil or criminal law perspective would be deemed constitutionally adequate.[39] The effective transmission of notice to both juvenile and parent or guardian was particularly defective in the *Gault* situation and courts of all description have almost always viewed the notice requirement as a major component of due process. The IJA/ABA *Juvenile Justice Standards* in its *Standards Relating to Adjudication* note in *Standard 1.1(A)* that "[e]ach jurisdiction should provide by law that the filing of a written petition giving the respondent adequate notice of the charges is a requisite for adjudication proceedings to begin."[40] Of course, the IJA/ABA guidelines were promulgated some thirteen years after *In re Gault*, and reflect simple after-the-fact recognition in model statutory form what should have been standard operating procedure in pre-*Gault* juvenile law. Without notice, the juvenile, his or her parents or guardian and the child's legal counsel are at a loss to begin preparation to defend against a particular charge or charges. The amazing thing about the *Gault* lower court proceedings was that Arizona and most other jurisdictions at the time treated "notice" as an unnecessary criteria.

---

37. *Id.* at 33.

38. *Id.*

39. The Court cited in footnote #23 the cases which stated the necessary criteria for adequate notice in a criminal context. These were *Cole v. Arkansas*, 333 U.S. 196 (1948) and *In re Oliver*, 333 U.S. 257 (1948). For what constitutes adequate notice in the civil context, the Court cited *Armstrong v. Manzo*, 380 U.S. 545 (1965) and *Mullane v. Central Hanover Trust Co.*, 339 U.S. 306 (1950).

40. *IJA/ABA Juvenile Justice Standards, Standards Relating to Adjudication* 3 (1980).

2. Right to Counsel

In perhaps the most important and far-reaching portion of the majority opinion, the Court extended the right to counsel guarantee of the Sixth Amendment most recently developed in the 1963 *Gideon*[41] decision to juveniles. The majority, however, made it clear—perhaps because of the multiple definitions of delinquency then existing—that they were referring only to[42]

> [a] proceeding where the issue is whether the child will be found to be "delinquent" and subjected to the loss of his liberty for years...The juvenile needs the assistance of counsel to cope with problems of law, to make skilled inquiry into the facts, to insist upon regularity of the proceedings, and to ascertain whether he has a defense and to prepare and submit it. The child requires the guiding hand of counsel at every step in the proceedings against him.[43]

Concluding that the due process clause of the Fourteenth Amendment demands nothing less, Justice Fortas remarked that a lawyer must be appointed for a juvenile whose delinquency was of such character that it "may result in commitment to an institution in which the juvenile's freedom is curtailed...."[44] In 1967, however, this automatic constitutional right to a lawyer in a juvenile court delinquency adjudication was nothing short of a paradigm shift in juvenile court practice. Nonetheless, if one were carefully reading the judicial tea leaves of the Warren Court's liberal majority, this extension seemed both logical and natural. Given the development of the parallel right to counsel in adult criminal practice since the 1930s,[45] the

---

41. *Gideon v. Wainwright*, 372 U.S. 335 (1963).

42. 387 U.S. at 36.

43. *Id.*

44. 387 U.S. at 41.

45. *See, e.g., Powell v. Alabama*, 287 U.S. 45 (1932). This was the infamous "Scottsboro Case" involving the rapid trial and conviction on capital rape of nine illiterate black youngsters arrested when taken off a Southern Railway freight train at Paint Rock, Alabama on March 25, 1931, and taken to the Jackson County Courthouse at Scottsboro, Alabama. The case was eventually appealed to the United States Supreme Court where Justice Sutherland for the majority ruled that the "Scottsboro Boys" as they were known, were not accorded the right to counsel "in any substantial sense" and such treatment by the Alabama authorities violated the defendants' Fourteenth Amendment due process rights. For an intriguing factual and historical account of this litigation and its cultural overtones, *see* DAN T. CARTER, SCOTTSBORO: A TRAGEDY OF THE AMERICAN

right to counsel for juveniles, while path-breaking, should not have been considered such a radical departure from *stare decisis*. The *Gault* majority were noticeably disturbed about the commitment of a juvenile to an institution (in Gault's case for six years) without appropriate legal representation.

3. Privilege Against Compulsory Self-Incrimination

In the appeal at the state level, the Supreme Court of Arizona rejected Gault's contention that he should have been advised that he need not incriminate himself. It said, "We think the necessary flexibility for individualized treatment will be enhanced by a rule which does not require the judge to advise the infant of a privilege against self-incrimination."[46] Note here the underlying historical premise at work. Like most state appellate courts who were forced to consider the issue, the Supreme Court of Arizona was most reluctant to import a constitutional "right" theretofore applicable only to adult criminal defendants into a *parens patriae* tribunal. The words "flexibility" and "individualized treatment" were *parens patriae* terms of art that obviously covered a multiplicity of due process sins in the juvenile court system of the 1960s. The Arizona judges were not recalcitrant; they were simply following what they believed to be both logic and precedent when they refused to allow the adult practice of "pleading the Fifth" into a children's court. Recognition of such a right to them— like the vast majority of their brethren in other states—would open the door to a perceived flood of counterproductive "legalizing" techniques that would dismember the juvenile court. The stakes were high here and the Arizona judiciary was not about to break new ground in the traditional handling of delinquency cases. Probably

---

SOUTH (rev. ed. 1979) and JAMES E. GOODMAN, STORIES OF SCOTTSBORO (1994). *Johnson v. Zerbst*, 304 U.S. 458 (1938), applied Sixth Amendment right to counsel in *federal* criminal cases holding, among other things, that to conduct one's own defense without a lawyer in a federal criminal trial amounts to a jurisdictional violation of the Sixth Amendment requirement and dispossessed the court of jurisdiction to hear the case without counsel present, unless the defendant waived that right; *Griffin v. Illinois*, 351 U.S. 12 (1956), ruled that indigent adult criminal defendants are entitled to a transcript of their trial in order to facilitate a possible appeal; *Douglas v. California*, 372 U.S. 353 (1963), held that indigent adult defendants are entitled to free legal representation on a *first* appeal; and *Gideon v. Wainwright*, 372 U.S. 335 (1963), guaranteed the right to counsel for all non-capital indigent felony defendants in adult criminal proceedings.

46. 99 Ariz. at 191, 407 P. 2d at 767–68.

second only in controversy to the right to counsel, the invocation of a right to remain silent in a delinquency hearing was tantamount to dealing the *parens patriae* juvenile court a significant body blow.

After discussing at length the differential impact of such decisions as *Miranda v. Arizona*,[47] and the earlier decisions of *Haley v. Ohio*[48] and *Gallegos v. Colorado*[49] on the totality of the juvenile court process, the Court ruled that "[T]he constitutional privilege against self-incrimination is applicable in the case of juveniles as it is with respect to adults."[50] The Court did note, however, "that special problems may arise with respect to waiver of the privilege by or on behalf of children, and that there may well be some differences in technique ...depending upon the age of the child and the presence and competence of parents."[51] In this connection, the juvenile must be advised further that he or she does not have to testify or make a statement if either does not so choose. The *Gault* majority placed a great deal of importance on the grant of this constitutional protection to juveniles. A key to their thinking perhaps resides in their comparison of a delinquency adjudication to a felony prosecution on the adult level. Rarely in the preceding sixty-six years of juvenile court history did one find a judge who was receptive to the invocation of a right to remain silent being accorded to a child charged with a delinquent act. One of the prominent benchmarks of the *parens patriae* court was its use of information, most often freely volunteered by the juvenile, the parents, or both. To place in the hands of the child, or, more appropriately, the child's counsel, the benefit of silence in the face of a delinquency allegation, was a plus for civil liberties, but a decided minus for juvenile court traditionalists. Justice Fortas, however, was not going to let this moment pass without making sure that lower courts, the bar, the police and the public at large were aware of why this privilege could now be invoked by a juvenile defendant. Said he:[52]

> The privilege against self-incrimination is, of course, related to the safeguards necessary to assure that admissions or confessions are reasonably trustworthy, that they are

47. 384 U.S. 436 (1966).
48. 332 U.S. 596 (1948).
49. 370 U.S. 49 (1962).
50. 387 U.S. at 55.
51. *Id.*
52. 387 U.S. at 47.

not the mere fruits of fear of coercion, but are reliable expressions of the truth.... One of its purposes is to prevent the State, whether by force or by psychological domination, from overcoming the mind and will of the person under investigation and depriving him of the freedom to decide whether to assist the State in securing his conviction. It would indeed be surprising if the privilege against self-incrimination were available to hardened criminals but not to children.[53]

Gerald Gault's confession regarding the phone call to Mrs. Cook that emerged in evidence during the Arizona proceedings was of no particular legal moment to the United States Supreme Court. The entire proceeding surrounding Gault's delinquency determination was fatally defective because there apparently was no valid confession in the record that would support a commitment order to the state training school for six years. The "facts," such as they were, that were developed by the Arizona juvenile court were constitutionally infirm. Paulsen[54] notes incredulously that "[t]he juvenile court judge was quite unclear about the legal basis for the adjudication of [Gault's] delinquency." Thus we have a confused jurist who subsequently admitted at Gerald Gault's *habeas corpus* hearing that "I might be wrong."[55]

4. Confrontation and Cross-Examination

Eroding the *parens patriae* doctrine even further, the Court held that "absent a valid confession, a determination of delinquency and an order of commitment to a state institution cannot be sustained in the absence of *sworn testimony* subjected to the opportunity for *cross-examination* in accordance with our law and constitutional requirements."[56] (Emphasis added). This particular ruling was motivated, no doubt, by the former widespread practice of allowing abundant hearsay and other unsworn testimony to be routinely introduced in juvenile proceedings. This free exchange of information, some factual, some anecdotal, some blatantly violative of the rule against

53. *Id.*
54. Paulsen, *supra* note 2, at 235.
55. 387 U.S. at 8, n. 5.
56. 387 U.S. at 57.

hearsay, was all part and parcel of the non-adversary thesis of social casework practice introduced at the very inception of juvenile justice.[57] To be charged with an offense, juvenile or adult, on the unsworn allegations of an absent complaining witness comports more with the practices of a Star Chamber proceeding than with a proceeding designed, in theory at least, to accord a child's "best interests" paramount importance. No fair system of justice should be premised upon a cluster of institutional practices and rules that would forbid an accused individual the elementary right to confront his or her accuser and to examine witnesses both favorable and unfavorable. The confrontation clause and the right to examine and cross-examine witnesses were simply not part of the American juvenile court practice structure pre-1967. From 1899 until 1967, the cumulative cultural tradition in the juvenile court viewed constitutional fundamentals such as these in a negative and pejorative sense.

These four holdings: (1) Notice of charges, (2) Right to counsel, (3) Right to be free from compulsory self-incrimination, and (4) Right to confrontation and cross-examination comprised the narrow *ratio decidendi* of the decision which, in the fullness of time, has become *the* leading case in juvenile law in the twentieth century. The Supreme Court's lengthy opinion combining both constitutional law and high Court scolding of the methods and practices of American juvenile courts would have shocked the earlier guardians of the *parens patriae* grail. Regrettably, *Gault* raised more legal and social policy questions than it answered. Admittedly, it initially threw the entire juvenile justice establishment in the United States temporarily off-balance and admittedly, it gave solace to civil libertarian interests that believed juvenile justice must somehow be brought in line with the parallel criminal justice revolution of that era.

5. What *Gault* Did Not Decide

After announcing new criteria for juvenile due process, the Supreme Court was quite eager to point out that it would not consider "the impact of these constitutional provisions upon *the totality*

---

57. *See generally* Joel F. Handler, *The Juvenile Court and the Adversary System: Problems of Function and Form,* 1965 Wis. L. Rev. 7; Hyman S. Lippman, *Treatment of Juvenile Delinquents in National Conference of Social Work, Proceedings* 314 (1945); and PAULINE V. YOUNG, SOCIAL TREATMENT IN PROBATION AND DELINQUENCY (1937).

of the relationship of the juvenile and the state."[58] (Emphasis added). The majority carefully avoided the issue of the extension of any of these rights into either the pre-adjudicatory or dispositional stages of delinquency litigation.

But even at the adjudicatory phase, the decision did not hold that *all* procedural guarantees applicable to an adult accused would apply with equal force in delinquency proceedings. Seemingly conscious of its pioneering effort, the Court repeated the view expressed earlier in *Kent*[59] "that while 'We do not mean...to indicate that the hearing... must conform with all the requirements of a criminal trial...we do hold that the hearing must measure up to the essentials of due process and fair treatment.'"[60] In addition to this self-imposed restriction, the Court refused to reach such issues as (1) whether or not hearsay testimony may be freely admitted in a juvenile proceeding, and, if so, to what extent;[61] (2) whether guilt "beyond a reasonable doubt" or simply by a "preponderance of the evidence" should be the appropriate burden of proof standard in delinquency adjudications;[62] (3) whether the minor has a right to a transcript or other

---

58. 387 U.S. at 13.

59. 383 U.S. 541, 555 (1966).

60. 387 U.S. at 30.

61. For example, in some jurisdictions there was no constitutional objection to the use of hearsay against a minor, *Holmes' Appeal*, 379 Pa. 599, 109 A. 2d 523 (1954), *cert. denied*, 348 U.S. 973 (1955). The better reasoned cases, however, hold that hearsay testimony is inadmissible in juvenile court proceedings and reject findings of delinquency based solely upon hearsay. *See, e.g., In re L. Z.*, 396 N.W. 2d 214 (Minn. 1986); *In re Kevin G.*, 80 Misc. 2d 517, 363 N.Y.S. 2d 999 (Fam. Ct. N.Y. Co. 1975); *In re Johnson*, 214 Kan. 780, 522 P. 2d 330 (1974); *Krell v. Mantell* 157 Neb. 900, 62 N.W. 2d 308 (1954); *In re Ross*, 45 Wash. 2d 654, 277 P. 2d 335 (1954); *In re Sippy*, 97 A. 2d 455 (D.C. Mun. Ct. App. 1953); *In re Contreras*, 109 Cal. App. 2d 787, 241 P. 2d 631 (1952); *People v. Fitzgerald*, 244 N.Y. 307, 155 N.E. 584 (1927); and *Miller v. State*, 82 Tex. Cr. 495, 200 S.W. 389 (1917). In this connection Sheldon Glueck noted that "[l]oftiness of the motives of a juvenile court can be an insufficient exchange for hearsay or neighborhood gossip or the inability of the child to examine the witnesses from whom the social investigator obtained his information." Problems of Delinquency 327 (Sheldon & Eleanor Glueck eds. 1959).

62. While the quantum of proof required for conviction "beyond a reasonable doubt" had never been questioned in the adult system, no specific standard had been established to adjudicate "delinquency" of a serious nature in juvenile court by 1967. Like so many other areas of juvenile law at the time, some juvenile courts applied the "preponderance of the evidence" standard, *e.g., In re Bigsby*, 202 A. 2d 785 (D.C. Mun. App. 1964); *State v. Ferrell*, 204 S.W. 2d 692 (Tex. Civ. App. 1947); *People v. Lewis*,

record of the proceedings;[63] (4) whether there exists a right to appeal from a finding of delinquency in such proceedings;[64] and (5) whether or not a juvenile judge, in finding the youth delinquent, must state on the record the grounds for such a determination since the judge is also the trier of fact?

Gault was correspondingly silent on some of the broader questions of criminal procedure that have a crucial bearing on the ultimate question of guilt or innocence. For example, does a juvenile charged with the commission of a delinquent act have a constitutional right to trial by jury?[65] In 1971, the United States Supreme Court answered

---

260 N.Y. 171, 183 N.E. 353 (1932); and *State ex rel. Berry v. Superior Court,* 139 Wash. 1, 245 Pac. 409 (1926); some the "clear and convincing proof" standard, *e.g., Lynch v. Lichtenthaler,* 85 Cal. App. 2d 437, 193 P. 2d 77 (1948); *Jensen v. Housley,* 279 Ark. 742, 182 S.W. 2d 758 (1944); *First Nat'l Bank v. Ford,* 30 Wyo. 110, 216 Pac. 691 (1923); while the "beyond a reasonable doubt" standard was approved in *In re Urbasek,* 38 Ill. 2d 535, 232 N.E. 2d 716 (1967) and in *In re Madik,* 233 App. Div. 12, 251 N.Y. Supp. 765 (1931).

63. An adequate record for appellate review is a stenographic transcript of the juvenile court hearing. Although the "right" to appeal is not constitutionally mandated, it is clear that the Fourteenth Amendment prevents discriminatory denials of appeal in criminal cases, *e.g., Dowd v. United States ex rel. Cook,* 340 U.S. 206 (1957) and *Cochran v. Kansas,* 316 U.S. 255 (1942).

64. The allowance of an appeal is really not a "right" in the strict constitutional sense of the term. The United States Supreme Court has yet to rule that a defendant in an adult criminal proceeding has a "right" to appellate review. But, *Griffin v. Illinois,* 351 U.S. 12 (1956) held that if a jurisdiction affords the right to appeal a criminal conviction, then the Equal Protection clause mandates that indigent defendants who cannot afford a transcript be given the right to a free transcript for appellate review. Since the *Gault* decision, most jurisdictions provide in some manner or form a basis for appellate review of juvenile court rulings. These statutes are not uniform and there is considerable variation in language. However, both the *Uniform Juvenile Court Act* of 1968 in § 59 and the 1959 *Standard Juvenile Court Act* in § 28 provide that an "aggrieved party" may appeal from an order of a juvenile court.

65. Pre-*Gault* juvenile law on the jury trial issue was regulated by and large by the dual concepts of the *parens patriae* doctrine and the *equitable* nature of delinquency proceedings. In other words, juries were not employed. Nineteenth-century cases in Illinois and in New Hampshire held that children were entitled to a trial by jury in a *criminal* prosecution, *e.g., People ex rel. O'Connell v. Turner,* 55 Ill. 280 (1870) and *State v. Ray,* 63 N.H. 406 (1885). Later twentieth-century cases in these same states, however, took a contrary view, namely, *Lindsey v. Lindsey,* 257 Ill. 328, 100 N.E. 892 (1913) and *Petition of Morin,* 95 N.H. 518, 68 A. 2d 668 (1949). The decision of *McKeiver v. Pennsylvania,* 403 U.S. 528 (1971) settled the jury trial issue in federal constitutional law against such a right, although there are a number of jurisdictions that allow a jury trial for juve-

that question in the negative in the *McKeiver*[66] decision. Since 1971, however, there has been widespread debate about the allowance of a jury trial for juveniles tried in juvenile court for serious delinquency. Nonetheless, that debate has had little effect on the jury issue in those jurisdictions that continue to disallow juvenile juries. What has happened in the waiver context has probably lessened the demand for juries in most juvenile courts since *McKeiver* was decided. In *federal* delinquency cases, likewise, a concensus has emerged that juries are not constitutionally required.[67]

Regardless of the clear preference for avoiding jury trials in delinquency adjudications, there are some states that provide either by statute or by decisional law for jury trials in an adjudicatory hearing.[68] The 1980 *Juvenile Justice Standards*[69] "recommends that jury trials be made available in juvenile proceedings as a matter of

---

niles either by legislative enactment or by case decision. The *McKeiver* case did not foreclose state experimentation with juvenile court juries, but ruled only that a jury trial was not mandated by the United States Constitution.

66. *McKeiver v. Pennsylvania*, 403 U.S. 528 (1971).

67. In this connection *see United States v. Torres*, 500 F. 2d 944 (2d Cir. 1974) and *United States v. Hill*, 538 F 2d 1072 (4th Cir. 1976).

68. One of the earlier cases was *R.L.R. v. State*, 487 P. 2d 27 (Alaska 1971). In the 1990s, several jurisdictions have passed statutes that afford this right to juveniles. Representative examples include *Colorado* — COLO. REV. STAT. ANN § 19-2-501 (West Supp. 1995); *Massachusetts* — MASS. GEN. LAWS ANN. ch. 119, § 55A (West 1993); *Montana* — MONT. CODE ANN. § 41-5-521(1) (1995); *New Mexico* — N.M. STAT. ANN. § 32A-2-16(A) (Michie 1995); *Texas* — TEX. FAM. CODE ANN. § 54.03(c) (West Supp. 1995); and *Wyoming* — WYO. STAT. ANN. § 14-1-223(c) (1994). In the same year that *In re Gault* was decided, Normen Dorsen and Daniel Rezneck, appellate counsel for Gerald Francis Gault in the United States Supreme Court, supported the proposition that trial by jury should be equally applicable to hearings in juvenile courts where *delinquency* was at issue. They wrote that "[j]uvenile court judges have no demonstrated superiority to juries in determing whether a law violation has been committed.... Other values of the jury system...are as applicable for juveniles as for adult offenders." Normen Dorsen & Daniel A. Rezneck, *In re Gault and the Future of Juvenile Law*, 1 Fam. L.Q. 1 (Dec. 1967).

69. *IJA/ABA Juvenile Justice Standards, Standards Relating to Adjudication, Standard 4.1 Trial by jury* notes "A. Each jurisdiction should provide by law that the respondent may demand trial by jury in adjudicatory proceedings when respondent has denied the allegations in the petition," and "B. Each juridiction should provide by law that the jury may consist of as few as [six] persons, and that the verdict of the jury must be unanimous." *Id.* at 51.

state public policy."[70] Two final issues left unresolved by the *Gault* majority were, first, whether or not a juvenile should enjoy a right to a "public" hearing[71] and, secondly, should a juvenile incarcerated in juvenile detention pending a hearing on the merits of a petition be entitled to release on bail?[72]

C. *In re Gault* and the Assault on *Parens Patriae*

The majority opinion in the *Gault* decision was, in fact, two opinions in one. The first or what one might call the "constitutional law opinion" set out the four procedural steps that affected juvenile

---

70. *IJA/ABA Juvenile Justice Standards, supra* note 69, at 51.

71. On the question of "public access" to juvenile court proceedings that involve delinquency, the *IJA/ABA Juvenile Justice Standards* comes out in favor of a right of access. *Standard 6.1 Right to a public trial*, states that "[e]ach jurisdiction should provide by law that a respondent in a juvenile court adjudication proceeding has a right to a public trial." *Id*. at 70. The *Commentary* section after *Standard 6.1*, states in part that "[i]t would appear that the best solution is to assure the respondent a right to a public trial.... With advice of counsel, he or she may waive this right." *Id*. at 72. The right of an adult charged with crime to have a "public" trial was commanded by the United States Supreme Court in *In re Oliver*, 333 U.S. 257 (1948). However, because the Court in *Gault* did not rest its various rulings on the need to prevent disparity of treatment between juvenile and adult, it is debatable whether it will eventually command a "public trial" for juveniles. By its failure to rely on the Equal Protection Clause, combined with the recognition that the juvenile court does have unique features worth saving, it is presumptuous to assume that the Supreme Court will command such a federal constitutional requirement even for juveniles tried in juvenile court on felony-type delinquency petitions.

72. The bail question remains unsettled as the juvenile court nears its centennial. Bail has generally been considered a "non-issue" in juvenile law largely because most juveniles are released outright to the custody of a parent of guardian. At the time of *In re Gault* in 1967, the weight of authority on this subject was decidedly *not* in favor of granting bail to juveniles. Since *Gault*, there have been a number of states who still follow pre-*Gault* authority and disallow bail for minors, relying instead on alternative release criteria. The potential is present, however, for the bail question to again arise due to the steady "recriminalization" of juvenile justice since the mid-1970s. Samuel M. Davis notes that "bail should not be accorded a child as a matter of right,...because the child may be in need of care, supervision, or protection that might be denied him or her without proper inquiry into the conditions and environment into which he or she will be released." SAMUEL M. DAVIS, RIGHTS OF JUVENILES: THE JUVENILE JUSTICE SYSTEM 3-58.5–3-58.6 (2d ed. 1996).

courts nationwide when delinquency and loss of liberty were at issue. The second or "policy opinion" was highly critical of the juvenile court apparatus in America not only in the sixties, but much further back in time. It is to this second, or "policy" portion of the opinion that will now be discussed.

Justice Fortas and his majority colleagues railed against the doctrinal development of *parens patriae* employed by juvenile courts since their inception. In addressing the issues of treatment and rehabilitative care, long the mainstay of child saving Progressives, Fortas noted that[73]

> These results were to be achieved without coming to conceptual and constitutional grief, by insisting that the proceedings were not adversary, but that the State was proceeding as *parens patriae*. The Latin phrase proved to be a great help to those who sought to rationalize the exclusion of juveniles from the constitutional scheme; *but its meaning is murky and its historic credentials are of dubious relevance.* (Emphasis added).

By 1967, American juvenile justice had, in fact, begun to suffer both "conceptual and constitutional grief" at the hands of the *parens patriae* juvenile court. Throughout the twentieth-century American juvenile courts had rested content in the way they handled children and their attendant legal problems. Now, in the late 1960s, came a United States Supreme Court ruling that literally threw cold water on one of the most cherished precepts of juvenile law.

In re Gault[74] effectively abolished the *parens patriae* doctrine in the adjudicatory stage of a delinquency case. The juvenile judge, the probation staff and the juveniles were now legally separated from a Siamese-like relationship that had existed among them since the turn of the century. Indeed, something had gone very wrong with a system that was designed to help, but, during the course of six-and-a-half decades became a system flawed by changing times and changing legal doctrine. Nine years before the *Gault* case, law professor Francis A. Allen had warned that[75] "[t]he semantics of 'socialized justice'

---

73. 387 U.S. 1, 16 (1967).
74. 387 U.S. 1 (1967).
75. Francis A. Allen, *The Borderland of the Criminal Law: Problems of Socializing Criminal Justice*, 32 Soc. Service Rev. 116 (1958).

are a trap for the unwary...." He then added this cogent observation;[76] "if the measures taken result in the *compulsory loss of the child's liberty*...the impact on the affected individual is *essentially a punitive one.*" (Emphasis added). The almost global commingling in the 1960s and in prior years of delinquency definitions with acts and statuses having little to do with serious law violation created a conundrum for the Court. Recognizing that its decision would immediately impact a wide range of previously sacrosanct policies, the Court wisely chose to limit its holding to cases of delinquency where a loss of liberty was a possibility.

"Socialized justice" in Allen's turn of phrase had reached a point by 1967 where it encumbered a number of children who were being hauled into juvenile courts on a variety of charges, many of which still harkened back to late nineteenth- and early twentieth-century conceptions of "pre-delinquency." These *status* offenses, so-called, were the alleged precursors to more serious law violation, or so conventional wisdom maintained. The vice in juvenile court operation by the 1960s was that its everyday practices—while benevolent in rhetoric—was punitive in practice. Nonetheless, no one connected with the juvenile court establishment wished to face this reality and this abdication of purpose paved the way for a pedestrian dispute like that of Gerald Francis Gault to reconstruct a major portion of juvenile law. Recall that Gault was sentenced to what amounted to nearly a six-year incarceration on "facts" that were not fully developed, on a statute the juvenile court judge was not totally conversant with, and on "testimony" of no one other than the juvenile, his parents and the probation officer. The real tragedy of Gerald Francis Gault's case was not only the cavalier treatment accorded him by the Arizona juvenile court, but also by the fact that Gault's situation was not unique—it happened on a regular basis in countless other juvenile tribunals throughout the land. There was a double standard at work here. An adult charged with the same offense would have received, at most, a short jail term and a small fine, or both. The question troubling Justice Fortas was *why* did a juvenile accused of the same behavior, end up behind bars in a state training school for nearly six years? The answer was simple: the juvenile court who committed Gault was doing so under a broad grant of power it assumed under *parens patriae.*

---

76. *Id.*

What is left of *parens patriae* after *Gault's* "constitutional domestication"[77] of the juvenile court? Today few would deny that, in theory at least, the chancery influence in serious delinquency adjudications is no longer present. *Gault* re-introduced the criminal procedure model in delinquency adjudication. In reviving a more adversarial approach to delinquency hearings, the United States Supreme Court played down the *parens patriae* influence, for *parens patriae* does not mix well with an adversary posture. Although the majority opinion was not entirely free of ambiguity, it is believed that the "worst of both worlds" rationale comes as close as any in justifying the *Gault* holding. This is a sad commentary on twentieth-century juvenile court practice. Sad all the more because on the cusp of the twenty-first century, we are apparently in a retrograde posture in both juvenile delinquency adjudication and in juvenile corrections.

In the favored position of hindsight, looking back at the work of the American juvenile court in its first century of operation, one can perhaps simply conclude that the court's rhetoric outpaced its reach. The *parens patriae* heart of the child saving juvenile court was really not aimed directly at dealing with the amoral, violent and predatory delinquency that has emerged in postmodern America. The *parens patriae* juvenile court was a court constructed around the principle that the state could intervene coercively in the lives of certain youngsters when their teenage behavior flashed semaphoric signals of potential degeneration and lawlessness. As a socio-legal agency of child welfare, the court could attempt to change, both for the short and for the long run, a child's life chances. The *Gault* decision forced the juvenile court as an institutional component of the American legal system to face the issue of whether or not the *parens patriae* juvenile court had the "right" to intervene in the lives of minors unconstrained by simple due process. The answer was no. In that context, most would probably agree that *Gault* was correct. The *parens patriae* power in its pure form was both constitutionally suspect and correctionally overbroad. Far too many children were being committed on a routine basis to state institutions under omnibus delinquency definitions that made a mockery of simple justice. While the Supreme Court did not emphasize it, perhaps in the back of the justice's minds dwelt a very real concern for the mischief caused by sixty-plus years of rather vague juvenile court legislation and its attendant interpreta-

---

77. Paulsen, *supra* note 2.

tion by the nation's juvenile bench. The juvenile court has always been a creature of statutory law. That law can be changed, modified or even abolished by legislative will. The differential definitions of delinquency contained in many juvenile codes in the 1960s and before literally invited judicial abuse. In 1904, it was noted in the *Proceedings of the National Conference on Charities and Correction*[78] that "[o]ur country has inherited the powers of the ancient Court of Chancery...Our judges have recently discovered in these principles *very large and unsuspected powers and have used them.*" (Emphasis added). Certainly between 1904 and 1967, an enormous accretion of power evolved in the hands of the juvenile bench. This accretion was aided, of course, by a rapid proliferation of social welfare based delinquency statutes that had no penal law counterpart in precision of language. Legislation of any kind must, of necessity, be somewhat general in nature because lawmakers cannot possibly provide in advance for all the contingencies that might occur. Nonetheless, juvenile court legislation was a separate case in point. Platt[79] observed in his first edition account of the forces that established the Chicago juvenile court that legislation

> brought within the ambit of governmental control a set of youthful activities that had been previously ignored or handled informally. It was not by accident that the behavior selected for penalizing by the child savers—drinking, begging, roaming the streets, frequenting dance halls and movies, fighting, sexuality, staying out late at night, and incorrigibility...

was behavior that had a pre-delinquent slant. What Platt could also have said was that these behavioral markers laid the foundation for widespread legislative enactment of additional statutes that penalized a congeries of annoying, but relatively harmless, youthful behavior. As noted earlier, by 1927, every jurisdiction in the nation except Maine and Wyoming had enacted some form of juvenile code. Between 1927 and 1967, these statutes grew in the types of proscribed behavior and in the vagueness of language describing that behavior. The tendency during this era was to lump together offenses only for children with

---

78. Charles R. Henderson, *Theory and Practice of Juvenile Courts* in *Proceedings of the National Conference on Charities and Correction* 358, 364 (1904).

79. ANTHONY M. PLATT, THE CHILD SAVERS: THE INVENTION OF DELINQUENCY 139 (1969).

those which were a clear violation of case or statutory criminal law. Once this took place, behaviors which should have been separated both for doctrinal and practical purposes, became fungible—like different sizes and grades of grain being commingled in one large batch. Once this occurred, the unwitting groundwork was laid for a constitutional judgment on delinquency adjudication in the juvenile court. Thus the original legal sin of differential delinquency definitions was a major component in the critical essay portion of the *Gault* majority opinion.

Coincident with these early twentieth-century developments in statutory ambiguity came an equally significant development from a purely judicial perspective. Until the founding of the juvenile court, children tried in adult criminal courts were cast in an adversary posture against the state with the court itself taking a traditionally "passive" or referee role in the entire affair. With the establishment of the juvenile court and its rapid proliferation throughout the country by the late 1920s, the role of the juvenile judge became crucial. Lawyers, of course, were not generally welcome in juvenile courts. Few ever ventured into a juvenile court on behalf of a child client. Because of the representational vacuum left by the almost self-imposed absence of advocates generally, juvenile court judges undertook to place themselves squarely in the middle of the controversies coming before them. Instead of playing a traditional umpire role, the judges, in effect, became a *de facto party* to the controversy before them. On the surface, such a change passed virtually unnoticed and uncommented upon for many years.[80] Its eventual impact, however, caused a shift in emphasis in juvenile litigation that would ultimately bring the entire system into constitutional disrepute. As a *party*, juvenile judges felt obliged to delve more deeply into the myriad "causes" of delinquency since the aim of the system was rehabilitating the youth employing the teachings of positive criminology. The juvenile judge now began wearing two hats—one representing the coercive power of the state as *parens patriae*—the other ostensibly representing the juvenile to see to it that the child's "best interests" were protected and advanced.

---

80. But in 1913, Roscoe Pound noted that "the powers of the court of star chamber were a bagatelle compared with those of American juvenile courts....If those courts chose to act arbitrarily and oppressively they could cause a revolution quite as easily as did the former [Star Chamber]." Roscoe Pound, *The Administration of Justice in the Modern City*, 26 Harv. L. Rev. 302, 322 (1913).

Time and circumstance have shown that this role ambiguity of the juvenile bench created more problems than solutions. Abraham S. Blumberg[81] noted in 1979 that

> [a]ctually, attempts at social engineering by the "child savers" was not inspired by benevolence or humanitarianism but *rather* an ironfisted need to control youthful nonconformity in the guise of relieving children of the impact of the adult criminal process. Their romantic paternalism was grounded in a distrust and abhorrence of what they saw as the corrupting, evil influence of cities upon the waves of poor immigrant youth....It is of course a fiction that a child who is adjudged "delinquent" in the course of a "socialized" process is not a "criminal" and does not have a "record." (Emphasis in original).

From the 1920s until the emergence of the Warren Court in the 1950s, juvenile delinquency gradually became more pervasive and socially threatening. During the lengthy pre-*Gault* era, the judicial scale began to tip noticeably toward the direction of state intervention in an array of delinquency petitions camouflaged under the *parens patriae* doctrine. The "two-hats" theory of decision-making remained, as it had for most of the century prior to the 1960s, a mere rhetorical gloss. Even as late as the early 1960s, some juvenile court jurists were quite eager to reaffirm the long-standing role of *parens patriae* in the delinquency context. Writing three years prior to the *Gault* decision, Ohio juvenile court judge Rhea Brown[82] noted that

> The general conclusions to be drawn on this subject are that because of the disabilities that...accompany infancy, children are not entitled to freedom from restraints and training as adults are. Since the wise parent not only can, but does restrain and correct his child, when it is necessary and when because of the failure or incapacity of the parent, it is necessary for the state to take over these parental functions, it cannot be said that the child is being deprived of his liberty without due process of law, or denied the

---

81. Abraham S. Blumberg, Criminal Justice: Issues and Ironies 292–93 (2d ed. 1979).

82. Rhea Brown, *The Constitutional Problems of the Juvenile Court Law,* 50 Women L.J. 89, 103 (1964).

equal protection of the laws, or any other rights protected by the Bill of Rights.

Few would quarrel with Judge Brown regarding what a wise and compassionate parent would do regarding appropriate discipline, restraint and correction. The truth of the matter was, and is, that children who become emmeshed in the juvenile justice system rarely have the luxury of wise parental surrogates; otherwise, they would never enter the system in the first place. But, having made a decision to intervene for whatever reason does not, the Warren Court said, give the state *carte blanche* authority to play the parental role in a manner equally as officious, uncaring and insensitive as a juvenile's natural parents might under similar circumstances. Apparently, many juvenile court judges up to the very eve of the *Gault* decision continued to cling to the notion that because the doctrine of *parens patriae* was both historically and philosophically compatible with their own notions of justice, attacks on the concept were both ill-advised and conceptually misplaced. Likewise, a plethora of juvenile jurists could still take comfort in the dicta constantly repeated since 1899 that juvenile delinquency was a *civil status*, not a criminal act. In the mid-1950s, Chief Justice Stern of the Supreme Court of Pennsylvania epitomized the grip *parens patriae* had on the judiciary. In speaking to the issue of the type of proceeding commonly handled by juvenile courts in his state, Justice Stern said that[83]

> The proceedings...are not in the nature of a criminal trial but constitute merely a civil inquiry or action looking to the treatment, reformation and rehabilitation of the minor child. *Their purpose is not penal but protective...* to check juvenile delinquency and to throw around a child, just starting, perhaps, on an evil course and deprived of proper parental care, the strong arm of the State acting as *parens patriae.* The State is not seeking to punish an offender but to salvage a boy who may be in danger of becoming one, and to safeguard his adolescent life....No suggestion or taint of criminality attaches to any finding of delinquency by a Juvenile Court. (Emphasis added).

---

83. *Holmes' Appeal,* 379 Pa. 599, 603–04, 109 A. 2d 523, 525, *cert. denied,* 348 U.S. 973 (1955).

Contrast that language from a high state court in the 1950s with this language by Justice Fortas in 1967 in *Gault*:[84] "[t]he juvenile offender is now classed as a 'delinquent.'...It is disconcerting, however, that this term has come to involve only slightly less stigma than the term 'criminal' applied to adults." By 1967, the term "delinquency" was behaviorally amorphous. The *Harvard Law Review* noted that "[i]n *Gault* the Court dispelled the illusion...that procedural safeguards [for delinquents] were determined by interpretation of juvenile court statutes, not the Constitution."[85] The language employed by Justice Stern in the case of *Holmes' Appeal*,[86] was a classic example of our perennial pertinacity regarding the *parens patriae* doctrine in the service of social justice. But its rhetorical ability to persuade was wearing dangerously thin. In 1956, one year after the Pennsylvania decision in *Holmes' Appeal*, the United States District Court for the District of Columbia in *In re Poff*[87] noted that when a minor commits an act which would otherwise be an adult crime, due process requires that the child be advised beforehand that he or she is entitled to effective assistance of counsel in the District of Columbia juvenile court. The *Poff* court noted that[88]

> The government urges upon this Court that the constitutional guarantee of the right to assistance of counsel in all criminal prosecutions is not applicable to proceedings before the Juvenile Court to determine delinquency of a child,...[y]et by some sort of rationalization, under the guise of protective measures, we have reached a point where rights once held by a juvenile are no longer his. Have we now progressed to a point where a child may be incarcerated and deprived of his liberty during his minority by calling that which is a crime by some other name?

In 1957, a United States District Court in New Jersey[89] had before it a *habeas corpus* proceeding involving a finding of delinquency under the New Jersey Juvenile Court Act. The state contended, among

---

84. 387 U.S. 1 (1967).

85. Note, *Procedural Due Process at Juvenile Sentencing for Felony*, 81 Harv. L. Rev. 821, 829 (1968).

86. *Holmes' Appeal*, 379 Pa. 599, 109 A 2d 523 (1955).

87. 135 F. Supp. 224 (D.D.C. 1955).

88. *Id.* at 225–26.

89. *Application of Johnson*, 178 F. Supp. 155 (D.C.N.J. 1957).

other things, that traditional due process does not apply to a juvenile in a state delinquency proceeding. In answer to that argument, the court replied that such a contention "…must surely have been intended to mean only that the rigor of certain judicial and correctional procedures ordinarily applied in cases of adult offenders, need not be applied in cases of juvenile offenders. It cannot mean that the constitutional protections of fundamental fairness are to be constricted."[90] In another District of Columbia decision in 1958,[91] Judge Holtzoff ruled that "[p]recious constitutional rights cannot be diminished or whittled away by the device of changing names of tribunals or modifying the nomenclature of legal proceedings. The test must be the nature and the essence of the proceeding rather than its title."[92] Thus by the late 1950s there was a growing unease in some jurisdictions about the grip that *parens patriae* still exerted on juvenile tribunals and its stifling effect on due process. The dicta in *Poff, Johnson* and *Dickerson* were clear indications that when a juvenile was charged with a liberty-depriving act of delinquency, due process and fair treatment demanded that the child be given at least basic procedural protections. In fact, the United States Supreme Court specifically cited both *Poff* and *Johnson* in its majority opinion in *Gault.*[93]

While there was no doubt that the *Gault* holding erased *parens patriae* in the adjudicatory segment of a delinquency hearing, the Court took special care to note that *parens patriae* should not be considered moribund in *other phases* of juvenile justice. Repeating the admonition he had made earlier in *Kent*,[94] Justice Fortas stated clearly that "We do not mean…to indicate that the hearing to be held must conform with *all* of the requirements of a criminal trial or even of the usual administrative hearing; but we do hold that the hearing must measure up to the essentials of due process and fair treatment."[95] (Emphasis added). In his concurring opinion in *Gault*, Justice Black saw due process rights for juvenile through his long-advocated total incorporation prism that he had championed since his famous dissent in

---

90. *Id.* at 160.
91. *United States v. Dickerson*, 168 F. Supp. 899 (D.D.C. 1958).
92. *Id.* at 902.
93. *Application of Johnson* was cited in f.n. 8, 387 U.S. at 12 and *In re Poff*, was cited in f.n. 55, 387 U.S. at 35.
94. 383 U.S. 541 (1966).
95. *Id.* at 562.

Adamson v. California[96] in 1947. Justice Black wrote that "[a]ppellants are entitled to these rights, not because of 'fairness, impartiality and orderliness—in short, the essential of due process' require them ...but because they are specifically and unequivocally granted by provisions of the Fifth and Sixth Amendments which the Fourteenth Amendment makes applicable to the States."[97] According juveniles "the essentials of due process" in a *delinquency* determination left open both the pre-adjudicatory and the dispositional stages of a delinquency case to further speculation. The high court wisely chose to sidestep those two areas not only out of a sense of judicial reserve and a "this case only" approach in *Gault*, but also out of a policy choice that apparently *sub silentio* approved of a *parens patriae* application in these beginning and ending stages. The *Gault* majority was aware of the then recently released document titled *A Report of The President's Commission On Law Enforcement And Administration of Justice*. In a portion of that voluminous national recital on crime in the United States, the *Report* noted that "[d]elinquency is not so much an act of individual deviancy as a pattern of behavior produced by a multitude of pervasive societal influences well beyond the reach of action by any judge, probation officer, correctional counselor or psychiatrists."[98] In distancing itself from constitutionally intruding into the intake and dispositional components of juvenile justice, the Supreme Court was at least allowing the *parens patriae* concept to remain viable in those two areas of practice.

In re Gault[99] shifted the *parens patriae* focus from the basic legal question of guilt or innocence in the fact-finding portion of the proceedings to the intake and dispositional processes whereby a broader discretionary decision-making process was demanded. The Court left the more preventive and penologically-oriented intake and dispositional phases intact for continued employment of the *parens patriae* ideology. In sum, there was a constitutional trade-off at work here. The evaporation of *parens patriae* in the adjudicatory phase was compensated for by allowing it to remain as a force for prevention and rehabilitation—two of the major historical goals undergirding the court's formation.

---

96. 332 U.S. 46 (1947).

97. 387 U.S. at 61.

98. *Report of the President's Commission on Law Enforcement and Administration of Justice: The Challenge of Crime in a Free Society* 80 (1967).

99. 387 U.S. 1 (1967).

Chapter Seven

The Juvenile in the Arms of the Court— Disposition

A. Routine Sanctions and the Influence of Positive Criminology

The symbiotic relationship between positive criminology and the juvenile court has been one of the few constants in the juvenile justice century. If one were to reflect on a time line for this association, one would probably have to assume a very close relationship for about the first seventy-five years of the court's life. The last quarter of the twentieth century, however, has been an era shorn of the rehabilitative ideal in general and especially in delinquency litigation.

Positivism in criminology traces its beginnings to that remarkable trio of Italians: Cesare Lombroso, Raffaele Garofalo and Enrico Ferri.[1] Positivism employs at least two major constructs in its quest for identifying the etiology of juvenile deviance—science and technique. Science in the sense that the positive approach to criminality studies the individual by means of the application of non-judgmental statistical, medical and psychological analyses coupled with a methodology that winnows out, where possible, biases that would otherwise sully the enterprise. Technique in the sense that positivism enlists a variety of social science and medical disciplines and their collective wisdom to promote the rehabilitative ethos of the *parens patriae* court. It was standard child saving gospel that social and medical science in the early twentieth century held all the answers to both prevention and cure. Although not specifically employed in the pio-

---

1. *See generally* Philip Jenkins, *The Radicals and the Rehabilitative Ideal, 1890–1930,* 20 CRIMINOLOGY 347 (Nov. 1982); *The Positive School of Criminology: Three Lectures by Enrico Ferri* (Stanley E. Grupp ed. 1968); Marvin E. Wolfgang, *Criminology and the Criminologists,* 54 J. Crim. L.C. & P.S. 155 (1963); Marvin E. Wolfgang, *Pioneers in Criminology: Cesare Lombroso (1835–1909),* 52 J. Crim. L.C. & P.S. 361 (Nov.–Dec. 1961); ENRICO FERRI, CRIMINAL SOCIOLOGY (J.I. Kelly & John Lisle trans. 1917); and CESARE LOMBROSO, CRIME: ITS CAUSES AND REMEDIES (1911).

neering child saving literature, the juvenile court began operation under what Francis A. Allen called the "rehabilitative ideal."[2] This term epitomized both the rationale for and the therapeutic milieu of a separate court for children. In short, the argument went, if the antecedents of deviant and criminogenic behavior can be identified, that behavior can be modified. The juvenile court was society's unique institutional solution to the heretofore illusive search for a politico-legal response to juvenile delinquency.

The intake and adjudicatory phases of a delinquency case were mere necessary preliminaries to the assumed supermarket of therapeutic social services available to the child. The dispositional phase of the process was the gateway to the child savers Nirvana—treatment, benevolence, restoration and prevention. As originally conceived, the dual dispositional alternatives of probation or institutional placement were considered logical choices. Of these two, probation was the heart of the court's treatment and rehabilitative regimen. The founders viewed the probationary prong of the disposition segment to be the one area where an individual trained in social science techniques could fulfill the *parens patriae* promise to the juvenile. As Marygold S. Melli noted,[3] "[t]he new court was developed on a non-adversarial clinical-therapeutic model. Its primary role was to determine what course of treatment was necessary to rehabilitate the juvenile." This somewhat unorthodox quasi-medical model of correction placed probation at the apex of its programmatic efforts to reform troubled youth.

---

2. FRANCIS A. ALLEN, THE BORDERLAND OF CRIMINAL JUSTICE (1964) denoted the rehabilitative ideal in the following language:

> a complex of ideas which, perhaps, defies an exact definition. The essential points, however, can be identified. It is assumed, first, that human behavior is the product of antecedent causes. These causes can be identified as part of the physical universe, and it is the obligation of the scientist to discover and to describe them with all possible exactitude. Knowledge of the antecedents of human behavior makes possible an approach to the scientific control of human behavior. Finally...it is assumed that measures employed to treat the convicted offender should serve a therapeutic function; that such measures should be designed to affect changes in the behavior of the convicted person in the interests of his own happiness, health, and satisfaction and in the interest of social defense. *Id.* at 26.

3. Marygold S. Melli, *Juvenile Justice Reform in Context*, 1996 Wis. L. Rev. 375.

By 1899, probation and its earlier successes were well known to the juvenile court's Victorian organizers and it afforded them a ready-made laboratory for implementing the tenets of positive criminology. Social workers, psychologists, sociologists, psychiatrists and other less formally trained personnel moved rapidly into the juvenile justice system as the network of juvenile courts burgeoned between 1899 and the late 1920s. From about 1930 until the present day, probation has remained a major dispositional fixture in the treatment armamentarium of American juvenile courts. However, since the 1970s, probation practice in the serious delinquency context has changed to meet both political and judicial demands of a more conservative ideology.

The other historical prong of the dispositional phase is institutional commitment. Juveniles who are either not amenable to mainstream probation or who are perceived to be public safety risks, or both, are more institution-eligible than their less culpable cohorts. The nineteenth century laid the institutional groundwork for the twentieth-century carceral framework. While variations are numerous in structure, programs, staff and funding sources, all carceral institutions have one common denominator—security. Custody has primacy and rehabilitation programs, if any, are often a distant second. During the last half of the twentieth century, probation and institutional confinement have given way to a more varied dispositional menu. The variety encountered is largely dependent upon the size, location, and community culture in a particular region of the country. Because a juvenile judge must be able to fashion a disposition for three separate types of children, the dispositional options necessarily expanded as caseloads increased. By mid-century, the original dual options of probation or incarceration had expanded to include such alternatives as restitution with or without probation, community service performance, youth and family counseling, referral to an external social service or mental health agency, intensive probation, residential placement in specific community group homes, foster home placement, and forestry camp or wilderness programs run by state or private foundations or agencies. These certainly do not exhaust the list, but they are examples of the range of dispositions that some juvenile judges have at their disposal.

By the 1950s, public enthusiasm for the work of the juvenile court was eroding. With the increase in the flow of information created by television and other sophisticated news-gathering agencies, Americans who thought about it at all were beginning to conclude that the juvenile court's performance simply did not measure up to the vision of its founders. The "worst of both worlds" was impinging on the delinquent minor far earlier than either *Kent* or *Gault* had imagined. Yet, at mid-century, juvenile correction at the institutional level and even at the community level was a very low visibility concern to most of the public. "Treatment" for the juvenile could be either community-based or institutional and in certain cases incarceration *per se* was often seen as a superior form of social control. Within certain institutional milieus, the youngster could in fact be introduced to that promised social service supermarket. But here again, rhetoric often outpaced reality and the available treatment resources were often marginal at best. As with probation, the sanction of incarceration carried with it a cruel irony. Under *parens patriae*, the state became the parent substitute, yet no one would seriously entertain the presumption that a bureaucratic sovereign could in any real way measure up to most parents, even those with significant parental deficits. Juvenile institutions—reformatories, training schools or industrial schools—were populated by lost children in a lost world at the mercy of social engineers and wardens who spoke of benevolence but who practiced retribution. Rehabilitation was often little more than a smoke and mirrors game. The entire edifice was exposed to the light of constitutional scrutiny in *In re Gault*[4] and the courts and the public thereafter took away with them a radically changed view of the juvenile court and of juvenile justice in general after 1967.

   Gault, however, did not address the dispositional phase of juvenile court practice. What *Gault* did do was to restructure procedural due process in delinquency adjudications and raise broad public policy issues involving the process and management of an increasingly criminogenic generation of children. Prior to the 1980s, dispositional options in many jurisdictions had collected around a more or less standard set of criteria exemplified by the provisions contained in the *Uniform Juvenile Court Act* of 1968. This model legislation was drafted by the respected National Conference of Commissioners on Uniform State Laws. The Act established four dispositional benchmarks for both deprived and delinquent children: (1) a commitment for disposition of a "deprived child" to include the juvenile being allowed to remain with parents or guardian under court supervision; temporary custody with another person or agency designated by the

---

4. 387 U.S. 1 (1967).

court; or a transfer of the juvenile to a juvenile court in another state where the facts so warrant; (2) placing the juvenile on probation; (3) placing the juvenile in "an institution, camp, or other facility for delinquent children operated under the direction of the court [or other local public authority;"][5] or (4) committing the child to a designated state department for youth or to an appropriate institution for delinquent children.[6]

Secure institutional placement was not generally considered the norm for most juveniles coming to the court charged with an act of delinquency. Probation had become so institutionalized as a dispositional option, that most juvenile judges would defer to that sanction unless there was clear indication of a need for tighter control. However, practices varied widely throughout the United States and some juvenile courts would almost invariably sentence even mildly delinquent or dependent children to confinement for reasons that were often not entirely clear. Through the 1960s, children were being committed to institutional placement for both serious maladaptive behavior and for so-called "status" offenses.

In theory at least, a disposition to an institution presupposes a lack of either treatment alternatives in the community, or a public safety concern for both the youngster and the wider population. Of course, all of this presupposes a deliberative process by the juvenile bench. But as *Gault* graphically revealed, some children were committed to secure facilities on the flimsiest evidence and at the whim and caprice of the judge. The language in the *Gault* majority opinion revealed a sense of distrust, not only because of the facts developed in the case, but also with juvenile dispositions generally. By the late 1960s, evidence had accumulated that many juvenile courts were employing the disposition power to "warehouse" children in secure institutions who should never have been there in the first place. These youngsters— some delinquent and some dependent—were there because of a multitude of factors going far beyond "black letter" legal criteria. Here as elsewhere in juvenile justice, *circumstance* and *context* far more than "the law" came together in the dispositional phase of juvenile proceedings to render irrelevant principled legal doctrine and penological wisdom.

---

5. *Uniform Juvenile Court Act* § 31 (1968).
6. *Id.*

One of the slippery slopes that conveyed these children into institutional confinement was the vague and often global statutory definitions of "delinquency" that placed in the judge's hands almost *carte blanche* power to find a minor delinquent. Gerald Francis Gault was a textbook example of a recipient of this loose and poorly crafted legislative criteria.

B. Delinquency Statutes and the Demise of the Condemnation Sanction

Following the early Illinois practice, statutes in other jurisdictions were enacted using language similar to that in the 1899 legislation. But with the passage of time and as social science became more role dominant in juvenile court philosophy, many states added language to their delinquency definitions not found in either the early juvenile codes or in penal legislation generally. The word "delinquent" became a legal screen behind which hid a number of euphemistic quasi-legal wrongs. The inclusion of behavioral markers as statutory delinquency was all well and good so long as those markers were more or less consonant with their penal law counterparts. However, it quickly became apparent that lawmakers as well as juvenile court judges were caught up in a child savers public relations campaign that early on completely changed the face of juvenile codes. The idea of early intervention to thwart further protocriminal behavior in youth necessarily demanded a statutory base that was accordion-like; one that could expand or contact as new data either revealed or undermined contemporary delinquency theory. These rather remarkable statutory proscriptions allowed juvenile courts to become roving commissions to seek out and "treat" errant youth under their *parens patriae* power. Few would contend that the juvenile court has no proper function beyond its delinquency jurisdiction. However, the question "[d]oes inclusion in the delinquency definition of children who are not offenders but may be in need of protection complicate the concepts of the juvenile court?"[7] was never asked. In the socio-legal culture of the pioneering years of juvenile court expansion, no stock was taken of the issue of overcriminalizing the juvenile court by oversocializing its statutory base. In their heady desire to rescue children

---

7. Sol Rubin, *The Legal Character of Juvenile Delinquency*, 261 Annals 1, 2 (Jan. 1949).

from the more rigid and formalistic criminal law, the early juvenile court devotees failed to isolate a *bona fide* condemnation sanction for "true" delinquency. Had they done so at this nascent stage of juvenile court development, the history of this institution may well have been decidedly different. But, condemnation was not a part of *parens patriae* and few, if any, child savers were willing to indulge in so alien an idea. Thus, a key component of the penal law was swept away in delinquency definitions as part of the wider abolition of criminal law doctrine in juvenile justice generally. Fifty years into the juvenile court's existence, Sol Rubin[8] made an interesting comment when he noted that "[i]f the child's behavior is dangerous to community well-being, delinquency is indicated. If, however, *the child* and *not* the community, is in danger, the child needs protection, *but delinquency is not indicated*." (Emphasis added).

By the late 1940s, more and more evidence was accumulating that indicated that the label "delinquent" bore a stigma of some proportion. For example, the Supreme Court of Virginia in a 1946 decision stated:[9]

> The judgment against a youth that he is delinquent is a serious reflection upon his character and habits. The stain against him is not removed merely because the statute says no judgment in this particular proceeding shall be deemed a conviction for crime or so considered. The stigma of conviction will reflect upon him for life. It hurts his self-respect. It may, at some inopportune, unfortunate moment, rear its ugly head to destroy his opportunity for advancement and blast his ambition to build up a character and reputation entitling him to the esteem and respect of his fellow men.[10]

In the same year that *In re Gault*[11] was decided, the Lyndon Johnson administration published its *magnum opus* on the American crime problem entitled *The Challenge of Crime in a Free Society*.[12] That

---

8. *Id.* at 3.

9. *Jones v. Commonwealth*, 185 Va. 335, 38 S.E. 2d 444 (1946).

10. *Id.* at 341–42, 38 S.E. 2d at 447.

11. 387 U.S. 1 (1967).

12. *Report of the President's Commission on Law Enforcement and Administration of Justice: The Challenge of Crime in a Free Society* (1967).

main document and the accompanying nine *Task Force Reports* on various aspects of American criminality represented "the combined work of 19 commissioners, 63 staff members, 175 consultants and hundreds of advisors."[13] Besides the nine *Task Force Reports*,[14] the study included *Research Studies* and *Selected Consultants' Papers*. The *Task Force Report: Juvenile Delinquency and Youth Crime*[15] consumed a total of 428 pages and reinforced statements such as those made by the Supreme Court of Virginia. It stated:[16]

> So long as the community's classification of a young person remains informal, the likelihood that it can be modified by changing circumstances remains possible. *But the official labeling of a misbehaving youth as delinquent places him in a clear category which is difficult to escape.* Once a youth is stamped delinquent, the resources of the police, the court services, the schools and other official agencies respond to him on the basis of that label, *in a manner different from those without the label.* Further, this label becomes known to the public, whose view of the individual then becomes colored by it. (Emphasis added).

Public policy choice fueled by the rhetoric of the anti-legalist child savers accounted for much of the statutory language that worked its way into the juvenile codes of the United States by the year 1927. Terms such as "truant," "idle," "wayward," "incorrigible," "disobedient," "beyond control of parent or guardian," and others connoted a peculiar statutory list more expressive of socio-psycho-cultural dysfunctions than ones denoting criminal behavior *per se*. These terms did not then and do not now have any adult counterparts in the general criminal law. But, by institutionalizing expressions of distaste in statutory language, lawmakers unwittingly failed to isolate the informal social control sanction of *condemnation*. By removing all traits of condemnation from juvenile law, juvenile codes removed a major

---

13. *Id.* at v., *Summary.*

14. These nine included the following: *The Police; The Courts; Correction; Juvenile Delinquency and Youth Crime; Organized Crime; Science and Technology; Assessment of Crime; Narcotics and Drugs; and Drunkenness.*

15. *Task Force Report: Juvenile Delinquency and Youth Crime, Report on Juvenile Justice and Consultants' Papers, Report of The President's Commission on Law Enforcement and Administration of Justice* (1967).

16. *Id.* at 360.

reinforcing element in the sociology of sanctions. Condemnation can and often does play a role in correction, although it was not so viewed during the halcyon days of juvenile court expansion.

Throughout the history of the American juvenile court, expansive statutory definitions of delinquency reflect the classical paradigm of overcriminalization. We have excessively relied on juvenile courts to perform tasks ill-suited to them, and, in the process have created acute problems of juvenile law administration. By condemning categories of activity under the "delinquency" label that on the adult level lack condemnatory characterization, legislatures have handicapped the enforcement of juvenile law against genuinely threatening conduct.

Writing on the problems of public intoxication in the November, 1967 issue of *The Annals of the American Academy of Political and Social Science*, Gerald Stern noted that[17]

> The effectiveness of the criminal justice system depends upon the respect it commands as an impartial forum. By failing to dispense due process in all cases, the entire system is weakened. Moreover, by handling cases which are regarded as non-criminal in nature, the system breeds disrespect for its institutions.

If we simply substitute the word "juvenile" for the word "criminal" in the above passage, its admonition would still be valid. In the same issue of *The Annals*, Sanford H. Kadish[18] writes "One hopes that attempts to set out the facts and to particularize the perils of overcriminalization may ultimately affect the decision of the legislatures." But precious few "facts" and "perils" of overcriminalization have caught the attention of lawmakers in dealing with juvenile codes throughout the century.

As noted earlier, Judge Edward F. Waite[19] warned: "Has not the time arrived when no tribunal should claim the title of juvenile court, implying in its origin and major application a jurisdiction and proce-

---

17. Gerald Stern, *Public Drunkenness: Crime or Health Problem?*, 374 Annals 153 (Nov. 1967).

18. Sanford N. Kadish, *The Crisis of Overcriminalization*, 374 Annals 170 (Nov. 1967).

19. Edward F. Waite, *How Far Can Court Procedure Be Socialized Without Impairing Individual Rights?*, 12 J. Crim. L. & Criminology 339, 340 (Nov. 1921).

dure followed wholly on the parental idea, without distinction in aim and essential method between delinquent, dependent and neglected wards of the state...?" In the juvenile justice century, Judge Waite's warning has regretfully gone largely unheeded. It was believed by some observers that the *Gault* holding would ignite law reforms to address this issue by promulgating legislation that would separate the truly delinquent from the dependent and neglected child. Apparently, that simply has not taken place. One still can peruse juvenile codes that commingle the delinquent with other non-criminal categories. "Juvenile delinquency," says Paul W. Tappan,[20] "implies a special age range, a more or less distinct court jurisdiction, and a concept of status." He then makes this crucial observation: "There is the further, most significant and more difficult problem of *the behavior* denoted by that term. Here is real confusion in the purpose, philosophy, and the content of the law—and a bewilderment to match in the practices of the courts."[21] (Emphasis added). In 1940, law professors Jerome Michael and Herbert J. Wechsler in their noted casebook on criminal law[22] said that

> [T]he determination of the kinds of behavior to be made criminal involves three major problems: (1) What sorts of conduct is it both desirable and possible to deter; (2) what sorts indicate that persons who behave in those ways are dangerously likely to engage in socially undesirable behavior in the future; (3) will the attempt to prevent particular kinds of behavior by the criminal law do less good, than harm, as measured by their other harmful results.[23]

---

20. Paul W. Tappan, Juvenile Delinquency 15 (1949).

21. *Id.* In *White v. Reid*, 125 F. Supp. 647 (D.D.C. 1954), the court noted that
   Unless the institution is one whose primary concern is the individual's moral and physical well-being, unless its facilities are intended for and adopted to guidance, care, education and training rather than punishment, unless its supervision is that of a guardian, not that of a prison guard or jailor, it seems clear a commitment to such institution is by reason of conviction of crime and cannot withstand an assault for violation of fundamental Constitutional safeguards. *Id.* at 650.

22. Jerome Michael & Herbert J. Wechsler, Criminal Law and its Administration (1940).

23. *Id.* at 11.

Of course, Michael and Wechsler were not discussing juvenile law at all here, but, that exclusion aside, what they did say about criminal law doctrine is most apropos to the delinquency jurisdiction of the juvenile court. Labels notwithstanding, delinquency jurisdiction is Janus-faced—it looks in both directions! In one direction it sees delinquency as a violation of the state penal code, while in the opposite direction it sees delinquency as as nothing more than a congeries of behavioral acts that are child-specific having no criminal law nexus. When statutory language involving two entirely different types of behaviors are melded into one generic proscription, theoretical and practical concerns become confused.

John C. Watkins, Jr.[24] notes that

> Legitimate state force against the various depredations of the adult criminal element find expression in criminal law through the so-called "principle of legality."...Professor Jerome Hall says this principle has two corollaries: "penal

---

24. John C. Watkins, Jr., *Isolating the Condemnation Sanction in Juvenile Justice: The Mandate of In re Gault*, in CRITICAL ISSUES IN CRIMINAL JUSTICE 492 (R.G. IACOV-ETTA & DAE H. CHANG eds. 1979). In 1959, Frederick Sussman compiled a list of thirty-three behavioral patterns or acts that would possibly trigger a delinquency petition under most juvenile codes of the era. Collectively, they were:
(1) violating any law or ordinance; (2) habitually truant; (3) associates with thieves, vicious or immoral persons; (4) incorrigible; (5) beyond control of parent or guardian; (6) growing up in idleness or crime; (7) so deports self as to injure self or others; (8) absents self from home without just cause or without consent; (9) immoral or indecent conduct; (10) habitually uses vile, obscene, or vulgar language in public; (11) knowingly enters or visits a house of ill repute; (12) patronizes, visits policy shop or gaming place; (13) habitually wanders about railroad yards or tracks; (14) jumps on train or enters cars or locomotive without authority; (15) patronizes saloon or dram shop; (16) wanders streets at night while not on lawful business; (17) patronizes public pool room or bucket shop; (18) immoral conduct around school or public place; (19) engages in illegal occupation; (20) engages in occupation dangerous or injurious to self or others; (21) smokes cigarettes or uses tobacco in any form; (22) frequents places the existence of which is a law violation; (23) addicted to drugs; (24) disorderly; (25) begging; (26) uses intoxicating liquor; (27) makes indecent proposal; (28) loiters, sleeps in alleys, vagrant; (29) runs away from state or charitable institution; (30) found on premises occupied or used for illegal purposes; (31) operates motor vehicle dangerously while under influence of liquor; (32) attempts to marry without consent in violation of law; and (33) given to sexual irregularities. FREDERICK SUSSMAN, LAW OF JUVENILE DELINQUENCY 21 (1959).

statutes must be strictly construed, and they must not be given retroactive effect." The first corollary is particularly relevant to delinquency legislation.

Hall's "strict construction" comment refers, in part, to the penal law's careful attention to the *criminal act* as the triggering device for possible prosecution. Note that the emphasis on *the act* is likewise an acceptance of classical criminology's emphasis on that self-same component. *Per contra*, the argument goes, the "act" of delinquency is not of the same order as the "act" of an adult in crime perpetration. Quite the contrary say the juvenile court apologists. The "act" of delinquency is merely the necessary legal predicate for state intervention under *parens patriae* in order to look at *the child as a child*—not for the "act" the child committed! Here we have positive criminology writ large. At the end of the juvenile justice century, one might well ask how in good conscience could this legal sleight of hand have dominated juvenile court practice for so long? More likely than not, very little serious policy choice *queries* were voiced in this field until the last quarter of the twentieth century. But even in this frame of reference, attention has focused more on age, offense and sanction than on wider reform efforts in statutory delinquency definitions. Again, Tappan was clearly on point in 1949 when he remarked that "[a]n evolving jurisprudence of delinquency has been less sure of its ground in this issue of conduct to be made taboo, perhaps than any other branch of law."[25] In that observation, Tappan in a sense laid bare the issue that has plagued juvenile justice since its inception—"conduct to be made taboo." Taboo implies ostracism and community condemnation. Condemnation implies some form of punishment in either the sacred or secular realm, or perhaps in both. What the architects of the juvenile court failed to consider was that by decoupling criminal-based delinquency from its condemnation moorings, they set the stage for a jurisprudence of contradiction. Certainly law can be and often seems inconsistent. But law cannot be consistently inconsistent decade after decade in its keystone jurisprudential role. By abandoning condemnation and taboo in its delinquency jurisdiction in 1899, the juvenile court *as an institution* set itself up for the buffeting winds of change that have plagued it in the years since the mid-1970s.

---

25. Tappan, *supra* note 20, at 16.

C. The Dispositional Dilemma of the Status Offender

The so-called "status offender" is a generic term often applied to what originally was termed a "dependent" child, or, in more modern acronyms CHINS (child in need of supervision): JINS (juvenile in needs of supervision); MINS (minor in need of supervision); or YINS (youth in need of supervision) or some other variant. An important and continuous policy debate surrounds the question of whether or not the juvenile court should retain jurisdiction over these youth. One of the key components in this debate is the question of whether status offense activity is predictive of future delinquent behavior? The assumption is that if non-criminal behavior patterns progress into criminal (*i.e.*, delinquency) activity, then the juvenile court should retain jurisdiction over these children for dispositional purposes. However, there is no unanimity on this latter point. Joseph G. Weiss[26] notes that in self-report data he studied, juveniles tend to commit *both* status offenses and delinquent acts.

From the early juvenile codes to the present, legislatures have dichotomized, at least to some degree, the behavior of juveniles indicative of either true delinquency or offenses only for children. In studying crime and deviance throughout the life cycle, Robert J. Sampson and John H. Laub[27] note that "we contend that childhood antisocial behavior (*e.g.*, juvenile delinquency, conduct disorder, violent temper tantrums) is linked to a wide variety of troublesome adult behavior ..."[28] Their statement of "linkage" of antisocial behaviors in youth to adult criminality is reinforced in other research and in the literature on life course criminality[29] that lends credence to the retention of

---

26. Joseph G. Weiss, Jurisdiction and the Elusive Status Offender: A Comparison of Involvement in Delinquent Behavior and Status Offenses (1980).

27. Robert J. Sampson & John H. Laub, *Crime and Deviance Over the Life Course: The Salience of Adult Social Bonds*, 55 Am. Soc. Rev. 609 (1990).

28. *Id.* at 611.

29. *See, e.g.*, Avshalom Caspi, *Personality in the Life Course*, 53 J. Personality & Social Psy. 1203 (1987); Marvin Wolfgang, Terence Thornberry & Robert Figlio, From Boy to Man: From Delinquency to Crime (1987); Criminal Careers and "Career Criminals" (Alfred Blumstein, Jacqueline Cohen, Jeffrey Roth & Christy Visher eds. 1986); Travis Hirschi & Michael Gottfredson, *Age and the Explanation of Crime*, 89 Am. J. Soc. 552 (1983); and Sheldon Glueck & Eleanor Glueck, Delinquents and Nondelinquents in Perspective (1968).

status offense jurisdiction in the juvenile court. In an early address before the International Convention of Chiefs of Police in St. Louis in 1921, August Vollmer[30] noted that besides what he termed "mental peculiarities and abnormalities" such life course events as "drunken and immoral parents, bad companions, poverty, unemployment and unsatisfied interests"[31] were some of the major determinants of delinquency in his view. It cannot be gainsaid that the "unruly," "dependent" or "status offender" child is a major concern of the juvenile court if for no other reason than there are few other institutional arrangements charged by statute to deal with such a population. Still, the feeling persists in some quarters that juvenile court hegemony over the status offender is misplaced and that the social welfare establishment should assume more or even all of the responsibility in dealing with these youth. This debate is certainly not over and will continue to be a point of contention as we move into century twenty-one. The focus here, however, is how American juvenile courts have handled the status offender, especially in the years subsequent to *In re Gault*.[32]

A decade after *Gault*, the Supreme Court of Appeals of West Virginia had occasion to decide a case[33] coming before it from the Calhoun County Juvenile Court involving a youngster, age sixteen, by the name of Gilbert Harris. It seemed that young Harris was confined in a state forestry camp for boys because he had been adjudged delinquent for missing school for some fifty days. Up until this particular proceeding, the juvenile had never been charged with any act of delinquency, yet he was ordered to be incarcerated for nearly a year beyond the legal age of mandatory school attendance. Harris was mildly retarded and had a facial disfigurement, and, as the court noted, "Petitioner was ridiculed and shunned by his classmates...."[34] After setting forth the provisions of the state statute dealing with delinquent children, Justice Neely noted that the West Virginia laws "fail to meet the equal protection, substantive due process, and the cruel and unusual punishment standards because they permit the classification and treatment of status offenders *in the same manner* as

---

30. August Vollmer, *Predelinquency*, 14 J. Crim. L. & Criminology 279 (1923–24).
31. *Id.* at 280.
32. 387 U.S. 1 (1967).
33. *State ex rel. Harris v. Calendine*, 233 S.E. 2d 318 (W. Va. 1977).
34. *Id.* at 322.

criminal offenders."[35] (Emphasis added). The appellate court was clearly disturbed that a juvenile could be held in state custody for truancy with no prior juvenile record and noted that

> Since the class to which status offenders belong had been created under authority of the State's inherent and sovereign *parens patriae* power...and not under the plenary powers of the state to control criminal activity and punish criminals,...status offenders must be treated in a fashion consistent with the *parens patriae* power, namely, they must be helped and not punished,...otherwise their classification becomes invidious, and accordingly, unconstitutional.[36]

Justice Neely then concluded his opinion by remarking that "no status offender in any event, regardless of incorrigibility, may be incarcerated in a secure, prison-like facility, which is not devoted exclusively to the custody and rehabilitation of status offenders. We emphasize here that State parsimony is no defense to an allegation of deprivation of constitutional rights."[37] In the same year as the *Callendine* ruling, the Appellate Court of Illinois decided an appeal[38] from the Juvenile Division of the Circuit Court of Cook County. Bonnie Jean Terrile, age thirteen, was adjudged an habitual truant and committed to the Chicago Parental School, a state institution for truants. The evidence revealed that the juvenile had been absent from her regular public school classes some 126 days. For the court, Justice Stamos stated that[39]

> The purpose of the compulsory school attendance law...is to assure that all children receive a minimum education... punishment is clearly *not* a legitimate interest. However, the State may not pursue a governmental purpose, albeit legitimate and substantial, by means which abridge fundamental liberties more broadly than necessary. *The purpose must be achieved by means of the least restrictive viable alternative.* (Emphasis added).

In overturning the commitment to the Chicago Parental School, the court remarked that "the record is devoid of evidence that commit-

---

35. *Id.* at 324.
36. *Id.* at 326.
37. *Id.* at 331.
38. *Chicago Board of Education v. Terrile*, 361 N.E. 2d 778 (Ill. 1977).
39. *Id.* at 781.

ment is the least restrictive alternative."[40] The concept of least restrictive alternative is amplified in the *IJA/ABA Juvenile Justice Standards*[41] as follows:

> In choosing among statutorily permissible dispositions, the court should employ the least restrictive category and duration of disposition that is appropriate to the seriousness of the offense, as modified by the degree of culpability indicated by the circumstances of the particular case, and by the age and prior record of the juvenile. The imposition of a particular disposition should be accompanied by a statement of the facts relied on in support of the disposition and the reasons for selecting the disposition and rejecting less restrictive alternatives.

The *Juvenile Justice Standards* here recognize the obvious: that no statutory formulation can establish in advance the multitude of factors that can persuade a judge to either increase or decrease a juvenile commitment order. The least restrictive alternative concept embraces the idea that the court should look to the sanction least restrictive in terms of custodial management. This is in keeping with the long-held criminological view that the deeper a juvenile penetrates the carceral system, the more difficult it is to return that youngster to society as a productive citizen. The least restrictive alternative doctrine, however, did not emerge from either criminology or from juvenile law. Its first application appeared in 1960 in the First Amendment case of *Shelton v. Tucker*.[42] Subsequently, the doctrine was adopted by appellate courts in criminal cases involving the collateral attacks on sentences under the "cruel and unusual punishment" clause of the Eighth Amendment and in other contexts as well.[43] The least restrictive al-

---

40. *Id.* at 782.

41. *IJA/ABA Juvenile Justice Standards, Standards Relating to Disposition* § 34.1 (1980).

42. 364 U.S. 479 (1960).

43. *See, e.g., Adams v. Carlson*, 368 F. Supp. 1050 (E.D. Ill. 1973): *In re Foss*, 112 Cal. Rptr. 649, 519 P. 2d 1073 (1974); *In re John H.*, 48 App. Div 2d 879, 369 N.Y.S. 2d 196 (1975); *L.E.A. v. Hammergren*, 294 N.W. 2d 605 (Minn. 1980); *Egan v. M.S.*, 310 N.W. 2d 719 (N.D. 1981); *West Virginia ex rel. H.K. v. Taylor*, 289 S.E. 2d 673 (W. Va. 1982); *In re Darlene C.*, 301 S.E. 2d 136 (S.C. 1983); *In re D.L.D.*, 327 N.W. 2d 682 (Wis. 1983); *In re V.G.*, 331 N.W. 2d 632 (Wis. 1983); *A.O. v. State*, 456 So. 2d 1173 (Fla. 1984); *R.P. v. State*, 718 P. 2d 168 (Alaska Ct. App. 1986); *Glenda Kay S. v. State*, 732 P. 2d 1356 (Nev. 1987); *In re Michael G.*, 44 Cal. 3d 283, 243 Cal. Rptr. 224,

ternative rubric has also been employed in cases involving contempt of court by a juvenile.[44]

Because the status offender represents such a diverse group of behavioral characteristics, state law on disposition for these youth is far from uniform. Whether one views Sussman's lengthy 1959 criteria for juvenile court intervention and disposition as legitimate is probably academic today. Since *In re Gault*,[45] a number of legislatures have removed some of the more behaviorally vague criteria for intervention in the status offense category in order to tighten juvenile court jurisdiction. For those offenses that remain in the juvenile codes falling within the "status" criteria, the federal government moved to begin the deinstitutionalization of these children when President Gerald R. Ford signed the *Juvenile Justice and Delinquency Prevention Act of 1974*.[46] In the dispositional context, one of the major provisions of this legislation was to actively encourage state jurisdictions to prohibit status offenders from being incarcerated and to remove those juveniles currently in carceral institutions. In a notable book[47] on the continued failings of the juvenile justice system *post-Gault*, Ira M. Schwartz states that "[w]hile the federal agenda and the voices of reformers were calling for deinstitutionalization and the emptying of the training

---

747 P. 2d 1152 (1988); and *In re B.S.*, 549 N.E. 2d 695 (Ill. 1989). In the 1990s, several states, among them Arkansas, Iowa, Louisiana, and North Carolina began employing the "least restrictive alternative" in their statutory schemes.

44. *See, e.g., In re Ann M.*, 525 A. 2d 1054 (Md. 1987) and *A.A. v. Rolle*, 604 So. 2d 813 (Fla. 1992).

45. 387 U.S. 1 (1967).

46. 42 U.S.C. § 5601 *et seq.* (1974). This legislation is premised upon a Congressional finding that "understaffed, overcrowded juvenile courts, probation services, and correctional facilities are not able to provide individualized justice or effective help" to juveniles who are in trouble. 42 U.S.C. § 5601(a)(2) (1974). It is noted by John R. Bird, Marcia L. Conlin & Geri Frank, *Children in Trouble: The Juvenile Justice System* in ch. 11, LEGAL RIGHTS OF CHILDREN (Robert M. Horowitz & Howard A. Davidson eds. 1984), that

> [w]ith this legislation, Congress provides federal grants to state and local programs for education, prevention, diversion, and treatment...As a condition of participating in JJDPA's formula grant program, states must cease the practice of confining status offenders in secure detention centers and institutions as well as the practice of placing children in adult jails. *Id.* at 469–70.

47. IRA M. SCHWARTZ, (IN)JUSTICE FOR JUVENILES: RETHINKING THE BEST INTERESTS OF THE CHILD (1989).

schools, an entirely different agenda was emerging in the states."[48] Schwartz documents what he calls "the disconnect between federal juvenile justice policy and the developments in the states."[49] He then comments almost with an air of resignation that "[t]he *Juvenile Justice and Delinquency Prevention Act* of 1974 has had little impact on reforming the juvenile justice system."[50] The "disconnect" alluded to by Schwartz probably encapsulates as well as any the forces beyond federal legislation that ran counter to the aim of this 1974 legislation. By that date, the winds of change were blowing steadily through statehouse and courthouse alike. When Lyndon B. Johnson's *Report of the President's Commission on Law Enforcement and Administration of Justice* was published in 1967, it contained what was essentially a politically liberal agenda for rescuing the juvenile court from its errant history. The *Task Force Report: Juvenile Delinquency and Youth Crime*[51] had a total of thirty-two consultants, sixteen of whom were either university professors or individuals employed by national think tanks or research organizations. Most of these individuals were tutored in the positive approach to criminality and many were politically liberal. Their recommendations—while both positive and creative—all had at bottom the infusion of more federal funding for both the juvenile court itself and its various satellite institutions of prevention and control. In short, the *President's Commission* report was a decidedly liberal agenda foisted upon an increasingly skeptical and conservative American public. With the arrival of the Nixon administration in 1969, the groundwork was laid for a reassessment and reevaluation of the entire criminal justice edifice.

Although the *Juvenile Justice and Delinquency Prevention Act* was signed into law in 1974, by that time the United States Supreme Court had decided a series of cases in the 1960s and early 1970s that portended change in the "business as usual" approach to both juvenile court fact-finding and dispositional options. For example, *Kent v. United States*[52] and *In re Gault*[53] collectively had established basic due process criteria to be employed in a waiver hearing and in the ad-

48. *Id.* at 7.
49. *Id.* at 16.
50. *Id.* at 17.
51. *Supra* note 15.
52. 383 U.S. 541 (1966).
53. 387 U.S. 1 (1967).

judicatory stage of a delinquency proceeding, respectively. In 1970, the Court ruled in *In re Winship*[54] that the adult criminal law burden of proof "beyond a reasonable doubt" standard would henceforth be required in cases of felony-type delinquency. This change in the burden of proof reflected the Court's concern about the hertofore loose "preponderance of the evidence" totem utilized almost universally by juvenile courts up to that time. *Winship's* holding also raised the level of debate over whether or not delinquency in general and serious delinquency in particular was still a relevant jurisdictional component of juvenile justice. Following close on the heels of the *Winship*[55] ruling came the 1971 decision of *McKeiver v. Pennsylvania*.[56] The *McKeiver* court broke with what many presumed would be a series of juvenile cases following the "selective incorporation" principle enunciated by the Warren Court during the 1960s in adult criminal procedure. In *McKeiver*, the Court ruled that although individual states were free to utilize a jury in juvenile courts as the fact-finder, the United States Constitution did not require a trial by jury in a juvenile court in delinquency proceedings. A reading of the opinion by Justice Blackmun reveals that he and his majority colleagues were still very troubled about juvenile rehabilitation and the continuing failure of the system to live up to its late nineteenth-century ideals. Noting that at least twenty-nine states and the District of Columbia deny a juvenile a jury trial in delinquency proceedings, Blackmun remarked that "[i]f a jury trial were to be injected into the juvenile court system as a matter of right, it would bring with it into that system the traditional delay, the formality and the clamor of the adversary system and, possibly, the public trial."[57] This the Court was unwilling to champion. At mid-decade in 1975, the Court in *Breed v. Jones*[58] granted to juveniles the protection of the Fifth Amendment's "double jeopardy" clause wherein a juvenile is protected from adult prosecution subsequent to the initiation of adjudicatory proceedings in a juvenile court for the same offense.

Kent, Gault, Winship, McKeiver and *Jones* had all involved questions of either procedural fairness or questions regarding the adequacy

---

54. 397 U.S. 358 (1970).
55. *Id.*
56. 403 U.S. 528 (1971).
57. *Id.*at 550.
58. 421 U.S. 519 (1975).

of the fact-finding process. Never had the United States Supreme Court been so actively involved in juvenile court proceedings. It seemed by 1975 that the Court was well on its way toward a complete re-shaping of the entire juvenile justice adjudicatory apparatus. This "trend" was not lost upon politicians, lawmakers and the general public. There seemed to be an increasingly pervasive view that the juvenile court's delinquency jurisdiction, especially that segment dealing with the more serious felony-type behavior, was in a terminal state of existence. What was apparently happening between the mid-1960s and the mid-1970s was, in Barry C. Feld's words "[t]he decline in deference to the professionalism and benevolence of rehabilitative experts" and "an increased emphasis on procedural formality, administrative regularity, and the rule of law."[59] But the Supreme Court's activist agenda did not mention the status offender at all. The Court was primarily interested in bringing specific constitutional protections to those juveniles whose liberty interests were at risk because of a felony-type delinquency charge. Unfortunately, status offenders were also at risk of being incarcerated, despite the passage of the *Juvenile Justice and Delinquency Prevention Act.*[60] By 1974, research indicated that there were approximately 65,000 juvenile status offenders incarcerated in custodial institutions. During this era, "liberals popularized the conclusion that state enforced rehabilitation ultimately resulted in the victimization of juveniles," but "conservatives came to offer a vastly different critique: child-saving contributed to *the victimization of the public.*"[61] (Emphasis added). Yet despite all good intentions, the 1974 legislation made little initial headway. Schwartz[62] was incredulous when, after being sworn in as Administrator of the Office of Juvenile Justice and Delinquency Prevention in January, 1979, he noted that between 1975 and 1979, the admission rates for status offenders in custodial institutions had not significantly decreased! States *were* decarcerating status offense juveniles at one end of the correctional pipeline, but were also continuing to funnel in new admitees at the

---

59. Barry C. Feld, *Criminalizaing the American Juvenile Court,* 17 *Crime & Justice: A Rev. of Research* 197, 205 (Michael Tonry ed. 1993).

60. 42 U.S.C. § 5601 *et seq.* (1974).

61. Francis T. Cullen, Kathryn M. Golden & John B. Cullen, *Is Child Saving Dead?: Attitudes Toward Juvenile Rehabilitation in Illinois,* as quoted in THE NEW JUVENILE JUSTICE 231 (Martin L. Forst ed. 1995).

62. Schwartz, *supra* note 47.

other end to take up the population slack! Clearly, the states' policies were at odds with the mandate of the JJDPA.

Legislation in the juvenile justice field has often been enacted to address certain perceived systemic ills. The JJDPA was motivated, in part, by a series of federal district court opinions in the early to mid-1970s documenting numerous abusive practices suffered by juveniles in state custodial lockups, many of whom were status offenders.[63] The impact of the JJDPA, however, was finally beginning to reap results some fifteen years after its passage. Barry Krisberg and James Austin note[64] that "[i]n 1989, only 2,245 status offenders were in public facilities. However, another 6,863 were housed in privately operated facilities, for a total of 9,098."[65] Thus, over time, state jurisdictions reduced status offender incarceration from approximately 65,000 in 1974 to 9,098, or a reduction in round figures by 56,000 youths by the beginning of the 1990s. Along with such decarceration has come a concomitant move in another sector to incarcerate a large number of youth. Since 1967, America has witnessed the beginnings of the almost total eclipse of the *parens patriae* juvenile court in matters of serious delinquency and its dispositional retrenchment.

D. The Demise of Rehabilitative Penology in Juvenile Delinquency Dispositions

In his concluding remarks delivered in the Louis D. Brandeis Memorial Lectures at Brandeis University in March, 1960, David L. Bazelon, Circuit Judge on the United States Circuit Court of Appeals for the District of Columbia, made a remark that is relevant but often ignored. Said Bazelon,[66] "Crime and criminals belong very much to their particular time and place. They grow out of very specific social settings. Moreover, any system of sanctions and any system of reha-

---

63. In this connection *see Nelson v. Heyne*, 355 F. Supp. 451 (N.D. Ind. 1972); *aff'd* 491 F. 2d 352 (7th Cir. 1974), *cert. denied*, 417 U.S. 976 (1975); *Inmates of Boys' Training School v. Affleck*, 346 F. Supp. 1354 (D.R.I. 1972); *Morales v. Turman*, 364 F. Supp. 166 (E.D. Tex. 1973). The *Morales* case was continuously in the federal courts for over a decade. *See Morales v. Turman* 569 F. Supp. 332 (E.D. Tex. 1983).

64. BARRY KRISBERG & JAMES F. AUSTIN, REINVENTING JUVENILE JUSTICE (1993).

65. *Id.* at 74.

66. Closing remarks of the Hon. David L. Bazelon, United States Circuit Judge, Louis D. Brandeis Memorial Lecture, Brandeis University, Waltham, Mass., March 14, 1960.

bilitation applies to and within a society." The "time and place" of both juvenile delinquency and juvenile delinquents were changing even as Bazelon spoke. It is generally conceded that the *parens patriae*, social service, rehabilitative juvenile court had reached its zenith by the end of the 1950s. Thereafter, there began a slow but steady feeling among the juvenile justice *cognoscenti* that there was something amiss about this institution and the manner in which it went about its assigned tasks.

In their book *The Good Society*,[67] Robert N. Bellah and his co-authors identify a salient point. Institutional authorities as individual human beings bespeak institutional success and failures. They quote anthropologist Mary Douglas where she said that "[t]he most profound decisions about justice are not made by individuals as such, but by individuals thinking within and on behalf of institutions."[68] Since 1960, institutional change across a broad spectrum of American society has occurred. Juvenile court dispositional practices lagged behind changing practices on the adult level largely because of the continuing grip of positivism. However, the 1970s brought into focus some of the parallel changes occurring in criminal justice policy involving adult correction. Douglas' "individuals thinking within and on behalf of" the institutional arrangement called adult corrections surmised that rehabilitative penology was moribund. Many of the recommendations in the 1967 *Challenge of Crime in a Free Society* report were viewed by policymakers as mere positivistic boiler-plate. The arrival of Richard Milhouse Nixon in the White House with his administration's "law and order" rhetoric had its impact. Adult criminality was rapidly being reconfigured back into a classical-neoclassical mind set which would ultimately lead to significant changes in sanction practices for adult offenders. Cesare Bonesana Beccaria's famous 1764 essay titled *Dei delitti e delle pene* (Essay on Crimes and Punishment) was being dusted off and read once again by conservative politicians, academics and jurists. Beccaria's social contract thoughts struck an extremely responsive audience in the post-1960, post-Warren era of the 1970s. He maintained, among other things, that the legislature, not the judiciary, should be the source of law; that the state has an inalienable right to punish and that there should

---

67. Robert N. Bellah, Richard Madsen, William M. Sullivan, Ann Swidler & Steven M. Tipton, The Good Society (1991).

68. *Id.* at 13, quoting Mary Douglas, How Institutions Think 124 (1986).

be proportionality between offense and punishment. Further, Beccaria persuasively argued that *the act* is the true measure of criminal harm, not the intent of the actor and that penalties are matters best handled by the legislature, not by the judiciary.[69] Up through the 1960s, the concepts of the indeterminate sentence, probation and parole, inmate classification procedures, prison treatment programs and the juvenile court idea itself collectively exemplified criminological positivism at its best—but times were changing—especially in the sentencing and dispositional arena. From the early 1930s to the late 1960s, a veritable army of social science and medical professionals had waged what was often considered by them to be a "holy war" on classical and neoclassical notions of crime and punishment. Yet, despite all their efforts, crime in the United States continued to rise. Political scientist James Q. Wilson[70] noted in 1975, in looking back at President Lyndon B. Johnson's crime study that "there was not in being [in 1967] a body of tested or even well-accepted theories as to how crime might be prevented or criminals reformed..." Like its erstwhile predecessor, the *Wickersham Commission Report*[71] of 1931, the 1967 *Report of the President's Commission on Law Enforcement and Administration of Justice* was a gargantuan piece of governmental research that was flawed from its inception. Changes in sentencing policies and other more conservative trends that emerged in the 1970s either disregarded or marginalized most of the major recommendations of the 1967 study. The majoritarian political philosophy of the 1970s regarding criminal punishment was not beholden to the same set of ukases propounded by the political inventor of The Great Society.

While the juvenile court in the immediate post-*Gault* era still clung to most of the tenants of positivism in dispositional decisions, the criminal courts were poised to make a retrogressive move in sentencing policy. However, the appearance of such retrogression was chimerical, for in reality, nothing much had changed. There was little retrogression simply because there had been so little progression. Classical and neoclassical

69. These and other classical principles can be found in CESARE BONESANA BECCARIA, AN ESSAY ON CRIMES & PUNISHMENT (Henry Padlucci trans. 1963).

70. JAMES Q. WILSON, THINKING ABOUT CRIME 56 (1975).

71. Known officially as the *National Commission on Law Observance and Enforcement*, but referred to more often by the name of the U.S. Attorney General who spearheaded the effort, George Wickersham.

policies still dominated American corrections notwithstanding what few inroads positivism had made. Between 1970 and 1976, for example, a series of widely read books and articles were published by respected academics, journalists and other policymakers that moved adult penal policy solidly back into the classical-neoclassical camp where it has remained to this day.[72] The gist of this "revisionist" literature argued for the removal of adult corrections from the "treatment business" altogether. Because this spate of new literature was flowing from some very highly respected sources, politicians, lawmakers and academics all came together in common cause for a revived classical-neoclassical penal agenda. At first blush, this melding of divergent interests seemed bizarre to say the least. Nonetheless, the common strand apparently uniting this critical mass was a deeply held belief that adult corrections was ineffective in rehabilitating offenders and that most of its positivistic ideology was bankrupt. The proponents of this "new" criminology, in the words of Donal E. J. MacNamara,[73] accepted "prisons as a societal necessity..., an end to coerced institutional treatment...abolition or severe *constraints* on parole and acceptance of a deterrent-retributive-punitive rationalization for dealing with offenders." (Emphasis in original). The old but comforting assumptions of classical-neoclassical thought, long entrenched in the criminal law as unassailable doctrine, had once again emerged, phoenix-like from the shattered assumptions and treatment rhetoric of positive criminology.

The great thinkers and commentators of classical and neo-classical criminology tended to be more applied than theoretical in their prescriptions for change. They were not social scientists in the twentieth-

---

72. In chronological order they were: FRED GRAHAM, THE SELF-INFLICTED WOUND (1970); AMERICAN FRIENDS SERVICE COMMITTEE, STRUGGLE FOR JUSTICE (1971); MARVIN E. FRANKEL, CRIMINAL SENTENCES: LAW WITHOUT ORDER (1972); NORVAL MORRIS, THE FUTURE OF IMPRISONMENT (1974); Robert Martinson, "What Works?—Questions and Answers About Prison Reform," 35 Public Interest 22 (1974); DAVID FOGEL, WE ARE LIVING PROOF: THE JUSTICE MODEL FOR CORRECTIONS (1975); DOUGLAS LIPTON, ROBERT MARTINSON & JUDITH WILKS, THE EFFECTIVENESS OF CORRECTIONAL TREATMENT: A SURVEY OF TREATMENT EVALUATION STUDIES (1975); *New York State Report of the Citizen's Inquiry on Parole and Criminal Justice*, PRISON WITHOUT WALLS (1975); JAMES Q. WILSON, THINKING ABOUT CRIME (1975); ERNEST VAN DEN HAAG, PUNISHING CRIMINALS: CONCERNING A VERY OLD AND PAINFUL QUESTION (1975); ANDREW VON HIRSCH, DOING JUSTICE: THE CHOICE OF PUNISHMENTS (1976) and SAMUEL YOCHELSON & STANTON E. SAMENOW, THE CRIMINAL PERSONALITY (1976).

73. Donal E. J. MacNamara, *Medical Model in Corrections: 'Requiescat in pace,'* as quoted in ANNUAL EDITIONS: CRIMINAL JUSTICE 80/81 208 (1980).

century idiom, but rather men who probably would have conceived themselves more as political sociologists of penology! Because of their practical and applied bent, they were chiefly interested in pre-positivistic "legal" explanations of crime and criminality. They placed certainty and order above all other concerns. In the process, they infused adult criminal justice with a measure of consistency and predictability. Their hedonistic calculus combined with what could be described as an administrative-legal criminology, while crude and somewhat metaphysical by modern standards, endures in criminal law doctrine. Their collective views on the criminal law, crime and punishment were robustly embraced by post-*Gault* lawyers, politi-cians and others who had the power to both persuade and to legis-late. Near the end of the 1970s, C. Ray Jeffrey[74] noted that "the lawyer and the politician are so committed to a given view of human nature and justice that an impossible gap has been created between the behavioral sciences and the criminal justice system." In the final thirty years of the twentieth century, criminal justice policymakers have, with few exceptions, identified themselves with the tenets and philosophies of Jeremy Bentham, Cesare Bonesana Beccaria, Sir Robert Peel, Sir William Blackstone and others of similar persuasion. Their task has been made easier when nagging doubts about rehabili-tative penology were expressed by noted men of letters and re-searchers. Public clamor also aided in the process. Thus by the late 1970s, adult penal policy had taken a markedly right turn towards a sociopolitical conservatism of significant dimension. The administra-tive and legal criminology of the eighteenth and nineteenth centuries seems oddly "new"[75] in the late twentieth century. Such a turn of events could not help but have an impact on the dispositional criteria of adjudicated delinquents.

What occurs in criminal justice policy may or may not correspond-ingly occur in juvenile justice. However, throughout the sixties and

---

74. C. Ray Jeffrey, *Criminology as an Interdisciplinary Behavioral Science,* as quoted in CRIMINOLOGY: NEW CONCERNS 17, 33 (Edward Sagarin ed. 1979).

75. Using the term "new criminology" here may be misleading to some extent. In Richard Spark's words, "claims to novelty, in criminology as elsewhere, are bound to be transient things: somebody, someday, is going to come along with a newer criminology a still newer criminology, a newest criminology, and so on." Richard F. Sparks, *A Critique of Marxist Criminology,* as quoted in 2 *Crime & Justice: An Annual Rev. of Research* 160 (Norval Morris & Michael Tonry eds. 1980). As used here, however, the term refers simply to what is perceived to be a renewed embrace of classical and neo-classical ideas in contemporary punishment dialog.

seventies, there were a number of observers of the American juvenile court who believed its rehabilitation rhetoric rang as hollow as did that of adult corrections. The demise of rehabilitative penology in the juvenile court was simply an event waiting to happen. The writings of Norval Morris, Robert Martinson, David Fogel, James Q. Wilson, Ernest Van den Haag, Andrew von Hirsh and Donal E. J. MacNamara, among others, cast a pall over the juvenile court's dispositional premises, especially as it related to the serious, predatory delinquent. Juvenile courts in the 1970s began employing judicial waiver under the *Kent*[76] criteria more frequently to divest themselves of juveniles whom they perceived to be beyond reclamation under the *parens patriae* formula. Also in this connection, legislation began to be enacted to allow not only judicial waiver, but prosecutorial waiver as well. "Ultimately," says Feld,[77] "waiver involves the choice of appropriate disposition of offenders who chronologically happen to be juveniles. The distinction between treatment as a juvenile and punishment as an adult...has no criminological significance other than its legal consequences." The "legal consequences," however, were both serious and long-term. Serious, in the sense that *potentially* lengthier sentences may be given by either a judge or jury and serious in the sense that both negative collateral consequences[78] and death-eligibility may accrue to the new juvenile "convict." While broader constitutional protections may allow for a fairer guilt-determining process, if bargained justice is sacrificed, the juvenile convict faces an array of sanctions far more onerous than he or she would have faced in a juvenile court disposition. In addition to the notable increase in the waiver option, post-*Gault* legislative exclusion statutes added another classical dimension to juvenile justice. Here, the legislative intent was quite clear. Such legislation preempts juvenile court jurisdiction over an age-specific and conduct-specific cohort of juveniles who, in the legislative mind, are "adult" in all but chronological age. In speaking to this issue, Feld[79] remarks that "[l]egislatively defining adulthood entails both empirical judgments and value choices." From an empirical

---

76. 383 U.S. 541 (1966).

77. Feld, *supra* note 59, at 238.

78. On the broad issue of the collateral consequences attendant upon a conviction of crime as an adult, *see Special Project: The Collateral Consequences of a Criminal Conviction*, 23 Vand. L. Rev. (1970).

79. Feld, *supra* note 59, at 239.

point of view, there was an accumulating body of data that indicated that serious juvenile criminality was rapidly getting out of hand. In a 1996 National Institute of Justice *Research Preview* entitled "Youth Violence, Guns, and Illicit Drug Markets,"[80] it is noted that

> The perception that violence is on the rise is supported by data showing a sharp increase in violent crime among juveniles since the mid 1980s. Although the overall national homicide rate has not increased over the past 20 years, homicides by youth under the age of 24 have grown significantly in recent years. Between 1985 and 1992, the rate of homicide by young people, the number they committed with guns, and the arrest rate of nonwhite juveniles for drug offenses have more than doubled....

This report then notes ominously that "...children who are now younger (about ages 5 to 15) represent the future problem, because they are larger cohorts than the current 18-year-old group."[81] In May, 1994, the Office of Juvenile Justice and Delinquency Prevention published a *Fact Sheet* titled "Juvenile Violent Crime Arrest Rates 1972–1992." In that document it is noted that

> the rate of juvenile Violent Crime Index arrests remained relatively constant from 1972 through the late-1980s. In fact, the violent crime arrest rate was near its low point for this period in 1987. In 1990, however, the juvenile violent crime arrest rate broke out of its historic range and by 1992 had reached its highest level in the last 20 years.[82]

The Juvenile Violent Crime Index includes four offenses: murder, forcible rape, robbery and aggravated assault. The *Fact Sheet* concludes that "[i]n the late 1980s *something changed*. A change which is bringing more and more juveniles into the justice system charged with a violent offense."[83] (Emphasis added). Schwartz[84] notes that

---

80. National Institute of Justice (NIJ), *Youth Violence, Guns, and Illicit Drug Markets* (June, 1996).

81. *Id.*

82. Office of Juvenile Justice & Delinquency Prevention (OJJDP), *Juvenile Violent Crime Arrest Rates 1972–1992, Fact Sheet #14* 1 (May, 1994).

83. *Id.* at 2.

84. Schwartz, *supra* note 47, at 34.

"[t]he rates of serious juvenile crime increased sharply in 1985." In March, 1996, OJJDP stated that[85]

> Demographic experts predict that juvenile arrests for violent crimes will more than double by the year 2010, given population growth projection and trends in juvenile arrests over the past several decades.... Juvenile violent crime arrests are increasing, but only a fraction of youth (one-half of 1 percent) is arrested for violent crimes each year. We can interrupt this escalation of violence based on identified positive and negative characteristics—protective and risk factors—that are present or lacking in communities, families, schools, peer groups, and individuals.

In the waiver context alone, OJJDP reported in its *Fact Sheet #18* entitled "Delinquency Cases in Juvenile Court, 1992,"[86] that "[i]n 1992, 11,700 delinquency cases were transferred by a juvenile court judge. Transfers increased 68% between 1988 and 1992...." Adding the recent findings by OJJDP on children excluded from juvenile court jurisdiction by statutory mandate, Susan Guarino-Ghezzi and Edward J. Loughran[87] remark

> that specific exclusions are in addition to the upper age boundaries of juvenile court jurisdiction that automatically exclude all juveniles beyond age fifteen, sixteen or seventeen, depending on the state. Such age boundaries are believed to account for 176,000 youths per year under the age of eighteen, regardless of their offense.[88]

Looking at these figures from simply a narrow time frame from the late eighties to the early nineties, one would have to conclude that both waiver and exclusion provisions enacted since the mid-1970s have significantly changed the face of juvenile court dispositional practice. Some observers of the juvenile court now ask, given facts such as the above, whether we are simply in yet another cycle of dispositional alternatives?

---

85. Office of Juvenile Justice & Delinquency Prevention (OJJDP), *Combating Violence and Delinquency: The National Juvenile Justice Action Plan* 1 (March, 1996).

86. Office of Juvenile Justice & Delinquency Prevention (OJJDP), *Delinquency Cases in Juvenile Court, 1992, Fact Sheet #18* 2 (July, 1994).

87. SUSAN GAURINO-GHEZZI & EDWARD J. LOUGHRAN, BALANCING JUVENILE JUSTICE (1996).

88. *Id.* at 17.

Thomas J. Bernard, in a provocative little book[89] published in 1992, contends that "[t]here is a cyclical pattern in juvenile justice policies in which the same sequence of policies have been repeated three times in the last two hundred years."[90] He further argues that "[p]ast experience suggests that these [post-1975] policies will fail and that they will eventually be abandoned as the cycle of juvenile justice moves to its next stage."[91] While there are many naysayers and abolitionists who are quite ready to debunk Bernard's thesis, he does at least have history on his side and history often has the unsettling habit of repeating itself. Lacking a crystal ball to forecast a future policy shift to abandon the delinquency jurisdiction of the juvenile court for serious law violations, the late twentieth-century emphasis on juvenile accountability and punishment may yet prove to be only a temporary culture-driven legal expediency. On the other hand, the entire *corpus* of juvenile law may be jettisoned to be replaced by some other formal institutional arbiter of social control we have yet to envisage. The point for the here and now as the juvenile court celebrates its century mark is that we are faced with a youth population far different from that we faced in the closing years of the nineteenth century. Contemporary American culture both drives, defines and reinforces juvenile crime through numerous outlets including our media-driven thirst for the bizarre, things salacious, things violent and just simply "things." Children are assaulted by the psychological and structural deficits in the family, the school, the peer group and the urban "hood." The drug trade alone in this nation has become a teenage cultural weapon of mass destruction. The social control mechanisms that existed for youth in 1899 are not the social control mechanisms for youth in 1999. Juvenile justice dispositional policy cannot help but be driven in large measure by the structural landscape of the late twentieth century. The apparent return to a classical-neoclassical *modus operandi* in juvenile court delinquency dispositions can be seen in some ways as simply a groping for solutions to problems that have been and probably will continue to be intractable. Judge Bazelon's comments uttered in 1960 that "[c]rime and criminals belong very much to their particular time and place"[92]

---

89. THOMAS J. BERNARD, THE CYCLE OF JUVENILE JUSTICE (1992).
90. *Id.* at 3.
91. *Id.* at 8.
92. Bazelon, *supra* note 66.

are peculiarly apt today. In juvenile justice, structure drives policy. So long as we live in a cultural structure that seems to marginalize so many crucial socialization processes for a significant segment of underclass children, we will continue to be faced with an enormous delinquency rate. In that event, we cannot expect for policy choices to be other than punitive in dispositional options for the seriously delinquent.

But there is an even more distressing and troubling phenomena "out there" that many would not associate with the recriminalization of the juvenile court. The end of the juvenile justice century finds the nation's population, cultural, racial and ethnic, far removed from those of a century earlier. What we have in the United States in the late twentieth century is a child and teenage population that, on the one hand, is more adult-like, while on the other, is even more vulnerable than their 1899 counterparts. The adult-child or child-adult dyad has changed. Both here and elsewhere, but especially here in the United States, the very concept of childhood and adolescence has been reconfigured. Today we have a pre-pubescent and teenage population that is viewed by the adult world dangerously close to the same way medieval society viewed their children—simply as "little adults." Once this re-identification is absorbed into the culture, the law will likewise begin adopting its doctrine to such a state of affairs. In matters of delinquency, if our legal and cultural constructs combine to re-imagine children as adults in miniature form, such re-imagination can produce significant policy changes. If a twentieth-century juvenile court has laid the foundation for a vectoring off of its delinquency jurisdiction to a twenty-first-century criminal court, a significant reason for such a spin-off can be laid at the doorstep of the new image of legal "infancy."

The United States Supreme Court cases of the 1960s began the nascent re-imaging process, although probably inadvertently. *Kent*[93] and *Gault*[94] in particular were the judicial spearhead of a wider "rights-based" jurisprudence for children that accelerated a cultural process already in existence. By the end of the 1970s there was in place a small but critical body of constitutional caselaw that had judicially exhaulted "childhood" to almost adulthood status in juvenile

---

93. 383 U.S. 541 (1966).
94. 387 U.S. 1 (1967).

law. This change certainly did not go unnoticed in the larger society and as juvenile delinquency became more perverse and was reported with more frequency, the socio-cultural artifact of delinquency as a "childhood" phenomena began to rapidly evaporate.

The last thirty years of the 1900s have seen the American juvenile court's moorings to its *parens patriae* anchor cut loose. *Parens patriae* is a particularly good *philosophical* base for dispositions premised on the delinquent as child. It is decidedly *not* a good philosophical base upon which to premise the delinquent *as an adult*. *Parens patriae* held both an actual and symbolic perspective for the child saving juvenile court. When *In re Gault*[95] disconnected *parens patriae* from delinquency, the juvenile courts' institutional legitimacy was at risk. Note Justice Fortas' words in *Gault:*[96] "it is important, we think, that the claimed benefits of the juvenile process should be candidly appraised...it is urged that the juvenile benefits from the informal proceedings of the court...one in which a fatherly judge touched the heart and conscience of every youth...."[97] Then, citing "a recent study" by sociologists Stanton Wheeler and Leonard S. Cottrell, Jr.[98] Fortas noted that "when the procedural laxness of the 'parens patriae' attitude is followed by stern disciplining, the contrast may have an adverse effect upon the child, who feels that he has been deceived or enticed."[99] All of this, in sum, then led the Justice to intone that "[u]nder our Constitution, the condition of being a boy does not justify a kangaroo court."[100] Laxity produces deception which, in turn, is one of the hallmarks of a "kangaroo court." Laxity in both procedure and in dispositional outcomes were carefully nurtured and institutionalized in the *parens patriae* juvenile court. Gerald Francis Gault's case, in effect, legally deconstructed *parens patriae* in delinquency adjudications and found it wanting in philosophy, in procedure and in dispositional choice.

As earlier mentioned, the *Gault* ruling was a narrow one yet it has had profound reverberations in succeeding decades for delinquency

---

95. *Id.*

96. *Id.* at 21.

97. *Id.* at 25–26.

98. *Id.* at 26, citing Stanton Wheeler & Leonard S. Cottrell, Jr., *Juvenile Delinquency — Its Prevention and Control* (1966).

99. 387 U.S. at 26.

100. 387 U.S. at 28.

dispositions involving felony-type malfeasance. The particular language employed in some segments of the majority opinion became an epiphany for the reconstruction of childhood. The American juvenile court had often employed its delinquency jurisdiction pretextually to encumber numbers of children in a questionable jurisdictional net and now the United States Supreme Court was prepared to finally right that wrong. The Court, paradoxically, also opened a door to what many would consider an atavistic reversion to a more punitive dispositional practice in juvenile justice. An examination of one important segment of that practice follows.

Chapter Eight

The Juvenile in the Arms of the State — Capital Punishment

A. Juvenile Crime and the Ultimate Sanction: The Constitutional Arguments

Capital punishment evokes both rational and irrational responses from a wide audience. Like religion, the proponents and opponents of the death penalty have claims that are staked out not only in theology, but also in moral philosophy, politics, criminology, law and what Michael L. Perlin[1] would label "OCS" or "ordinary common sense." Violent juvenile crime, especially homicide,[2] in combination with a decreased sense of institutional integrity in the operation of the juvenile court in recent years have forced us into a penological dilemma. In this state of affairs the capital sanction for selected death-eligible juveniles seems entirely appropriate. The urge to pun-

---

1. MICHAEL L. PERLIN, THE JURISPRUDENCE OF THE INSANITY DEFENSE 287–294 (1994). In speaking directly to the issue of the defense of insanity, but in comments also relevant to many other legal issues including capital punishment for juveniles, Michael Perlin remarks that "OCS is an incomplete and imperfect tool by which to assess criminality. Anthropologists have shown that the content and style of expression of common sense varies markedly from one place to another." *Id*. at 291.

2. *See generally* Office of Juvenile Justice & Delinquency Prevention (OJJDP), *Juvenile Violent Crime Arrest Rates 1972–1992, Fact Sheet #14* (May, 1994); National Institute of Justice (NIJ), *Juvenile Homicides* (August, 1995); and National Institute of Justice (NIJ), *Youth Violence, Guns, and Illicit Drug Markets* (June 1996). In this connection, the 1996 Report of the National Criminal Justice Commission titled *The Real War on Crime* notes alarmingly in the chapter captioned "Youth Violence and Juvenile Justice" that

> Until the 1980s, the biggest threats to young people were car accidents and suicide....The death rate of homicide in the 1980s of young people aged 15 to 19 increased by 61 percent. Between 1986 and 1992 alone, the number of children in the United States killed by firearms jumped 144 percent, compared to a 30 percent increase for adults. *Id*. at 130–131.

See also Robert Davis & Sam V. Meddis, *Random Killings Hit a High*, USA TODAY, Dec. 5, 1994, at 1A.

ish juveniles as adults through either the waiver or exclusion statute route is simply part of a broader societal trend in the past thirty years to narrow dispositional options for violent predatory delinquency. The national press began voicing concern about serious juvenile crime in the 1970s. For example, in 1975, *Newsweek* published a major piece[3] on juvenile crime and noted, among other things, that "[t]he statistics on child criminals are awesome. Juvenile crime has risen by 1,600 per cent in twenty years [1955–1975]. More crimes are committed by children under 15 than by adults over 25—indeed, some authorities calculate that half of all crimes in the nation are committed by juveniles." The article's author, warming to his subject, then continued:[4]

> In Atlanta, juvenile arrests for arson have tripled since 1970, and in New York, since 1972, burglary and rape charges against juveniles have nearly doubled....In Florida, a 15-year-old boy is sentenced to death for sexually molesting and murdering a 12-year-old girl....Six New York teenagers, one of them 13, are charged with murdering three impoverished men in their 70s and 80s....A boy of 12 in Phoenix carries a .38 revolver to school and holds his horrified teacher and classmates at gun point for an hour before surrendering.

In speaking directly to the point of implementing the capital sanction for juveniles, the article notes that "[t]wo years ago Georgia decided that capital felonies could be tried in adult courts at 13, and this year [1975] New Mexico lowered to 15 the age at which defendants could be tried for first-degree murder."[5] In 1978, in an article in the legal magazine *Juris Doctor*,[6] Lucy Komisar writes that

> It is true that most states have tried to design their new laws to separate the serious delinquent from the minor offender, *but the legislators' patience with all juvenile delinquency is clearly running out. The general trend now is to view offenders less as children to be helped and more as criminals to be punished.*...The media and the state legis-

---

3. Jerrold Footlick *et al.*, *Children and the Law*, NEWSWEEK, Sept. 8, 1975, at 66.
4. *Id.*
5. *Id.* at 70–71.
6. Lucy Komisar, *Putting Johnny in Jail*, JURIS DOCTOR, June–July 1978, at 16.

latures say get tougher, stop "mollycoddling" serious offenders and start treating them more like adults.[7] (Emphasis added).

Ten years later in a piece by Martha Middleton in a respected weekly
of the legal profession,[8] she quotes Donna Hamparian, then the Director of the Ohio Serious Juvenile Offender Project, stating that juveniles are "'not thought of as children today... [t]hey're thought of as
offenders, felons, murderers.'"[9] These comments and countless others
that were voiced in the seventies and eighties in a number of media
outlets set a generally conservative, anti-rehabilitation, pro-punish-
ment tone for juvenile sanctions. In many ways, some of these pronouncements were foreshadowed by the retributive literature of the
early and mid-1970s. Other commentators with varying political, religious and social constituencies joined forces in the debate and the tone
was set for an arguably retrogressive dispositional policy in juvenile
justice that mirrored the public's genuine anxieties. We can look back
on the 1970s as the decade in which juvenile law began a halting but
steady absorption of some of the more conservative penological tenets
prevalent in adult criminal law administration. Elevating the "nothing
works"[10] dictum by sociologist Robert Martinson to almost liturgical
reverence, the rehabilitative ideal in both adult and juvenile corrections went into eclipse. This gradual waning of rehabilitation was par-
alleled by another more pernicious assumption that punishment *qua*
punishment was a worthy goal in its own right both for adults and for
juveniles. While certainly not everyone agreed with this shift in emphasis, the punishment paradigm became the new bright star in the
correctional constellation. As noted in earlier chapters, the decade preceding this correctional shift in perspective—the 1960s—was a time
of both ferment and reappraisal in juvenile law. With the end of the
Warren Supreme Court and the beginning of the Burger Court and the
Nixon administration's "war on crime," strategic operations to amend
the *parens patriae* juvenile court began in earnest. Since 1969, there
has been very little abatement in that effort.

---

7. *Id.* at 19, 23.

8. Martha Middleton, *Punishment or Parenting for Child Criminals?*, NAT'L L.J.,
Apr. 18, 1988, at 1–20.

9. *Id.* at 20.

10. *See* Robert Martinson, *What Works?—Questions and Answers About Prison
Reform*, 35 Public Interest 22 (1974).

Doubtless both violent teenage and sub-teen criminality (especially drug-driven, inner city homicide) will continue to be a serious socio-legal issue. It has dominated public policy choice since the seventies and it will continue to do so after the juvenile court's centennial anniversary.[11] Whether and to what extent this recriminalization of the juvenile court will impact serious juvenile violence is debatable. What is less debatable, however, is the economic, educational, social and familial neglect driven by a minimalist political agenda that has fueled this problem over the final three decades of the twentieth century. Juvenile courts and their satellite social service and treatment agencies of all description have suffered from this state of affairs.

Since the juvenile court and the law it administers is entirely a creature of statute, it was only a matter of time after the turbulent 1960s before legislatures began to react to the public mood for more punitive measures to deal with juvenile violence.[12] The cacophony of appeals to "get tough" with juveniles in general and violent juveniles in particular signaled an attitude change in the body politic. Teenage homicide suspects were rapidly being perceived as less eligible for continued juvenile court disposition. For the lawmakers themselves, this shift away from the *parens patriae* juvenile court for a cohort of predatory amoral delinquents to a criminal court for their trial and punishment was both good politics and good policy. It was, at one and the same time, a reaffirmance of the dual role that general and

---

11. *See, e.g.,* MURIEL GARDINER, THE DEADLY INNOCENTS: PORTRAITS OF CHILDREN WHO KILL (1985); Anastasia Toufexis, *Our Violent Kids,* TIME, June 12, 1989, at 52–58. CHARLES EWING, WHEN CHILDREN KILL: THE DYNAMICS OF JUVENILE HOMICIDE (1990); Edward D. Tolley, *The Execution of America's Children,* 6 Ga. St. U.L. Rev. 403 (1990) and *Beyond the Teen-Age Gun,* N.Y. TIMES, June 28, 1978, at 30.

12. Because of rising crime rates, actual or perceived, state lawmakers began opting for a more aggressive waiver policy that would, in some cases, effectively by-pass traditional waiver criteria established in *Kent v. United States* in 1966. Prosecutorial waiver and the enactment of exclusion statutes began to be employed to strengthen the hand of the state. The National Advisory Commission on Criminal Justice Standards and Goals (1973) rejected statutory waiver. The Commission recommended, instead, that a *mandatory* judicial waiver hearing be held before a juvenile was transferred to a criminal court for trial. Likewise, the earlier *Task Force Report: Juvenile Delinquency and Youth Crime* (1967) rejected statutory waiver and recommended the employment the "least restrictive alternative" principle in juvenile sentencing. Both recommendations were largely ignored.

special deterrence was meant to fulfill. General in the sense that the new punitive "message" would hopefully be heard by potential teenage killers and special in the sense that the spectra of recidivism would be foreclosed for the condemned juvenile. What this spate of lawmaking did not address was whether American society was a willing foil to sanction capital punishment for juveniles regardless of age or maturity level. An even more bedeviling conundrum was whether, assuming death eligibility in a particular case, our post-modern culture had finally bitten the *parens patriae* bullet and was amenable to sanctioning death for juveniles as a criminal justice policy choice? A crucial inquiry embedded within such a conundrum asks whether certain non-legal, *youth specific criteria*, should be factored in to a decision as weighty as the death penalty? Correspondingly, should juvenile justice policymakers consider the fact that four well-respected national professional organizations in the United States had gone on record opposing the death penalty for youth under age eighteen?[13] By the same token, Amnesty International reported that between 1979 and the early 1990s, only eight juveniles had been executed worldwide, yet three of these eight occurred in the United States.[14] No one would suggest that this execution rate is reflective of a floodgate response to increasingly severe juvenile criminality. What this evidence does reflect, however, is that the nation that gave birth to the juvenile court is the only non-third world, post-industrial society on the planet to continue to hold out the death penalty as a viable and *potential* legal sanction for juvenile crime! That reflection, in turn, raises an even more troubling issue that haunts the juvenile court in the last decade of the twentieth century. That issue is this: despite public criticism, confusion in purpose and contradiction in practice, are we ready to jettison juvenile court jurisdiction in homicide cases in order to reify our "culture of punishment?"[15] To address that question, attention will be focused on judicial pronouncements from the Supreme Court of the United States.

---

13. These four were: the American Bar Association; the American Law Institute; the National Council of Juvenile and Family Court Judges; and the National Council on Crime and Delinquency.

14. The remaining five were executed in Bangladesh, Rwanda, Pakistan and Barbados.

15. Perlin, *supra* note 1, at 445.

B. The Juvenile Death Penalty Issue and the United States Supreme Court

Seeking guidance from the opinions of the Supreme Court of the United States is not considered to be a risky venture in the broad field of criminal justice practice. Since the denouement of the Warren Court's liberal block and their agenda for change in the early 1970s, the Court has moved rather rapidly in the direction of endorsing both a conservative and a communitarian ideology in crime control. Rather than establishing mechanistic legal rules and then requiring the states to fall in line behind those rules, the Court, under two post-Warren Chief Justices (Warren E. Burger and William J. Rehnquist), has been far more sensitive to community standards, values and indeed prejudices than its 1960s predecessor. Because of this apparent willingness to take into consideration the pulse of the commonweal in matters of punishment, the Court has moved almost in lockstep with the parallel state efforts to recriminalize juvenile justice.

Putting children to death in this country is by no means a practice of recent vintage.[16] As early as 1642 in Plymouth Colony, a sixteen-

---

16. M. Watt Espy and John Ortiz Smykla have documented a total of 88 executions of juveniles under the age of eighteen in the United States between 1900 and 1959. There was an apparent moratorium on juvenile executions from 1960 until well after the decision of *Furman v. Georgia*, 408 U.S. 238 (1972). The ESPY FILE data on juvenile executions in the twentieth century ceases after the year 1959. According to Victor L. Streib, Dean and professor of law at the Claude W. Pettitt College of Law, Ohio Northern University, nine juveniles have been executed in the United States for offenses committed while under age eighteen between January 1, 1973 and June 10, 1997. These nine were: Charles Rumbaugh (Texas, 1985); J. Terry Roach (South Carolina, 1986); Jay Pinkerton (Texas, 1986); Dalton Prejean (Louisiana, 1990); Johnny Garrett (Texas, 1992); Curtis Harris (Texas, 1993); Frederick Lashley (Missouri, 1993); Ruben Cantu (Texas, 1993); and Chris Burger (Georgia, 1993). Rumbaugh, Roach, Pinkerton, Garrett and Burger were Caucasian. Prejean, Harris and Lashley were African-American and Cantu was Latino. There have been no additional juvenile executions since Chris Burger was put to death in Georgia on December 7, 1993. For a complete and compelling discussion of juvenile executions in the United States from January 1, 1973 to June 30, 1996, *see* Victor L. Streib, *The Juvenile Death Penalty Today: Present Death Row Inmates Under Juvenile Death Sentences and Death Sentences and Executions for Juvenile Crimes, January 1, 1973 to June 30, 1996,* Ohio Northern University School of Law (July 2, 1996). Thus, assuming the correctness of both the ESPY FILE and the data collected by Dean Streib in his *Monograph*, ninety-seven juveniles who committed a crime while under age eighteen have been executed by civil authority in the United States between January, 1900 and June, 1997. Add to this total the 114 executions document-

year-old boy by the name of Thomas Graunger was executed for allegedly committing the crime of beastiality—a mortal offense for both body and soul under Puritan law.[17] As noted earlier by M. Watt Espy,[18] the record of juvenile executions in America during the nineteenth century exceeded the less empirical estimates of many commentators. One reason for this may have been the fact that birth registration data during that century was often inaccurate and haphazard and thus investigators were hobbled by that deficiency. Twentieth-century execution data on the executions of individuals under the age of eighteen collected from both the Espy File at The University of Alabama and from data supplied this author by Professor Victor L. Streib of the Pettit College of Law at Ohio Northern University, document a total of ninety-seven juveniles executed in the United States from 1900 through mid-year 1997.[19] Whether one would characterize such data as troubling or not would depend, in part, upon one's view of capital punishment *per se* and one's stance on juvenile executions in particular. The United States Supreme Court has clearly raised the level of debate in recent years and we will begin with a look at that Court's approach to juvenile executions.

Age and conduct are the two minimum legal criteria to trigger juvenile court jurisdiction. In juvenile homicide situations, the "conduct" of the youngster is generally considered the least controversial aspect of the issue. The real debate involves chronological age at time of crime commission and whether a minor of a certain age is, in fact,

---

ed by the ESPY FILE for juveniles during the nineteenth century and at the end of the twentieth century, assuming no additional executions take place between mid-1997 and December 31, 1999, the United States will have executed a total of 211 individuals whose crimes was committed while they were under age eighteen. Dean Streib notes in his *Monograph* that

> [a]s of June 30, 1996, forty-seven persons were on death row under death sentences received for juvenile crimes....Although all were age sixteen or seventeen at the time of their crimes, their current [1996] ages range from seventeen to thirty-seven....Texas has been by far the largest death row for juvenile offenders now [1996] holding seventeen (36%) of the national total of forty-seven juvenile offenders. *Id.* at 9.

17. In this connection *see* NEGLEY K. TEETERS & JACK H. HEDBLOM, HANG BY THE NECK (1967).

18. 114 juveniles under age eighteen executed between 1800 and 1899.

19. *Supra* note 16.

a "juvenile" or an "adult" for sanctioning purposes.[20] In other words, does the fact that a particular teenager or pre-teen commits first-degree murder have a legal bearing on the criminal responsibility issue in homicide? As late as February, 1939, Frederick Woodbridge in a widely-read law review article,[21] noted that

> [t]he criminal law has been built upon the theory that a person should be held criminally responsible only for acts which he intends to commit. This in turn is based upon the theory of freedom of the will, despite modern psychological theories. This theory of freedom of the will and the requirement of intent is still the basis of the common law of crimes.[22]

Further on, Woodbridge remarks that

> It has been suggested that the establishment of juvenile or children's courts, with consequent provisions that children under certain specified ages shall not be guilty of any crime (usually with some exceptions such murder or treason) shall be held responsible as "delinquents" only, will do away to a great extent with the age lines of responsibility of infants. This has had some effect upon the criminal responsibility of children, *but in the cases exempted the question still arises.*[23] (Emphasis added).

Woodbridge's comments made some sixty years ago still have relevancy.[24] The postmodern debate on juvenile executions in the United States Supreme Court centers around four decisions rendered since 1982.[25] In reviewing these decisions in sequence, one must conclude

---

20. Capital punishment for juveniles is prohibited outright by either case law or by statutory proscription in thirty-one states and the District of Columbia. Thirty-six states and the District of Columbia set age seventeen as the upper age limit for juvenile court jurisdiction.

21. Frederick Woodbridge, *Physical and Mental Infancy in the Criminal Law*, 87 U. Pa. L. Rev. 426 (1939).

22. *Id.*

23. *Id.* at 437.

24. For a more contemporary example of the defense of "infancy" in the post-*Gault* juvenile court, *see* Andrew Walkover, *The Infancy Defense in the New Juvenile Court*, 31 U.C.L.A. L. Rev. 503 (1984).

25. *Eddings v. Oklahoma*, 455 U.S. 104 (1982); *Thompson v. Oklahoma*, 487 U.S. 815 (1988); *Stanford v. Kentucky*, 492 U.S. 361 (1989); and *Missouri v. Wilkins*, 492

that the post-*Gault* Supreme Court has moved closer to the "community standards" approach to capital punishment for juveniles than heretofore existed.

In *Eddings v. Oklahoma*,[26] Monty Lee Eddings, age sixteen, was found guilty of first degree murder by the District Court of Creek County, Oklahoma, upon a plea of *nolo contendere* for the shotgun slaying of an Oklahoma Highway Patrol officer who had ordered Eddings and his companions to pull over. The death penalty statute in Oklahoma at the time provided for the trial judge, in passing sentence on a death-eligible defendant, to take into consideration "any mitigating circumstances" as well as aggravating ones, in reaching a decision. At his sentencing hearing, the trial judge ruled that the State of Oklahoma had proven each of three aggravating circumstances beyond a reasonable doubt. Turning to the issue of mitigation, the court ruled *as a matter of law* that other than the factor of youth, it could *not* consider Eddings emotional disturbance nor his faulty upbringing in a clearly dysfunctional family setting. Eddings was thereupon sentenced to death and the Court of Criminal Appeals of Oklahoma affirmed,[27] concluding that youth alone, balanced against evidence of sufficient aggravation, was insufficient to overturn the trial judge's decision. Noting that all statutory aggravating circumstances had been established, the Court of Criminal Appeals then declared that[28]

> [Eddings] also argues his mental state at the time of the murder. He stresses his family history saying he was suffering from severe psychological and emotional disorders, and that the killing was in actuality an inevitable product of the way he was raised. There is no doubt that petitioner has a personality disorder. But all the evidence tends to show that he knew the difference between right and wrong at the time he pulled the trigger, and that is the test of criminal responsibility in this State. For the same reason, the petitioner's family history is useful in explaining why he

believed the way he did, but it does not excuse his behavior.[29]

On *certiorari* to the Supreme Court of the United States, that Court, in a 5–4 decision, vacated the sentence of death handed down by the Oklahoma courts under the authority of *Lockett v. Ohio*.[30] Justice Powell, joined by Justices Brennan, Marshall, Stevens and O'Connor held that Edding's sentence of death was imposed without any serious consideration of *all* mitigating factors as counseled by *Lockett*. Said Justice Powell:[31]

> We find that the limitations placed by these [Oklahoma] courts upon the mitigating evidence they would consider violated the rule in Lockett. Just as the State may not by statute preclude the sentencer from considering any mitigating factor, neither may the sentencer refuse to consider, *as a matter of law*, any relevant mitigating evidence. In this instance, it was if the trial judge had instructed a jury to disregard the mitigating evidence Eddings proffered on his behalf.[32] (Emphasis in original).

In footnote #11 of its opinion, Justice Powell cited excerpts from the *Twentieth Century Task Force on Sentencing Policy Toward Young Offenders*.[33] A key statement in that document read that

> [A]dolescents, particularly in the early and middle teen years, are more vulnerable, more impulsive, and less self-disciplined than adults. Crimes committed by youths may be just as harmful to victims as those committed by older persons, but they deserve less punishment because adolescents may have less capacity to control their conduct and to think in long-range terms than adults.[34]

Apparently, the majority in *Eddings* was reinforcing the premise that both the *capacity* issue and the *limited time horizon* issue were crucial components in a proper determination of whether to capitally

---

29. *Id.*

30. 483 U.S. 586 (1978).

31. *Eddings v. Oklahoma*, 455 U.S. at 113.

32. *Id.* at 113–14.

33. *Task Force on Sentencing Policy Toward Young Offenders, Confronting Youth Crime* (1978).

34. *Id.* at 7.

punish a juvenile. *Eddings* was somewhat unique, however, in the fact that the Court's decision rested on an issue that was not argued in the application for *certiorari*. In effect, the Court was able to side-step the specific issue of the constitutionality of the death penalty for juveniles under age sixteen at time of crime commission. That avoidance technique, however, was short lived.

On June 29, 1988, the Court decided another case from Oklahoma involving a juvenile and the law's ultimate penalty. In *Thompson v. Oklahoma*,[35] a fifteen year old boy by the name of William Wayne Thompson was charged with the brutal murder of his former brother-in-law. The evidence strongly suggested that the killing took place, at least in part, because the defendant knew his brother-in-law was abusing his [Thompson's] sister. Under Oklahoma's waiver statute,[36] Thompson was transferred to the District Court of Grady County, Oklahoma, to be tried as an adult. A trial on the merits resulted in the defendant being convicted of first-degree murder and sentenced to death. On appeal to the Oklahoma Court of Criminal Appeals, that court affirmed the sentence.[37] On further appeal to the United States Supreme Court, that Court, per Justice Stevens in a 4–1–3 opinion, held that the "cruel and unusual punishment" clause[38] of the Eighth Amendment to the United States Constitution forbids a state to execute a juvenile "who was under 16 years of age at the time of his or her offense."[39] In deciding the weighty question of the applicability of the Eighth Amendment to a state's countervailing argument that it has the legal right and duty to capitally sanction certain teenage killers, the Court looked at three concepts. First, it canvassed state legislation and that legislations' treatment of chronological age in capital punishment statutes. It then turned its attention to the behavior of juries and how they react in juvenile homicide cases, and finally the Court looked at the proportionality argument between the death penalty and a juvenile's culpability. *Thompson*

---

35. 487 U.S. 815 (1988).

36. OKLA. STAT ANN. tit. 10, § 1112(6) (West 1987).

37. *Thompson v. Oklahoma*, 724 P. 2d 780 (Okla. Cr. App. 1986), *vacated*, 487 U.S. 815 (1988).

38. The Eighth Amendment reads: "Excessive bail shall not be required, nor excessive fines imposed, nor cruel and unusual punishment inflicted." U.S. CONST. amend. VIII. Justice Kennedy did not take part in the *Thompson* deliberations.

39. *Thompson*, 487 U.S. at 838 (Stevens, J., plurality opinion).

raised the thorny issue, by the late 1980s, of what interaction, if any, the juvenile justice system should have with adult criminal justice on the capital punishment question. The issue was joined by taking sides on one of two prongs of the argument. First, either continue to equate the juvenile justice system to the adult system and thereby support the death penalty for fifteen-year-old murderers employing the common law age differentials as the appropriate legal yardstick for culpability; or secondly, recognize that capital punishment as a sanction choice is in derogation of juvenile law doctrine because of a host of significant mitigative differences that juveniles bring with them to the culpability equation.

Referring back to its decision in *Eddings*,[40] the plurality in *Thompson*[41] were willing to acknowledge a juvenile's youth as a compelling mitigating factor in capital cases. The majority opinion took special note of the fact that in 1988, thirty-seven jurisdictions authorized capital punishment, but of that number, eighteen states disallowed the death penalty for juveniles under age sixteen. Looking further into state practice as a guide, the Court noted that nineteen states[42] had not even addressed the age limit issue as it related to the death penalty. Thus, in theory at least, a child of very tender years could potentially be death-eligible in these nineteen jurisdictions because there was neither legislation nor decisional law establishing an age floor for imposition of capital punishment. Taking one of their decisional cues from the fact that eighteen states prohibited imposition of the death penalty for juveniles under age sixteen and combining that cue with the additional facts that respected national[43] and international organizations[44] strongly objected to the death penalty for mi-

---

40. 455 U.S. 104 (1982).

41. 487 U.S. 815 (1988).

42. As of 1988, the following states had not enacted statutory minimums for death eligibility nor was there any decisional law in those jurisdictions that apparently addressed that issue: Alabama, Arizona, Arkansas, Delaware, Florida, Idaho, Louisiana, Mississippi, Missouri, Montana, Oklahoma, Pennsylvania, South Carolina, South Dakota, Utah, Vermont, Virginia, Washington, and Wyoming. Also, on the date of the *Thompson* decision, the federal government had no minimum age for death eligibility.

43. *Supra* note 13.

44. Amnesty International in its *amicus curiae* brief for the petitioner reported that of the 11,000 documented executions worldwide between 1979 and 1988, only eight were for crimes committed by children under the age of eighteen. Brief of *Amicus Curiae*, Amnesty International in Support of Petitioner, at 23–24.

nors, the plurality concluded that death-eligibility for a fifteen-year-old juvenile would "offend civilized standards of decency."[45] In her concurring opinion in *Thompson*, Justice O'Connor noted that in all those states that had established a chronological age floor for death eligibility, all had set age sixteen as that floor. She correspondingly observed that neither the Oklahoma legislature nor any other state legislative body had given any serious attention to the interplay and potential conflict between its capital punishment legislation and its statutes allowing juveniles to be prosecuted as adults. Since Oklahoma law had not at the time established any age floor for imposition of the capital sanction, O'Connor's concurrence in conjunction with the plurality opinion of Justices Stevens, Brennan, Marshall and Blackmun resulted in the vacating of Thompson's sentence. Thus the Court concluded that "the Eighth and Fourteenth Amendments prohibit the execution of a person who was under 16 years of age at the time of his or her offense."[46]

Reading together the *Thompson* plurality opinion and Justice O'Connor's concurrence, commentators and Supreme Court watchers alike generally concluded that age sixteen was the constitutional bright line for juvenile death eligibility absent some express legislative or case law variant. In 1989, the United States Supreme Court granted *certiorari* in two consolidated cases coming to it form the states of Kentucky[47] and Missouri.[48]

Although *Thompson* had apparently established an age line of sixteen for capital punishment in those jurisdictions who had no statutory or decisional law floor for death eligibility, there was still a great

---

45. 487 U.S. 815, 830 (1988).

46. *Id.* at 838. Could it be here that the majority was possibly harking back to the admonition of the 1671 "Capital Laws" of the New Plymouth Colony which read, in part:

> If a man have a stubborn or rebellious child, of sufficient years and understanding [viz.] *sixteen years of age,* which shall not obey the voice of his Father, or the voice of his Mother...then shall his Father and Mother lay hold on him, and bring him before the Magistrates assembled in Court, and testify unto them, that their Son is Stubborn and Rebellious, and will not obey their voice and chastisement, but lives in sundry notorious crimes; *such a Son shall be put to death,* or otherwise severly punished. New Plymouth GENERAL LAWS, ch. 2, "Capital Laws" §§ 13 & 14 (1671). (Emphasis added).

47. *Stanford v. Kentucky,* 492 U.S. 361 (1989).

48. *Missouri v. Wilkins,* 492 U.S. 361 (1989).

deal of dissonance about juveniles ages sixteen to eighteen who were charged with capital homicide. The proponents of capital punishment for certain juvenile felons were fond of noting that the original Illinois juvenile court statute of 1899 did *not* cover juvenile homicide. Furthermore, many lawmakers and their public supporters were of the opinion that even though the statutory jurisdiction of juvenile courts was raised in a majority of states to age eighteen by the late 1920s, there was sufficient statutory authority to buttress their argument that intentional juvenile homicide was beyond the pale of juvenile court power. Add to this the continuing and often contentious debate over what role psychiatry, psychology and sociology play in the juvenile culpability equation, and the groundwork was laid for another round in the capital punishment polemic.

Stanford v. Kentucky[49] and *Missouri v. Wilkins*[50] were cases whose factual backgrounds would test the true mettle of juvenile death penalty abolitionists. In *Stanford* and *Wilkins*, both juveniles committed felony-murder. On January 7, 1981, seventeen-year-old Kevin Stanford robbed a service station in Jefferson County, Kentucky, where the victim, Baerbel Poore, age twenty-one, was employed. During and after the robbery, Stanford and an accomplice raped and sodomized Poore. She was then taken to an isolated location where Stanford fatally shot her in the back of the head. When later asked by a corrections officer why he had killed the victim, Stanford replied that "'I had to shoot her, [she] lived next to me and she would recognize me.'"[51] A hearing was held in juvenile court and Stanford was waived to adult criminal court for trial. The juvenile was transferred to the circuit court, tried by a jury and found guilty of murder, first-degree sodomy, first-degree robbery and receiving stolen property. At the sentencing hearing, Stanford was sentenced to death and forty-five years in the penitentiary.[52]

On July 27, 1985, Heath Wilkins, age sixteen, murdered one Nancy Allen in Avondale, Missouri. Allen was a twenty-six year old mother of two small children working behind the sales counter of a store she and her husband jointly owned. The evidence in the case revealed that Wilkins, and his accomplice, Patrick Steven, had dis-

49. 492 U.S. 361 (1989).
50. 492 U.S. 361 (1989).
51. *Stanford v. Commonwealth*, 734 S.W. 2d 781, 788 (Ky. 1987).
52. *Id.* at 792.

cussed the robbery of this business as early as two weeks preceding the act. Wilkins stabbed Allen in the back and three additional times in the chest while his accomplice attempted to open the cash register. Begging for her life, Wilkins proceeded to stab the victim four more times in the neck, leaving her to die on the floor behind the counter. The two juveniles left the premises with approximates $450 in cash, liquor, cigarettes and checks. After apprehension, the Missouri juvenile court terminated its jurisdiction over Wilkins and certified him for trial as an adult under a Missouri statute permitting juveniles between the ages of fourteen and seventeen who have committed felonies to be tried in adult court. In subsequent proceedings, Wilkins was found guilty by a jury of first-degree murder and was capitally sentenced. The Supreme Court of Missouri affirmed the death sentence in face of the argument that it violated the Eighth Amendment.[53] In an interesting twist to the case, Wilkins dismissed his appointed counsel and waived his right to counsel. He plead guilty to all charges[54] and informed the trial judge that he preferred death over life imprisonment without parole.[55] Nonetheless, the Supreme Court of Missouri would not allow Wilkins to be unrepresented in a capital murder case and requested the state public defender to join the litigation as *amicus curiae* and to argue the merits of the defendant's case for purposes of review.

On June 26, 1989, the United States Supreme Court announced its decision in these two consolidated cases under the caption of *Stanford v. Kentucky*.[56] At that time, the composition of the Court was such that most commentators could, with a fair degree of accuracy, determine the proponents and opponents of juvenile capital punishment. Those justices opposing death as a legal sanction for juveniles were Justices Blackmun, Brennan, Marshall and Stevens. Arrayed on the opposite of the issue were Chief Justice Rehnquist and Justices Kennedy, Scalia and White with Justice O'Connor as a "swing" vote somewhere between the two camps.

Justice Scalia authored the majority opinion in *Stanford*. He began by framing the issue to be "whether the imposition of capital punishment on an individual for a crime committed at 16 or 17 years of age

---

53. See *State v. Wilkins*, 736 S.W. 2d 409, 417 (Mo. 1987).
54. *Id.* at 410–11.
55. *Id.* at 411.
56. 492 U.S. 361 (1989).

constitutes cruel and unusual punishment under the Eighth Amendment."[57] Thus presented, Scalia and Chief Justice Rehnquist and Justices White, O'Connor and Kennedy joined in affirming the sentences upheld by both the Supreme Courts of Kentucky and Missouri, respectively. Justice Blackmun, Brennan, Marshall and Stevens dissented.

In upholding the constitutionality of the death penalty for sixteen- and seventeen-year-old juveniles, Justice Scalia remarked that[58]

> [t]he thrust of both Wilkins' and Stanford's arguments is that imposition of the death penalty on those who were juveniles when they committed their crimes falls within the Eighth Amendment's prohibition against 'cruel and unusual punishments'....Neither petitioner asserts that his sentence constitutes one of 'those modes or acts of punishment that had been considered cruel and unusual at the time that the Bill of Rights was adopted.'...Nor could they support such a contention. At that time, the common law set the rebuttable presumption of incapacity to commit any felony at the age of 14, and theoretically permitted capital punishment to be imposed on anyone over the age of 7....Thus petitioners are left to argue that their punishment is contrary to the 'evolving standards of decency that mark the progress of a maturing society.'[59]

The "evolving standards of decency" dicta from the 1958 opinion of *Trop v. Dulles*[60] is notoriously vague and open-ended, but the Court has employed this phraseology in a number of cases involving the Eighth Amendment. In an attempt to reign in that standard, Justice Scalia in footnote #1[61] remarked that "[w]e emphasize that it is *American* conceptions of decency that are dispositive, rejecting the contention of petitioner and their various *amici*...that the sentencing practices of other countries are relevant."[62] (Emphasis in original). Scalia discounted Stanford and Wilkin's contention that the Court should look to the practice in other nations to discern whether Amer-

---

57. 492 U.S. at 364–65.
58. 492 U.S. at 368–69.
59. *Id.*
60. 356 U.S. 86, 101 (1958).
61. 492 U.S. at 361.
62. *Id.*

ican standards of decency measure up to some international norm. In concluding the footnote, he noted that "they [international standards] cannot serve to establish the...Eighth Amendment prerequisite..."[63] Finding no "national concensus" that would direct the Court to determine that death eligibility for sixteen- and seventeen-year-olds is cruel and unusual, the Court let stand the sentences upheld by the Kentucky and Missouri courts.

Legal historians have generally concluded that the "cruel and unusual punishment" clause in the Eighth Amendment derives from certain language contained in the 1689 English Bill of Rights via the Virginia Declaration of Rights of 1776. While there is some disagreement, most scholars of legal history would probably affirm that the framers of the Eighth Amendment sought to prohibit some of the more common forms of egregious *torture* that was commonplace in the criminal justice sanctioning policies of Tudor and Stuart England. Those draconian penalties for capital crimes included such notorious barbarities as death by drawing, by crucifixion, by pressing, by burning at the stake, burning in oil, burial alive and disembowelment, followed by drawing and quartering.[64] "The framers [of the Eighth Amendment] clearly did not believe that such then common punishments as lashing, branding, ear-cropping, or execution by hanging or firing squad were cruel and unusual."[65] These sanction modes were simply not conceived as being either "cruel" or "unusual" in the 1791 punishment calculus of post-colonial America. One must also concede that this particular language in the Eighth Amendment preceded by 108 years the founding of the juvenile court in the United States.

If Raoul Berger[66] and other legal scholars are correct, we must conclude that the cruel and unusual punishment language embodied

---

63. *Id.*

64. *See, e.g.,* GEORGE IVES, A HISTORY OF PENAL METHODS (1914); Anthony F. Grannuci, *'Nor Cruel and Unusual Punishment Inflicted': The Original Meaning*, 57 Cal. L. Rev. 839 (1969); LARRY CLARK BERKSON, THE CONCEPT OF CRUEL AND UNUSUAL PUNISHMENT (1975); and WALTER BERNS, FOR CAPITAL PUNISHMENT: CRIME AND THE MORALITY OF THE DEATH PENALTY (1979).

65. Gregory Bassham, *Rethinking the Emerging Jurisprudence of Juvenile Death*, 5 Notre Dame J.L. Ethics & Pub. Pol'y. 467, 468 (1991).

66. RAOUL BERGER, DEATH PENALTIES: THE SUPREME COURT'S OBSTACLE COURSE (1982).

in the Eighth Amendment incorporated by reference *the common law meaning* of the words "cruel" and "unusual." This means that insofar as can be determined, capital punishment for serious felonies was accepted by the framers of the Eighth Amendment as a legal given. This, among other reasons, is apparently why the Rehnquist Court's conservative phalanx has had no doctrinal qualms in upholding the imposition of the death penalty for certain adult felons. Since both Stanford and Wilkins were tried *as adults*, the Court's analysis is true to form. To a conservative public, such reasoning concludes the matter. Doctrinally, however, the matter is not so easily foreclosed; only the focus of inquiry is shifted. The inquiry now seems to be whether or not the Eighth Amendment should ever afford a legal shield against capital punishment for juveniles under age eighteen by incorporating a legal construct into its language that was non-existent in 1791? That construct, of course, is the term *delinquency*. To the child savers and the Progressive reformers, delinquency was premised on childhood as a distinct and unique legal artifact. From 1899, a body of legislation and case law has emerged that has treated childhood—until recently—differently than childhood was treated at the time of the adoption of the Bill of Rights. Yet, throughout the twentieth century, American society and the American judicial process has never come to a concensus on just exactly what "childhood" is. Pre-1899 law provided a defense of "infancy" for minors under the age of seven.[67] Between that age and fourteen, the law rebuttably presumed incapacity to entertain criminal intent or *mens rea*. At age fourteen, the juvenile became, in the Latin idiom, *doli capax*[68] and was treated, for purposes of the criminal law, as if he or she were a responsible adult. This legal dividing line between innocence and culpability was unmoving and its application left a number of children between ages fourteen and above at risk and death-eligible. While prosecutorial discretion and jury nullification did play a mitigating role in the avoidance of juvenile executions between 1791 and 1899, still the criminal law's policy was the common law's policy—*childhood* ended at age fourteen and the defense of infancy was unavailing beyond that point.

---

67. For a discussion of the entire issue, *see* Woodbridge, *supra* note 21.

68. The Latin term implying the capability of forming criminal intent or having sufficient intelligence to discern right from wrong. *See* BLACK'S LAW DICTIONARY 570 (4th ed. 1951).

When the Illinois legislature enacted the first juvenile statute, their collective motives were not seriously challenged. After this legislation had been enacted, teenagers up to age sixteen and then later up to age eighteen in most states came under the protective mantle of *parens patriae*. Although to some the juvenile court idea was both novel and philosophically disturbing, one must also remember that a narrow range of criminal acts, particularly homicide, was generally *excluded* from juvenile court legislation. However, this exclusion was not global in nature and as other states began establishing juvenile courts, statutory language became muddled. Some legislation would specifically exclude homicide, others were silent on the issue. By the 1930s, there seemed to be a general feeling that even children who kill may be far better off in the juvenile court than in criminal court. Thus, depending upon statutory definitions of delinquency, it would be possible for a juvenile court to exercise jurisdiction over a teenage or younger homicide suspect and retain jurisdiction over that youngster until age twenty-one.

Between 1899 and the mid-1970s there occurred a series of "paradigm shifts"[69] in numerous fields of endeavor, juvenile law included. But despite these rearrangements, the core philosophy of juvenile law and practice remained relatively intact—juvenile delinquents were to be "helped" by the juvenile court, not further harmed. As mentioned in the previous chapter, however, there was a growing disillusionment with the effectiveness of both adult and juvenile rehabilitation programs by 1975. The poverty of correctional programs in American penology was starkly revealed in the September 9–13, 1971, prison riot at the Attica Correctional Facility in New York state. That incident and the numerous post-mortems written by journalists and scholars alike propelled criminal corrections at all levels into the national spotlight. While not immediate, the Attica incident probably

---

69. David Reidy remarks that:

Every community arises out of and remains embedded in some common ground which it achieves and then takes for granted. This common ground constitutes the community's dominant paradigm...Paradigms, a shared sense of meaning maintained over time, makes it possible for communities to exist...[p]aradigms make possible a communal reality, a world beyond self,...[a] community that evolves into or achieves a new paradigm undergoes a paradigm shift. This shift in that which binds the community together changes the community and its very foundation. David A. Reidy, Jr., *The Law, Dominant Paradigms and Legal Education*, 39 Kan. L. Rev. 415, 421–23 (1991).

began to fuel subliminal but long-continuing doubts about the aptness of sanctions meted out in American juvenile courts. With an increase in teenage homicides, especially the anonymous stranger-victim killings, immense public pressure and media fulmination was exerted on both prosecuting authorities and juvenile court judges to remove teenage murder suspects from the juvenile court altogether. The paradigm shift was in motion.

In 1972, the year following the Attica disturbance, the United States Supreme Court decided a case that became a *cause celebre* in capital punishment litigation. In *Furman v. Georgia*,[70] the Supreme Court paved the way for a complete overhaul of state capital punishment legislation. In an odd *per curiam* opinion where all nine justices wrote,[71] the Court impliedly invited the several states to return to their legislative drawing boards to re-draft death penalty legislation to comport with newly-announced constitutional requirements. That invitation was accepted and subsequent so-called "guided discretion" death penalty legislation replaced pre-*Furman* law.

The *Furman* case may have also been the catalyst for much of the current debate over the juvenile death penalty. The *Furman* "majority" ruled that the punishment of death was not *per se* a violation of the Eighth Amendment.[72] *Furman* revamped capital punishment law for adults, but it also established the constitutionality of the death penalty for age-specific, death-eligible juveniles who would be tried in adult criminal courts by virtue of waiver or exclusion legislation. In other words, the common law interpretation of "cruel and unusual" is an execution-friendly interpretation, both for adults and for juveniles tried as adults. Thus, a realistic assessment of post-*Furman*

---

70. 408 U.S. 238 (1972).

71. Actually, there was no distinct "plurality" opinion as such in *Furman*. Three justices (Douglas, Stewart and White) ruled against unbridled jury *discretion* in allocating death to some convicts and not to others, while Justices Brennan and Marshall held to the view that capital punishment *in any form* was unconstitutional *per se*. Cobbled together, these five loosely congruent opinions comprised a "majority" sufficient to overturn Furman's Georgia conviction and render unconstitutional all state capital punishment statutes that granted juries total discretion as to sanction choice.

72. But, according to Malcolm E. Wheeler, "the decision beclouds more than it clarifies regarding the constitutionality of capital punishment per se and the scope of the eighth amendment in general." Malcolm E. Wheeler, *Toward a Theory of Limited Punishment II: The Eighth Amendment After Furman v. Georgia*, 25 Stan. L. Rev. 62 (1972).

adult capital punishment litigation in conjunction with the *Stanford-Wilkins* ruling, leads one to believe that the Eighth Amendment's "cruel and unusual punishment" clause holds out little promise for blunting juvenile executions for those over age sixteen. The under sixteen-year-old juvenile may or may not be death-eligible, depending upon such factors as (1) the jurisdiction's waiver legislation language; (2) whether or not an exclusion statute is in force; (3) whether the jurisdiction has a statutory "floor" for juvenile death eligibility; and (4) how the highest court in a particular jurisdiction interprets the language of both the majority and the dissents in *Eddings*,[73] *Thompson*,[74] and *Stanford-Wilkins*.[75] Given the diversity of organic law coupled with the dissonance endemic within the appellate judiciary over capital punishment for juveniles, a "national" policy on the issue is probably foreclosed. But the problem runs deeper than simply acknowledging a paradigm shift that occurred in the 1970s.

A doctrinal fault line has fractured concensus in juvenile law for a number of years. On one side of the line is the contention that juvenile courts should exercise exclusive hegemony over *all* teenage wrongdoing, including serious felony-type teen and sub-teen malfeasance. This view roughly comports with the *parens patriae* model of juvenile justice in its pristine form. The other side of the fault line takes a quite different approach. It adopts the view that legal "childhood" or "juvenileness"[76] is so gossamer, so ephemeral and so accordion-like that in the last thirty years of the juvenile justice century,

---

73. 408 U.S. 238 (1972).
74. 487 U.S. 815 (1988).
75. 492 U.S. 361 (1989).
76. A term employed by William S. Geimer. He explains it as follows:
   "juvenileness" is a single-edged sword which cuts through a young person's constitutional rights.... Juvenileness is, in one sense, contextual. That is, juveniles live their lives in places and situations where adults have "legitimate interest" to be balanced against juveniles' assertions of right.... Juvenileness is, in another sense, philosophical. That is, it consists of a set of assumptions about young people — some demonstrably false, some occasionally accurate, some half-valid. William S. Geimer, *Juvenileness: A Single-Edged Constitutional Sword*, 22 Ga. L. Rev. 949, 950–52 (1988).
On the issue of "childhood" and its construction and reconstruction in American culture, *see* Lloyd deMause, *The Evolution of Childhood* in The History of Childhood (deMause ed. 1974) and LaMar T. Empey, *The Social Construction of Childhood and Juvenile Jusitce* in The Future of Childhood and Juvenile Justice (LaMar T. Empey ed. 1979).

American society has "re-imagined" childhood completely out of its historic *parens patriae* mold and into at least a quasi-adult mold for a specific group of children. By deconstructing the *parens patriae* rubric for teenage killers, the American juvenile court has come full-circle in its first century of operation.

In re Gault[77] provided the opening wedge into an ethos of distrust that has enveloped American juvenile courts since the seventies. Not only has the Supreme Court of the United States, but state appellate tribunals and the general public all have exhibited a profound distrust of the juvenile court *as an institution*. Part of the price we pay for this distrust is the moral dilemma we confront regarding the juvenile death penalty. This distrust, however, did not burst forth *eo instante* as a direct repercussion of the *Gault* holding. Regretfully, it was developing over a lengthy period of time prior to 1967. From a combination of ill-crafted juvenile legislation driven by the often inflated and ill-conceived notions of social science, in conjunction with a juvenile court bench largely unskilled in applying *valid social science data* in dispositional decisions, we have arrived at the terminus of the juvenile justice century. Paradoxically, as we look to century twenty-one, we are surrounded by clarion calls for both abolition and retention of the juvenile court. Paradoxically also, juvenile homicide is probably the major socio-legal artifact fueling this debate.

C. Postmodern Criminology and the Juvenile Death Penalty

In 1976, in the very midst of the re-emergence of the recriminalization of the juvenile court, two men trained in the litany of positivism and "value-free" scientific assessment of human behavior made some rather startling observations. Samuel Yochelson and Stanton Samenow[78] became convinced that the study of crime and criminality through traditional sociological and psychological methods were unavailing. In his study of violent teenage behavior and violent childhood behavior in general as a clinical psychologist, Samenow took what to many then and still now consider an unorthodox view. Samenow wrote that

---

77. 387 U.S. 1 (1967).
78. Samuel Yochelson & Stanton E. Samenow, The Criminal Personality (1976).

we are persuaded by emerging facts to *discard sociologic and psychologic theories of causation* in favor of a careful probe into the criminal's thinking and action patterns. Basically we could establish *no causal connection* between the way a criminal thinks and acts and the circumstances of his life. Sociologic and psychologic explanations *were abandoned, as well as the mental illness concept,* because they stood in the way of an effective process of change. The use of such time-honored concepts [as sociological and psychological explanations of crime] has hardly altered the national crime picture.[79] (Emphasis added).

By factoring out both sociological and psychological theories of crime and giving environmental indices short shrift, Samenow relegated much of modern twentieth-century criminology to the trash heap. Although these comments and others were radical, the Yochelson and Samenow work was a virtual *tour de force* for those advocating the abandonment of the rehabilitative ideal in much of American penology in the 1970s.

In his *Stanford* opinion,[80] Justice Scalia caustically marginalized any positivistic approach to decode the etiology of juvenile homicide. In commenting on the claims of both Stanford and Wilkins that because of their youth they were both less mature and consequently less morally or legally culpable, Scalia wrote:[81]

In support of these claims, petitioners and their supporting *amici* marshall an array of *socioscientific evidence* concerning the psychological and emotional development of 16 and 17-year-olds.... But as the adjective "socioscientific" suggest ...it is not demonstrable that no 16-year-old is "adequately responsible" or significantly deterred.... The battle must be fought, then, on the field of the Eighth Amendment; and in that struggle *socioscientific, ethicoscientific or even purely scientific evidence is not an available weapon....* We have no power under the Eighth Amendment to substitute our belief in the scientific evidence *for the society's apparent skepticism.*[82] (Emphasis added).

79. *Id.* at vii.
80. 492 U.S. 361 (1989).
81. *Id.* at 377–78.
82. *Id.*

Contrast Scalia's language here in 1989 with the language employed by Justice Fortas in *Kent v. United States*[83] twenty-three years earlier: "[t]he objectives [of the juvenile justice system] are to provide measures of guidance and rehabilitation for the child and protection for society not to fix criminal responsibility, guilt and punishment. The State is parents patricide rather than prosecuting attorney and judge."[84] Clearly, the *Kent* decision did not involve a wanton act of murder and clearly Justice Fortas was extolling the continued virtues of the juvenile court apparatus as he saw it, not expressing an opinion on juvenile homicide. Yet, a major disconnect in juvenile justice had emerged within that twenty-three-year time frame. A clue to such a disconnect may be gleaned from the *Kent* opinion in another context. Justice Fortas noted the *dual* role that juvenile courts must play in the handling of child lawbreakers. On the one hand there was the "guidance and rehabilitation" role; on the other, the "protection for society" role. While not mutually exclusive, these two prongs of juvenile jurisprudence have been the Archilles heel of the juvenile court throughout most of its existence. The year following *Kent*, the same jurist writing for the same Court created even more dissonance between the rehabilitative ideal and the public safety prongs in *In re Gault*.[85] *Gault* was the wedge in the door that opened the juvenile court to the 1970s paradigm shift. In employing the procedural due process device that had animated the Warren Court's "revolution" in adult criminal law, the *Gault* majority effectively criminalized by reference the delinquency work of the juvenile court in the minds of most Americans. It mattered not that there were important subset criteria that could significantly alter the *Gault* holding in specific cases. What came out of *In re Gault* was a "message" that proclaimed that the United States Supreme Court had now granted adult "rights" in delinquency cases to delinquents so therefore let's treat delinquents "like adults." This mind-set gathered momentum as media accounts of teenage homicide became more prevalent. When some notorious cases of random and sometimes planned murders occurred in the 1980s, the public, the courts and the prosecutorial and legislative establishments were ready and willing to hold juveniles like Thompson, Stanford and Wilkins fully responsible *as adults* for their misdeeds.

---

83. 383 U.S. 541 (1966).
84. *Id.* at 554–55.
85. 387 U.S. 1 (1967).

For these juveniles and others like them over the age of sixteen whose crimes are reflective of amorality run amok, the *Stanford* and *Wilkins* decisions should be fair warning. The United States Supreme Court has now drawn its "bright line" at age sixteen, despite what other jurisdictions have done in that regard. The area of contention for death-eligibility now will focus on the under sixteen juvenile who commits capital murder. For this population, one of the issues that surely will be on the agenda at the end of the juvenile justice century will be whether or not "socioscientific," "ethicoscientific" or "purely scientific evidence," in Justice Scalia's lexicon, can be deployed in aid of both prevention and treatment of sub-sixteen, serious, predatory delinquency?

United States Supreme Court justices are certainly not alone in their apparent disdain of criminological tenets. The American public likewise is not overly supportive of some of the more questionable criminological ukases. Like the juvenile court itself, criminology has consistently promised more than it could deliver. This means-end conflict has blinded both the wider public and the policymakers alike to recognize any real contributions criminology may bring to the juvenile violence question. Yet, data is "out there" that strongly suggests that this cone of violence the nation is experiencing at the hands of some delinquents may not be nearly as epidemic as it appears. Relative to the issue of providing *applied* public choice options for the diminution of serious, predatory delinquency, criminology is generally found wanting. Nonetheless, a caveat is in order here. Since Martinson's "nothing works" thesis appeared in 1974, there has been some promising, but little known research, that seems to indicate that we may be on the verge of isolating some of the causal antecedents of violent predatory delinquency. For example, in their 1987 article[86] Diane C. Dwyer and Roger B. McNally note that "[r]ecent research on very violent youth, those who commit murder, produces some intriguing findings that should caution us to this deterrence response and suggest other alternatives to be examined for the violent few."[87] Citing the research of Dorothy O. Lewis and others in the *American Journal of Psychiatry*,[88] Dwyer and McNally note that "the re-

86. Diane C. Dywer & Roger B. McNally, *Juvenile Justice: Reform, Retain, and Reaffirm*, 51 Fed. Probation 47 (Sept. 1987).

87. *Id.* at 49.

88. Dorothy O. Lewis *et al., Biopsychosocial Characteristics of Children Who Later Murder: A Prospective Study*, 142 Am. J. Psychiatry 1161 (Oct. 1985).

searchers document the childhood neuropsychiatric and family characteristics prior to the commission of the act. The profile of these children included psychotic symptoms, major neurological impairment, a psychotic first-degree relative, violent acts during childhood, and severe physical abuse."[89] These authors then go on to note that notable social science studies such as the Marvin Wolfgang birth cohort data[90] which tracks chronic delinquency *after* its commission must be supplemented with data like that generated by Lewis and her colleagues. Recent data assembled by J. David Hawkins[91] cites a quote by Judge David Mitchell, chief judge of the Juvenile Court of Baltimore County, Maryland, who observed that "[i]t is of no value for the court to work miracles in rehabilitation if there are no opportunities for the child in the community. Until we deal with the environment in which they live, *whatever we do in the courts is irrelevant.*"[92] (Emphasis added). Hawkins also identified what he termed "risk factors for violence."[93] These include:

(1) Availability of guns; (2) community law/norms favorable to crime; (3) media portrayal of violence; (4) low neighborhood attachment/community disorganization; (5) extreme economic deprivation; (6) poor family management practices; (7) excessively severe or inconsistent punishment; (8) parental failure to monitor their children's activities; (9) antisocial behavior of early onset [in school]... aggressiveness in grades K–3; (10) persistent antisocial behavior first exhibited in adolescence; and (11) [associating] with peers who engage in problem behavior (for example, drug abuse, delinquency, violence, sexual activities, or dropping out of school).[94]

In its monograph titled *Combating Violence and Delinquency: The National Juvenile Justice Action Plan*, the Office of Juvenile Justice and Delinquency Prevention notes that

---

89. Dwyer & McNally, *supra* note 86, at 49.

90. MARVIN WOLFGANG, ROBERT FIGLIO & THORSTEN SELLIN, DELINQUENCY IN A BIRTH COHORT (1972).

91. J. David Hawkins, *Controlling Crime Before It Happens: Risk-Focused Prevention,* as quoted in National Institute of Justice (NIJ), *Juvenile Homicides* (August, 1995).

92. *Id.* at 10.

93. *Id.* at 11–13.

94. *Id.*

[j]uvenile violent crime arrests are increasing, but only a fraction of youth (one-half of 1 percent) is arrested for violent crimes each year. We can interrupt this escalation of violence based on identified positive and negative characteristics...that are present or lacking in communities, families, schools, peer groups, and individuals.[95]

In its 1994 publication[96] on strategies to combat violent delinquency, the OJJDP states that "[r]ecent research has documented the behavioral pathways and factors that contribute to serious, violent, and chronic juvenile crime.[97] It cited the research efforts of individuals such as David Huizinga, Rolf Loeber, Terence P. Thornberry,[98] Cathy S. Widom,[99] and Carolyn A. Smith and Terence P. Thornberry,[100] to mention but five. In their recent in-depth coverage of American criminality, James Q. Wilson and Joan Petersilia[101] include in their edited work a chapter entitled "Investing in Criminal Justice Research" co-authored by Alfred Blumstein and Joan Petersilia.[102] In addressing the issue of the importance of research in both criminal justice and in criminology, Blumstein and Petersilia note that by the mid-1990s, "one sees a significant accumulation of research findings and insights *that were not available ten years earlier.*"[103] (Emphasis added). They then speak to a point directly related to comments such as those uttered by Justice Scalia in his *Stanford* opinion regarding the empirical research enterprise. Going directly to the point, they write:[104]

---

95. Monograph, *Combating Violence and Delinquency: The National Juvenile Justice Action Plan —Summary* (March, 1996).

96. Office of Juvenile Justice & Delinquency Prevention (OJJDP), *Program Sumary: Comprehensive Strategy for Serious, Violent and Chronic Juvenile Offenders* (June, 1994).

97. *Id.* at 6.

98. David Huizinga, Rolf Loeber & Terence Thornberry, *Urban Delinquency and Substance Abuse*, Office of Juvenile Justice & Delinquency Prevention (OJJDP) (1993).

99. Cathy S. Widom, *The Cycle of Violence,* National Institute of Justice (NIJ) (Oct., 1992).

100. Carolyn A. Smith & Terence Thornberry, *The Relationship Between Childhood Maltreatment and Adolescent Involvement in Delinquency and Drug Use*, paper presented at the Society for Research on Child Development, New Orleans, La. (March, 1993).

101. CRIME (James Q. Wilson & Joan Petersilia eds. 1995).

102. *Id.* at 465.

103. *Id.*

104. *Id.* at 471.

Another important factor *inhibiting* more significant efforts by the NIJ [National Institute of Justice] derives from the inherent perspective on empirical research held by *the majority of the legal profession,*...In the legal profession generally, there is no comparable *tradition* [as in medicine] for empirical research. The counterpart legal research involves searching for cases or statutes that address the issues of the case....Thus, the search for generalizable knowledge that is the essence of empirical research—*and that should provide a basis for public policy—is not a central aspect of legal professional work.*[105] (Emphasis added).

In its general animus toward the findings and the insights elicited by empirical social science research, the legal profession has strong allies among the general public. Quoting from a 1983 article[106] in his book on the insanity issue,[107] Michael L. Perlin writes that

Ellsworth and Ross...endorse the symbolic perspective: it is the idea of the death penalty rather than its application that elicits strong public support. The public's attitudes are expressive rather than instrumental,...Retentionists thus see the death penalty as having 'enormous symbolic value as an expression of a no-nonsense stand in the war on crime.'[108]

The "symbolic value" of death eligibility for juveniles over age sixteen is now both legally endorsed and publicly supported. The question now becomes whether or not our postmodern criminology of the past fifteen years or so can produce any *public policy basis* for restricting death eligibility to youngsters under age sixteen? Charles Ewing, in his work on juvenile homicide,[109] states that "[j]uveniles who kill challenge longstanding and widely held conceptions of childhood and adolescence and create a serious dilemma for the criminal

---

105. *Id.*

106. Phoebe Ellsworth & Lee Ross, *Public Opinion and Capital Punishment: A Close Examination of the Views of Abolitionists and Retentionists,* 29 Crime & Delinq. 116 (1983).

107. Perlin, *supra* note 1.

108. *Id.* at 369.

109. CHARLES EWING, WHEN CHILDREN KILL: THE DYNAMICS OF JUVENILE HOMICIDE (1990).

and juvenile justice system."[110] A child advocate faced with a juvenile client on trial for capital murder in an adult criminal court is often in a quandary. The vacuous nature of the "cruel and unusual punishment" clause of the Eighth Amendment sweeps too wide of the mark to be of any real value, especially under that Amendment's interpretation by the Rehnquist Court. On the other hand, the hostility to solid social science and criminological research findings by a large portion of the bench and bar places the advocate in an almost untenable position. The lawyer for the juvenile is oftentimes forced either to rely on constitutional premises that appellate courts largely regard as inapplicable, or, failing that, marshall sufficient criminological or other social science data that is suspect at best and rejected out of hand at worst. But, as Blumstein and Petersilia noted, social science in general and criminology in particular have made some significant empirical findings regarding kids who kill since the mid-1980s that *should* have a voice in the capital punishment debate regarding juveniles.

Depending upon the juvenile involved and his or her peculiar socio-psychological background, will depend on who the advocate should call for assistance. In most situations, the under-sixteen juvenile will be an individual involved in a high-profile case that, momentarily at least, draws extensive media coverage and local, if not national public interest. The "expressive" urge to punish may very well be "in the air." In those situations where the juvenile is foreclosed from realistically pleading insanity or "perfect" self-defense, the defendant will in all likelihood appear to be quite "normal" in psychosocial terms. It is here, if at all, that juvenile advocates must consider the employment of expert witnesses to give the court and jury a descriptive word-picture that reveals a troubled past. Both the court and the trier of fact in matters of this nature often wear a set of sociocultural and legal "blinders" that impede their ability to consider the etiological dynamics of the homicidal act. A forensic psychologist, a forensic sociologist and perhaps a forensic social worker may offer insights into the socialization and developmental background of the juvenile that could be probed by trial counsel. Lawyers themselves are simply not trained to "see" those things that these professionals encounter in their research and in their day-to-day practices. Forensic social workers, in particular, are a valuable resource in certain types of juvenile homicide litigation. These are individuals

---

110. *Id.* at 13.

trained to identify and explain the interface between human behavior and the social environment. Their testimony may allow trial counsel a "foot in the door" so to speak in making an argument for mitigation. These disciplines may afford insights—social, psychodynamic or environmental markers—that both the court and the jury may be able to relate to. Having said all of this, however, it would be sheer lighthearted optimism to predict consistent success in such cases. Many will be lost, probably most. Juries composed of lay men and women have been known to listen very carefully to all expert opinion on both sides of an issue and then, inexplicably, ignore or marginalize all of it; the same holds true if the juvenile is tried before a judge. Nonetheless, juveniles charged with capital murder would not be candidates for a bench trial, so one would have to look for persuasive evidence to be placed before a group of lay persons that they could both understand and identify with. The difficulty comes in piercing the "ordinary common sense" screen and the cultural hostility toward empirical research as it bears upon the dynamics of the homicidal act of the youngster on trial. Yet, postmodern criminological, medical, sociological and psychological research *does* have a role in proceedings such as this, if for no other reason than to operate as a counterweight to unexamined, untested and unverified "ordinary common sense."[111] But "OCS" has a powerfully seductive pull in the minds of judge and jury alike in juvenile homicide prosecutions. Arnold Binder, Gilbert Geis and Dickson Bruce[112] write that "unlike the physical sciences, social science suffers from commentary by those *outside its professional bounds* who nonetheless remain quite convinced that they thoroughly understand the forces at work to produce any human act."[113] (Emphasis added). Social science in general and especially criminology face a formidable struggle to convince "outsiders" of their merit. This is made all the more difficult when those charged with making and applying policy believe that they possess coequal or even superior wisdom to that of professional opinion in the field. Add to this the fact that criminology "embraces an uneasy mixture of explanatory, descriptive, political and normative concerns, and ranges well beyond the social sciences into the realms of

---

111. A term employed by Perlin, *supra* note 1.

112. ARNOLD BINDER, GILBERT GEIS & DICKSON BRUCE, JUVENILE DELINQUENCY: HISTORICAL, CULTURAL, LEGAL PERSPECTIVES (1988).

113. *Id.* at 92.

law and medicine, philosophy and social theory, policy science and politics"[114] and the problem become apparent. But despite such obstacles, it would simply be wrongheaded public policy to allow these insights and empirical research findings to go unexamined and have no place at the decisional table when the juvenile death penalty is debated. The causes of juvenile delinquency in general and juvenile homicide in particular are complex and multi-dimensional. At the end of the juvenile justice century, however, it would be most unfortunate if our post-industrial, information-intensive culture did not at least begin to seriously consider some of the empirical findings of postmodern criminology and its satellite disciplines in the juvenile life-death equation.

114. David Nelken, *Reflexive Criminology* as quoted in THE FUTURES OF CRIMINOLOGY 10 (David Nelken ed. 1994).

Chapter Nine

The End of the Juvenile Justice Century and the Juvenile Court's Postmodern Future

A. Is the Past the Prologue to Century Twenty-One?

In the *Preface* it was noted that we live in a world "that does not know how to define itself by what it is, but only by what it has just now ceased to be."[1] In his collection of essays on the postmodern condition, Walter Truett Anderson includes a selection by the French intellectual Michel Foucault whose 1978 work, *Discipline and Punish*[2] has become a widely-cited source in the on-going quest to unravel the socio-political and legal origins of imprisonment. In Foucault's essay "Strategies of Power"[3] he notes that beginning in the eighteenth century "[w]hat developed then, was a whole technique of human dressage by location, confinement, surveillance, the perpetual supervision of behavior and tasks, in short a whole technique of 'management'..."[4] The late nineteenth century saw Foucault's "technique of 'management'" in America blossom from its Illinois roots into a nationwide parallel universe for controlling children whose natural parents were unequal to the tasks of management within the nuclear family unit as envisaged by the child savers. Foucault also notes in this same essay that "the birth of the human sciences goes hand in hand with the installation of new mechanisms of power."[5] In the history of institutions and social movements, the meteoric rise and early judicial acceptance of the juvenile court was significantly advanced by the social science promise of rehabilitation, cure and

---

1. The Truth about the Truth: De-confusing and Reconstructing the Post-modern World 6 (Walter Truett Anderson ed. 1995).
2. Michel Foucault, Discipline and Punish (1978).
3. Foucault, *supra* note 2, at 43.
4. *Id.*
5. *Id.* at 44.

reintegration. In a nation then experiencing rapid urbanization, industrialization and immigration, a technique was devised to "manage" the youthful counterproductive spin-offs such forces unleashed. The juvenile court was, in Foucault's words, a "new mechanism of power." But it was also most surely conceived in terms where its power aspects were sufficiently masked by Progressive era idealism and the law's ready willingness to accord children some measure of behavioral license. The *parens patriae* concept allowed the juvenile court to be viewed as both parent and disciplinarian in one institutional matrix. This allowance provided a powerful incentive for juvenile courts to employ their "best interests" rubric in the service of statist aims. What is so amazing is that it took the judiciary nearly seventy years to come to the realization that even benevolent power can be egregiously misused. The "worst of both worlds" finally caught up with the juvenile court in the late 1960s. Since the *Gault*[6] decision, juvenile courts have been struggling with adjusting juvenile justice to criminal justice and often performing very poorly in the process. The last thirty years of the juvenile justice century has been witness to an uneasy accommodation by the juvenile court to widespread calls for either its outright abandonment, or, failing that, for the use of more formal and often more draconian social control mechanisms for the unrepentant, violent, predatory child criminal. The remaining jurisdictional segments of the juvenile court structure—dependency and neglect—have been almost totally disregarded in our national focus on serious delinquent behavior. Yet, in terms of fulfilling its *parens patriae* mission, dependency and neglect practices of the American juvenile court have not suffered the slings and arrows of outrageous polemic relative to their delinquency counterpart. In statehouse after statehouse filled with angry Puritans, the late twentieth century has witnessed a groundswell of juvenile code enactments that have placed certain categories of youth in a pre-1899 time warp. This atavistic state of affairs, however, has also been nurtured by a wide range of developments far removed from the juvenile court itself. In a real sense, the years since the 1970s have seen the juvenile court become more accommodating to punitive policy choices that have impinged upon its very legitimacy.

Thomas S. Szasz, the heterodox American psychiatrist whose works on law and mental illness have been widely read, widely

---

6. 387 U.S. 1 (1967).

praised and widely condemned,[7] made this interesting observation in the early 1970s:[8]

> To the child, control means care and love; to the adult, disdain and repression. Herein lies the fundamental dilemma and task of society:...[m]odern societies are well on their way to inverting this arrangement: they encourage parents to fake respect for their children and thus justify their failure to control them; and politicians to fake love for their fellow citizens and thus justify their efforts to exercise unlimited control over them.... *In the United States today there is a pervasive tendency to treat children like adults,* and adults like children....We should recognize the counterparts of this pattern: causing children to behave in an adult-like fashion which results in 'adulticism.'...[9] (Emphasis added.)

It is Szasz's concept of "adulticism" that has been one of the driving forces animating the recriminalization of the American juvenile court and in the constant call for its abolition! Where have all of these recriminalization/abolition arguments originated? Are they merely a historical footnote coming at the end of the juvenile court's first century of operation or are they the precursor to a completely different, completely refigured "juvenile" court in century twenty-one? That answer is yet to be determined. In the meantime, nonetheless, an excursus into some of the motivational mainsprings fueling this phenomena may be of value.

In 1991, Ira M. Schwartz and two other colleagues reported the results of a study commissioned by the Center for the Study of Youth Policy and conducted at the University of Michigan's noted Institute for Social Research.[10] In that study, these researchers found, for ex-

---

7. *See e.g.,* Thomas Szasz, Law, Liberty, and Psychiatry: An Inquiry into the Social Uses of Mental Health Practices (1963); Psychiatric Justice (1965); The Manufacture of Madness: A Comparative Study of the Inquisition and the Mental Health Movement (1970); The Myth of Mental Illness (1974); The Therapeutic State: Psychiatry in the Mirror of Current Events (1984); and Insanity: The Idea and Its Consequences (1987).

8. Thomas Szasz, The Second Sin (1973).

9. *Id.* at 1–2.

10. Ira M. Schwartz, Shenyang Guo & John J. Kerbs, *The Impact of Demographic Variables on Public Opinion Regarding Juvenile Justice: Implications for Public Policy,* 39 Crime & Delinq. 5 (Jan. 1993).

ample, that in a 1982 research project conducted by the Hubert H. Humphrey Institute of Public Affairs at the University of Minnesota, 73 percent of a cohort of 1,000 adults surveyed "believed that the primary purpose of juvenile court should be to treat and rehabilitate."[11] On the other hand, "[n]early 80% ... believed juvenile courts were too lenient on juveniles adjudicated for serious crimes."[12] In 1988, in a study sponsored by the National Council on Crime and Delinquency, Schwartz and his colleagues reported that in a "survey of over 1,100 Californians ... "[13] over "two thirds (68.4%) ... indicated that they supported a treatment and rehabilitation-oriented juvenile court ... "[14] while 62 percent voiced their disapproval for judges to sentence juvenile offenders the same way they would sentence adults. In a 1990 survey conducted by Schwartz and two other colleagues,[15] they found that "66 percent of all respondents felt juveniles who were found guilty of an offense should not receive the same sentence as adults."[16] Schwartz, Guo and Kerbs conclude from their overall findings in both Michigan and elsewhere that "the public prefers having juveniles accused of serious crimes (felonies) tried in adult courts. At the same time, public opinion does not favor giving juveniles the same sentences as adults or sentencing them to adult prisons."[17] Thus, they conclude that the public has, in recent years, become much more comfortable with the ideas of abolishing the *parens patriae* juvenile court. One would assume from this conclusion that Schwartz *et al.* view public opinion surveys through the prism of the *delinquency jurisdiction* of the court only—not opinion involving the less controversial non-criminal aspects of juvenile court practice. They note, "this [public opinion] raises serious questions about the future of the juvenile court with regard to the legal processing of juveniles accused of serious crimes."[18] On the other hand, these findings and others as well do not usually indicate what public

---

11. *Id.* at 6.
12. *Id.*
13. *Id.*
14. *Id.*
15. Ira M. Schwartz, Joan M. Abbey & William H. Barton, *The Perception and Reality of Juvenile Crime in Michigan,* Center for the Study of Youth Policy (Oct. 1990).
16. Schwart, Guo & Kerbs, *supra* note 10, at 7.
17. *Id.* at 24.
18. *Id.*

opinion might be for certain age-specific cohorts (under age sixteen, for example) who commit either homicide or other felony-type delinquency. Is there, for example, a significant body of public opinion in the 1990s that believe *all* serious delinquency cases under a certain age should be treated as "adult" crime and juveniles so charged tried in criminal courts subjected to adult sanctions? Is there a large segment of public opinion that *disagrees* with the United States Supreme Court's *Stanford-Wilkins* age differentiae for juvenile capital punishment, preferring either a lower or a higher age limit? These and other issues remain subject to fluctuation in the public's eye as delinquency either levels off, declines or rises. Public opinion is often fickle and is subject to notorious mood swings often based on anecdotal evidence having little, if any, real empirical validity. Yet, the Schwartz research does seem to indicate that if serious juvenile crime continues unabated during the latter 1990s and into the twenty-first century, lawmakers may be inclined to remove the delinquency jurisdiction from the court altogether. In that event, delinquency jurisdiction in the juvenile court may become lie a fly in amber—a historical jurisdictional relic of a past age. However, the "shop talk" in juvenile justice circles throughout the 1990s has been curiously ambivalent about both the longevity of and alternatives to retaining a separate court for youthful lawbreakers, with or without a delinquency component. This ambivalence is fueled by a continual dissonance between wanting to punish and wanting to save, between conservative and liberal political positions regarding the proper role of the court, and between our overall uneasiness about adult social control mechanisms applied to a congeries of behavioral indices symptomatic of adolescent life.

B. Retention, Abolition and Direction

The American juvenile court in the twentieth century was (and still is) a court designed to shield private problems from public view. Yet in an ironic twist of fate, the work of this court has become exceedingly "public" in the last three decades of the 1900s than many of its proponents would either wish or desire. This has occurred in no small measure because of the positions taken by a public that is more fractious, more unsure of itself in matters of penal policy in general and more willing to accede to the voices of classicism than ever before. The American public and its policymakers are seemingly enthralled with the imagination of the immediate—an imagination that is emmeshed in a conceptual vice that cannot see beyond what current practice may be doing to the juvenile court idea.

The public in our postmodern culture is badly splintered on the juvenile court retention-abolition issue. Unfortunately, the public that is consulted on numberless issues by numberless surveys may not be truly representative. As Robert N. Bellah and his colleagues so thoughtfully note,[19] "[a] mass of claimants organized into various pressure groups *is not a public....* Often our politicians and political parties debase the public by playing on its desires and fears: desire for private benefits...fear of those most in need of public provision."[20] (Emphasis added). This balkanization of the American "public" into numerous special interests who become special pleaders for their own parochial causes has had a deadening effect on true public discourse. Bellah further notes that present-day American culture and its public discourse does not come anywhere near the public discourse of past centuries. Despite our information-saturated society, in late twentieth-century America there is no overarching "discursive community capable of thinking about the common good..."[21] Because we live in a culture more interested in the individual good as an end in itself, such an emphasis has had a deleterious effect on the creation and promulgation of public policy. The juvenile court, one among a host of other American institutions, certainly suffers from such a state of affairs. In the retention-abolition hyperbole, little common ground is ever reached because our public discourse since the late 1960s in this field has focused on narrow, intensely held, excessively partisan positions.

The post-*Gault* juvenile court has been a court warding off oppositional interests in areas such as correctional treatment, punishment and juvenile responsibility in general. Despite the cumulative advances in social science and in the healing arts, juvenile court philosophy has been captured by a coterie of special interests that seek to advance their own agenda in the face of countervailing research and empirical fact. The United States has a late twentieth-century juvenile court that is heavily imbued with a punishment paradigm at all levels of delinquency practice and this paradigm in the court's paramount

---

19. ROBERT N. BELLAH, RICHARD MADSEN, WILLIAM M. SULLIVAN, ANN SWIDLER & STEVEN M. TIPTON, THE GOOD SOCIETY (1991).

20. *Id.* at 138–39.

21. *Id.* at 139.

jurisdictional segment threatens the existence of the court as originally conceived.

Justine Wise Polier, a noted family court jurist in New York City for a number of years, sadly remarked in the *Preface* to her 1989 book[22] that

> Americans have long been proud of being a child-centered, if not child-spoiling society. But we have rarely taken stock of the vast differences in the ways we cherish our own children, yet judge children who look or act in ways we dislike or disapprove....The drive for greater punishment, the transfer of more youthful offenders at younger ages to the Criminal Court system, and the further reduction of public aid appear as today's judgments....[23]

Law professor Irene Merker Rosenberg of the University of Houston believes that "the question of abolition has gone beyond mere academic discussion."[24] Professor Rosenberg is not convinced at all that trying delinquency cases in the criminal courts will reap the advantages claimed by various abolitionists. "It seems to me," says Rosenberg, "that underlying the views of the abolitionists, at least unconsciously, is a somewhat idealized or romanticized version of adult courts in which the criminal guarantees of the Bill of Rights are meaningfully enforced."[25] One of Rosenberg's opposites in the retention-abolition debate is law professor Janet E. Ainsworth of the University of Puget Sound. In a lengthy fifty-one page law review article,[26] professor Ainsworth examines the "invention" of childhood employing social constructivist theory. Quoting Arlene Skolnick's comment that "'[i]n the post-industrial era...the institutional and psychological basis for conceiving childhood and adulthood as distinct stages of live may no longer exist,'"[27] Ainsworth notes that in the 1990s, "we are witnessing the breakdown of the binary opposi-

---

22. Justine Wise Polier, Juvenile Justice in Double Jeopardy: The Distanced Community and Vengeful Retribution (1989).

23. *Id.* at xv.

24. Irene M. Rosenberg, *Leaving Bad Enough Alone: A Response to the Juvenile Court Abolitionists,* 1993 Wis. L. Rev. 163.

25. *Id.* at 173.

26. Janet E. Ainsworth, *Re-Imaging Childhood and Reconstructing the Legal Order: The Case for Abolishing the Juvenile Court,* 69 N.C. L. Rev. 1083 (1991).

27. *Id.* at 1103.

tion between child and adult, which provided the conceptual foundation of juvenile court jurisprudence."[28] Tying all of this in with the collapse of the rehabilitative ideal in corrections with what she sees as an apparent breakdown in the child-adult dyad in United States Supreme Court decisions, among others, Ainsworth argues for abolition because "the juvenile court now lacks a rationale for its continued existence other than sheer institutional inertia."[29] She then immediately qualifies the above comment by adding that "[a]ll things being equal, inertia might not be an insupportable basis for maintaining the juvenile court."[30] In employing the Rosenberg-Ainsworth dichotomous arguments over the future of the juvenile court, one is struck by both the intensity of their respective views and the arguments each marshall in support of their positions. Like excellent lawyers, they bring to the debate a mind-set focusing on those arguments and propose premises favorable to their own position.

Another dichotomous argument over the future of the juvenile court is carried on between two male law professor protagonists. Robert O. Dawson of the University of Texas at Austin and Barry C. Feld of the University of Minnesota present interesting but contrary views on the juvenile court's future. Feld is a widely published legal scholar of the juvenile court[31] who has done not only a significant amount of legal research, but has also been one of the rare breed in

---

28. *Id.*

29. *Id.* at 1118.

30. *Id.*

31. *See generally* Barry C. Feld, *Reference of Juvenile Offenders for Adult Prosecution: The Legislative Alternative to Asking Unanswerable Questions,* 62 Minn. L. Rev. 515 (1978); *Juvenile Court Legislative Reform and the Serious Young Offender: Dismantling the "Rehabilitative Ideal,"* 69 Minn. L. Rev. 141 (1981); *A Comparative Analysis of Organizational Structure and Inmate Subcultures in Institutions for Juvenile Offenders,* 27 Crime & Delinq. 336 (1981); *Delinquent Careers and Criminal Policy: Just Deserts and the Waiver Decision,* 21 Criminology 195 (1983); *Juvenile Court Meets the Principle of Offense: Legislative Change in Juvenile Waiver Statutes,* 78 J. Crim. L. & Criminology (1987); *In re Gault Revisited: A Cross-State Comparison of the Right to Counsel in Juvenile Court,* 34 Crime & Delinq. 393 (1988); *Juvenile Court Meets the Principle of Offense: Punishment, Treatment, and the Difference It Makes,* 68 B.U. L. Rev. 821 (1988); *The Punitive Juvenile Court and the Quality of Procedural Justice: Disjunctions Between Rhetoric and Reality,* 36 Crime & Delinq. 443 (1990); *Justice By Geography: Urban, Suburban, and Rural Variations in Juvenile Justice Administration,* 82 J. Crim. L. & Criminology 156 (1991); and JUSTICE FOR CHILDREN: THE RIGHT TO COUNSEL AND THE JUVENILE COURTS (1993).

the legal academy who looks beyond "the law" for answers that empirical social science may provide. Feld maintains that "[a]bolishing the juvenile court would force a long overdue and critical reassessment of the entire social construct of 'childhood'"[32] citing Ainsworth's 1991 law review article. To Feld, "[t]he fundamental shortcoming of the traditional juvenile court is not a failure of implementation but a failure of conception."[33] He then goes on to argue that the *parens patriae* juvenile court "was conceived as a social service agency in a judicial setting"[34] and that it is both philosophically and pragmatically dubious to expect a court with that type of organizational structure to continue to exist in the twenty-first century. Feld holds to a sincere and well-argued belief that the adult criminal courts could and should be modified in certain particulars to deal with the influx of juvenile caseloads. He notes that "[a]dult courts could impose shorter sentences for reduced culpability on a discretionary basis...[t]his could take the form of a formal 'youth discount' at sentencing."[35] Further on he notes that "[a] graduated age/culpability sentencing scheme could avoid some of the inconsistency and injustice associated with the binary either/or juvenile versus adult sentencing played out in judicial waiver proceedings."[36]

"The case against abolition," writes Robert O. Dawson of the University of Texas at Austin,[37] "is based on three clusters of arguments: 1) the notion that minors have less responsibility for their misconduct than do adults; 2) the greater rehabilitation potential of minors, justify greater devotion to resources; and 3) the avoidance of inappropriate legal rules."[38] One of the key arguments Dawson advances and one rarely touted in the literature as a reason for retention of the juvenile court is that "[a]n integral part of any juvenile justice system is a network of private, charitable, or religious institutions, facilities,

---

32. Barry C. Feld, *Criminalizing the American Juvenile Court*, 17 *Crime & Justice: A Rev. of Research* 197, 261–67 (Michael Tonry ed. 1993).

33. *Id.* at 256

34. *Id.*

35. *Id.* at 264.

36. *Id.* at 265.

37. Robert O. Dawson, *The Future of Juvenile Justice: Is It Time to Abolish the System?*, 81 J. Crim. L. & Criminology 136 (1990).

38. *Id.* at 145.

and programs"[39] that are regularly employed in the dispositional context. To Dawson, "[t]here really is no adult counterpart to this private segment of the juvenile system,... "[40] He concludes his plea for retention by mentioning the loss of control over status offenders, the spectre of dealing with the questionable practices of bail bondsmen for youngsters and last, but certainly not least, "the undeniable fact ...that children attract resources, both public and private."[41] These four divergent views by a quartet of legal scholars reflect a depth of analysis generally missing in the hurly burly pedestrian positions taken in "public opinion" polls and in legislative chambers. Their views are merely illustrative, not exhaustive. Divergent positions taken by others who have an equal interest in this issue reflect their own widely differing views and their own particular "slant" on the subject.[42] Like so much in the law, there are equities on both sides of this issue. A schism running through this debate has bedeviled this body of law since 1899 and is one that continues to defy rational solution, or so it would seem. That schism is the inability or unwillingness of lawmakers to discretely define the term "delinquency" in juvenile codes. We read and hear a great deal about trying *delinquents* as adults, dealing with *delinquents* more harshly, holding *delinquents* more responsible, and sanctioning *delinquents* more severely. Despite the call for treating delinquents as less eligible for juvenile court juris-

---

39. *Id.* at 148.
40. *Id.*
41. *Id.* at 155.
42. *See, e.g.,* Michael K. Burke, *This Old Court: Abolitionists Once Again Line Up the Wrecking Ball on the Juvenile Court When All It Needs Is a Few Minor Alterations,* 26 U. Tol. L. Rev. 1027 (1995); Charles E. Springer, *Rehabilitating the Juvenile Court,* 5 Notre Dame J.L. Ethics & Pub. Pol'y. 397 (1991); Seymour Gelber, *The Juvenile Justice System: Vision for the Future,* 41 Juv. & Fam. Ct. J. 15 (1990); Ira M. Schwartz, "The Next Twenty Years," ch. 5 in (IN)JUSTICE FOR JUVENILES 167 (1989); Katherine H. Ferderle, *The Abolition of the Juvenile Court: A Proposal for the Preservation of Children's Legal Rights,* 16 J. Contemp. L. 23 (1990); Martin Guggenheim, *A Call to Abolish the Juvenile Justice System,* 2 Children's Rights Rep. 7 (1978); Barry Krisberg, Ira Schwartz, Paul Lisky, & James F. Austin, *The Watershed of Juvenile Justice Reform,* 32 Crime & Delinq. 5 (1986); Francis B. McCarthy, *Should Juvenile Delinquecy Be Abolished?,* 23 Crime & Delinq. 196 (1977); H. Ted Rubin, *Retain the Juvenile Court?: Legislative Developments, Reform Directions and the Call for Abolition,* 25 Crime & Delinq. 281 (1979): Steven Wizner, & Mary F. Keller, *The Penal Method of Juvenile Justice: Is Juvenile Court Delinquency Jurisdiction Obsolete?,* 52 N.Y.U. L. Rev. 1120 (1977); and Marvin Wolfgang, *Abolish the Juvenile Court System,* 2 Cal. Lawyer 12 (1982).

diction, there remains a troubling legislative spaghetti bowl of statutory provisions whose wording should be reinvestigated in light of contemporary punitive orientations. If the juvenile court abolitionists ultimately win the day and convince governors and state legislatures to truncate the delinquency jurisdiction of the court, the question then becomes: Do we now abolish *all* definitions of delinquency, or do we carve out a segment of juvenile criminality—felonious but non-lethal—that will still demand the attention of the juvenile court? If so, do we then establish an age limit for exclusive jurisdiction, regardless of offense, and, if so, at what age division? What an informed public should debate, both within and without the academy, is this: How can postmodern American society deal with these differential definitions of delinquency that have held a reasonable solution hostage to our retention of the juvenile court as an institution? An answer to that question would measurably facilitate the untying of the Gordian knot of juvenile criminality and the juvenile court's response to it. While not necessarily *the* complete answer to the juvenile court conundrum, it would certainly facilitate a more rational and communitarian discourse. American juvenile codes are creatures of the legislative will and they can be changed by that will. But this body of law has been enveloped in a complex web of contradictions that has often tended to compromise its ability to both deal with the serious delinquent and to protect the public. A legislative agenda that would forthrightly address the issue of delinquency categories by age, by conduct and by sanction may save the juvenile court from extinction as we know it. For example, legislation should address the chronological age *floor* for death eligibility for juveniles charged with capital murder. Correspondingly, legislation should also address the upper age limits for delinquency jurisdiction. Debate should center on whether or not to revive the original Illinois statutory upper age limits of sixteen, with dependency and neglect jurisdiction arguably remaining at eighteen. The waiver issue should also command a thoughtful reassessment.[43] A definitive age line should be established, perhaps on the common law model, at age fourteen. If fourteen is

---

43. The waiver rationale has not always lived up to its purported purpose, that is, a device to remove violent, dangerous and predatory juveniles out of juvenile court and into criminal court. The Office of Juvenile Justice and Delinquency Prevention (OJJDP) of the U.S. Department of Justice reported in 1995, that 16.6% of waived juveniles nationwide were involved in violent criminal activity, whereas 83.3% were charged with property offenses. *See generally* Office of Juvenile Justice and Delinquency Prevention,

agreed upon, then the "floor" issue would be determined for capital punishment unless a higher statutory age limit is enacted following the Supreme Court's *Stanford-Wilkins* pronouncement. If age sixteen is the upper age for delinquency jurisdiction, then who between the ages of fourteen and sixteen should be removed to adult criminal court for trial on charges less than capital homicide? Here debate should center, among other things, on crime type, evidence of culpable mental state, use of weapon or not, prior juvenile record, aggravating and mitigating circumstances, choice of victim, amenability to juvenile justice treatment, and any other relevant social science data that can assist the court in its waiver determination. The matter of prosecutorial waiver and exclusion legislation that targets juveniles below age sixteen for adult prosecution should be considered presumptively suspect. If legislation can tighten the multiform definitions of delinquency by discarding their non-criminal triggers, juvenile courts would be far better equipped to direct their attention toward more appropriate offense-specific dispositional alternatives. A well-written and thoughtfully crafted body of organic juvenile law would at least give the juvenile, the court and the correctional establishment a firmer sense of purpose about both the juvenile court and about juvenile justice. As previously noted, one of the negative hallmarks of the pre-*Gault* juvenile court was its loss of institutional integrity in the minds of the public at large. While certainly not a panacea for *all* the ills of the court, statutory modification of the delinquency jurisdiction would be a healthy beginning. American juvenile courts are classic examples of a judicial system operating under statutory mandates that diminish rather than inspire confidence in their work product. Compassion fatigue with all of that term's implications sealed the fate of the *parens patriae* juvenile court in serious delinquency cases in the late 1960s. The court as an institution had promised much, but delivered little. The public embraced the juvenile court early on as a truly *American* solution to an increasingly intractable problem. After the 1950s, however, there developed enormous unease about the efficacy of the court's child saving mission. That unease, coupled with a slow but ominous rise in delinquency rates and a greater willingness to punish youthful malefactors, came to a head in the constitutional litigation of the 1960s. Compassion, broadly conceived, has always

Howard Snyder and Melissa Sickmund, *Juvenile Offenders and Victims: A Focus on Violence* 17 (May, 1995).

been an unarticulated major premise in juvenile court operation. But, with the *Kent*[44] and *Gault*[45] decisions abroad in the law and the nation moving toward an era where adolescence was being redefined, the old Progressive shibboleths were no longer deemed as relevant as they once were. Compassion for juveniles, especially those ethnic and class-specific youngsters who were then (and now) crowding the juvenile court dockets, seemed terribly out of fashion. Rehabilitation in the juvenile court, except for a small number of low visibility programs, had long since taken on the trappings of a smoke and mirrors game that was making a mockery of the state as super parent. The truly regretful fact of the matter was this: the juvenile court had always promised both treatment and rehabilitation for its wards. That promise, however, was premised upon a late nineteenth-early twentieth-century view of the child as one who had earlier in his or her life been *habilitated* (made fit or equipped) to ultimately become a productive societal member. The juvenile court would intercede in this effort in order that the youngster could be *rehabilitated* or placed in a previous state of being once he or she had gone astray and violated a juvenile code. The juvenile court was the institutional arm of the benevolent patriarch who would now lead the child back to the path of rectitude, habilitation and lawful middle-class behavior. That idea worked very well for a brief span of years when the juvenile court's client population had been exposed at least to some modicum of socialization or habilitation *before* their court appearance. However, when the adolescent caseload of the court began to be overwhelmed by children who had *never* been ever marginally socialized or habilitated, the pious rhetoric of benevolent treatment and *re*habilitation rang empty. If a child has never experienced habilitation in a secure family setting or other appropriate social milieu before he or she comes before a juvenile court, how legitimate is it to expect the state as *parens patriae* to *rehabilitate* that juvenile? The prefix "re" before the term habilitate would seem to suggest making "anew" or remaking into a former state of being. The tragedy of the juvenile justice century is that American juvenile courts lost their ability to rehabilitate their charges precisely because the American adult (and often teenage) underclass lost both its will and its tenuous ability to habilitate its offspring from birth. The juvenile court, recognizing early on

---

44. 383 U.S. 541 (1966).
45. 387 U.S. 1 (1967).

this weak partnership between court and parent, shifted emphasis to a quasi-preventive mode of operation, the idea being to prevent delinquent behavior by coercively intervening before the child reached legal adulthood. This was made legally palatable by encouraging legislatures to enact delinquency definitions having no statutory counterpart in other areas of enacted law. The hope here was that through this legislative grant of power, the juvenile court would serve as parental alter-ego in a preventive context. The history of the conflation of delinquency definitions post-1899 indicated that the legislatures were approvingly entering into a compact with their juvenile courts to recast the court into a preventive role that often overreached the bounds of legitimate state intervention. But, even in their nascent preventive mode, American juvenile courts never completely conceived their mission to be one of delinquency prevention *per se.* Prevention, if it exists at all, exists primarily anterior to judicial intervention. Todd Clear[46] notes that "[c]rime prevention can be thought of as occurring in several domains of action.... We may target social forces [or]...[f]inally, we may target the conditions under which crimes occur,..."[47] The most that one can hope for in *post facto* juvenile court intervention with delinquents is that through occasional therapy that shows solid social science or medical success, through natural maturation and through a huge dose of episodic good luck, the youngster will emerge from association with the system a better person. Unfortunately, in most cases, that hope is nothing more than sheer optimism on the same order as the child saving rhetoric of the early twentieth century. Juvenile corrections is often ill-equipped to "target the offender" and to provide individualized treatment resources. Moreover, the juvenile court as an institution has neither the mandate nor the resources at its disposal to target either the wider social forces or the social conditions at work that breed delinquent behavior. The legislative reformulations, the renewed urge to punish, the conversion of childhood to Szasz's "adulticism," and the recent calls for abolition of the post-*Gault* juvenile court may simply be just another *ex post facto* apology. An apology for this society's benign and not-so-benign neglect of a population segment whose importance in the postmodern social scheme of things has been devalued and deemphasized for the past several decades.

46. Todd Clear, Harm in American Penology: Offenders, Victims, and Their Communities (1994).
47. *Id.* at 183.

In a January, 1997, newspaper *Commentary* entitled "An arsonist's letter points to deeper ills,"[48] black syndicated columnist Bill Maxwell of St. Petersburg, Florida, printed excerpts from a letter written by one Everette Carter, a seventeen-year-old black male charged with the crime of arson in the burning of a St. Petersburg church in October, 1996. The letter was addressed by the juvenile to the white pastor of the burned church which the juvenile attended, and read in part as follows:

Dear Mr. Paster:

This is Emory Carter. this letter is to let you no that it was not your falt what I did the only person to blame is me and I can't say it in words But if I could I would rebuild the church.... Its sad that this world so full of hate But it's the truth theres even Biger crime than we notic so many young are going to waste. So many strong young men full of pride But they just Don't care that there dieing for no resan ... all I can do is ask for forgiveness and god. and I hope that youl say yes ... its so hard to Believe a young man could holed up so much waight and til it explodes. that's all I got to say for now all got to say is that I am truly sorry please forgive me.[49]

That letter and its pathetically written message speaks volumes about the state of childhood in some of the less fortunate strata of postmodern America. The Everette Carters of this land are clear examples of the non-habilitated youngsters that dominate the juvenile dockets at the end of the juvenile justice century. They have become our worst case scenario, a Dickensian visage, dominating and skewing political discourse, public philosophy and public choice. Polier[50] summed up the plight of children like Everette Carter and countless others like him when she noted that "[t]he lessening concern for youths who [live] in and would be returned to lives of poverty in deprived areas [play] a dominant role in the decline of juvenile justice."[51] What century twenty-one holds for both the juvenile court and for its socially

---

48. Bill Maxwell, *An arsonist's letter points to deeper ills,* Tuscaloosa (Ala.) News, Jan. 29, 1997, at 7A.

49. *Id.*

50. Polier, *supra* note 22.

51. *Id.* at 160. *See also* Arloc Sherman, Wasting America's Future (1994).

marginalized caseload is still an open question. Perhaps wiser and more pragmatic minds will prevail to reinvigorate the institution with a new sense of purpose, *a new twenty-first-century Progressivism* with a new ethos of child saving aimed at those children today who are far more at risk, relatively speaking, than those immigrant vagabond youngsters in the Illinois summer of 1899.

References

A Report of the Labors of John Augustus for the Last Ten Years, in Aid of the Unfortunate, Boston: Wright & Hasty (1852).

Abraham, Henry J., *Freedom and the Court: Civil Rights and Liberties in the United States*, New York: Oxford University Press (1967).

Ainsworth, Janet E., "Re-Imaging Childhood and Reconstructing The Legal Order: The Case for Abolishing the Juvenile Court," 69 *North Carolina Law Review* 1083 (1991).

Allen, Francis A., *The Borderland of Criminal Justice: Essays in Law and Criminology*, Chicago: The University of Chicago Press (1964).

———, "The Borderland of the Criminal Law: Problems of Socializing Criminal Justice," 32 *Social Service Review* 116 (1958).

———, *The Decline of the Rehabilitative Ideal: Penal Policy and Social Purpose*, New Haven: Yale University Press (1981).

Alers, Miriam S., "Transfer of Juvenile from Juvenile to Criminal Court," 19 *Crime and Delinquency* 519 (1973).

American Broadcasting Company, "Youth Terror: The View from Behind the Gun," TV Documentary, June 28, 1978.

American Civil Religion (Donald G. Jones & Russell E. Richey eds.), San Francisco: Mellen Research University Press (1990).

Baker, Harvey H., "Procedures of the Boston Juvenile Court," in *Preventive Treatment of Neglected Children* (Hastings H. Hart ed.), New York: Russell Sage Foundation (1910).

Bassham, Gregory, "Rethinking the Emerging Jurisprudence of Juvenile Death," 5 *Notre Dame Journal of Law, Ethics and Public Policy* 467 (1991).

Bazemore, Gordon & Mark Umbreit, "Rethinking the Sanctioning Function in Juvenile Court: Retributive or Restorative Responses to Youth Crime," 41 *Crime and Delinquency* 296 (1995).

Beccaria, Cesare Bonesana, *An Essay on Crimes and Punishment* (Henry Padlucci trans.) New York: Macmillan (1963). (Originally published in 1764).

Bellah, Robert N., "American Civil Religion in the 1970s," in *American Civil Religion* (Donald G. Jones & Russell E. Richey eds.), San Francisco: Mellen Research University Press (1990).

Bellah, Robert N., et al., *The Good Society*, New York: Alfred A. Knopf (1991).

Berger, Raoul, *Death Penalties: The Supreme Court's Obstacle Course*, Cambridge: Harvard University Press (1982).

Berkson, Larry C., *The Concept of Cruel and Unusual Punishment*, Lexington, MA: Lexington Books (1975).

Berlin, Isaiah, "Two Concepts of Liberty," Inaugural Lecture, Oxford University, England, October 31, 1958.

Bernard, Thomas J., *The Cycle of Juvenile Justice*, New York: Oxford University Press (1992).

Berns, Walter, *For Capital Punishment: Crime and the Morality of the Death Penalty*, New York: Basic Books (1979).

Besharov, Douglas, J., *Juvenile Justice Advocacy: Practice in a Unique Court*, New York: Practicing Law Institute (1974).

Bevan, Anuerin, *In Place of Fear*, New York: Simon & Schuster (1952).

"Beyond the Teen-Age Gun," *New York Times*, June 28, 1978, p. 30.

Binder, Arnold, Gilbert Geis & Dickson Bruce, *Juvenile Delinquency: Historical, Cultural, Legal Perspectives*, New York: Macmillan (1988).

Bird, John·R., Marcia L. Conlin & Geri Frank, "Children in Trouble: The Juvenile Justice System," in *Legal Rights of Children* (Robert M. Horowitz & Howard A. Davidson eds.), New York: McGraw-Hill (1984).

Bishop, Donna M. & Charles E. Frazier, "Transfer of Juveniles to Criminal Court: A Case Study and Analysis of Prosecutorial Waiver," 5 *Notre Dame Journal of Law, Ethics and Public Policy* 281 (1991).

Bishop, Donna M., Charles E. Frazier & John C. Henretta, "Prosecutorial Waiver: A Case Study of Questionable Reform," 35 *Crime and Delinquency* 179 (1989).

Bishop, Donna M., et al, "The Transfer of Juveniles to Criminal Court: Does It Make a Difference?," 42 *Crime and Delinquency* 171 (1996).

Black, Donald & Albert J. Reiss, Jr., "Police Control of Juveniles," 35 *American Sociological Review* 63 (1970).

Black, Henry C., *Black's Law Dictionary*, 4th ed., St. Paul: West (1951).

Blackstone, Sir William, *Commentaries on the Laws of England*, vols. 1 & 4, (William Draper Lewis ed.), Philadelphia: Rees Welch & Co. (1898).

Bloch, Herbert A. & Frank T. Flynn, *Delinquency: The Juvenile Offender in America Today*, New York: Random House (1956).

Blumberg, Abraham S., *Criminal Justice: Issues and Ironies*, 2d ed., New York: New Viewpoints (1979).

Bork, Robert H., *Slouching Towards Gomorrah: Modern Liberalism and American Decline*, New York: Harper-Collins (1996).

Bortner, M.A., "The Young Offender: Transfer to Adult Court and Subsequent Sentencing," 6 *Criminal Justice Journal* 281 (1983).

———, "Traditional Rhetoric, Organizational Realities: Remand of Juveniles to Adult Court," 32 *Crime and Delinquency* 54 (1986).

Boswell, Mary Jane, *Notes*, "Where Have All the Children Gone? The Supreme Court Finds Pretrial Detention of Minors Constitutional: *Schall v. Martin*," 34 *DePaul Law Review* 733 (1985).

Bradbury, Dorothy E., *Five Decades of Action for Children: A History of the Children's Bureau*, Washington, DC: U.S. Government Printing Office (1962).

Bremmer, Robert, "A Note on the Role of Social Workers in the Reform Movement," in *Perspectives on Social Welfare: An Introductory Anthology* (Paul Weinberger ed.), New York: Macmillan (1969).

Brieland, Donald, Lela B. Costin & Charles R. Atherton, *Contemporary Social Work: An Introduction to Social Work and Social Welfare*, 2d ed., New York: McGraw-Hill (1980).

Brown, Rhea, "The Constitutional Problems of the Juvenile Court Law," 50 *Women Law Journal* 89 (1964).

Burke, Michael K., "This Old Court: Abolitionists Once Again Line Up the Wrecking Ball on the Juvenile Court When All It Needs Is a Few Minor Alterations," 26 *University of Toledo Law Review* 1027 (1995).

Caldwell, Robert G., *The Red Hannah: Delaware's Whipping Post,* Philadelphia: University of Pennsylvania Press (1947).

Carter, Dan T., *Scottsboro: A Tragedy of the American South,* Baton Rouge, LA: Louisiana State University Press (rev. ed. 1969).

Caspi, Avshalom, "Personality in the Life Course," 53 *Journal of Personality and Social Psychology* 1203 (1987).

Champion, Dean, "Teenage Felons and Waiver Hearings: Some Recent Trends, 1980–1988," 35 *Crime and Delinquency* 577 (1989).

Children and Families First: A Mandate for America's Courts, National Council of Juvenile and Family Court Judges (1995).

Chute, Charles, *John Augustus: First Probation Officer: John Augustus' Original Report of His Labors, 1852,* Montclair, NJ: Patterson-Smith Reprint Series (1939).

Chute, Charles & Majorie Bell, *Crime, Courts and Probation,* New York: Macmillan (1956).

Clear, Todd R., *Harm in American Penology: Offenders, Victims, and Their Communities,* Albany, NY: State University of New York Press (1994).

Clear, Todd R. & Vincent O'Leary, *Controlling the Offender in the Community,* Lexington, MA: Lexington Books (1983).

Cohen, Lawrence E., *Delinquency Dispositions: An Empirical Analysis of Processing Decisions in Three Juvenile Courts,* National Criminal Justice Information Service (NCJIS), Washington, DC: U.S. Government Printing Office (1975).

Coke on Littleton (Francis Hargrave & Charles Butler eds.), London: J. & W.T. Clark (1809). (Also known as *First Part of the Institutes of the Lawes of England).*

Combating Violence and Delinquency: The National Juvenile Justice Action Plan, Office of Juvenile Justice & Delinquency Prevention

(OJJDP), Washington DC: U.S. Government Printing Office (March, 1996).

Cox, Steven M. & John J. Conrad, *Juvenile Justice,* Dubuque, IA: William C. Brown (1978).

Crime (James Q. Wilson & Joan Petersilla eds.), San Francisco: Institute for Contemporary Studies (1995).

Criminal Careers and 'Career Criminals,' (Alfred Blumstein, Jacqueline Cohen, Jeffrey Roth & Christy Visher eds.), Washington, DC: National Academy Press (1986).

Croxton, Tom A., "The Kent Case and Its Consequences," 7 *Journal of Family Law* 1 (1967).

Cullen, Francis T., Katheryn Golden & John B. Cullen, "Is Child Saving Dead?: Attitudes Toward Juvenile Rehabilitation in Illinois," in *The New Juvenile Justice* (Martin L. Forst ed.), Chicago: Nelson-Hall (1995).

Current Events: "Juvenile Court Celebrates Thirtieth Birthday," 15 *American Bar Association Journal* 329 (June, 1929).

Dalzell, George W., *Benefit of Clergy and Related Matters,* Winston-Salem, NC: J.F. Blair (1955).

Davis, Robert & Sam V. Meddis, "Random Killings Hit a High," *USA Today,* Dec. 5, 1994, p. 1A.

Davis, Samuel M., *Rights of Juveniles: The Juvenile Justice System,* 2d ed., New York: Clark Boardman Callaghan (1996).

———, "The Jurisdictional Dilemma of the Juvenile Court," 51 *North Carolina Law Review* 195 (1972).

Dawson, Robert O., "The Future of Juvenile Justice: Is It Time to Abolish the System?," 81 *Journal of Criminal Law and Criminology* 136 (1990).

Delinquency and Social Policy (Paul Lerman ed.), New York: Praeger (1970).

Delinquency Cases in Juvenile Court, 1992, Fact Sheet #18, Office of Juvenile Justice & Delinquency Prevention (OJJDP), Washington, DC: U.S. Government Printing Office (July, 1994).

deMause, Lloyd, "The Evolution of Childhood," in *The History of Childhood* (Lloyd deMause ed.), New York: Harper Torchbooks (1975).

Dorsen, Norman & Daniel A. Rezneck, "In re Gault and the Future of Juvenile Law," 1 *Family Law Quarterly* 23 (1967).

Douglas, Mary, *How Institutions Think*, Syracuse, NY: Syracuse University Press (1986).

Dwyer, Diane C. & Roger B. McNally, "Juvenile Justice: Reform, Retain and Reaffirm," 51 *Federal Probation* 47 (1987).

Ellsworth, Phoebe C. & Lee Ross, "Public Opinion On Capital Punishment: A Close Examination of the Views of Abolitionists and Retentionists," 29 *Crime and Delinquency* 116 (1983).

Espy, M. Watt & John Ortiz Smykla, *Executions in the United States, 1608–1991: The Espy File* computer file. 3rd ICPSR ed. Compiled by John Ortiz Smykla, The University of Alabama. Ann Arbor, MI: Inter-University Consortium for Political and Social Research producer and distributor, 1994.

Ewing, Charles, *When Children Kill: The Dynamics of Juvenile Homicide*, Lexington, MA: Lexington Books (1990).

Fagan, Jeffrey & Elizabeth P. Deschenes, "Determination of Juvenile Waiver Decisions for Violent Juvenile Offenders," 81 *Journal of Criminal Law and Criminology* 314 (1990).

Federle, Katherine H., "The Abolition of the Juvenile Court: A Proposal for the Preservation of Children's Legal Rights," 16 *Journal of Contemporary Law* 23 (1990).

Feld, Barry C., "A Comparative Analysis of Organizational Structure and Inmate Subcultures in Institutions for Juvenile Offenders," 27 *Crime and Delinquency* 336 (1981).

———, "Criminalizing the American Juvenile Court," 17 *Crime and Justice: A Review of Research* 197 (Michael Tonry ed.), Chicago: The University of Chicago Press (1993).

———, "Delinquent Careers and Criminal Policy: Just Deserts and the Waiver Decision," 21 *Criminology* 195 (1983).

———, "In re Gault Revisited: A Cross-State Comparison of the Right to Counsel in Juvenile Court," 34 *Crime and Delinquency* 393 (1988).

———, "Justice by Geography: Urban, Suburban, and Rural Variations in Juvenile Justice Administration," 82 *Journal of Criminal Law and Criminology* 156 (1991).

———, *Justice For Children: The Right to Counsel and the Juvenile Courts*, Boston: Northeastern University Press (1993).

———, "Juvenile Court Legislative Reform and the Serious Young Offender: Dismantling the 'Rehabilitative Ideal,'" 69 *Minnesota Law Review* 141 (1981).

———, "Juvenile Court Meets the Principle of Offense: Legislative Change in Juvenile Waiver Statutes," 78 *Journal of Criminal Law and Criminology* 471 (1987).

———, "Juvenile Court Meets the Principle of Offense: Punishment, Treatment, and the Difference It Makes," 68 *Boston University Law Review* 821 (1988).

———, "Reference of Juvenile Offenders for Adult Prosecution: The Legislative Alternative to Asking Unanswerable Questions," 62 *Minnesota Law Review* 515 (1978).

———, "The Punitive Juvenile Court and the Quality of Procedural Justice: Disjunctions Between Rhetoric and Reality," 36 *Crime and Delinquency* 443 (1990).

Ferdinand, Theodore N., "History Overtakes the Juvenile Justice System," 37 *Crime and Delinquency* 204 (1991).

Ferri, Enrico, *Criminal Sociology* (J.I. Kelly & John Lisle trans.), Boston: Little, Brown (1917).

Ferster, Elyce Z. & Thomas F. Courtless, "The Beginning of Juvenile Justice: Police Practices and the Juvenile Offender," 22 *Vanderbilt Law Review* 567 (1969).

Ferster, Elyce Z., Edith N. Snethen & Thomas F. Courtless, "Juvenile Detention: Protection, Prevention or Punishment?," 38 *Fordham Law Review* 161 (1969).

Finkelstein, M. Marvin, *et al., Prosecution in Juvenile Courts: Guidelines for the Future*, National Institute of Law Enforcement & Criminal Justice (NILECJ), Washington, DC: U.S. Government Printing Office (1973).

Fitzherbert, Sir Anthony, *New Natura Brevium*, 8th ed., London: H. Lintot (1755).

Fogel, David, *We Are Living Proof...The Justice Model for Corrections*, Cincinnati: Anderson (1979).

Footlick, Jerrold *et al., Children and the Law, Newsweek*, Sept. 8, 1975, p. 66.

Foucault, Michel, *Discipline and Punish*, New York: Pantheon Press (1978).

Fox, Sanford, J., *Modern Juvenile Justice: Cases and Materials*, St. Paul: West (1972).

Frank, Henriette G., Jerome Amalie & Hofer Amalie, *Annals of the Chicago Woman's Club for the First Forty Years of Its Organization*, Chicago: Chicago Woman's Club (1916).

Frank, Jerome, *Law and the Modern Mind*, New York: Coward-McCann (1935).

————, "The Place of an Expert in a Democratic Society," in *The Selected Writings of Judge Jerome Frank: A Man's Reach* (Barbara Frank Kristein ed.), New York: Macmillan (1965).

Frankel, Marvin, E., *Criminal Sentences: Law Without Order*, New York: Hill & Wang (1972).

Friedman, Lawrence M., *A History of American Law*, 2d ed., New York: Simon & Schuster (1985).

Friendly, Henry J., "The Bill of Rights as a Code of Criminal Procedure," 53 *California Law Review* 929 (1965).

Gardiner, Muriel, *The Deadly Innocents: Portraits of Children Who Kill*, New York: Basic Books (1985).

Garlock, Peter D., "Wayward Children and the Law, 1820–1900: The Genesis of the Status Offense Jurisdiction of the Juvenile Court," 13 *Georgia Law Review* 341 (1979).

Gaurino-Ghezzi, Susan & Edward J. Loughran, *Balancing Juvenile Justice*, New Brunswick, NJ: Transaction (1996).

Gaylin, Willard *et al., Doing Good: The Limits of Benevolence*, New York: Pantheon Books (1978).

Geimer, William S., "Juvenileness: A Single-Edged Constitutional Sword," 22 *Georgia Law Review* 949 (1988).

Gelber, Seymour, "The Juvenile Justice System: Vision for the Future," 41 *Juvenile and Family Court Journal* 15 (1990).

Glueck, Sheldon, *The Problems of Delinquency*, Boston: Houghton-Mifflin (1959).

Glueck, Sheldon & Eleanor Glueck, *Delinquents and Non-Delinquents in Perspective,* Cambridge: Harvard University Press (1968).

Goodman, James E., *Stories of Scottsboro,* New York: Pantheon Books (1994).

Goring, Charles, *The English Convict: A Statistical Study,* London: Darling & Son (1913).

Graham, Fred, *The Self-Inflicted Wound,* New York: The Free Press (1970).

Grannuci, Anthony F., "'Nor Cruel and Unusual Punishment Inflicted': The Original Meaning," 57 *California Law Review* 839 (1969).

Griffin, Brenda S. & Charles T. Griffin, *Juvenile Delinquency in Perspective,* New York: Harper & Row (1978).

Guggenheim, Martin, "A Call to Abolish the Juvenile Court System," 2 *Children's Rights Reports* 7 (1978).

Hagan, John & Jeffrey Leon, "Rediscovering Delinquency," 42 *American Sociological Review* 587 (1982).

Hale, Sir Matthew, *The History of the Pleas of the Crown,* London: T. Payne (1778).

Hall, Jerome, *General Principles of Criminal Law,* 2d ed., Indianapolis: Bobbs-Merrill (1960).

Hammond, John Lawrence & Barbara Hammond, *The Town Labourer,* London: British Home Office (1941).

Handler, Joel F., "The Juvenile Court and the Adversary System: Problems of Function and Form," 1965 *Wisconsin Law Review* 7.

Harno, Albert J., "Some Significant Developments in Criminal Law and Procedure in the Last Century," 42 *Journal of Criminal Law, Criminology and Police Science* 427 (1951).

Hawkins, J. David, "Controlling Crime Before It Happens: Risk-Focused Prevention," in *Juvenile Homicides,* National Institute of Justice (NIJ), Washington, DC: U.S. Government Printing Office (August, 1995).

Henderson, Charles R., "Theory and Practice of Juvenile Courts," in *Proceedings of the National Conference on Charities and Correction* (1904).

Hirschi, Travis & Michael Gottfredson, "Age and the Explanation of Crime," 89 *American Journal of Sociology* 552 (1983).

Holstein, Sherry B., *Comment*, "Slamming the Door on Prodigals: Changing Conceptions of Childhood and the Demise of Juvenile Justice," 9 *Northern Kentucky Law Review* 517 (1982).

Horowitz, Robert M. & Howard A. Davidson, *Legal Rights of Children*, Colorado Springs, CO: McGraw-Hill (1984).

Huizinga, David, Rolf Loeber & Terence Thornberry, "Urban Delinquency and Substance Abuse," Office of Juvenile Justice and Delinquency Prevention (OJJDP), Washington, DC: U.S. Government Printing Office (1993).

Hurley, Thomas D., *Origin of the Illinois Juvenile Court Law*, Chicago: The Visitation and Aid Society (1907).

Hurst, James W., *The Growth of American Law: The Law Makers*, Boston: Little, Brown (1950).

Huxley, Aldous, *Brave New World Revisited*, New York: Harper (1960).

IJA/ABA Juvenile Justice Standards, Standards Relating to Adjudication, Cambridge: Ballinger (1980).

———, *Standards Relating to Disposition*, Cambridge: Ballinger (1980).

———, *Standards Relating to Interim Status*, Cambridge: Ballinger (1980).

———, *Standards Relating to the Juvenile Probation Function*, Cambridge: Ballinger (1980).

———, *Standards Relating to Juvenile Records and Information Systems*, Cambridge: Ballinger (1980).

———, *Standards Relating to Police Handling of Juvenile Problems*, Cambridge: Ballinger (1980).

Inciardi, James A., *Criminal Justice*, 5th ed., New York: Harcourt Brace (1996).

Ives, George, *A History of Penal Methods*, London: Stanley Paul (1914).

Jeffrey, C. Ray, "Criminology as an Interdisciplinary Behavioral Science" in *Criminology: New Concerns* (Edward Sagarin ed.), Beverly Hills, CA: Sage (1979).

Jenkins, Phillip, "The Radicals and the Rehabilitative Ideal, 1890–1930," 20 *Criminology* 347 (1982).

Jensen, Gary F. & Dean G. Rojek, *Delinquency and Youth Crime*, 2d ed., Prospect Heights, IL: Waveland Press (1992).

Justice for the Child (Margaret K. Rosenheim ed.), New York: Free Press (1962).

Juvenile Homicides, National Institute of Justice (NIJ), Washington, DC: U.S. Government Printing Office (August, 1995).

Juvenile Violent Crime Arrest Rates 1972–1992, Fact Sheet #14, Office of Juvenile Justice and Delinquency Prevention (OJJDP), Washington, DC: U.S. Government Printing Office (May, 1994).

Kadish, Sanford H., "The Crisis of Overcriminalization," 374 *Annals of the American Academy of Political and Social Science* 170 (1967).

Kahn, Alfred J., "Social Work and Control of Delinquency," in *Delinquency and Social Policy* (Paul Lerman ed.), New York: Praeger (1970).

Kean, A.W.G., "The History of the Criminal Liability of Children," 53 *Law Quarterly Review* 364 (1937).

Keiter, Robert B., "Criminal or Delinquent? A Study of Juvenile Cases Transferred to Criminal Court," 19 *Crime and Delinquency* 528 (1973).

Kfoury, Paul R., "Confidentiality and the Juvenile Offender," 17 *New England Journal on Criminal and Civil Confinement* 55 (1991).

——, "Prosecutorial Waiver of Juveniles Into Adult Criminal Court: The Ends of Justice... or the End of Justice?," 5 *Nova Law Journal* 487 (1981).

——, "Relinquishment of Jurisdiction For Purposes of Criminal Prosecution of Juveniles," 8 *Northern Kentucky Law Review* 377 (1981).

Komisar, Lucy, "Putting Johnny in Jail," *Juris Doctor*, June–July 1978, p. 16.

Krisberg, Barry & James F. Austin, *The Children of Ishmael: Critical Perspectives on Juvenile Justice*, Palo Alto, CA: Mayfield (1978).

——, *Reinventing Juvenile Justice*, Newbury Park, CA: Sage (1993).

Krisberg, Barry *et al.*, "The Watershed of Juvenile Justice Reform," 32 *Crime and Delinquency* 5 (1986).

Lee, Deborah A., *Comment*, "The Constitutionality of Juvenile Preventive Detention: Schall v. Martin—Who Is Preventive Detention Protecting?," 20 *New England Law Review* 341 (1984–85).

Lemert, Edwin M., *Instead of Court: Diversion in Juvenile Justice*, Center for Studies of Crime and Delinquency, Chevy Chase, MD: National Institute of Mental Health (1971).

Levesque, Roger J.R. & Alan J. Tompkins, "Revisioning Juvenile Justice: Implications of the New Child Protection Movements," 48 *Washington University Journal of Urban and Contemporary Law* 87 (1995).

Lewis, Dorothy O. *et al.*, "Biopsychosocial Characteristics of Children Who Later Murder: A Prospective Study," 142 *American Journal of Psychiatry* 1161 (1985).

Lindsey, Ben, "The Juvenile Laws of Colorado," 18 *Green Bag* 126 (1906).

————, "The Juvenile Court of Denver," in *International Prison Commission, Children's Courts in the United States: Their Origin, Development and Results* (1904).

Lippman, Hyman S., "Treatment of Juvenile Delinquents" in *Proceedings, National Conference of Social Work*, New York: Columbia University Press (1945).

Lipton, Douglas, Robert Martinson & Judith Wilks, *The Effectiveness of Correctional Treatment: A Survey of Treatment Evaluation Studies*, New York: Praeger (1975).

Lombroso, Cesare, *Crime: Its Causes and Remedies* Boston: Little, Brown (1911).

Lou, Herbert H., *Juvenile Courts in the United States*, Chapel Hill, NC: University of North Carolina Press (1927).

McCarthy, Francis B., "Should Juvenile Delinquency Be Abolished?," 23 *Crime and Delinquency* 196 (1977).

MacNamara, Donal E.J., "Medical Model in Corrections: 'Requiescat in Pace,'" in *Annual Editions: Criminal Justice 80/81*, Guilford, CT: Dushkin (1980).

Mack, Julian W., "The Juvenile Court," 23 *Harvard Law Review* 104 (1909–10).

Maestro, Marcello T., *Voltaire and Beccaria as Reformers of the Criminal Law*, New York: Columbia University Press (1942).

Margolin, Arnold D., "The Element of Vengeance in Punishment," 24 *Journal of Criminal Law and Criminology* 755 (1933).

Martinson, Robert, "What Works?—Questions and Answers About Prison Reform," 35 *Public Interest* 22 (1974).

Maxwell, Bill, "An arsonist's letter points to deeper ills," *Tuscaloosa* (Ala.) *News*, January 29, 1997, p. 7A.

Melli, Marygold S., "Juvenile Justice Reform in Context," 1996 *Wisconsin Law Review* 375.

Mellinkoff, David, *The Language of the Law*, Boston: Little, Brown (1963).

Mennel, Robert M., "Attitudes and Policies Toward Juvenile Delinquency in the United States: A Historiographical Review," 4 *Crime and Justice: An Annual Review of Research* 191 (Michael Tonry & Norval Morris eds.), Chicago: The University of Chicago Press (1983).

Michael, Jerome & Herbert J. Wechsler, *Criminal Law and its Administration*, Mineola, NY: Foundation Press (1940).

Middleton, Martha, "Punishment or Parenting for Child Criminals?," *National Law Journal*, April 18, 1988, p. 1.

Milsom, S.F.C., *Historical Foundations of the Common Law*, London: Butterworths (1969).

Morris, Norval, *The Future of Imprisonment*, Chicago: The University of Chicago Press (1974).

National Advisory Commission on Criminal Justice Standards and Goals, U.S. Department of Justice, Washington, DC (1973).

National Commission on Law Observance and Enforcement (The Wickersham Commission), Washington, DC: U.S. *Government Printing Office* (1931).

Nelken, David, "Reflexive Criminology," in *The Futures of Criminology* (David Nelken ed.), Thousand Oaks, CA: Sage (1994).

Neumeyer, Martin H., *Juvenile Delinquency in Modern Society*, New York: D. Van Nostrand (1949).

New York State Report of the Citizen's Inquiry on Parole and Criminal Justice, Prison Without Walls (1975).

Nibecker, F.H. "Education of Juvenile Delinquents," 23 *Annals of the American Academy of Political and Social Science* 483 (1904).

Note, "Misapplication of the Parens Patriae Power in Delinquency Proceedings," 29 *Indiana Law Journal* 475 (1953–54).

Note, "Procedural Due Process at Juvenile Sentencing for Felony," 81 *Harvard Law Review* 821 (1968).

Note, "Rights and Rehabilitation in the Juvenile Courts," 67 *Columbia Law Review* 281 (1967).

Oppenheimer, Heinrich, *The Rationale of Punishment*, London: University of London Press (1913).

Orfield, Leonard B., *Criminal Procedure From Arrest to Appeal*, Westport, CT: Greenwood Press (1947).

Packer, Herbert L., *The Limits of the Criminal Sanction*, Stanford, CA: Stanford University Press (1968).

Paulsen, Monrad G., "Children's Court—Gateway or Last Resort?," 72 *Case and Comment* 3 (Nov.–Dec. 1967).

———, "The Constitutional Domestication of the Juvenile Court," 1967 *Supreme Court Review* 233.

Perlin, Michael L., *The Jurisprudence of the Insanity Defense*, Durham, NC: Carolina Academic Press (1994).

Pickett, Robert S., *House of Refuge: Origins of Juvenile Reform in New York State*, Syracuse, NY: Syracuse University Press (1969).

Piliavin, Irving & Scott Briar, "Police Encounters With Juveniles," 70 *American Journal of Sociology* 206 (1964).

Pisciotta, Alexander W., "Treatment on Trial: The Rhetoric and Reality of the New York House of Refuge, 1857–1935," 29 *American Journal of Legal History* 151 (1985).

Platt, Anthony M., *The Child Savers: The Invention of Delinquency*, Chicago: The University of Chicago Press (1969).

———, *The Child Savers: The Invention of Delinquency*, 2d ed., Chicago: The University of Chicago Press (1977).

Plucknett, Theodore F.T., *A Concise History of the Common Law*, Boston: Little, Brown (1956).

Polier, Justine W., *Juvenile Justice in Double Jeopardy*, Hillside, NJ: Lawrence Erlbaum Associates (1989).

Pope, Carl E., "Blacks and Juvenile Crime: A Review," in *Criminal Justice System and Blacks* (Daniel Georges-Abeyie ed.), New York: Clark Boardman (1984).

Pound, Roscoe, *Criminal Justice in America,* Cambridge: Harvard University Press (1945). (Originally published in 1930).

————, *Interpretations of Legal History,* Cambridge: Harvard University Press (1946). (Originally published in 1923).

————, "The Administration of Justice in the Modern City," 26 *Harvard Law Review* 302 (1913).

————, "The Causes of the Popular Dissatisfaction With the Administration of Justice," 19 *American Bar Association Report* 395 (1906).

Prevention and Treatment of Neglected Children (Hastings H. Hart ed.), New York: Arno Press (1910).

Prize Essays on Juvenile Delinquency, Philadelphia: Edward C. & John Biddle (1855).

Problems of Delinquency (Sheldon Glueck & Eleanor Glueck eds.), Boston: Hougton-Mifflin (1959).

Program Summary: Comprehensive Strategy for Serious, Violent and Chronic Juvenile Offenders, Office of Juvenile Justice & Delinquency Prevention (OJJDP), Washington, DC: U.S. Government Printing Office (June, 1994).

Radzinowicz, Leon, *A History of English Criminal Law and Its Administration From 1750*, New York: Macmillan (1948).

————, *In Search of Criminology,* London: Heinemann Educational Books (1961).

Reidy, David A., Jr., "The Law, Dominant Paradigms and Legal Education," 39 *Kansas Law Review* 415 (1991).

Rembar, Charles, *The Law of the Land: The Evolution of Our Legal System*, New York: Simon & Schuster (1980).

Rendleman, Douglas R., "*Parens Patriae*: From Chancery to the Juvenile Court," 23 *South Carolina Law Review* 205 (1971).

Report From the Select Committee on Criminal and Destitute Juveniles, Together With the Proceedings of the Committee in The Child and the State (Grace Abbott ed.), New York: Greenwood Press (1968). (Originally published in 1938).

Report of the Committee of the Chicago Bar Association (1855).

Roberts, Albert R., *Juvenile Justice: Policy, Programs and Services*, Chicago: Dorsey Press (1989).

Rosado, Lourdes M., "Minors and the Fourth Amendment: How Juvenile Status Should Invoke Different Standards for Search and Seizure on the Street," 71 *New York University Law Review* 762 (1996).

Rosenberg, Irene M., "Leaving Bad Enough Alone: A Response to the Juvenile Court Abolitionists," 1993 *Wisconsin Law Review* 163.

———, "*Schall v. Martin:* A Child is a Child is a Child," 12 *American Journal of Criminal Law* 253 (1984).

Ross, Thomas, "The Rhetorical Tapestry of Race: White Innocence and Black Abstraction," 32 *William and Mary Law Review* 1 (1990).

Rossum, Ralph A., "Holding Juveniles Accountable: Reforming America's Juvenile Justice System," 22 *Pepperdine Law Review* 907 (1995).

Rubin, H. Ted, *Juvenile Justice: Policy, Practice and Law*, 2d ed., New York: Random House (1985).

———, "Retain the Juvenile Court? Legislative Developments, Reform Directions and the Call for Abolition," 25 *Crime and Delinquency* 281 (1979).

———, *The Courts: Fulcrum of the Justice System*, Pacific Palisades, CA: Goodyear (1976).

Rubin, H. Ted & Richard S. Schaffer, "Constitutional Protections for the Juvenile," 44 *Denver Law Journal* 66 (1967).

Rubin, Sol, *The Law of Criminal Correction*, St. Paul: West (1963).

———, "The Legal Character of Juvenile Delinquency," 261 *Annals of the American Academy of Political and Social Science* 1 (1949).

Sampson, Robert J. & John H. Laub, "Crime and Deviance Over the Life Course: The Salience of Adult Social Bonds," 55 *American Sociological Review* 609 (1990).

Schlossman, Steven L., *Love and the American Delinquent: The Theory and Practice of 'Progressive' Juvenile Justice, 1825–1920*, Chicago: The University of Chicago Press (1977).

Schlossman, Steven L. & Michael Sedlak, "The Chicago Area Project Revisited," 29 *Crime and Delinquency* 398 (1983).

Schramm, Gustav L., "Philosophy of the Juvenile Court," 261 *Annals of the American Academy of Political and Social Science* 101 (1949).

Schwartz, Ira M., *(In)justice for Juveniles: Rethinking the Best Interest of the Child*, Lexington, MA: Lexington Books (1989).

Schwartz, Ira M., Joan M. Abbey & William H. Barton, *The Perception and Reality of Juvenile Crime in Michigan*, Center for the Study of Youth Policy, Ann Arbor, MI: University of Michigan (1990).

Schwartz, Ira M., Shenyang Guo & John J. Kerbs, "The Impact of Demographic Variables on Public Opinion Regarding Juvenile Justice: Implications for Public Policy," 39 *Crime and Delinquency* 5 (1993).

Sellin, Thorsten, "Corrections in Historical Perspective," 23 *Law and Contemporary Problems* 585 (1958).

Sherman, Arloc, *Wasting America's Future*, Children's Defense Fund, Boston: Beacon Press (1994).

Sieh, Edward, "From Augustus to the Progressives: A Study of Probation's Formative Years," 57 *Federal Probation* 67 (1993).

Simon, Johnathan, "Power Without Parents: Juvenile Justice in a Postmodern Society," 16 *Cardozo Law Review* 1363 (1995).

Simonsen, Clifford E., *Juvenile Justice in America*, 3d ed., New York: Macmillan (1991).

Smith, Bruce, "Municipal Police Administration," 26 *Annals of the American Academy of Political and Social Science* 1 (1929).

Smith, Carolyn A. & Terence Thornberry, "The Relationship Between Childhood Maltreatment and Adolescent Involvement in Delinquency and Drug Use," paper presented at the Society for Research on Child Development, New Orleans, LA, March, 1993.

Smykla, John O., *Probation and Parole: Crime Control in the Community*, New York: Macmillan (1984).

Snedden, David S., *Administration and Educational Work of American Juvenile Reform Schools,* New York: Columbia University Press (1907).

Snyder, Howard & Melissa Sickmund, *Juvenile Offenders and Victims: A Focus on Violence,* Office of Juvenile Justice and Delinquency Prevention (OJJDP) Report, Pittsburgh: National Center on Juvenile Justice (May, 1995).

Society for the Reformation of Juvenile Delinquents, Documents Relating to the House of Refuge (Hastings H. Hart ed.) (1832).

Sparks, Richard F., "A Critique of Marxist Criminology," in 2 *Crime and Justice: An Annual Review of Research* 160 (Norval Morris & Michael Tonry eds.), Chicago: The University of Chicago Press (1980).

Special Project: "The Collateral Consequences of a Criminal Conviction," 23 *Vanderbilt Law Review* 941 (1970).

Springer, Charles E., "Rehabilitating the Juvenile Court," 5 *Notre Dame Journal of Law, Ethics and Public Policy* 397 (1991).

Standards and Guides for Detention of Children and Youth, Hackensack, NJ: National Council on Crime and Delinquency (1961).

Standard Juvenile Court Act, 6th ed., Hackensack, NJ: National Council on Crime and Delinquency (1959).

Stern, Gerald, "Public Drunkenness: Crime or Health Problem?," 374 *Annals of the American Academy of Political and Social Science 153 (1967).*

Streib, Victor L., *The Juvenile Death Penalty Today: Present Death Row Inmates Under Juvenile Death Sentences and Death Sentences and Executions for Juvenile Crimes, January 1, 1973 to June 30, 1996,* Ada, OH: Ohio Northern University School of Law (July 2, 1996).

Struggle for Justice, A Report on Crime and Punishment in America, American Friends Service Committee, New York: Hill & Wang (1971).

Sussman, Frederick, *Law of Juvenile Delinquency,* rev. ed., New York: Oceana (1959).

Sutherland, Edwin H. & Donald R. Cressey, *Principles of Criminology,* 7th ed., New York: J.B. Lippincott (1966).

———, *Criminology*, 9th ed., New York: J.B. Lippincott (1974).

Szasz, Thomas, *Insanity: The Idea and Its Consequences*, New York: John Wiley (1987).

———, *Law, Liberty, and Psychiatry: An Inquiry Into the Social Uses of Mental Health Practices*, New York: Macmillan (1963).

———, *Psychiatric Justice*, New York: Macmillan (1965).

———, *The Manufacture of Madness: A Comparative Study of the Inquisition and the Mental Health Movement*, New York: Harper & Row (1970).

———, *The Myth of Mental Illness: Foundations of a Theory of Personal Conduct*, New York: Harper & Row (1974).

———, *The Second Sin: Some Iconoclastic Thoughts on Marriage, Sex, Drugs, Mental Illness, and Other Matters*, Garden City, NJ: Doubleday (1973).

———, *The Therapeutic State: Psychiatry in the Mirror of Current Events*, Buffalo, NY: Prometheus Books (1984).

Tappan, Paul W., *Crime, Justice and Correction*, New York: McGraw-Hill (1960).

———, *Juvenile Delinquency*, New York: McGraw-Hill (1949).

Task Force Report: Juvenile Delinquency and Youth Crime, The President's Commission on Law Enforcement and Administration of Justice, Washington, DC: U.S. Government Printing Office (1967).

Task Force on Sentencing Policy Toward Young Offenders, Confronting Youth Crime, New York: Twentieth Century Fund (1978).

Taylor, Hasseltine B., *Law of Guardian and Ward*, Chicago: The University of Chicago Press (1935).

Teeters, Negley K. & Jack H. Hedblom, *Hang By The Neck*, Springfield IL: Charles C. Thomas (1967).

Teitelbaum, Lee E., "Youth Crime and the Choice Between Rules and Standards," 1991 *Brigham Young University Law Review* 351.

Terry, Robert M., "The Screening of Juvenile Offenders," 58 *Journal of Criminal Law, Criminology and Police Science* 179 (1967).

The Challenge of Crime in a Free Society, Report of the President's Commission on Law Enforcement and Administration of Justice, Washington, DC: U.S. Government Printing Office (1967).

The Child, the Clinic and the Court, (Jane Addams ed.), New York: New Republic (1925).

The Criminal Law Revolution and Its Aftermath: 1960–1975 (Anthony E. Scudellari, John G. Miles, Jr., Richard E. Crouch & George F. Knight eds.), Washington, DC: Bureau of National Affairs (1975).

The Future of Childhood and Juvenile Justice (LaMar T. Empey ed.), Charlottesville, VA: University of Virginia Press (1979).

The New Juvenile Justice (Martin L. Forst ed.), Chicago: Nelson Hall (1995).

The Positive School of Criminology: Three Lectures by Enrico Ferri (Stanley E. Grupp ed.), Pittsburgh: University of Pittsburgh Press (1968).

The Report of the National Criminal Justice Commission, The Real War on Crime (Steven R. Donziger ed.), National Center on Institutions and Alternatives, New York: Harper-Collins (1996).

The Rhetoric of Law (Austin Sarat & Thomas R. Kearns eds.), Ann Arbor, MI: The University of Michigan Press (1996).

The Social Services: An Introduction, 2d ed., (H. Wayne Johnson ed.), Itasca, IL: F.E. Peacock (1986).

"The Supreme Court, 1966 Term," 81 *Harvard Law Review* 171 (1967).

The Truth About the Truth: Deconfusing and Reconstructing the Post-modern World (Walter Truett Anderson ed.), New York: Tarcher-Putnam (1995).

"The Youth Crime Plague," *Time,* July 11, 1977, pp. 18–30.

Thomas, Charles W. & Shay Bilchik, "Prosecuting Juveniles in Criminal Courts: A Legal and Empirical Analysis," 76 *Journal of Criminal Law and Criminology* 439 (1985).

Timasheff, Nicholas S., *One Hundred Years of Probation, 1841–1941,* New York: Fordham University Press (1941).

Tolley, Edward D., "The Execution of America's Children," 6 *Georgia State University Law Review* 403 (1990).

Toufexis, Anastasia, "Our Violent Kids," *Time,* June 12, 1989, p. 52–58.

Towne, Arthur W., "Shall the Age Jurisdiction of Juvenile Courts Be Increased?," 10 *Journal of Criminal Law and Criminology* 493 (1920).

Uniform Juvenile Court Act, Philadelphia: National Conference of Commissioners on Uniform State Laws (1968).

van den Haag, Ernest, *Punishing Criminals: Concerning a Very Old and Painful Question,* New York: Basic Books (1975).

Vold, George B., *Theoretical Criminology,* New York: Oxford University Press (1958).

Vold, George B. & Thomas J. Bernard, *Theoretical Criminology,* 3d ed., New York: Oxford University Press (1986).

Vollmer, August, "Predelinquency," 14 *Journal of Criminal Law and Criminology* 279 (1923–24).

von Hirsh, Andrew, *Doing Justice: The Choice of Punishments,* New York: Hill & Wang (1976).

Wagner, Susan, *Casenote,* "Constitutional Law—State Classification of Certain Juvenile Offenders To Be Tried as Adults—Does It Offend Equal Protection or Due Process Rights of Juvenile Defendant," 29 *Journal of Family Law* 201 (1991).

Waite, Edward F., "How Far Can Court Procedure Be Socialized Without Impinging Individual Rights?," 12 *Journal of the American Institute of Criminal Law and Criminology* 339 (1921).

Walkover, Andrew, "The Infancy Defense in the New Juvenile Court," 31 *University of California Los Angeles Law Review* 503 (1984).

Wallace, John A. & Marion M. Brennan, "Intake and the Family Court," 12 *Buffalo Law Review* 442 (1963).

Watkins, John C., Jr., "Isolating the Condemnation Sanction in Juvenile Justice: The Mandate of *In re Gault,*" in *Critical Issues in Criminal Justice* (R.G. Iacovetta & Dae H. Chang eds.), Durham, NC: Carolina Academic Press (1980).

Weiss, Joseph G., *Jurisdiction and the Elusive Status Offender: A*

Comparison of Involvement in Delinquent Behavior and Status Offenses, Washington, DC: U.S. Government Printing Office (1980).

Welch, Thomas A., "*Kent v. United States and In re Gault:* Two Decisions in Search of a Theory," 19 *Hastings Law Journal* 29 (1967).

Wheeler, Malcolm E., "Toward a Theory of Limited Punishment II: The Eighth Amendment After Furman v. Georgia," 25 *Stanford Law Review* 62 (1972).

Wheeler, Stanton & Leonard S. Cottrell, Jr., *Juvenile Delinquency: Its Prevention and Control*, New York: Russell Sage Foundation (1966).

White, James B., "Imagining the Law," in *The Rhetoric of Law* (Austin Sarat & Thomas R. Kearns eds.), Ann Arbor, MI: The University of Michigan Press (1994).

Widom, Cathy S., *The Cycle of Violence*, National Institute of Justice (NIJ), Washington, DC: U.S. Government Printing Office (Oct., 1992).

Wigmore, John H., *A Treatise on the Anglo-American System of Evidence in Trials at Common Law*, 3d ed., Boston: Little, Brown (1940).

———, "Juvenile Courts vs. Criminal Courts," 21 *Illinois Law Review* 375 (1926).

Williams, William A., *The Contours of American History*, Chicago: Quadrangle Books (1961).

Wilson, James Q., *The Moral Sense*, New York: The Free Press (1993).

———, *Thinking About Crime*, New York: Basic Books (1975).

———, *Varieties of Police Behavior*, Cambridge: Harvard University Press (1968).

Wizner, Stephen & Mary F. Keller, "The Penal Model of Juvenile Justice: Is Juvenile Court Delinquency Jurisdiction Obsolete?," 52 *New York University Law Review* 1120 (1977).

Wolfgang, Marvin, "Abolish the Juvenile Court System," 2 *California Lawyer* 12 (1982).

——, "Criminology and the Criminologist," 54 *Journal of Criminal Law, Criminology and Police Science* 155 (1963).

——, "Pioneers in Criminology: Cesare Lombroso (1835– 1909)," 52 *Journal of Criminal Law, Criminology and Police Science* 361 (1961).

Wolfgang, Marvin, Robert Figlio & Thorsten Sellin, *Delinquency in a Birth Cohort*, Chicago: The University of Chicago Press (1972).

Wolfgang, Marvin, Terence Thornberry & Robert Figlio, *From Boy to Man: From Delinquency to Crime*, Chicago: The University of Chicago Press (1987).

Woodbridge, Frederick, "Physical and Mental Infancy in the Criminal Law," 87 *University of Pennsylvania Law Review* 426 (1939).

Yochelson, Samuel & Stanton E. Samenow, *The Criminal Personality*, New York: Jason Aronson (1976).

York, Cynthia M., *Casenote*, "Constitutional Law—Pretrial Preventive Detention—Pretrial detention of an accused juvenile delinquent who poses a serious threat of recidivism does not violate due process. *Schall v. Martin*, 104 S. Ct. 2403 (1984)," 62 *University of Detroit Law Review* 145 (1984).

Young, Pauline V., *Social Treatment in Probation and Delinquency*, New York: McGraw-Hill (1937).

Youth Violence, Guns and Illicit Drug Markets, National Institute of Justice (NIJ), Washington DC: U.S. Government Printing Office (June, 1996).

Zalman, Marvin & Larry J. Siegel, *Criminal Procedure: Constitution and Society*, Belmont, CA: West-Wadsworth (1997).

Zimring, Franklin E., "The Treatment of Hard Cases in American Juvenile Justice: In Defense of Discretionary Waiver," 5 *Notre Dame Journal of Law, Ethics and Public Policy* 267 (1991).

Author Index

Subject Index